THE PLANTATION
OF ULSTER

About the Author
Jonathan Bardon was born and educated in Dublin, but has spent most of his life as a teacher and lecturer in Belfast. Author of many books on Irish history, including the widely-praised *A History of Ulster*, he has an outstanding reputation as a narrative historian of rare ability.

THE PLANTATION OF ULSTER

The British Colonisation of the North of
Ireland in the Seventeenth Century

JONATHAN BARDON ∾

Gill & Macmillan

Gill & Macmillan
Hume Avenue, Park West, Dublin 12
with associated companies throughout the world
www.gillmacmillanbooks.ie

© Jonathan Bardon 2011, 2012
978 07171 5447 0
First published in hard cover 2011
First published in paperback 2012

Index compiled by Helen Litton
Typography design by Make Communication
Print origination by Carole Lynch
Cartography by Design Image
Printed by ScandBook AB, Sweden

The paper used in this book comes from the wood
pulp of managed forests. For every tree felled,
at least one tree is planted, thereby renewing
natural resources.

A CIP catalogue record for this book is available
from the British Library.

5 4 3 2

To Carol

and in memory of Dermot Neary, Martin Godfrey, Bridgheen McWade and Robert J. Hunter

CONTENTS

In 1603, two dynasties fell.

Elizabeth I died childless: the Tudors lost the Crown. And Hugh O'Neill surrendered to the English: over a thousand years of Gaelic monarchy ended.

O'Neill died in despair in 1616. But history had not abandoned him.

He left a daughter, Sorcha O'Neill, who married an Irish aristocrat, a Magennis of Iveagh. Ten generations later, one of her descendants became Lady Glamis. In 1900, she had a daughter—Elizabeth Bowes Lyon.

Elizabeth was the mother of Elizabeth Windsor. In 1952, she became the Queen of Great Britain and Northern Ireland.

Elizabeth II embodied a dynasty which Elizabeth I had been at pains to destroy.

DOUGLAS CARSON, 17 JUNE 2011

PREFACE

In seeking the origins of Northern Ireland's present discontents, historians and social scientists alike are again and again brought back to the British colonisation of Ulster in the seventeenth century. Attempting to find explanations has long been a concern of this author, who, in addition to teaching Irish history during a long career in further and higher education, has at various times been involved in curriculum programmes for schools (including Cultural Heritage and Education for Mutual Understanding), in writing radio and television programmes on Irish history, in the Community Relations Council and in the teaching of prisoners at the Maze Prison (where he taught exactly the same programme of Irish history to both loyalist and republican inmates).

Many widely held assumptions about the Plantation of Ulster can be shown to be flawed or, if not, in need of some refinement. Some argue—as indeed did those who wrote pamphlets to encourage colonisation—that the land was 'utterly depopulated'. It was not, even though the ruthless campaigning and destruction of food supplies as Crown forces closed in on Ulster in 1600–1603 had, by slaughter and famine, greatly reduced the numbers of native Irish there.

It is not true that those 'deserving Irish' who received estates were deliberately assigned the poorest, most infertile land. James I's determination to remove all the natives from the estates of the leading planters came to nothing. Of course the Catholic Gaelic gentry were left with almost nothing in the province by the end of the century, but most of the Irish—reduced in status, with burdensome rents and uncertain tenures—remained to farm the land. The slow process by which Catholic natives lost access to the choicest lands began only at the very end of the seventeenth century.

Many will be surprised that three amongst the most energetic planters were Catholics. Sir Randal MacDonnell, Earl of Antrim, brought large numbers of Presbyterian Lowlanders onto his land even before the official plantation had got under way; George Touchet, 18th Baron Audley, had seen to the erection of some of the plantation's most impressive castles and fortifications—notably Ballynahatty, Castlederg and Castle Curlews—up to his death in 1617; and, to the consternation of the government, Sir George Hamilton of Greenlaw, together with his relatives, as well as befriending Irish priests and Jesuits made his well-managed estate in the Strabane area a haven for Scottish Catholics seeking refuge from the oppressions of the Kirk.

Despite the confiscation of its lands and frequent persecutions, the Catholic Church in Ulster appears to have become stronger, better organised and more fervent during the period of plantation. To some extent this was even with the connivance of local planters; some London Companies infuriated the authorities by favouring Catholic priests on their lands, if only because they were model tenants who paid their rents promptly.

During the late sixteenth and early seventeenth centuries far more Scots leaving their homeland settled in Poland and Scandinavia than in Ulster. The great Scots migration to the north of Ireland began only in the 1650s and reached a peak in the 1690s. The assumption that religious and cultural differences kept British colonists and Gaelic Irish, and their descendants, as rigidly separate ethnic groups does not stand up to close scrutiny. There was far more intermingling than is generally acknowledged; otherwise British surnames, such as Hume, Adams and Sands, would not be found amongst Catholic nationalist activists, nor would native Irish ones, such as O'Neill, McCusker and Maginnis, be found amongst Protestant unionist politicians.

Despite jaundiced observations in government reports commissioned by James I, the British colonisation of most of Ulster was largely achieved. Perhaps as many as 35,000 English and Scots had settled in the province by 1622; but, as this book is at pains to point out, the greatest influx occurred in the second half of the seventeenth century. Up to a quarter of a million British crossed over to Ireland between 1586 and 1700, most of them to Ulster—a greater number than crossed the Atlantic from the Iberian Peninsula between 1500 and 1600.

That the Plantation of Ulster had a profound effect on the history of Ireland thereafter is universally acknowledged. It is less well known that it impinged significantly on developments on the other side of the Irish Sea. The City of London was persuaded by James I, very much against its inclinations, to become deeply involved in the plantation. Though the return on the great sums invested was meagre enough, the City was mercilessly hounded by Charles I for failing to adhere strictly to the conditions laid down. This was not the only reason for London coming down firmly on the side of Parliament, but it was a major one, ultimately ensuring the Royalists' defeat in the Civil War.

In September 1718 a seventy-ton vessel, the *Maccullum*, set out from Derry Quay across the Atlantic. With the Rev. James Woodside at their head, about a hundred passengers disembarked at Boston. This could be regarded as the beginning of a great and sustained exodus from Ulster to North America. By 1775 at least 100,000 and perhaps as many as 200,000 had left Ulster for Colonial America, and the migration began again once King George III had given official recognition to the United States of America in 1783.

Even greater numbers emigrated in the nineteenth century. Americans referred to these immigrants as the 'Scotch-Irish'. By this time most of these people had been in Ulster for several generations. The majority were Presbyterians, descended from Scots who had earlier colonised Ulster; however, there were nearly as many members of the Church of Ireland (Anglican settlers principally of English origin), drawn from a wider area, and considerable numbers of Catholics of native Irish stock, as indicated by surname evidence, many of whom became Protestants soon after landing. The striking fact is that very few Scots had yet—at least in the eighteenth century—emigrated directly from Scotland to Colonial America.

These 'Scotch-Irish' and their descendants were to play a pivotal role in the shaping of the United States. They and their forebears had long experience of building fortifications in hostile territory, of felling timber and clearing the land for the plough and of engaging woodkerne, tories, raparees and other native Irish who resented their intrusion. They were to become energetic pioneers in the 'back country', pushing the frontiers of European settlement in North America inexorably westwards. Famously, they and their descendants provided the United States with many presidents, generals and entrepreneurs.

Even more Protestants left Ulster for America in the nineteenth century than in the previous one, but by then Catholic Irish were arriving in greater numbers. As Prof. Don Akenson has pointed out, there are far more citizens in the United States of Ulster Protestant descent than of Irish Catholic descent: the Scotch-Irish had a century head start in which to increase their numbers. Akenson also refers to detailed surveys which show that those claiming Irish Catholic ancestry are far more prosperous today than those claiming Scotch-Irish ancestry—almost certainly because those Irish escaping hunger and destitution sought refuge in booming industrial cities, while the region of the Appalachians and the South suffered prolonged economic blight.

The tragedy for Ireland was that the conquest and colonisation of Ulster took place at a time when western and central Europe were rent by bitter religious divisions. Events and developments thereafter, not only in Ireland but also on the other side of the Irish Sea, prevented wounds sustained earlier from healing over. The outcome was a dangerously fractured society in the north. In this, Northern Ireland is not unique in Europe: in Belgium the divisions between French and Flemish-speakers are acute, but at least the Belgians have not been killing each other over their differences. In Northern Ireland, memories of previous dispossessions and massacres passed down from one generation to another. Ancient hatreds welled to the surface in bitter violence in 1969 that soon surpassed that of 1920–22 and made the region the most continuously disturbed part of Europe since the ending of the Second World War. By the end of the millennium a total of 3,651 men, women and children lost their lives in Northern Ireland as a direct result of the violence. Though shorter-lived, the much bloodier ethnic slaughter accompanying the break-up of Yugoslavia in the 1990s grimly demonstrated what could happen in an all-out conflict in Northern Ireland. Yet the era of terrorism and sectarian murders was brought to an end, and during the twenty-first century, and at the time of writing, a remarkable peace has prevailed.

Material informing virtually all the observations made above can be found in a wide range of scholarly works. In a book of this scope the author is especially reliant on the published findings of specialists. I hope that these writers will consider acknowledgement of their work in the references and bibliography in part an expression of my gratitude. William Roulston was particularly generous in making some of his unpublished material available to me and in providing advice on sources. Carol Tweedale, Margaret Bannon, Nonie Murray and Victor Blease valiantly undertook the task of reading draft chapters to comment on how the text might be received by the non-specialist, and their advice urging further clarification was much appreciated. Patrick Speight, Alison Finch, Norbert Bannon, the late Timothy McCall, Trevor Parkhill, Aodán Mac Póilin, Bill (W. H.) Crawford and Don Akenson provided many invaluable insights, as did a group of men of my own vintage who meet once a month in Belfast to discuss Ireland's past, the island's present condition and the country's literary heritage. They are Maurice Blease, Victor Blease, Douglas Carson, David Coffey, Brian Garrett, Liam Kearney, John Knox, Eddie McCamley, Alister McReynolds, Frank Murray, Peter Spratt and Barry White. My thanks also to the staffs of the Linen Hall Library, Queen's University

Library, Belfast Central Library and the Public Record Office of Northern Ireland and to Natasha McGowan, Sean Hughes, Tim Smyth and Laura Spence for their interest and support.

'Now I would like to visit more of those places I've been reading about in your book,' my wife, Carol, said to me on the day I submitted the main text to the publishers. Next morning we set off from Belfast, starting at Charlemont Fort and Castlecaulfield. Driving by the western shores of Lough Neagh, we stopped to climb up to Tullaghoge, the magnificent view over so much of Ulster making it plain why the O'Neills had chosen it as their inauguration site. We called at Bellaghy Bawn, the Vintners' impregnable-looking fortification, and then on to Dunluce; this romantic ruin in a beautiful setting we had been to many a time, but now we saw it for what it was, a planter's castle. (The newly written government guide leaflet is so informative that it was at once added to the bibliography.) On our return journey we halted to admire the imposing seventeenth-century defensive wall at Glenarm before calling in at Ballygalley to view the castle adorned with tourelles in the Scots baronial style. The following evening we walked around the Bishop's Castle at Ballylumford and Castle Chichester at Whitehead and along the surviving defences put up by Sir Arthur Chichester at Carrickfergus. Then—fighting our way through briars, nettles and farm equipment—we struggled around Dalway's Bawn, the most complete bawn in Ulster.

The province bristles with evidence of the plantation in stone. Western Ulster boasts many of the finest: Castle Murray, commanding an exquisite view across Donegal Bay; Donegal Castle, sensitively restored; the menacing defences of Monea; the handsome Watergate in Enniskillen; Termon McGrath, near Pettigo, one of the grandest and least visited ruins in the area; and, probably the most rewarding of all, Tully Castle, on the southern shore of Lower Lough Erne.

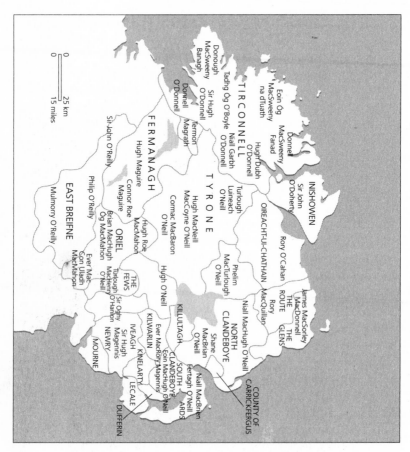

Map 1: Lordships in Ulster c. 1590 (from Mallory and McNeill, *The Archaeology of Ulster*)

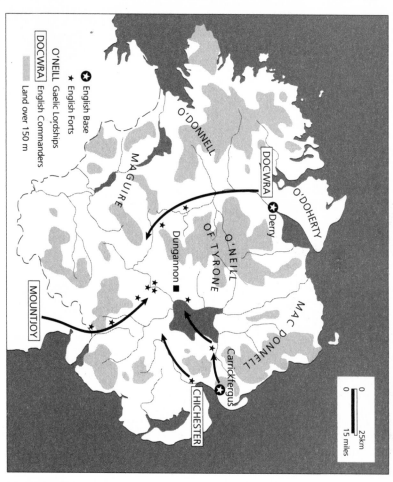

Map 2: Lord Deputy Mountjoy's campaign against the Earl of Tyrone and his allies, 1600–1603 (from Mallory and McNeill, *The Archaeology of Ulster*)

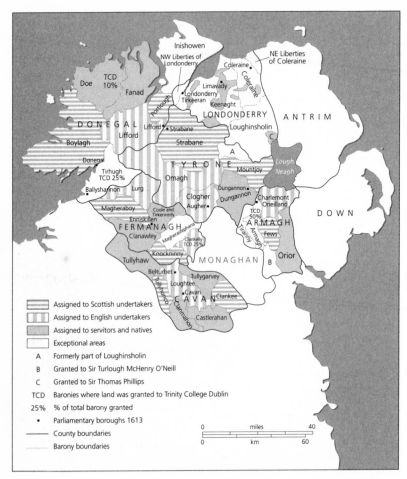

Map 3: The Plantation of Ulster, 1609–13. Antrim and Down were not included in the scheme, as those counties were already being colonised by British brought in by Sir Hugh Montgomery, Sir James Hamilton, Sir Randal MacDonnell and Sir Arthur Chichester (from a map by T. W. Moody and R. J. Hunter in Moody, Martin and Byrne, *A New History of Ireland, IX*).

Map 4: The rebellion in Ulster and north Leinster, October 1641 to February 1642
(from Perceval-Maxwell, *The Outbreak of the Irish Rebellion of 1641*)

TIME-LINE

The reign of Elizabeth I (1558–1603)

Ireland	Great Britain	Elsewhere
1562: Hugh O'Neill taken into protective custody by Sidney	1562: Shane O'Neill in London	
		1571: Ottoman Turks defeated at Lepanto
1572: Thomas Smith lands at Strangford		1572: St Bartholomew's Day massacre of Huguenots
1573: Earl of Essex begins attempt to colonise eastern Ulster; Smith killed		
1585: Scheme for Plantation of Munster drawn up; Hugh O'Neill becomes Earl of Tyrone		1585: Raleigh sends out English settlers to Roanoke in Virginia
	1587: Execution of Mary Queen of Scots	
	1588: Spanish Armada	
		1592: St Patrick's College founded at Salamanca
1594: Nine Years' War begins		
1598: Tyrone's victory at the Yellow Ford		1598: Edict of Nantes; death of Philip II
1601: Irish and Spanish defeated at Kinsale		
		1602: Red Hugh O'Donnell dies at Simancas

The reign of James I (1603–25)

Ireland	Great Britain	Elsewhere
1603: Tyrone submits at Mellifont	1603: Tyrone and Rory O'Donnell meet James I in London; O'Donnell made Earl of Tyrconnell	
1604: Derry incorporated as a city	1604: Hampton Court conference	
1605: Chichester sworn in as Lord Deputy; Upper Clandeboye and Great Ards divided between Sir Hugh Montgomery, James Hamilton and Sir Conn O'Neill	1605: Gunpowder Plot	
		1606: Foundation of St Anthony's Franciscan College, Louvain
1607: Flight of the Earls		1607: First permanent English settlement of Virginia at Jamestown
1608: Rebellion of Sir Cahir O'Doherty; six counties in Ulster surveyed and escheated		1608: Tyrone and Tyrconnell in Rome; death of Tyrconnell; John Smith president of Virginia
1609: Plan of plantation for six confiscated counties in Ulster		1609: Irish swordsmen arrive in Sweden
1610: British undertakers assigned lands in Ulster	1610: London Companies' agreement with Crown to take part in Plantation of Ulster	1610: Murder of Henry IV of France
1611: Carew's survey of British colonisation of Ulster		
1613: Bodley's survey of Plantation of Ulster; incorporation of Londonderry, Coleraine, Belfast and twenty other Ulster towns		
1614: Bodley's second survey		
1615: Conspiracy of Gaelic gentry in Ulster		
1616: Bodley's third survey		1616: O'Neill dies in Rome
1618: Pynnar begins survey of Plantation of Ulster		1618: Bohemian Revolt begins the Thirty Years' War

The reign of James I (1603–25) *contd.*

Ireland	Great Britain	Elsewhere
		1620: Crew of *Mayflower* land at Plymouth Rock; Battle of White Mountain, near Prague; Ulster planter Robert Davies amongst the defeated
1622: Commission which includes survey of Plantation of Ulster ('Phillips Survey')		
	1623: Buckingham and Prince Charles depart to seek hand of Infanta in marriage	

The reign of Charles I (1625–49)

Ireland	Great Britain	Elsewhere
		1625: Failed English expedition to Cádiz
1626: Charles I offers 'graces' to Irish subjects in return for subsidies		
		1627: England at war with France; failed expedition to La Rochelle, during which Ulster planter Sir Ralph Bingley killed on the Ile de Rhé
	1628: Assassination of Buckingham	
	1629: 'Eleven Years' Tyranny' begins	
1632: Wentworth appointed Lord Deputy		1632: Gustavus Adolphus, King of Sweden, killed at Battle of Lützen
	1635: Star Chamber trial results in fine and surrender of Londonderry charter by City	
1636: Voyage of the *Eagle Wing*		
	1638: National Covenant in Scotland	

The reign of Charles I (1625–49) *contd.*

Ireland	Great Britain	Elsewhere
1639: 'Black Oath' imposed in Ulster	1639: First Bishops' War	1639: *Catechismus*, first book in Irish in roman type, printed in Brussels
1640: Charles I's second Irish Parliament	1640: Second Bishops' War; 'Long Parliament' begins to sit	1640: Eoghan Roe O'Neill defends Arras against the French
1641: Rebellion in Ulster; massacres; alliance of Ulster Irish and Old English	1641: Execution of Strafford (Wentworth)	
1642: Confederation of Kilkenny; Monro (veteran of Lützen) at Carrickfergus; Eoghan Roe O'Neill lands in Co. Donegal	1642: Adventurers' Act, offering confiscated land in Ireland in return for loans; English Civil War begins	
	1645: Royalists defeated at Naseby	
1646: Eoghan Roe O'Neill's victory at Benburb		
		1648: Peace of Westphalia ends Thirty Years' War
1649: Fever sweeps Ireland	1649: Execution of Charles I	

The Commonwealth (1649–60)

Ireland	Great Britain	Elsewhere
1649: Cromwell in Ireland; massacres at Drogheda and Wexford		
		1650: Since 1600 up to 40,000 Scots have settled in Poland and up to 30,000 in Scandinavia
1653: Sir Phelim O'Neill captured and executed	1653: Cromwell made Lord Protector; Act of Satisfaction to arrange transplantation to Connacht	
		1655: Vaudois Protestants massacred at Piedmont
	1658: Death of Cromwell	

The reign of Charles II (1660–85)

Ireland	Great Britain	Elsewhere
1660: Charles II proclaimed King in Dublin	1660: Charles II enters London	
1662: First Court of Claims	1662: Act of Settlement	
		1663: Colonisation of Carolinas begins
		1665: Dutch and English at war
	1666: Great Fire of London	
		1680: Turks besiege Buda; charger captured ('Byerley Turk'), later present at Boyne in 1690; Penn granted Pennsylvania
		1681: Turks besiege Vienna
	1681: Execution of Archbishop Oliver Plunkett	
1682: Construction of Long Bridge over Lagan at Belfast begins		

The reign of James II (1685–9)

Ireland	Great Britain	Elsewhere
		1685: Louis XIV revokes Edict of Nantes
1687: Tyrconnell appointed Lord Deputy		
1688: Thirteen apprentice boys close the gates of Derry to Lord Antrim's army	1688: William of Orange lands at Torbay; James II flees to France	

The reign of William III and Mary (1689–1702)

Ireland	Great Britain	Elsewhere
1689: Siege of Derry ends; Battle of Newtownbutler; Schomberg lands in Co. Down	1689: William and Mary joint monarchs	
1690: William III wins Battle of the Boyne	1690: Royal Navy defeated by French at Beachy Head	
1691: Battle of Aughrim; Treaty of Limerick		
	1692: Massacre of MacDonalds at Glencoe	1692: Salem witch trials
1695: Irish Parliament enacts first Penal Laws against Catholics	1695: First of 'Seven Ill Years' of famine in Scotland	

The reign of Anne (1702–14)

Ireland	Great Britain	Elsewhere
1704: Act to Prevent the Further Growth of Popery		1704: Battle of Blenheim
		1706: Battle of Ramillies
1707: Belfast Castle destroyed by fire	1707: Union of English and Scottish Parliaments	

Chapter 1

'A PRINCE'S PURSE AND POWER MUST DO IT': ELIZABETH AND GAELIC ULSTER

FAILED ATTEMPTS TO PLANT THE ARDS AND CLANDEBOYE

In November 1571 Sir Thomas Smith persuaded Queen Elizabeth to grant him the lands of the Ards Peninsula and of Upper Clandeboye in eastern Ulster. Provost of Eton, vice-chancellor at Cambridge and a privy councillor, Smith was certain that the only way to restore the Crown's hold on Ireland was by 'plantation', that is, colonisation by loyal English subjects who would bring civility, order and the Protestant faith to the barbarous people there. In a pamphlet outlining his plans, Smith made it clear that he intended to sweep away the native Irish, except for 'churls' to plough the soil: 'Every Irishman shall be forbidden to wear English apparel or weapon upon pain of death. That no Irishman, born of Irish race and brought up Irish, shall purchase land, bear office, be chosen of any jury.'[1] The Queen's secretary, Sir William Cecil, Lord Burghley, was so confident of the success of this scheme that he invested £33 6s 8d in it.

Smith's enterprise was doomed from the outset. Only about a hundred prospective planters set foot at the village of Strangford on 31 August 1572. Led by Smith's son, also called Thomas, the interlopers advanced north through the woods of the Dufferin to Newtownards, only to find that the Lord of Upper Clandeboye, Sir Brian MacPhelim O'Neill, had responded by sweeping through north Down, burning abbeys and other buildings which might give shelter to the English. Smith had to seek refuge in Ringhaddy Castle, and it was in vain that he appealed to Dublin for help. For his part Sir William Fitzwilliam, the Queen's Lord Deputy, was furious when he heard of the expedition. Had not Brian O'Neill been knighted recently for his services to the Crown against Shane O'Neill of Tyrone?

Might not this ill-considered scheme set Ulster aflame at a time when Munster was in full insurrection?

In October 1573 an Irish servant stabbed and killed Sir Thomas's son; his body was then boiled and fed to the dogs. By then a more grandiose enterprise was already under way. On 16 August 1573 a second expedition set out from Liverpool. Its leader, Walter Devereux, Earl of Essex, was so certain of success that he had mortgaged most of his extensive English and Welsh estates to raise ten thousand pounds to finance the project. The Queen—grateful for Essex's service in crushing Northumberland's rebellion and in foiling the escape attempt by Mary Queen of Scots from Tutbury—had granted him all of Clandeboye, the Route, the Glens of Antrim, the island of Rathlin and much else besides, from the sea west to the River Bann and Lough Neagh. She paid half the cost of the thousand soldiers he brought over with him.

Dispersed by a northerly wind, the expedition had an uncertain beginning. Essex took refuge on the Copeland Islands until he could sail for Carrickfergus. Faced with such a large intruding force, Sir Brian made cautious submission. 'I took him by the hand', Essex reported, 'as a sign of his restitution to her Highness's service.' The chief of Clandeboye was not impressed, however, when Essex took ten thousand head of his cattle into custody, and after a fortnight he bribed the guards at Carrickfergus to release them. Essex pursued Sir Brian in vain, and the cattle were secreted at Massereene.

The gentlemen colonists soon lost enthusiasm, and little was achieved. In November 1573 Essex wrote in complaint to the Queen:

> Two great disadvantages I find in this little time of my continuance here. The first by the adventurers, of whom the most part, not having forgotten the delicacies of England, and wanting the resolute minds to endure the travail of a year or two in this waste country, having forsaken me, feigning excuses to repair home where I hear they give forth speeches in dislike of the enterprise to the discouragement of others. The second, that the common hired soldiers, both horsemen and footmen, mislike of their pay.[2]

He hanged some Devon men for attempted desertion and imprisoned Captain William Piers, Constable of Carrickfergus, for showing friendship with Sir Brian. The Queen kept her faith in Essex and made him Governor of Ulster, but the enterprise fared no better the following year. The earl had assured Elizabeth that he 'would not willingly imbrue his hands with more blood than the necessity of the cause requireth'. In fact he shed a great deal of blood, and to little effect.

Essex restored peace with Sir Brian, but this was to occasion a unique act of treachery. When the agreement was made, Essex and his principal followers accepted an invitation to a feast in Belfast Castle in October 1574. The Annals of the Four Masters, written by Franciscan friars in Donegal Abbey between 1632 and 1636, recorded the outcome:

> They passed three nights and days together pleasantly and cheerfully. At the expiration of this time, as they were agreeably drinking and making merry, Brian, his brother, and his wife, were seized upon by the Earl, and all his people put unsparingly to the sword—men, women, youths, and maidens—in Brian's own presence. Brian was afterwards sent to Dublin, together with his wife and brother, where they were cut in quarters. Such was the end of their feast.[3]

Next year Essex slaughtered a band of O'Neills taking refuge on an island at Banbridge and wreaked havoc deep into the province when he made war on the most powerful lord in Ulster, Turlough Luineach O'Neill of Tyrone. Another act of barbarity followed that summer. Essex was determined to break the growing power of the MacDonnells of the Glens. Three frigates and other vessels set out from Carrickfergus on 20 July 1575 commanded by Francis Drake, already famous for his seizure of a Spanish treasure convoy at Nombre de Díos, Panama, the year before. On board were 380 men under Captain John Norris, Constable of Belfast and son of a Groom of the Stole who had been executed for adultery with Anne Boleyn.

The assault fleet reached Arkill Bay on the east side of the island of Rathlin on the morning of 22 July. The castle on the island was garrisoned by only fifty soldiers, but the MacDonnells had moved their women and children there for safety. The MacDonnells fought to prevent a landing, but the English, Essex reported, 'did with valiant minds leap to land, and charged them so hotly, as they drave them to retire with speed, chasing them to a castle which they had of very great strength'. For four days the castle was pounded by ship's cannon; without a well, its wooden ramparts destroyed by red-hot cannon balls and its gate breached, it could not hold out for long. The garrison surrendered at dawn on 26 July on condition that their lives were spared; but as the newly appointed Lord Deputy, Sir Henry Sidney, reported:

The soldiers, being moved and much stirred with the loss of their fellows that were slain, and desirous of revenge, made request, or rather pressed, to have the killing of them, which they did all . . . There were slain that came out of the castle of all sorts 200 . . . They be occupied still in killing, and have slain that they have found hidden in caves and in the cliffs of the sea to the number of 300 or 400 more.

Essex relayed to the Queen information received from his spy that the Lord of the Glens, Sorley Boy MacDonnell, had 'stood upon the mainland of the Glynnes and saw the taking of the island, and was like to run mad for sorrow (as the spy saith), turning and tormenting himself, and saying that he had then lost all that ever he had'. Elizabeth did not reprove Essex for the cruelty he had authorised; on the contrary, he was told to inform Captain Norris 'that we will not be unmindful of his good services', and she added in her own hand:

If lines could value life; or thanks could answer praise, I should esteem my pen's labour the best employed time that many years had lent me . . . Your most loving cousin and sovereign E.R.[4]

Essex declared to the Queen: 'For my part I will not leave the enterprise as long as I have any foot of land in England unsold'; but there was no disguising his failure. Lord Deputy Sidney came north in September and found Clandeboye 'utterly disinhabited', Kinelarty 'desolate and waste' and Carrickfergus 'much decayed and impoverished'; and he observed that Rathlin was 'veri easy to be wonne at any tyme but very chardgious and hard to be held'.[5] Granted the title of Earl Marshal, Essex retired to Dublin, where he died of dysentery in September at the age of thirty-six. The Lord Deputy felt that a better man might have been successful, and he continued to urge the Queen to promote 'the introduction of collonys of English and other loyal subjects, whereby a perpetuall inhabitation would have ensued to be a recompense as well of that which was spent', and build up the 'strength of the country against all forreyne invasion'. The Essex fiasco, however, led Sidney to conclude that such a scheme was 'no subject's enterprise, a prince's purse and power must do it'.[6]

So, indeed, it proved.

'THE PURCHASE OF THAT PLOT IS, AND HATH BEEN, VERY DEAR': PLANTING LAOIS AND OFFALY

In 1575 Sidney was serving for the seventh time as Lord Deputy, the Queen's chief governor in Ireland. He was one of a new breed of English administrators who believed that all Ireland should be brought to adopt English law and the reformed religion, and to submit to the power of the Crown. He had, however, to operate within the limited resources Elizabeth was prepared to make available. For most of her reign Elizabeth had no wish to be a conqueror of Ireland. Her view would change only when war with Spain made the island a vulnerable western flank imperilling England's security.

By the fifteenth century the Crown remained in control only of the coastal towns and an area around Dublin between Dundalk and Bray and inland to Naas, known as the Pale. Beyond the Pale, descendants of the first Norman conquerors had become independent warlords, and the English, Welsh and Flemings they had brought with them had become ever more gaelicised. The author of the *Libelle of Englyshe Polyce* (1436) pointed out that 'the wylde Yrishe' had regained so much of the island that

Our grounde there is a lytell cornere
To all Yrelande in treue comparison.[7]

Elizabeth's father, Henry VIII, had restored the Crown's authority over much of the country. In part this had been achieved by punitive military campaigns, but he had also put his faith in the power of persuasion. He had set out his thoughts in a long letter in 1540—to 'bring Irish captains to further obedience', and to recover royal lands the King suggested 'circumspect and politic ways . . . which thing must as yet rather be practised by sober ways, politic drifts, and amiable persuasions'.[8] The outcome was that Gaelic lords were invited to hold their lands by English feudal law; they were to drop their traditional Irish titles and give up their lands to the King, receiving them back immediately with English titles. To facilitate the process, Henry had himself proclaimed King of Ireland in 1541.

One by one nearly all the lords submitted and received fresh English titles. In short, this policy of 'surrender and regrant' enjoyed considerable success, and Elizabeth continued to implement it when it seemed appropriate. The granting of new titles, however, did not guarantee a genuine extension of royal power and English law. When the ten-year-old Edward VI came to the throne in 1547 his Lord Protectors listened to the advice of those who sought subjugation and not co-operation. His successor, Mary, then had given her full support to those at court who thought that tough military action was the only lesson the rebellious Irish would understand.

When she had come to the throne in 1558 Elizabeth was not short of advice on what should be done with Ireland. The problem was that much of this advice was contradictory, and, as a result, she vacillated between conciliation and military punishment. As Ireland was a constant drain on the royal finances, the advocates of conciliation often won the day; but as her reign progressed, the pressure on Elizabeth to apply a military solution became ever stronger. This was the era of European discovery, when the Spanish and Portuguese were establishing colonies in the New World. Could Ireland be an English Hispaniola where loyal subjects could be planted? Not only might these colonies bring 'civility' to a barbarous land and secure devotion to the Protestant religion but also they could more than recoup the costs of conquest. The population of England was rising fast, and certainly there was no shortage of younger sons of gentlemen who were inheriting nothing at home petitioning Elizabeth's court, and that of the Lord Deputy in Dublin Castle, for permission to carve out new patrimonies for themselves in Ireland.

Sidney was a persuasive advocate of plantation, that is, of colonisation as a long-term solution. He was deeply critical, however, of the first major Tudor plantation in Ireland. Queen Mary had authorised repeated campaigns into the island's interior in an attempt to extend the frontiers of the Pale westwards. Two midland counties had been confiscated from the Irish there and renamed: Laois became 'Queen's County' and Offaly was titled 'King's County' after Mary's husband, King Philip II of Spain. There followed an ambitious scheme to colonise these two counties with loyal subjects. The Gaelic nobles were either executed or expelled, but a proposal to drive out or slaughter all the native Irish inhabitants of the counties had been rejected on the grounds that it would be 'a marvellous sumptuous charge'. In return for rent payable to the Crown, land was allocated to 'Englishmen born in England or Ireland'—most of the colonists, in fact, were families from the Pale.

This plantation could hardly be regarded as a success. The principal Gaelic families in the midlands—the O'Connors, O'Mores and O'Dempseys—rebelled at least a dozen times in the ensuing decades. They were still rebelling during Sir Henry Sidney's last years in office. The Lord Deputy gave local English commanders a free hand, with grim results: in

1577 Robert Hartpole, Constable of Carlow, added to the catalogue of atrocities carried out in Elizabeth's name when more than fifty O'Mores were treacherously massacred at Mullaghmast, Co. Kildare. The hope was that the royal government could make a profit; in practice, the cost of protecting the colonists and crushing the surviving dispossessed was ruinous. Sidney ruefully observed that the 'revenue of both the countries countervails not the twentieth part of the charge, so that the purchase of that plot is, and hath been, very dear'.[9]

GAELIC ULSTER: 'THE GREAT IRISHRY'

More than any other part of Ireland, Ulster was beyond the Pale. It remained the most Gaelic, least anglicised and most independent of the four provinces. John de Courcy, a knight from Cumbria, had invaded northwards in 1177 and conquered the coastlands of Down and Antrim. Those who came after him extended this Earldom of Ulster along the north coast and even built a fortress on Inishowen, Greencastle, arguably the most remote Norman castle in western Europe. The earldom, however, was always a precarious marchland. In Down (which did not become a county until 1570) it never extended further west than the motte-and-bailey castles of Dromore and Duneight, for example. Then, in the fourteenth and fifteenth centuries, these lands, never more than lightly settled, were all but lost to the Crown.

Emerging from their woody fastness of Glenconkeyne, the descendants of Áed Buidhe O'Neill—a former king of Tír Eoghain—crossed the Lower Bann and carved out a new lordship for themselves from the shattered remnants of the earldom. The Whites of the Dufferin abandoned their inheritance on the western shores of Strangford Lough for the safety of the Pale, while the Savages, driven out of Moylinny (the valley of the Six Mile Water), hung on precariously to the southern tip of the Ards. The Magennises and MacCartans engulfed central and southern Down, while the O'Neills of Clann Aodha Buidhe emerged as the principal Gaelic lords of eastern Ulster: they dominated a sweep of territory extending from Larne inland to Edenduffcarrick (now Shane's Castle, near Randalstown) and taking in the castle of Belfast and north Down, including much of the Ards Peninsula. This territory the English called Clandeboye after the ruling family which had conquered it. Carrickfergus—built by de Courcy with the largest keep in Ireland and now a royal castle—was left isolated, described in 1468 as 'a garrison of war . . . surrounded by Irish and Scots, without succour of the English for sixty miles'.[10]

One freshly arrived English family, however, had established itself on Ulster's southern frontier. Sir Nicholas Bagenal, a knight from Staffordshire, had been forced to leave England in 1539 to escape justice after committing unspecified crimes. He served as military adviser to Conn Bacach O'Neill, who, after he had been made the 1st Earl of Tyrone, obtained a pardon for him. By the beginning of Elizabeth's reign Sir Nicholas had been granted the abbey lands of Newry, where he made good progress in developing a town. He was also Marshal of the Queen's Army in Ireland, a title he was able to pass on to his son Sir Henry.[11]

In contrast with Gaelic Ulster, subject only to intermittent and ineffective interference by the English Crown, another part of the Gaelic world was meanwhile succumbing to the power of Edinburgh. Assisted by the Campbells, James IV of Scotland in 1476 forced the surrender of the MacDonalds, the ruling family, and absorbed the Isles into his kingdom. One branch of the MacDonalds, the Lords of Islay and Kintyre, fought a desperate rearguard action. It was in the Glens of Antrim, acquired as a result of a marriage alliance in 1399 between John Mór MacDonald and Margery Bisset, the last heiress of a Norman family long settled there, that these MacDonalds (known in Ireland as MacDonnells) found refuge. As the sixteenth century progressed, the Antrim MacDonnells extended their lordship to the Route, where they subdued the MacQuillans, and southwards to the frontier of Clandeboye. These MacDonnells made marriage alliances with all the leading families of Ulster, including the Savages, and brought with them MacNeills, MacAllisters, MacKays and Macrandalbanes from Kintyre and Gigha, and from the Rinns of Islay the Magees, after whom Islandmagee is named. Others ranged backwards and forwards from the Isles to serve as mercenaries for the Gaelic lords of Ulster. To the English Crown these Gaelic-speaking Scots were just as much a threat as the native Irish. The Irish Council in Dublin was so alarmed that it sent this despatch to Henry VIII in 1533:

The Scottes also inhabithe now buyselley a greate parte of Ulster, which is the king's inheritance; and it is greatlie to be feared, oonles that in short tyme they be driven from the same, that they . . . woll, by little and little soe far encroche in acquyinge and wynninge the possessions there, with the aide of the kingis disobeysant Irishe rebelles, who doo nowe ayde theym therein after soche manner, that at lengthe they will put and expel the king from his whole seignory there.[12]

The most extensive area in Ireland under complete Gaelic control was centred on Ulster and long known to officials in Dublin Castle—when they were not calling it the 'Land of War'—as the 'Great Irishry'. The most powerful native rulers in all of Ireland were the O'Neills of Tír Eoghain, a much larger lordship in area than the present county of Tyrone. Amongst those subject to them were O'Cahans (now O'Kanes), O'Hagans, O'Devlins, O'Quinns and O'Mullans, each with a subordinate lord. Second only to Tír Eoghain was Tír Chonaill, rather larger than the present county of Donegal, a lordship ruled by the O'Donnells which had sway over the O'Dohertys of Inishowen, the O'Gallaghers of Glenveagh, the MacDavitts, the O'Boyles and three branches of the MacSweeneys, descendants of Hebridean mercenaries known as *gallóglaigh,* or gallowglass. Other leading Gaelic families of Ulster, often obliged to resist attempts by O'Neills and O'Donnells to become their overlords, were the Maguires of Fermanagh, the O'Reillys of Cavan, the O'Hanlons of Armagh and the MacMahons of Monaghan.

LORDS, GENEALOGISTS, LAWYERS, PHYSICIANS, HARPERS AND POETS

Though ravaged by Vikings and overrun in parts by Anglo-Normans, great swathes of Ulster had never been conquered or settled by outsiders—at least not since warrior chiefs and their followers, driven west by Roman legions from Britain and Gaul, had subjugated indigenous inhabitants to carve out new kingdoms for themselves in Ireland. Most Gaelic lords of the north could trace their ancestry back at least to early Christian times. Here society had been able to evolve with remarkably little dislocation imposed from outside; here many ancient traditions, beliefs, customs and practices, which had once prevailed in much of Celtic-speaking Europe north of the Alps, had not been lost. That is not to say that Gaelic society in Ulster had remained much the same as it had been in early Christian times: though often condemned by Elizabethan officials as 'barbarous' and devoid of 'civility', the native Irish here were constantly adapting to developments elsewhere.

Elizabethan Ulster bristled with small castles known as tower-houses, much like border peels (small fortified towers on the frontier between Scotland and England) and hardly different from tower-houses of the ruling classes in the most anglicised parts of Ireland. A typical tower-house was a single tall rectangular keep, at least twelve metres high and slightly tapered, with two towers flanking the main entrance connected by a bold arch. Constructed for defence—often at the expense of comfort—these were the residences of Gaelic lords and their centres of power.

The title of a principal lord was simply that of his lineage: for example, the ruler of Tír Eoghain in Lord Deputy Sidney's day, Turlough Luineach O'Neill, was simply Ó Néill, usually translated as 'the O'Neill'. The inauguration rituals of Irish chiefs were very archaic—originally they were treated as a wedding of a king to his kingdom. The ceremonies were usually held on ancient Neolithic or Bronze Age sites. The site had to include a special slab or flagstone and a sacred tree or a *doire*, a grove of oak trees—for example, Derrygonnelly in Co. Fermanagh means the 'oak grove of the O'Connollys', where this family had the right to inaugurate the Maguire lord. For the O'Donnells the site was near Kilmacrenan at the Rock of Doon, next the holy well Tobar Eithne, whose waters were said to run blood whenever an O'Donnell was about to suffer a violent death. The O'Neills of Tír Eoghain were inaugurated standing on the 'Stone of Kings', shaped like a huge chair, at Tullaghoge—when he smashed it to pieces in 1601 Lord Deputy Mountjoy knew the symbolic importance of his act. After being circled three times, the newly installed lord had placed in his hands a white rod, *an tslat sheilbhe*, 'the rod of possession', to symbolise the transfer of legal ownership of the title: the O'Donnell chosen lord was given the rod by the coarb (*comharba*, a church dignitary regarded as a saint's successor) of the monastery of St Columcille at Kilmacrenan. Then a shoe was put on the lord's foot by his *uirrí*, his principal vassal, in O'Neill's case by the Lord O'Cahan.[13]

The extent of each lordship—known to the English as a 'country' and to the Irish as an *oireacht*—was in a constant state of flux. Partly this was the result of expansion of the ruling family from the top downwards. As the seventeenth-century scholar Dualtach Mac Firbhisigh explained, 'as the sons and families of the rulers multiplied, so their subjects and followers were squeezed out and withered away'.[14] This process could be rapid because Gaelic lords practised serial monogamy, sending one wife back to her father after a few years and taking on another. Hugh O'Neill, the last Earl of Tyrone, had five wives. This could lead to fierce disputes on the death of a lord: primogeniture was not yet the norm, and the successor could in theory be chosen as the 'worthiest' by the high-born from any member of the *deirbhfhine*, 'certain family', a very large group which included first cousins and extended over four generations. The reality was that a man from the ruling family might make himself lord so long as he was popular enough and powerful enough to do so.

As a way of limiting disputes, a ruling lord would nominate a *tánaiste*, 'second in position', to succeed him. The Maguires of Fermanagh were able to pass on the succession from father to son in this way for more than two centuries, but they were unusual. Until the accession of Red Hugh O'Donnell in 1592, Tír Chonaill in particular was frequently convulsed by succession disputes. The practice of taking wives one after another could rapidly swell the ranks of the eligible. In the fifteenth century Turlough O'Donnell had eighteen sons by ten different women and fifty-nine grandsons in the male line. Mulmory O'Reilly of East Bréifne, which became Co. Cavan, had fifty-eight grandsons when he died, in 1566.[15] Illegitimate male children were not excluded from the right of succession. Fosterage was a custom of ancient origin, designed to maintain good relations with neighbours; girls were sent away between the ages of seven and fourteen, and boys between seven and seventeen. Turlough Luineach O'Neill, Lord of Tír Eoghain, for example, was so called because he had been fostered with the O'Luneys of Munterloney.

Each noble family had therefore to ensure the careful maintenance of genealogies. This was a key function of the classes made up of families who followed as hereditary occupations the various learned professions as historians, physicians, jurists, harpers and poets. These formed a literate, professional class. Many of them were widely read, but in one important respect Gaelic Ulster was behind most of western and central Europe: it was not yet participating in the print revolution, and well into the seventeenth century important works, such as the Annals of the Four Masters, circulated only in manuscript. The lands assigned to these professionals were often held free of tribute and exactions, and they were exempt from military service, known as the *gairm sluaigh* or 'calling out' of the army. There was considerable overlap between these men and 'erenagh' (*airchinneach*) and 'coarb' (*comharba*) families, responsible for the administration of church lands. In Co. Fermanagh the O'Breslin jurists, the physician O'Cassidys, the O'Fialain poets and the O'Cianain and O'Luinin historians were all erenaghs. Poets were more than composers of verse: they were almost pagan priests, like pre-Christian druids, and were believed to possess extraordinary powers—their curses were thought to be capable of bringing about the injury or even the death of those castigated.

The English referred to the native Irish legal system as 'Brehon Law', from *breitheamh*, a judge. The law texts compiled in the eighth and ninth centuries, though often quoted, were no longer used in everyday legal work. This customary law—strongly influenced by Roman law—was administered by brehons drawn from hereditary legal families, such as the MacCawells, who served the O'Neills of Tír Eoghain. These judges generally based their decisions after arbitration with both parties. Those who refused to agree to arbitration could have their property seized. Cases were usually held at the regular assemblies on a rath or a hill in each lordship. To ensure the enforcement of decisions it was customary to appoint sureties (*sláinte*, meaning 'protection')—important individuals who were pledged to intervene if necessary. English commentators were particularly appalled by the absence of criminal law. In England and the Pale, execution was the usual punishment for crimes; in Gaelic Ireland those convicted—even of murder—simply had to pay damages to the injured party. For theft, the *éiric*, or compensation, involved a payment of several times the value of the stolen goods. The *éiric* for murder, especially of someone of high status, could be very high: in Tír Chonaill in 1600 it was 168 cows. Often the 'whole kindred' of the murderer was responsible for producing the compensation decided on. The English generally referred to a 'whole kindred' in Gaelic Ireland as a sept.[16]

LANDS 'PARTIBLE AMONGST THE ISSUE MALE'

Crown officials strongly disapproved of the Gaelic system of land tenure and ownership. Lands were regularly redistributed, 'parted and partible amongst the issue male of any dying possessed thereof'. The English applied the term 'gavelkind', a custom of inheritance which operated in Kent, to this redistribution. Sir John Davies explained that 'after partition made, if any one of the sept died, his portion was not divided among his sons, but the chief of the sept made a new partition of all the lands belonging to that sept and gave to every one his part according to his antiquity'.[17] He was not alone in condemning such partitions, because the shifting of shares acted as a strong disincentive to improve lands or to erect permanent buildings.

In England and in the Pale, landowners depended primarily on rents for their income. Gaelic lords had their own demesne lands, such as the land around Enniskillen which the Lord Maguire 'manured with his own churls'. However, they relied principally on a wide range of exactions to maintain themselves, their families and their guests and, especially, to see to the upkeep of their troops. The English referred to arrangements for the free entertainment of the lord, his dependants and his fighting men as 'coyne and livery'. A Gaelic lord expected to have his party and his retinue fed, accommodated and entertained by the proprietor of the lands he was visiting or passing through. The burden of this free entertainment—

known as cuddies, from *cuid oidhche*, meaning a portion for the night—must have been heavy.

The costs involved in enduring the billeting of troops and of providing for fighting men were also high. The gallowglass were professional soldiers, described in 1600 as 'picked and selected men of great and mighty bodies, cruel without compassion . . . choosing rather to die than to yield the field, so that when it cometh to handy blows, they are quickly slain or win the field'. Their wages and provisions were known as *buannacht*, anglicised as 'bonnaght', and Crown officials often referred to warriors serving Gaelic lords in general as 'bonnaghts'. In wartime the great lords ordered an *éirí amach*, or uprising, of able-bodied men, the upper classes serving as horsemen and the freemen as footsoldiers, which the English called 'kerne' (from the Irish *ceithearn*).

The tribute to a lord was almost always levied in kind. Exactions included cattle, butter, 'cakes of bread', oats, beer for horseboys, food for hunting dogs, and a heriot, or death duty (usually his best beast), payable on the death of a tenant. Labour obligations included ploughing, reaping, cutting and drawing timber, and assistance in erecting tower-houses. Lords employed officers, hereditary seneschals known as *maoir*, to collect tribute and organise labour services. The *marasgal*, or marshal, organised the billeting of fighting men and the collection of associated levies. The O'Connellys were hereditary marshals to the MacMahons, and the O'Donnellys to the Tír Eoghain O'Neills—their perquisites included the heads and hides of cattle collected from vassals for O'Neill.[18]

LIVING OFF THE LAND

The O'Reillys seem to have been the only Gaelic family to establish a proper town in Ulster, namely Cavan, in their lordship of East Bréifne. Towns founded in the Earldom of Ulster had for the most part all but disappeared, such as Belfast, or had been reduced to modest villages, such as Strangford, Downpatrick and Coleraine. The only Norman foundation of any size was Carrickfergus, by far the largest town in Ulster. Ardglass, benefiting from its regular trade with the Pale, survived to replace Downpatrick as the main port for Lecale. On confiscated monastic lands beside Carlingford Lough, the Bagenals were making Newry a successful urban development. Some ecclesiastical centres such as Armagh could be described as towns, but others, notably Derry, were deserted. There was some nucleation around castles and tower-houses, but Ulster in Elizabeth's time was overwhelmingly rural.

A striking feature of Gaelic Ulster was that the most densely populated parts were to become areas where seventeenth-century British colonisation was to be most successful, including the river valleys of the Lagan, Clogher, Foyle, Lower Bann and Roe, much of Clandeboye and the Ards, north Armagh, east Fermanagh and much of Cavan. These were the most productive parts of the province. The economy was overwhelmingly dependent on agriculture. On fertile land in the glens and on the plains, rectangular fields were carefully fenced against domestic animals with wood cut from coppiced trees and the land turned over with a light plough drawn by a team of four 'garrons', or working horses. The plough was attached to horses' tails so as to cause the animals to halt if they should strike a rock or a stump, instead of continuing and so risking damage to the tackle. The poor used no more than a spade—a simple wooden implement with an iron sheath. Much of the arable land was cultivated in ridges, rather like American raised beds, to assist drainage in waterlogged areas, in the way that potatoes were grown in 'lazy beds' into the twentieth century. The broadcast seed corn favoured in Ulster was oats; some barley was grown for brewing and making *uisce beatha*, whiskey, but usually ale was made from malted oats or rye and flavoured with blackberries and herbs. Cutting, binding and stacking the corn made September the busiest time of the year. Just as ploughing by the tail horrified the English (it was forbidden by statute in the seventeenth century), so they were appalled by the Irish practice of burning the straw and chaff to leave the grain, rather than threshing it with flails. Most lords operated water mills for corn and for tucking wool, but many continued to use hand-querns to grind oats into meal.

The English consistently underestimated the importance of arable farming in Gaelic Ulster, but there is no doubt that cattle-raising was the basis of the rural economy. As each summer approached, herds were driven onto the hill slopes and drying fens and bogland. The herds and those who drove them were known collectively as *caoruigheacht*, anglicised as 'creaght'. Those accompanying the cattle erected temporary post-and-wattle thatched dwellings with circular walls, staying with their hounds to protect calves from wolves, and milking cows to make butter.[19] Then, in autumn, the cattle returned; after the harvest had been garnered in and fences had been broken up for winter fuel, the herds were brought to graze the long stubble and to manure the soil for next year's crop. This form of transhumance, known as 'booleying', often led outsiders to conclude mistakenly that the Gaelic Irish lived a nomadic existence. As yet there was little in the way of hay-making; only cattle reserved for breeding survived the slaughter of beasts before the winter set in. Cattle herds could be very large: in 1600 Turlough Luineach O'Neill's son, grandson and cousin each possessed two thousand head.[20] The upper classes made sure that there was enough pasture for grazing their warhorses. Domestic stock included garrons, pigs, fowl and sheep—wool was pulled rather than shorn. The Gaelic lords jealously guarded their fishing rights on rivers where salmon coming in from the ocean to spawn were trapped and salted (rather than smoked) to find a ready market abroad.

The population of Ireland in 1600 was probably no more than three-quarters of a million, reduced by climatic deterioration, disease and warfare from a peak of about a million in 1300. It is particularly difficult to estimate the population of Ulster, which, though it was one of four provinces, almost certainly had less than a quarter of the island's inhabitants.[21]

Trade was on a small scale. Tanned hides made up the bulk of exports, supplemented by coarse woollen mantles, linen, salted salmon and wolf hounds. The nobility had developed a taste for wine from Bordeaux and Spain, and this was Ulster's main import. Tír Chonaill lords often accepted wine in exchange for giving Spanish and French vessels permission to use Arran Island as a base for fishing for herring: one fifteenth-century O'Donnell chief was known as Turlough an Fhíona, 'of the wine'. Gaelic lords built their own coastal vessels, particularly in Tír Chonaill, and the constant traffic across the 'Waters of Moyle'—the North Channel—ensured that MacDonnells fashioned seasoned oak from the Glens of Antrim to build their fleets of galleys. Foreign vessels for the most part put in at Carrickfergus, Ardglass and Ballyshannon.

MANTLES, GLIBS, BONNYCLABBER AND THE 'KING OF SPAIN'S DAUGHTER'

The intense class-consciousness—indeed, the snobbery—of the nobility and men of the learned professions means that we know remarkably little not only about the landless labourers but also about better-off tenants, smiths and weavers. Fynes Moryson, secretary to Lord Deputy Mountjoy in the final years of Elizabeth's reign, wrote that the Gaelic lords regarded labourers and tenants at will as 'born slaves to till their ground and to do them all services'.[22] Though they appear to have been devoid of rights, they were not serfs—indeed, they could move freely from one lord to another—and as some Ulster proprietors were short of labour they sometimes went out of their way to attract families north from the Pale.

Farmers unable to afford tower-houses lived in what the English called 'coupled houses'. These were post-and-wattle dwellings with crucks (curved load-bearing timbers supporting the hipped thatched roof, springing from ground level or from a position within the side walls somewhat above the ground). Such structures were single-storey, mainly rectangular in plan, usually with a more or less centrally located door. Chimneys were rare, and smoke from the hearth in the centre of the house had to pass out through the door.[23] Some continued to occupy raths and crannógs (island dwellings from an earlier time).

The Armada castaway Captain Francisco de Cuéllar lived with the Irish in the far north-west for almost a year. He and other Spaniards without hesitation described the natives as 'savages':

> The men are all large-bodied, and of handsome features and limbs; and as active as the roe-deer. The most of the women are very beautiful, but badly got up. They do not eat oftener than once a day, and this is at night; and that which they usually eat is butter with oaten bread. They drink sour milk, for they have no other drink; they don't drink water, although it is the best in the world. On feast days they eat some flesh half-cooked without bread or salt, as that is their custom.

Edmund Campion, an English scholar subsequently tortured and gruesomely executed as a Jesuit traitor, commented on the menu of the Irish:

> Shamrocks, watercresses, roots and other herbs they feed upon, oatmeal and butter they cram together. They drink whey, milk and beef-broth, flesh they devour without bread, corn such as they have they keep for their horses.

Clearly, dairy produce formed the most important part of the diet. Oatmeal was often combined with butter—on one occasion the O'Donnells fell upon Shane O'Neill's warriors while they were holding out their helmets to be served raw oatmeal with melted butter poured over it. The churning of milk to make butter alongside grazing herds was a vital summer activity to ensure food over the winter. Heavily salted and flavoured with herbs, butter was often placed in wooden containers, known as raskins, and put into turf bogs, where it acquired a taste the English disliked. The need for butter as winter rations ensured that fresh milk was generally too precious to be drunk in any quantity, but buttermilk was widely consumed. Fynes Moryson wrote that the people 'esteem for a great dainty sour curds, vulgarly called Bonaclabbe'. This was *bainne clabair*, or bonnyclabber (clotted milk). Blood was sometimes drawn from below the ears of living cattle or horses and mixed with butter to form a jelly. Moryson adds that 'no meat they fancy so much as pork, the fatter the better'. Like other English observers, Moryson mentions the liking the Irish had for 'shamrock'—almost certainly this was wood sorrel (known to some today as 'Sour Sally'), rightly regarded as a piquant enhancement to a good, fresh salad. He wrote that they 'willingly eat the herb shamrock, being of a sharp taste, which as they run and are chased to and fro, they snatch like beasts out of the ditches'. Moryson commented on the liking for strong drink:

> When they come to any market to sell a cow or a horse, they never return home, till they have drunk the price in Spanish wine (which they call the King of Spain's Daughter), or in Irish 'usquebaugh' till they have out-slept two or three days' drunkenness. And not only the common sort, but even the lords and their wives, the more they want this drink at home, the more they swallow it when they come to it, till they be as drunk as beggars.

Indeed, Sir Josias Bodley, campaigning in Lecale in 1600, found priests there pouring 'usquebaugh down their throats by day and by night'.

Francisco de Cuéllar, though he admired the handsome men and was constantly encountering native girls 'beautiful in the extreme', was not impressed by their dress:

> They clothe themselves, according to their habit, with tight trousers and short loose coats of very coarse goat's hair. They cover themselves with blankets and wear their hair down to their eyes.

The 'goat's hair' was probably coarse sheep's wool, and 'blankets' were the mantles which were the most distinctive item of Irish dress. The mantle was an enveloping outer woollen cloak, tightly woven with curled nap raised with the aid of a teasel seed-head, the tufts treated with honey and vinegar to stop them uncurling. Moryson described the mantle as

> a fit house for an outlaw, a meet bed for a rebel, and an apt cloak for a thief . . . When it raineth, it is his pent-house, when it bloweth it is his tent, when it freezeth, it is his tabernacle. In summer he can wear it

loose; in winter, he can wrap it close; at all times he can use it; never heavy, never cumbersome.

Fighting men in particular liked to sport a 'glib', a thick roll of hair at the forehead. Campion observed: 'Proud they are of long crisped glibs, and do nourish the same with all their cunning: to crop the front thereof they take it for a notable piece of villiany'.[24]

Irish women seem to have been quite happy to expose their breasts in full in polite society and were not ashamed to be naked, as a Bohemian nobleman discovered in north Ulster in 1601. Just what Jaroslav z Donina was doing in O'Cahan's country in the middle of a devastating rebellion is impossible to say. There he encountered sixteen high-born women, all naked, with 'which strange sight his eyes being dazzled, they led him into the house' to converse politely in Latin in front of the fire. Joining them, the Lord O'Cahan threw all his clothes off and was surprised that the Czech baron was too bashful to do likewise.

THE PLANTATION OF MUNSTER AND THE 'NATIVE PLANTATION' OF MONAGHAN

Lord Deputy Sidney hoped that Turlough Luineach O'Neill, Lord of Tír Eoghain and the most powerful Gaelic magnate in Ireland, would die soon because of his 'ill diet, and continual surfeit'. Another royal official observed: 'Sir Turlough is very old and what with decay of nature through his age and overrun with drink which daily he is in, he is utterly past government'.[25] After heavy drinking sessions Turlough would lie unconscious for more than two days at a time. But this O'Neill had a tough constitution and was to live until 1595. Turlough had created a formidable Gaelic coalition by marrying Agnes Campbell, widow of James MacDonnell of the Glens and the Isles, and she had brought with her a large contingent of Scots mercenaries, *condottieri* known as Redshanks. In addition, her daughter Finola—known as Inghean Dubh, the 'dark daughter'—was married in turn to Hugh O'Donnell, Lord of Tír Chonaill. An urgent memorandum sent from Carrickfergus in 1580 warned Elizabeth of the danger this posed:

Here is a great bruit of 2000 Scots landed in Clandeboye. Turlough Luineach's marriage with the Scot is the cause of all this, and if her Majesty does not provide against her devices, this Scottish woman will make a new Scotland of Ulster. She hath already planted a good foundation; for she in Tyrone, and her daughter in Tyrconnell, do carry all the sway in the north.[26]

Elizabeth could do nothing in response: she had a rebellion to crush in the far south of Ireland.

The FitzGeralds of Munster, gaelicised descendants of the first Norman conquerors, deeply resented the erosion of their power and the growing insistence that they accept the reformed faith. In 1579 James FitzMaurice, cousin of the Earl of Desmond, Gerald FitzGerald, persuaded Pope Gregory XIII to fund an expedition of Italian and Spanish soldiers to assist an uprising. Landing at Smerwick on the Dingle Peninsula, they awaited reinforcements, which arrived in September 1580. But Lord Deputy Leonard Grey closed in with a formidable force soon after; the intruders surrendered the fort they had built, 'and then', Grey reported to the Queen, 'put I in certain bands, who straight fell to execution. There were 600 slain'.

It took another two years for the rebellion to be crushed. Great tracts of the south of Ireland were left in ruins, and a terrible famine swept across the land. Grey's secretary, Edmund Spenser, described the suffering of the inhabitants:

> They looked like anatomies of death, they spake like ghosts crying out of their graves; they did eat of the dead carrions, happy were they if they could find them, yea, and one another soon after . . . In a short space there were almost none left, and a most populous and plentiful country suddenly made void of man and beast.[27]

Walter Raleigh, a captain who had superintended the slaughter at Smerwick, was one of many who argued that now was the time to colonise the confiscated estates of the Earl of Desmond and his adherents. A hasty survey was made in 1584, and finally, in 1586, the decision was taken to settle people of English birth on the confiscated lands. The lands were divided into portions of between four thousand and twelve thousand acres, each to be granted to an 'undertaker', that is, a man who undertook to bring in a specified number of families to work the land—no Gaelic Irish tenants were permitted. Demand was strong, and eventually thirty-five undertakers were successful in getting estates. It was not long, however, before the Plantation of Munster began to run into trouble. The principal drawbacks in implementing the scheme were that the grants were too extensive, that not enough ordinary English farming families came over and that those that did were fatally exposed in the turbulent conditions following the outbreak of war in 1585 between England and Spain. The template of this plantation scheme was retained; with many lessons learnt, it was significantly modified when plans were being laid for the British colonisation of Ulster in the seventeenth century.[28]

The decision of Philip II of Spain to send his 'invincible' Armada north from Lisbon in 1588 deserves to be regarded as a major turning point in the history of Ireland. This was when the government in London felt that there was no alternative but to ensure the complete subjugation of the entire island for the sake of England's security. Otherwise, disaffected Irish, refusing to accept the Protestant faith of the established church, could provide a base for the Crown's Catholic enemies on the European mainland, turning Ireland into a dangerously vulnerable western flank in England's defences.

Of course the Spanish King's dream of conquering England soon turned to dust. Raked by cannon fire in the Channel and scattered by fireships, the Armada could do no other than take flight up the North Sea, around the Northern Isles and westwards, deep into the Atlantic. Many great galleons and other vessels, driven by storms, foundered on Ireland's western shores. Thousands drowned. More thousands were slaughtered on the orders of Lord Deputy Sir William Fitzwilliam. Nevertheless, there were at one stage some three thousand Armada survivors on Irish soil at a time when the Lord Deputy had at his command only about a thousand men.

Elizabeth was fortunate that the Spanish castaways were too exhausted, sick and demoralised to pose a serious threat. In addition, Gaelic lords in general were not yet ready to make common cause with them. All the same, the Armada was a wake-up call for the English Crown. Ireland clearly was now a pawn in European great-power rivalry. Decisive action was required to ensure that England's security was not gravely compromised by an unsure hold on that island.

Preoccupation with Munster and the Armada meant that the Crown could spare few men to bring Turlough Luineach O'Neill to heel. In any case, the wily lord, for all his defiance, generally avoided action which might unleash expeditions against him. The English government had an alternative and inexpensive ploy to reassert its influence and authority in Ulster: to shoe in a loyal and anglicised native Irish subject who could command the support of inhabitants there.

By English law, the rightful Earl of Tyrone was Hugh O'Neill, son of the murdered Matthew, son of the 1st Earl, Conn Bacach O'Neill, and brother of the murdered Brian, and whose close relative Shane had also been murdered. To be sure that he in turn would not be murdered, the infant Hugh had been taken to the Pale and given a good English education there. In 1585 Hugh O'Neill was formally granted the title of Earl of Tyrone and sent back to Ulster to promote obedience to the English Crown. Settling himself in Dungannon, the earl steadily increased his power in Tír Eoghain, slowly undermining the authority of the ailing Turlough. By 1590, however, it was the independent power of the Earl of Tyrone, not that of Turlough O'Neill, which was causing alarm in Dublin Castle.

When Hugh Roe MacMahon, the principal Gaelic lord in Co. Monaghan, made war on members of his family and raided cattle in the barony of Farney—the property of the Earl of Essex—Lord Deputy Fitzwilliam decided to teach him a lesson. In 1590 he led an expedition north from Dublin, captured Hugh Roe and hanged him. This punishment was followed by a partition of the extensive MacMahon lands. These estates were apportioned to five leading MacMahons and to the heads of some other prominent families in the area.

Dublin Castle was delighted with the results of this experiment. Not one of the owners of these comparatively modest estates would be strong enough to threaten rebellion—indeed, each was happy to pay taxes to the Crown in return for secure title to farms which they could pass on by English law to an eldest son. The Master of the Ordnance concluded that this sort of division was 'the soundest and surest way to bring Ireland to due obedience'.

Described as a 'native plantation', this exercise in social engineering, this application of the principle of divide and rule, was surely more effective than repeated expensive military expeditions. Indeed it was considered so successful that Co. Monaghan was not to be included in James I's Plantation of Ulster. A similar scheme was drawn up for the neighbouring O'Reilly lordship of East Bréifne, now renamed Co. Cavan. West Bréifne, which became Co. Leitrim, was another plum ripe for the picking—particularly after its lord, Sir Brian O'Rourke, had been hanged, drawn and quartered at Tyburn. One official described the planned 'native plantation' of Leitrim as 'indeed pleasing to God, highly profitable to the Queen, and the precedent of it a light and candle to their neighbours of the north to find out speedily the way to wealth, civility and obedience'. The Queen's Marshal, Sir Henry Bagenal, agreed with this view. He advised the break-up of the great Gaelic lordships of Ulster in this way: 'The chiefest, or rather the only means to reduce these barbarous people to obedience is to disunite them as all may be enforced to depend on the Queen'.[29]

THE NINE YEARS' WAR BEGINS

The Earl of Tyrone viewed these developments with mounting alarm, particularly when the Dublin government decided to break up the lands of the Maguires in Co. Fermanagh. All the Gaelic lords of the north felt directly threatened. When a sheriff approached Enniskillen with troops in 1593 this was too much for the Lord of Fermanagh, Hugh Maguire, who rose in rebellion. As one of the principal nobles in Ireland, the Earl of Tyrone was expected to campaign with the Queen's Marshal when he was in Ulster. O'Neill had a good record in this respect so far, and now he rode alongside Marshal Sir Henry Bagenal. After a hard-fought siege, Maguire was forced to surrender his island castle of Enniskillen early in 1594. Now it was the English who occupied the castle. Soon, however, it was they who were in danger.

The Earl of Tyrone made the fateful decision to change sides. He would champion the cause of the Gaelic lords of the north, leading them to resist the encroachment of the English Crown. For this strategy to succeed he would first have to end the centuries-old wasting rivalry between the O'Neills and the O'Donnells, and win the support of the MacDonnells. By his judicious marriage alliances Turlough Luineach had paved the way: the earl respectfully waited until the old man died, in 1595, before having himself proclaimed 'the O'Neill' and inaugurated at Tullaghoge. Red Hugh O'Donnell, the fifteen-year-old Lord of Tír Chonaill and son of Finola, had been captured by a ruse in 1587 and held captive in Dublin Castle. The earl, with many friends in the Pale and using bribes on a spectacular scale, organised a successful escape in 1592, and, assisted by O'Neill's men all the way, Red Hugh made his way north-west back to his castle at Ballyshannon. Though his frost-bitten big toes had to be amputated, Red Hugh was proclaimed 'the O'Donnell' shortly afterwards. The bond between the two lords would never thereafter be broken. Together they recovered Enniskillen for Maguire, and soon other English garrisons found themselves surrounded by hostile forces.

The hatred Sir Henry Bagenal, the Queen's Marshal, had for the earl played its part in precipitating the approaching war. In 1591 O'Neill eloped with Sir Henry's twenty-year-old sister, Mabel. Their marriage did not last long, Mabel dying five years later. Bagenal never forgave Tyrone and vented his feelings to the Queen's secretary, Lord Burghley: 'I can but accurse myself and fortune that my blood, which in my father and myself hath often been spilled in repressing this rebellious race, should now be mingled with so traitorous a stock and kindred'.[30]

'A QUICK END TO A SLOW PROCEEDING'

The Queen's Marshal was soon to experience the military power of a Gaelic Ulster united as never before. On 13 June 1595, returning after bringing supplies to Monaghan Fort, Bagenal was ambushed by Tyrone at Clontibret. There were, it was admitted, 'more hurt men in the late service than was convenient to declare'. It was evident that the natives had become accomplished in the use of firearms: Bagenal's cavalry commander observed 'that in no place whatsoever he had served in all his life he never saw readier or perfecter shot'.[31] Unlike his predecessors, who had relied on hiring mercenaries from the Scottish Isles, Hugh O'Neill raised a great host from his own lands. He armed not only his own freemen but also conscripted his peasantry, providing them with modern calivers, muskets and arquebuses and—with the help of some Spanish Armada castaways—giving them training and discipline. These 'bonaght' levies marched in companies carrying colours to the beat of drums and the skirl of pipes and were supported by 'kerne', light foot soldiers who could muster from any part of Ulster. O'Neill, his allied chiefs and their kinsmen, who formed the traditional warrior caste, made up the cavalry of this formidable army.

In 1598 the Irish Council in Dublin ordered another attempt to bring supplies to a beleaguered garrison, this time to Blackwater Fort in the heart of O'Neill's country. Reinforced by fresh troops from England, Bagenal led the largest expedition for many years in August. Shortly after leaving Armagh, the Marshal advanced into an elaborately prepared ambush. His army was all but annihilated, and Bagenal, raising his visor to rally his men, was shot through the head. This 'Battle of the Yellow Ford' was the most disastrous defeat the English ever suffered at the hands of the Irish.

All over the rest of the island, Gaelic lords rose up and clamoured to join with O'Neill and O'Donnell, even within sight of Dublin. The O'Mores furiously attacked the planters in King's County and Queen's County, and the Plantation of Munster disintegrated, the colonists being driven out, mutilated or killed. Elizabeth faced the real prospect of losing Ireland altogether. Not for the first time, O'Neill hesitated; his ambition was to be the unchallenged ruler of Ulster, not of Ireland as a whole, and now he hoped to win the Queen's acceptance of his rule. Elizabeth no longer had any wish to talk. Over the winter of 1598/9 troops were levied on an unprecedented scale across England, and rich contracts for food, munitions, camp equipment and medical supplies were made with London merchants.

The Queen chose Robert Devereux, 2nd Earl of Essex, as the man to lead her new army, with the exalted title of Lord Lieutenant. Leading the greatest army yet seen in Ireland, Essex did not do as he had promised: to meet Tyrone in the field. Instead he spent the summer of 1599 attempting to detach Leinster and Munster lords from O'Neill. Elizabeth fretted that her Lord Lieutenant was costing her a thousand pounds a day and urged him to put the axe 'to the root of that tree which hath been the treasonable stock from which so many poisoned plants and grafts have been derived'. As reports of aimless expeditions and inconsequential sieges were brought to her, Sir John Harrington observed: 'She walks much in her privy chamber, and stamps with her feet at ill news, and thrusts her rusty sword at times into the arras in great rage'.[32]

The news got worse. Sir Conyers Clifford and his army were overwhelmed by the O'Rourkes in the Curlew Mountains, and his head was sent to Red Hugh. Then, when Essex at last set out for Ulster at the end of August, troops began to desert. O'Neill and the Lord Lieutenant confronted each other at Ardee; but, instead of fighting, a curious parley followed on horseback in the middle of a stream entering the River Glyde near Dundalk. They met again with witnesses and agreed a six-week truce. The Ulster Irish retired, having made no concessions whatever.

'To trust this traitor upon oath is to trust a devil upon his religion', Elizabeth said in despair, scathingly describing the truce as a 'quick end made of a slow proceeding'.[33] Essex then suddenly deserted his post, returned to London and burst into the Queen's bedchamber to beg forgiveness. He was committed to the custody of Lord Keeper Egerton. The truce was extended to December 1599, but, while O'Neill wanted to maintain it, the English were preparing to renew the fight. Elizabeth was convinced that she must unstintingly use her treasure to defeat Tyrone. She also needed a man capable of steering her armies towards victory. That man was Charles Blount, Lord Mountjoy.

Chapter 2 ∽

| LA JORNADA DE IRLANDA

MOUNTJOY

Charles Blount, Lord Mountjoy, though only thirty-six years old when he was appointed Lord Deputy of Ireland in January 1600, believed himself to be in constant bad health. He took an afternoon nap in his tent when on campaign, and, his secretary Fynes Moryson informs us,

> he wore jerkins and round hose and cloaks lined with velvet, and white beaver hats, and besides his ordinary stockings of silk, he wore under boots another pair of woollen, with a pair of high line boot-hose, yea three waistcoats in cold weather, and a thick ruff, besides a russet scarf about his neck thrice folded under it. I never observed any of his age and strength to keep his body so warm . . . He took tobacco abundantly, which I think preserved him from sickness, especially in Ireland, where the foggy air of the bogs do most prejudice the health.

Mountjoy nevertheless inspired his men with greater success than any English commander before him, and he appeared fearless in battle. At different times his horse was shot under him, his greyhound running beside him was shot dead, and his chaplain, one of his secretaries and a gentleman of his chamber were killed in action close by him.

The new Lord Deputy planned to break the rebellion of the Ulster lords by laying waste the countryside and starving the people. He preferred to fight in winter, when it was more difficult for the Irish to hide in the leafless woods, when their stores of corn and butter could be burned and when their cattle down from their summer pastures could be more easily slaughtered. After the ignominious departure of Essex, O'Neill had been able to travel down to Munster to bring reassurance to his Gaelic allies there and to maintain a standing army of bonnaghts in the south under the command of Captain Richard Tyrrell. Mountjoy, however, swiftly dealt with the earl's southern supporters, despoiling Wicklow and scattering Tyrrell's force. Sir George Carew, Lord President of Munster, ensured that by the end of the year not a single castle in Munster remained in rebel hands.

In the spring, Mountjoy sent an expedition to Lough Foyle with the object of driving a wedge between the O'Neill and O'Donnell lordships. On 7 May 1600 an impressive fleet sailed out of Carrickfergus harbour with some four thousand soldiers and two hundred cavalry on board under the command of Sir Henry Docwra. Here, on the ancient ecclesiastical site of Derry, Docwra established his base. Using rubble from old buildings bound by mortar made by firing cockle-shells collected in the mud, his men completed the fortifications by the end of the summer. Red Hugh O'Donnell was close by, and any time the English ventured out the Irish fiercely attacked them and seized two hundred of their horses. Ships came in with fresh supplies and horses, and some Irish lords, who knew the countryside well, came over to the English side. They included Niall Garbh O'Donnell, who felt with some justice that he had as good a title to the chieftaincy of the O'Donnells as Red Hugh. Docwra overran Inishowen and began to fight his way upstream towards Strabane.

Meanwhile from the south the Lord Deputy approached the Moyry Pass, the gateway to Ulster, running between Dundalk and Newry. Red Hugh could only hope to evict Docwra with O'Neill's help, and that he could not do until the Earl of Tyrone had driven back Mountjoy. After weeks of intense fighting in foul weather, on the afternoon of Thursday 2 October the Irish advanced with pike and handgun in formidable array. Mountjoy threw five regiments against them, but after three hours of close fighting the English fell back in confusion.

The Lord Deputy had failed to break through Tyrone's elaborate defences at the pass. Nevertheless, the tide was beginning to turn against the Gaelic lords of Ulster. Only in the extremities of Munster and Connacht were there allies faithful to O'Neill still in arms. The 'Old English'—descendants of medieval Norman conquerors and those they had brought with them—stubbornly refused to join the Gaelic lords, much as they hated the government's attempts to force them to conform to the reformed religion. Elizabeth had no wish to negotiate a compromise peace. The only hope was substantial Spanish help.

'THE EXPEDITION MUST GO THIS YEAR': *SOCORRO* FOR IRELAND

On 16 May 1596 Red Hugh O'Donnell and Hugh O'Neill had written to the Prince of Asturias appealing to him to

> aid in his clemency this most excellent and just cause, that of asserting Catholic liberty and of freeing the country from the rod of tyrannical evil, and that, with the help of the Divine Majesty, he may win for Christ an infinite number of souls, snatching them from the jaws of Hell, and may wholly destroy or compel to return to reason the ministers of satanic fury and the impious disturbers of the Christian state.[1]

In 1598 the prince succeeded his father as Philip III of Spain. A pious and colourless king, Philip generally preferred to leave the direction of state affairs to others, but he was inclined to do what he could for the Ulster lords. On his accession Philip had unwisely sent away from court experienced and loyal servants bequeathed to him by his father. To replace these men the King had appointed his favourite, Francisco Gómez de Sandoval y Rojas, Duke of Lerma.

Fray Mateo de Oviedo (briefed by O'Neill's agent in Spain, Father Edmund O'Donnell) and Don Martín de la Cerdá assiduously lobbied Lerma to provide *socorro* (aid) to O'Neill and O'Donnell. A strong expeditionary force should be sent to Ireland. Without any serious support from juntas of councillors, Lerma warmed to the idea. In particular he liked the argument that a Spanish landing would so preoccupy Elizabeth in Ireland that she would be unable to continue authorising damaging English attacks on plate fleets coming from the Indies across the Atlantic. Lerma sent Cerdá to Ireland with silver, a thousand arquebuses with powder horns and a hundred quintals each of powder, lead and fuse, in three vessels under the command of Ensign Pedro de Sandoval. Putting in to Donegal Bay in April 1600, Cerdá held a conference of about sixty Gaelic leaders in Donegal Abbey. He was unable to promise an expedition, but his assurances and munitions did much to convince O'Neill and O'Donnell to fight on.

It was King Philip himself who made the decision to send an expedition. Rather unusually, he asserted himself, overruling councillors who assured him that the Spanish Empire had other priorities. In July he wrote that, if necessary, he would pay for the expedition out of his own pocket:

This enterprise must so further God's service, and the earnestness and zeal shown by the council for it must so animate those entrusted with its execution as to overcome all the difficulties unseen. I myself will see that the money is provided, even at the expense of what is necessary for my personal state. The expedition must go this year; to that end the council will put all in order with the utmost speed . . .[2]

In fact the expedition did not go that year. Archduke Albert in the Spanish Netherlands made desperate appeals for more men to fight the Protestant Dutch, and it looked as if troops would be needed to assist Savoyards against the French.

Meanwhile, in Ireland, O'Neill and O'Donnell were becoming increasingly desperate. Neither Mountjoy nor Docwra relaxed their campaigns of attrition during the winter of 1600/01. The men of Docwra's garrison 'sett divers Preys of cattle, & did many other services all the winter longe' with the help of Niall Garbh, 'without whose intelligence and guidance little or nothing could have been done of ourselves'.[3] Docwra was close to achieving his objective of separating Tír Chonaill from Tír Eoghain: Niall Garbh took Donegal Abbey, and Ballyshannon Castle was placed under siege. Cahir O'Doherty, Lord of Inishowen, came over to the English side, enabling Docwra to move against the MacSweeneys of Fanad. Mountjoy built a new fort at Mountnorris and from there raided deep into the Earl of Tyrone's country. At the beginning of April, Captain Edward Blaney and Captain Josias Bodley, employing '30 Arrows with Wild-fire', took one of O'Neill's greatest strongholds, the crannóg fortress of Lough Lurcan. A 'great store of butter, corn, meal, and powder, was burned and spoiled in the island, which all the rebels of that country made their magazine'.[4] Sir Arthur Chichester, using Carrickfergus as his base, ravaged Clandeboye, kept the MacDonnells at bay and crossed Lough Neagh in boats to create havoc on the western shores. In May 1601 he reported to Mountjoy:

We have killed, burnt, and spoiled all along the lough within four miles of Dungannon, from whence we returned hither yesterday; in which journeys we have killed above one hundred people of all sorts, besides such as were burnt, how many I know not. We spare none of what quality or sex soever, and it hath bred much terror in the people . . . and Tyrone himself lay within a mile of this place, but kept himself safe.[5]

This scorched-earth campaign was creating devastation in Ulster. A terrible man-made famine could be the only outcome. By now only the Spanish could save the cause of the Ulster lords.

A DIVIDED COMMAND

In January 1601 Don Martín de la Cerdá dropped anchor at Teelin, close to Slieve League, overlooking the most westerly point in Tír Chonaill. From La Coruña he had brought 2,000 arquebuses, 150 quintals each of powder, lead and fuse, and 20,000 ducats. But he brought also the bitter news of postponement. The best that Cerdá could do was to say that if the expedition had not come by the end of July the Gaelic lords would be free to negotiate terms. Much time was spent in discussing where a Spanish expeditionary force should land. In the end the Earl of Tyrone made it clear that if there were six thousand or more they should come to Waterford or Cork, if somewhat less to Limerick, and if less again to Donegal Bay.

In January 1601 France made peace with Savoy; Spanish troops would no longer be needed to defend Savoyards. Now Philip and Lerma were at one: the expedition to Ireland—*la jornada de Irlanda*—should be prepared without delay. A force of six thousand men was to be raised, made up of veterans from Galicia and the Azores, two thousand men already stationed in Lisbon and fresh recruits enlisted principally in Castile. Orders were issued for the making of ten thousand quintals of biscuit for the *jornada* in the ovens at La Coruña and Lisbon.[6]

The decision to send such a force to Ireland could not have been taken lightly. True, Philip III ruled many possessions in a far-flung empire. The Holy Roman Emperor was a member of his Habsburg dynasty and a firm ally. But Spanish world power was passing its zenith. Philip II had mortgaged American bullion in advance to pay foreign bankers; three times he had suspended payments to bankers, and he had left his son with an immense consolidated debt of 76,540,000 ducats. Spain was denuded of troops by the war in the Low Countries, the shortage of manpower made more acute by a plague in Castilian lands, which, between 1596 and 1602, led to the loss of half a million lives. Archduke Albert's attempts to achieve peace had broken down, and most of Spain's military resources were needed in Flanders, particularly when the Siege of Ostend, which was to last more than three years, began in June 1601.

The Low Countries would always be Spain's strategic priority. However, an expedition to Ireland would divert English troops away from assisting the Dutch and towards support for Mountjoy. The war against O'Neill and O'Donnell had been conducted at a ruinous cost to Elizabeth and had claimed the lives of some forty thousand soldiers. If the Spanish could ensconce themselves in Ireland they could use it for a base for the invasion of England, and place the Infanta Isabella, Archduke Albert's wife and Philip's sister, on the throne there. This would surely be a great victory for the Catholic cause.[7]

Don Diego de Brochero y Añaya accepted the post of naval commander of the expedition. A levy of seamen from Guipúzcoa, Biscay and Cuatro Villas included many English prisoners, together with forcibly impressed French and German sailors—Brochero did not relish the task of keeping a close eye on them. He was also troubled by the King's order that, once the soldiers and supplies were ashore, the ships were to be brought straight back to Spain. Don Juan del Águila, the captain-general in charge of the land forces, was a *maestre de campo* (colonel of a regiment) with a distinguished service record in Flanders, in Brittany and against the Turks. However, he had to be released from gaol to take up this command, having been convicted of ill-treating his men and dipping his hands into government funds. The King's decision to divide the command in this way between Brochero and Águila was to prove disastrous. In particular, Brochero, encouraged by Fray Oviedo, was sure that landfall should be made at Cork or Kinsale. Águila argued passionately against this, Munster being back in English control and too far away from the Ulster lords. His choice was Donegal Bay.

'THE SUCCOUR SENT BEING SO SMALL AND LANDED IN AN INCONVENIENT PLACE'

No decision on landfall had been arrived at as the Armada set sail from Lisbon down the Tagus at seven in the morning on 18 August 1601. Thirty-three ships crossed the bar at Belém at ten. Eleven of the ships had been brought from Andalusia by the admiral Don Pedro de Zubiaur, on board the largest vessel, a great galleon of 960 tons, the *San Felipe*. Águila, Brochero and Oviedo (now the titular Archbishop of Dublin) were together on another galleon, the *San Andrés*. Cerdá, having contracted malaria in Portugal, had been forced to stay behind. The destination still had not been resolved, and so, three hundred leagues from Ireland, Brochero called a conference in mid-ocean. Águila was firmly outvoted: Kinsale it had to be. All agreed that it was quite wrong to take the ships away once the men, provisions, munitions and equipment were taken ashore. Oviedo offered all his plate and Zubiaur his salary to pay the sailors to stay on; but, with a heavy heart, Brochero concluded that he had to follow the King's command.

The vote in favour of Kinsale had been partly influenced by the foul weather, which could make a voyage to the north-west a perilous one. Oviedo, very sick for most of the time, spoke of *malos temporales y tempestas*. The Armada was a month at sea before seeing Ireland at all, and then, off the Blaskets and Dursey Island, a violent storm scattered the fleet on 17 September. The *San Felipe* and six accompanying vessels became separated, and Zubiaur, after an abortive attempt to sail up to Donegal Bay, returned to Spain. He got the King's permission to make another attempt, but he was not to reach Ireland again until the beginning of December.

On 21 September, Brochero steered the rest of the ships into the Bandon Estuary, where Águila took over the walled town of Kinsale. Then the ships left. The number of effectives on board the Armada leaving Lisbon had been 4,432—well short of the 6,000 promised. Now, as a consequence of the storm off the Blaskets, Águila had only 3,500 men at most. In addition, Zubiaur's ships had been carrying the lion's share of the expedition's powder and match for his arquebuses. Then the captain-general received news which confirmed all his anxieties about Kinsale as a destination: two of O'Neill's firm allies in Munster, Florence MacCarthy and James FitzThomas—men expected to reinforce the Spaniards there without hesitation—had been seized by the English and imprisoned in the Tower of London. Donal Cam O'Sullivan Beare, Lord of Dunboy and the peninsula between Kenmare River and Bantry Bay, sent a message offering two thousand of his men to block Mountjoy's route and delay a siege until the arrival of the Ulstermen. In an extraordinary decision, Águila turned down this offer. Quite without justification, he did not trust this Irishman.

Zubiaur eventually got permission to sail to Ireland from La Coruña in November. He had with him only 621 men. Just as he was about to set off, the veteran Don Martín Manrique Padillo, Adelanto Mayor of Castile, wrote in disgust:

I do not consider as a reinforcement the expedition now being sent under Zubiaur. The reinforcement needed is one that will end the business once and for all, and not driblets like sips of broth, that will only prolong the agony, and allow the invalid to die after all. Little reinforcements will only cause the loss to be greater, and will give the

Queen an opportunity for sending with ease larger aid than can go from Spain. If the Irish do not see the Spaniards the stronger party, even for a week, they will not declare themselves against the Queen ... If with God's help the Earls be able to effect a junction with Don Juan del Águila, a good result may be hoped for, but there is a great fear that they may be defeated on the way, which would be a grievous thing, for the loss of all these good Catholics would have been brought about in consequence of the succour sent being so small and landed in an inconvenient place.[8]

AT KINSALE, 'AWAITING YOUR MOST ILLUSTRIOUS HIGHNESSES'

On 23 December 1601 Hugh O'Neill, Earl of Tyrone, was confident of victory. Here at Coolcarron, overlooking Belgooly in west Cork, he readied his great host for action to begin at the day's end. With him was the armed might of Gaelic Ulster: among those forming up with the O'Neills were MacDonnells from the Antrim Glens, Magennises of Down, O'Reillys from Cavan, Maguires of Fermanagh, O'Hanlons from Armagh, O'Haras from Antrim and MacMahons from Monaghan; and accompanying Tyrone's own gallowglass, musketeers and mounted warriors were contingents called up from his great lordship of Tír Eoghain, including O'Cahans, O'Hagans, O'Devlins, MacShanes, MacLavertys, Devines and O'Mullans. By his side was Red Hugh O'Donnell, Lord of Tír Chonaill. 'We are here awaiting your most illustrious highnesses', Águila had written to them; quickly surrounded by the English, he had been able to do no other than man the walls of Kinsale and send an appeal to the Ulster lords to join him.

The rebel lords agreed to risk all by traversing the length of the island in response. O'Donnell had been the first to begin the march south. Amongst those setting out from Tír Chonaill with Red Hugh and his O'Donnells were MacSweeneys, O'Gallaghers, MacDavitts, O'Boyles and O'Dohertys. Joining him at Ballymote in Co. Sligo were fighting men drawn from leading Connacht families, including O'Rourkes, O'Connors, MacDermotts and O'Kellys. This had been an epic trek of more than three hundred miles, with men wading swollen rivers, often up to the chest. In Tipperary, O'Donnell's host had memorably given an English army the slip by a forced march of forty miles through the night across the frozen Slievephelim Mountains. Reporting his failure to Lord Deputy Mountjoy, Sir George Carew, Lord President of Munster, had observed: 'The long march is incredible but, upon my reputation, I do assure your lordship it is true'.[9] After reaching the far south-west, Red Hugh had attracted to his standard O'Sullivan Beare, Lord of Dunboy, and other Gaelic contingents supplied principally by the MacCarthys and O'Driscolls. It was here, close to where west Cork meets Kerry, that the Basque admiral Zubiaur had brought in a small force of Spaniards at Castlehaven on 1 December.

In an attempt to draw the English away from Kinsale and to ensure that his men had sufficient provisions, O'Neill had ravaged north Leinster before advancing through the midlands, where he was joined by that dashing deserter from the forces of the Queen, Captain Richard Tyrrell. O'Neill and O'Donnell had rendezvoused at Bandon on 5 December before making camp a few miles north of Kinsale, at Coolcarron.

That Wednesday, 23 December, Pedro Blanco appeared in the Irish camp with Águila's final confirmation of the agreed battle plan. Blanco had been one of the few survivors of thousands cast ashore on Ireland's poorly charted Atlantic coasts when Armada vessels foundered there in 1588. O'Neill had engaged him as a personal servant. Now Blanco proved invaluable. Most attempting to steal past the English batteries and trenches encircling Kinsale had been captured and, after being interrogated, summarily hanged. Blanco had repeatedly avoided detection. Águila's battle plan, he translated for the Ulster lords, was that the Irish should advance at night, avoiding detection, to Ardmartin Hill, overlooking Kinsale. Then, at dawn, while the English would be facing north to meet this threat, the Spanish on a signal would sally out from the walls of Kinsale in attack.

Both O'Neill and O'Donnell had deep misgivings about this plan. All their victories over the English had been won by stealth, treachery and hit-and-run attacks in familiar countryside—above all by ambushing columns from the cover of woods and the protection of bogs. They would have preferred to stay put and wait for hunger and disease to destroy the forces of the Crown. Now Águila was asking them to face Mountjoy's forces in formal battle lines in the open—something O'Neill had always been careful to avoid. But Spanish captains sent from Castlehaven the day before urged the Gaelic lords to follow the plan. According to Ensign Pedro de Sandoval, the Earl of Tyrone 'began to complain very vehemently saying that . . . their people were not at all skilled for fighting in open country'.[10] Nevertheless, the advice of the Spanish captains prevailed.

Tyrone was bitterly disappointed that only eighty Spaniards had arrived from Castlehaven; Zubiaur had decided to keep the rest of his men to defend castles he occupied, the nearest of them at least two days' march from Kinsale. Nevertheless, those making ready for battle at Coolcarron felt certain of success; after all, the Irish and the Spanish together greatly outnumbered the encircled English. These men, for all the privations they had endured, were in good order and good spirits. Zubiaur's opinion of the thousand Munstermen led by O'Sullivan Beare to join the main Irish host was that 'these Irish are like game bucks, gallant and ready for travail and fighting'.[11]

'INFINITT MYSERYE GROWNE WEAKE AND FEINT WITH THEIR SPARE DIET'

Águila knew that all hope of reinforcement had gone. Just downstream of Kinsale, the English had taken the forts of Rincurran and Castle Park. Admiral Sir Richard Leveson's ships efficiently patrolled the Bandon River where it entered the sea. Mountjoy, who had arrived on 26 October, had erected platforms for his cannon and ordered the digging of trenches so deep they had to be scaled by ladders. Kinsale was completely surrounded. Águila was in, he admitted himself, *un hoyo* (a pit).[12] In addition, he was running short of provisions. In Lord President Carew's opinion, 'the Spaniards on there parts endure infinitt myserye growne weake and feint with their spare diet, being no other than water or rusk; dogs, cats and garrons is a feast when they can get it'.[13]

Actually the plight of the besieged was not nearly so desperate as that of the besiegers. Once the Irish had made camp at Coolcarron, Mountjoy's army was cut off from the rest of the Munster countryside. With skill and perseverance, Leveson had striven to bring reinforcements and supplies from Rochester and Barnstaple to land them at Oysterhaven, a creek adjacent to the Bandon Estuary. Now persistent westerly winds and violent storms had all but cut that supply line. Shortage of food and disease had been wreaking havoc on Mountjoy's army. In the extreme weather, sentinels were dropping dead at their posts. 'And it was most true that our men daily died in dozens', Fynes Moryson observed. At least six thousand men had been lost in this way—a number equivalent to all the reinforcements Mountjoy had been sent from England during the siege. 'I do not thinke a more miserable siedge hathe not been seene or so great a mortalite without a plage', Carew concluded. Writing that Wednesday, 23 December, Carew expressed his anxiety that the warhorses would become too weak from hunger to be capable of effective action: 'Our horses for want of forradge (which by reason of this long siedge the country cannot yield) do infinitly decay and espetiallye the last supplies, for the men fall sick and the horse perish'.[14] The same day the Lord Deputy sent a despatch to Sir Robert Cecil (son of Sir William), the Queen's secretary, reporting that 'in shorter time than is almost credible our new men were wholly wasted, and either by death, sickness or running away those companies and supplies grown altogether unserviceable'.[15]

From captured despatches and interrogation of prisoners, Mountjoy was aware that an attack was imminent. However, the story told later by Moryson—that in exchange for whiskey the battle plan had been revealed by a traitor in the Irish camp—is not corroborated elsewhere. At midnight the Earl of Tyrone, with Tyrrell and the Spaniards sent by Zubiaur in the van, began the two-mile march from Coolcarron. O'Donnell's force would follow to form the rearguard.

'MANIFEST WAS THE DISPLEASURE OF GOD': THE BATTLE OF CHRISTMAS EVE

Sir Henry Power, commanding an advance party of veteran troops, had been ordered out of the English camp to view the route O'Neill might be expected to take. Then, just before dawn, Power spotted the Irish lighting slow matches for their calivers and muskets, and he immediately informed Mountjoy. So too did another commander: 'A little before the break of day, Sir Richard Graeme, who had the guard of horse that night, sent word to the Lord Deputy that the scouts had discovered the rebels' matches in great numbers'. Mountjoy was with Carew and the Marshal, Sir Richard Wingfield, in their shelter built of turf. The Lord Deputy was about to go to bed, having decided that there would be no attack that night. Now, without hesitation, he gave the call to arms. A corporal dashed to the Earl of Thomond's camp with the news. Sir Henry Danvers readied the horse. Wingfield rode up to the scouts and sent back the intelligence that 'O'Neill was advanced horse and foot neere the toppe of the hill, where the Erle of Thomond first quartered within less than 2. musket shotte of the town'.[16]

On Ardmartin Hill, O'Neill had drawn up his men in battle order. Just then, however, the noise of martial preparation in the English camp made it patently clear that his presence had been detected. The element of surprise had gone. O'Donnell's army had not yet arrived. The earl could see no sign that Águila was about to sally out from the town. O'Neill had never won a victory by confronting the English directly in the open. He ordered his men back. As a violent squall briefly masked this manoeuvre, Tyrone retreated north-west about a mile over two streams to take refuge behind boggy ground.

O'Neill's men fired the first shots as English cavalry, commanded by Marshal Wingfield and the Earl of Clanrickard, galloped up. The boggy ground chosen by O'Neill proved no protection. Wingfield's men found a way round the ford, and, reinforced by the arrival of Power's regiment, the Marshal ordered a frontal assault. At first the main Irish battle of foot withstood the charge. The O'Neill's horsemen galloped forward to meet the English; in their traditional manner, they stalled, brandishing their spears.

Without hesitation, the English cavalry charged them. Immediately overwhelmed, the ranks of mounted Irishmen turned tail. As they fled, the Irish foot began to do the same. The English 'broke the gross which consisted of 1,500 men', Power explained; 'they were all of the country of Tyrone, this being such a fearful thing to the rest, that they all broke and shifted for themselves'.[17]

Only Tyrrell and the small Spanish contingent attempted to make a stand on nearby rising ground, but they were hacked down by Sir William Godolphin's cavalry. O'Donnell's men, finally appearing, witnessed the flight and, bewildered, joined in, throwing away their arms 'to run the lighter'. In their relentless pursuit the English inflicted a fearful slaughter, stopping only when their horses could go no further. Surrounded by bodies of the slain, Mountjoy knighted Clanrickard on the field of battle.

And what of Águila and his Spaniards? Hearing a *volée de joie* fired in Thomond's camp to celebrate the victory, Águila mistook it for O'Neill's expected signal. Sallying out from the walls, the Spaniards were quickly driven back, and, seeing English horsemen holding up seven Irish colours, they realised the battle was over.

The official journal recorded that corpses were strewn over 'almost two miles'. Dr Hippocrates D'Otthen, a surgeon serving with Mountjoy, reckoned that some 1,200 Irish had been killed. In the ensuing days more were to die from wounds and exposure. The English took no Irish prisoners. Offers of ransom were refused, and all captives were hanged. One report reaching Brussels stated that two hundred were strung up in front of the walls of Kinsale. Surviving Spaniards who had fought with Tyrrell—three captains, six ensigns and forty soldiers—had their lives spared. The journal recorded that 'the Spanish (which were hurt) were forthwith sent by the Lord Deputy to Kinsale to the Spanish commander to report to him this success'. The English casualties were extraordinarily low: according to D'Otthen, only three were killed.

The Spanish described the battle of Kinsale as a *derrota*, a rout. Moryson later reflected on the reasons for it:

> And how unprofitable their horse are, and of what small moment to help their foot, that one battell at Kinsall did aboundantly shewe, where the Irish horse and Foote being incouraged by the Spaniards to stand in the Playne field . . . by this forsaking of their foote, they might justly be said to be the chief cause of their overthrow. Their horses are of small stature, excellent amblers, but of little or no boldness and small strength either for battell or long marches . . . our English horsemen having deep war saddles and using pistols, as well as Speares and swords, and many of them having corsletts . . . our troops must need have great advantages over them.[18]

For the authors of the Annals of the Four Masters the battle marked the passing of an era:

> Manifest was the displeasure of God, and misfortune to the Irish of fine Fodhla . . . Immense and countless was the loss in that place; for the prowess and valour, prosperity and affluence, nobleness and chivalry, dignity and renown, bravery and protection, devotion and pure religion, of the Island, were lost in this engagement.[19]

Águila surrendered soon after. Red Hugh joined Zubiaur at Castlehaven, and after the Spanish there had laid down their arms he sailed to Spain in a vain attempt to persuade King Philip to send another expedition. O'Donnell died of fever a few months later at Simancas. O'Neill escaped the battlefield with only sixty men. Kinsale was Gaelic Ireland's Culloden: all the earl's triumphs had been wiped out during one hour's fighting that Christmas Eve. The fate of Ulster had been sealed. O'Neill, returned to Tyrone, fought on. The final subjugation of the north, fifteen months after Kinsale, was, however, inevitable. The way was clear for the most ambitious programme of confiscation and colonisation ever planned in western Europe: the Plantation of Ulster.

Chapter 3 ∾

| MELLIFONT

'A GOOD SUMMER'S JOURNEY'

Sir Henry Danvers, wounded during the Battle of Kinsale, crossed the Irish Sea to inform the Queen of her Lord Deputy's success, and, as John Stow recorded in his Annals of England, 'the xviii of January at night, bone-fiers were made at London, with ringing and otherwise rejoysing, for the newes out of Ireland, the victory of our English-men obtained there'.[1] The playwright Richard Venner dashed off a poem entitled 'England's Joy'. The fourth stanza reads:

> The Noble Lord, *Mount Joy* that Champion true:
> Of honours choise, in Virtues Chiualrie:
> Hath put to flight, that coward Rebell Crue
> Of proude *Tyrone,* and made the Spaniards flie.
> *Don John de Aquila* with all his traine:
> With little comfort are return'd to *Spaine.*[2]

Actually, after making his composition with Lord Deputy Mountjoy on 2 January 1602, Águila did not get a fair wind to return to Spain (in English ships paid for by Don Juan) until 16 March. The agreement included the stipulation that Zubiaur's men at Castlehaven should surrender all the castles they occupied in the area. Hearing that he had been refused pardon by Mountjoy, Donal Cam O'Sullivan Beare took back his castle at Dunboy and fortified Dursey Island with Spanish cannon. His resistance was determined but hopeless: Sir George Carew, Lord President of Munster, took Dursey by storm. Dunboy, however, did not fall until 18 June. Every man of the defending garrison was put to the sword.

One by one, other strongholds in Munster, Leinster and Connacht held by the Irish fell to English commanders and their allies. O'Sullivan Beare headed north with his people, including about five hundred fighting men.

Travelling between twenty and thirty miles a day, he had to construct a boat of sally rods, over which the skins of eleven horses were stretched, to take them with him, thirty at a time, across the River Shannon. By the time he reached the safety of O'Rourke's Leitrim Castle only eighteen fighting men, sixteen horseboys and one woman remained out of about a thousand who had set forth with him.

Fifteen months were to pass after the Battle of Kinsale before Mountjoy could bring the war to an end in Ulster. Once again he set about laying waste the countryside and destroying cattle and stores of food to starve the people into submission. His task was made easier by the submission, one by one, of lesser lords—including Randal MacDonnell, Lord of the Glens, who had returned from Kinsale with only forty survivors—and these were now expected to campaign alongside English troops.

However, the Queen made it clear that there was no question that the Earl of Tyrone himself should be allowed to sue for terms. She wrote to her Lord Deputy:

> We do require you very earnestly to be very wary in taking the Submissions of these Rebels . . . Next We do require you, even whilst the Iron is hot, so to strike, as this may not only prove a good Summer's Journey, but may deserve the Title of that Action which is the War's Conclusion. For furtherance whereof We have spared no Charge.

In her own hand the Queen wrote in the margin: 'We con you many Lauds for having so very nearly approached the villainous Rebel, and see no Reason why so great Forces should not end his Days'.[3]

'ALL MEANS TO FAMISH THEM'

In 1602 Mountjoy did have a good summer's journey in Ulster. He resumed the strategy he had been applying during the twelve months he had been campaigning in the north before the Spanish landing at Kinsale. He sought to find the enemy forces—often with the help of Irish guides in inhospitable territory—and engage them and destroy them. As well as taking into mercy Tyrone's increasingly pressed confederates, the Lord Deputy encircled the forces of O'Neill and O'Donnell with a ring of forts from Derry south along the Foyle, across the south-west borders of Tyrone at Newtownstewart, Omagh, Clogher and Augher, and in a line along the River Blackwater at Armagh, Mountjoy and, soon after, Charlemont. These he garrisoned with men ordered to harass the enemy constantly and to devastate the surrounding countryside. By the beginning of 1602 barely six square miles of Ulster lay beyond the range of his cavalry from a military outpost. No garrison or fort was more than a day's march from any of the others.[4] Since his opponents could take refuge in mountainous countryside and in the woods, Mountjoy systematically set about destroying their crops and slaughtering cattle.[5]

The Lord Deputy arrived in Newry on 10 June, and four days later he had reached the Blackwater. There he built a new fort, called Charlemount (later Charlemont) from a combination of his Christian name and title, with a garrison under the command of Captain Toby Caulfield. Sir Henry Docwra, Governor of Derry, had remained in Ulster throughout the Kinsale campaign. During this time his ally, Niall Garbh O'Donnell, had been able to hold Donegal Abbey, though he nearly lost it in September when an accidental fire detonated thirteen barrels of gunpowder, killing twenty-nine men and demolishing the defences. Docwra ordered the garrison to Assaroe on the River Erne to take the castle at Ballyshannon, long under siege. He himself was busy rounding up and killing those still in arms, including those who 'came into my hands alive, whome I caused the Souldiers to hewe in peeces with their swordes', and in July, Donal Ballagh O'Cahan, Tyrone's principal vassal, made submission.

Summoned with Chichester to join Mountjoy, Docwra observed: 'The axe was nowe at the root of the tree, & I may well say, the Necke of the Rebellion as good as utterlie broken'.[6] The Lord Deputy entered the smoking ruins of Dungannon without resistance. 'We have drunk your health in Dungannon', Mountjoy wrote to the Treasurer at Wars, Sir George Carey. 'Tyrone is turned a woodkerne'.[7] Docwra, after putting a garrison in Omagh Castle, joined the Lord Deputy at Dungannon on 26 June. Having laid waste much of eastern Ulster, Sir Arthur Chichester arrived next day, and there the three seasoned commanders held a conference. They agreed to continue and step up the policy of ravaging the countryside. As Mountjoy explained to the Queen's secretary in London, 'I will keep in these parts as long as I can see whether under the countenance thereof some plots I have laid for his head may the better go forward'.[8] By that the Lord Deputy meant the application of a scorched-earth policy, in the end the most effective tactic of all.

Tyrone, with only a few hundred men still by him, held out, moving between the fastness of Glenconkeyne and the woodlands of Fermanagh. Mountjoy advanced north to Tullaghoge and there destroyed the ancient inauguration site of the O'Neills:

The Lord Deputy spent some five Days about *Tullagh Oge,* where the Ô Neals were of old Custom created, and there he spoiled the Corn of all the Country, and Tyrone's own Corn, and brake down the Chair wherein the Ô Neals were wont to be created, being of Stone, planted in the open Field.[9]

Here, after the chief of the O'Hagans had submitted, Mountjoy reported that

we found every where men dead of famine, in so much that Ohagan protested unto us that between Tullogh Oge and Toome there lay unburied a thousand dead, and that since our first drawing this year to Blackwater, there were above three thousand starved in Tyrone.[10]

Mountjoy concentrated on seizing cattle and destroying corn as the harvest approached, and he ordered Docwra and Chichester to do likewise, reporting to London that 'for all Events we have spoiled and mean to spoil their Corn'.[11] This strategy of destroying the food supply of inhabitants was now applied more ruthlessly and strenuously than ever before.[12] The Annals of the Four Masters record that the English used 'harrows, pracas, scythes, and sickles to destroy ripe and unripe grain', and the Spanish received a despatch informing them that 'innumerable numbers of their people died from pure hunger and . . . some of them were eating one another'.[13] Nearly all the evidence, however, comes from the private and public despatches of the Queen's commanders and the accounts of Fynes Moryson. Chichester was a particularly enthusiastic advocate of devastation. He argued that it was not enough to pursue the Irish, 'the most treacherous infidels in the world', for 'a million swords will not do them so much harm as one winter's famine'.[14] On 2 July, Mountjoy wrote to Carew:

We do now continually hunt all their woods, spoil their corn, burn their houses, and kill so many churls, as it grieveth me to think that it is necessary to do this.[15]

O'Neill moved north to join the forces of Donal O'Cahan, and by the end of July the Lord Deputy was able to report to the Privy Council:

We can assure your lordships, that from O'Cane's country, where he now liveth, which is to the northward of his own country of Tirone, we have left none to give us opposition, nor of late have seen any but dead carcasses, merely starved for want of meat, of which kind we found many in divers places as we passed.[16]

By October, the Lord Deputy reported, all of Ulster west of the River Blackwater was devastated, save for the forests where O'Neill had taken his last refuge. Nevertheless, he added, for those still beyond his reach, 'there is growing so extreme a famine amongst them that there will be no possibility for them to subsist'.[17] So confident was he that Tyrone was all but finished that he felt able in November to lead an expedition to Connacht to extinguish the last embers of rebellion there.

The inevitable consequence of rounding up and slaughtering cattle and destroying crops and stores of butter and grain was a famine of great severity, as Moryson records:

Now because I have often made mention formerly of our destroying the Rebels Corn, and using all Means to famish them, let me by two or three Examples shew the miserable Estate to which the Rebels were thereby brought. Sir Arthur Chichester, Sir Richard Moryson, and the other Commanders . . . saw a most horrible Spectacle of three Children (whereof the eldest was not above ten Years old,) all eating and gnawing with their Teeth the Entrails of their Mother, upon whose Flesh they had fed 20 Days past, and having eaten all from the Feet upward to the bare Bones, roasting it continually by a slow Fire, were now come to the eating of her said Entrails in like sort roasted, yet not divided from the Body, being as yet raw.

Captain Trevor, Moryson continues, found women in the Newry district lighting fires in the fields

and divers little children driving out the Cattle in the cold Mornings, and coming thither to warm them, were by them surprised, killed, and eaten, which was at last discovered by a great Girl breaking from them by Strength of her Body, and Captain *Trever* sending out Soldiers to know the Truth, they found the Childrens Skulls and Bones, and apprehended the old Women, who were executed for the Fact.

Moryson describes 'Carcasses scattered in many Places, all dead of Famine'; common people surviving on 'Hawks, Kites, and unsavory Birds of Prey'; and Irish prisoners thrusting 'long Needles into the Horses of our English Troops, and they dying thereupon, to be ready to tear out one another's Throat for a Share of them'. He concludes that 'no Spectacle was more frequent in the Ditches of Towns, and especially in wasted Countries, than to see Multitudes of these poor People dead with their Mouths all coloured green by eating Nettles, Docks, and all things they could rend up above Ground'.[18]

SUBMISSION AT MELLIFONT

By February 1603 Mountjoy was looking forward to the end of O'Neill, 'the most ungrateful Viper to us that raised him', as those still in arms against the Queen were reduced to the status of 'banditoes'. Tyrone, however, was holding out in his fastnesses far more successfully than government officers expected, and his close followers 'could not be induced by any rewards of money, or pardons for their own estates or lives, to betray him'. As the English closed in, Elizabeth cancelled her previous instructions to her Lord Deputy and instructed him to offer a pardon.[19]

Sir Robert Cecil, the Queen's secretary, thought that there were many reasons for the war to be brought to a swift conclusion. The cost of the campaigning seemed to threaten the very solvency of the state and had required a drastic devaluation of the coinage used to pay the troops in Ireland: the intrinsic value of the new Irish coins was three-quarters less than those of the 'harps' they replaced.[20] The task of replenishing Mountjoy's army had stripped large parts of England and Wales of men of fighting age. In Cecil's words, 'this Land of Ire hath exhausted this land of promise'. Gaols were being emptied, vagabonds pressed and young men 'lifted' in Wales.[21] In addition, the demand for unconditional surrender and retribution could encourage Tyrone to escape to Spain; there he could put new life into Philip III's war with England at a time when Cecil was putting out feelers for the making of a peace. The Queen in any case was ill and did not appear to have long to live—was Tyrone holding out in the hope that Elizabeth's agreed successor, James VI of Scotland, would show him mercy? Mountjoy himself was eager to be in London when the Queen died and had been pressing members of the Privy Council to allow him to relinquish his command. The Lord Deputy changed tack and in February 1603 asked for permission to enter into negotiations with O'Neill. Cecil agreed.[22]

On 25 March, Mountjoy was staying with Sir Garret Moore, for many years Tyrone's close friend, on his estate of confiscated monastic land at Mellifont, Co. Louth. The Lord Deputy asked his relative, Sir Edward

Blount, and Sir William Godolphin to seek out O'Neill, hand him a written safe-conduct and bring him in.

The Queen died on 24 March, and the news was swiftly and secretly brought to Mountjoy during the night of 27 March. This brought a fresh urgency to the proceedings. The Lord Deputy kept the information to himself when the Earl of Tyrone arrived during the afternoon of 30 March. At the threshold of Mountjoy's room O'Neill fell to his knees and made a penitent submission. Asked to approach, O'Neill again went on his knees and for a full hour made protestations of repentance and loyalty. Tyrone put his submission in writing the following day: if the Queen would restore him to his dignities he would ever after remain a loyal subject, he would renounce the style and title of 'the O'Neill', he would abjure all foreign power (in particular dependence on the King of Spain), he would abide by English law and aid the Queen's magistrates, and he would resign all title to any lands except such as should be granted to him by Her Majesty's letters patent.

This submission Tyrone presented, again on his knees, to the Lord Deputy and the Council. With almost indecent haste Mountjoy promised pardon to him and his followers and restoration to his earldom. Fresh patents would be issued for the lands previously granted to him, with the exception of three hundred acres each to maintain the Mountnorris and Charlemont Forts, and of estates promised to two O'Neill lords who served the Crown: Sir Turlough MacHenry of the Fews (Tyrone's half-brother) and Henry Óg O'Neill, Shane O'Neill's grandson.

On 3 April, Mountjoy and Tyrone rode to Drogheda and next day to Dublin. On 5 April, Sir Henry Danvers arrived back from England with official letters announcing the Queen's death and declaring that James VI of Scotland was now also James I of England and Ireland. O'Neill wept when he heard the news; he claimed that his tears were from 'a tender sorrow for the loss of his sovereign mistress', but they were shed out of rage, Moryson believed.[23]

There were letters to be written. Tyrone wrote to Philip III of Spain to inform him that he had submitted and that he would be a faithful subject of King James. Mountjoy wrote to inform James that there was not a rebel left in Ireland who had not sued for mercy; he would wish to bestow this mercy on all but a very few, but on this matter he would like to know His Majesty's pleasure.[24]

Reappointed Lord Deputy on 12 April, and with the elevated title of Lord Lieutenant of Ireland a fortnight later, Mountjoy nevertheless chafed to return to the centre of power in England and, indeed, to the arms of his long-term mistress, Lady Penelope Rich. He was distracted, however, by unrest in Kilkenny and towns in Munster. These Catholic 'Old English' inhabitants had been treated with care while the war raged, for fear they might be tempted to join O'Neill and O'Donnell. Now tensions rose between them and Crown officials who were offended by their Catholicism. This was largely an exasperated outburst of religious fervour born of a forlorn hope that James I would grant Irish Catholics religious toleration. When the citizens of Cork rose in arms against Lord President Carew, Mountjoy felt he had no choice but to march south with some five thousand men to restore peace. The cowed townsmen had to swear allegiance to James I and desist from holding Catholic services in churches; but, much to the fury of several army commanders, Mountjoy allowed these Catholics to practise their religion in their own homes until the King decided otherwise.

'THESE PETTY LORDS WILL BE DEALT WITHAL AT PLEASURE'

This task completed, Mountjoy could now return to the business of putting flesh on the bones of what had been agreed at Mellifont. The servitors—army commanders and government officials who served the Crown—were dumbfounded at the restoration of the two principal rebel leaders: they were becoming convinced that the Earl of Tyrone had lost the war but won the peace. They also had confidently expected a generous share in the lands of the rebels they had defeated. Now they learnt that the great bulk of Tír Chonaill and Tír Eoghain would be returned to Rory O'Donnell and Hugh O'Neill. The immediate problem was that the treaty made at Mellifont ran completely counter to agreements and promises made by Mountjoy and other commanders during the final stages of the war with those lesser Gaelic lords who had submitted and joined the Crown forces against Tyrone.

To Mountjoy what had been agreed at Mellifont was sacrosanct. This meant that he was perfectly willing to go back on previous promises to others. Sir Henry Docwra was appalled. The assistance provided by the young Cahir O'Doherty in 1600 had enabled him to secure the entire peninsula of Inishowen and to command the narrows at the entrance to the Foyle, so vital for vessels bringing in supplies, munitions and reinforcements to Derry. Niall Garbh O'Donnell, by going over to Docwra and becoming 'the Queen's O'Donnell', had given the Crown forces control of the Finn Valley, with grazing essential for Docwra's warhorses. In addition, Niall Garbh proved a brave and accomplished commander who had thrust south-west and seized control of Donegal Abbey. Donal Ballagh O'Cahan had been slower to submit, but his decision to change sides had also been crucial in the final stages of the war.

Docwra travelled to Dublin in April 1603 to discover what Mountjoy intended. The meeting proved a difficult one. Sir Henry had promised that Niall Garbh would be made the Earl of Tyrconnell, and this had been confirmed by Mountjoy. Now Mountjoy had decided that Rory O'Donnell, who had submitted to him at Athlone in 1602 and was the brother of Red Hugh, should be the 1st Earl of Tyrconnell. Niall Garbh had accompanied Docwra to Dublin. According to Sir Henry, Mountjoy bluntly told Niall Garbh that 'yow are greatlie indebted vnto the state, for the entertainements you haue had & done little for . . . therefore yow shall not expect any further fauour from mee' and then sent him out of the room.[25] Docwra observed that he could not see why Mountjoy 'could think himself freed of his promises'. It is not difficult to agree with the Governor of Derry's judgement.[26] However, Docwra thought it politic not to argue Niall Garbh's case any further.

On 29 May 1603 Mountjoy, the Earl of Tyrone and Niall Garbh O'Donnell boarded the pinnace *Tremontana* at Dublin. Rory O'Donnell, expressing a fear that Niall Garbh would have him assassinated, travelled separately. On the passage to Holyhead they narrowly missed shipwreck, and, on the road from Beaumaris, O'Neill was pelted with stones and mud by women who had lost their menfolk in the Irish Wars.[27] In London the Gaelic lords were well received by King James. Mountjoy had little difficulty in persuading the King to uphold the Treaty of Mellifont. James issued a comprehensive pardon to the Irish lords for waging war on the Crown, and this was enshrined in statute as an Act of Oblivion. O'Donnell was made Earl of Tyrconnell, but Niall Garbh—by far the strongest O'Donnell—was given no more than a patent for his lands at Lifford.

Crown officers in Ireland were horrified to see Tyrone hold sway over almost three counties. The generous pardon infuriated the servitors. Sir John Harrington wrote in frustration:

I have lived . . . to see that damned rebel Tyrone brought to England, honoured and well liked . . . How I did labour after that knave's destruction! I adventured perils buy sea and land, was near starving, ate horseflesh in Munster, and all to quell that man, who now smileth in peace at those who did hazard their lives to destroy him: and now doth dare us old commanders with his presence and protection.[28]

As long as Mountjoy remained Lord Lieutenant of Ireland—a post he retained although he never returned to Ireland—the arrangements made at Mellifont and in London would stand. Meanwhile other lesser Gaelic lords, who had given so much valuable assistance to the Crown, were discovering that promises made to them were being broken. In a letter to Cecil in June 1602, Chichester had already signalled that such undertakings could be set aside, observing that when 'the greatest work be done'—that is, the war concluded—'these petty lords will be dealt withal at pleasure'.[29] This would have a baleful effect on the stability of Ulster for years to come.

Donal Ballagh O'Cahan had been Hugh O'Neill's chief *uirrí*, with a major role in the investiture of O'Neill as his *ceannfhine*, or overlord, at Tullaghoge. Indeed, still in his teens, he had saved O'Neill's life at the Battle of Clontibret in 1595, cutting off Captain Seagrave's arm just as he was about to plunge a dagger into the earl's chest. On transferring his allegiance to the Queen, he had been promised confirmation of possession of his ancestral lands in what was then still the county of Coleraine, with strongholds at Limavady and Dungiven. These promises made by Docwra had been confirmed by Mountjoy. Now the restoration of O'Neill meant that these undertakings to O'Cahan could not be kept. The billeting of men on O'Cahan's lands by Tyrone soon after illustrated O'Cahan's dependence. Docwra recalled how he had brought this up during his meeting with Mountjoy in Dublin:

> Then touching O'Caine I tould him how the Earle of Tyrone had sent men to be cessed vpon him ... My lord, said I, this is strange & beyond all expectation, for I ame sure your lordship cannot be vunmindfull, first of the agreement I made with him, wherein he was promised to be free & to hould his lands from the Crowne, & then your lordship ratified & approved the same vnto him vnder your hand, haue iterated it againe diuers and diuers times both by word of Mouth & writing, how shall I looke this man in the face when I shall knowe myself guilty directlie to haue falsified my word with him.[30]

Mountjoy responded that O'Cahan 'is but a drunken ffellowe, and soe base' and that 'wee must haue a Care to the Publique good, & give Contentment to my lord of Tyrone'. When Docwra carried this news back to O'Cahan, the young lord responded in fury that 'he was nowe vndone, & in worse case then before hee knewe vs' and bade 'the Devill take all English Men & as many as put theire trust in them'.[31]

Sir Cahir O'Doherty was more fortunate. In arms with Docwra from the age of fifteen, Cahir had been knighted for bravery by Docwra and given recognition as Lord of Inishowen. The only major concession he was forced to make under the new dispensation following Mellifont was to hand over the fertile island of Inch to the Earl of Tyrconnell. Turlough O'Neill, Lord of Sliocht Airt Uí Néill (the territory around Strabane and the power base of his grandfather Turlough Luineach O'Neill) had been one of Docwra's earliest allies. At his pivotal meeting with Mountjoy in Dublin, Docwra pleaded his case and again reminded the Lord Deputy of earlier promises made. Mountjoy made it clear that, like O'Cahan, he would be a dependant of the Earl of Tyrone. When Sir Henry asked that those Irishmen who had acted for him as his spies and guides be rewarded he was told bluntly 'that it was booteless to Motion for any landes for them'.[32]

These lesser Gaelic lords of the north were shortly to find that their position was even more precarious than it appeared. Mountjoy, once over in England, stayed there, leaving the elderly Sir George Carey in Dublin as head of the Irish administration. Carey, however, became the subject of an inquiry into charges of peculation during the debasement of the currency ordered by Elizabeth. He thought it wise to resign his post after only a year in office, and on 15 October 1604 Sir Arthur Chichester, the servitors' most vocal advocate, was appointed Lord Deputy in his place and was sworn in the following year. Mountjoy, who had been created Earl of Devonshire in July 1603, retained his title as Lord Lieutenant of Ireland, but he fell ill and died in 1606 at the age of forty-three—it has been suggested that he was the first high-profile English victim of addiction to tobacco.

The servitors were now to have their day. Meanwhile the British colonisation of Ulster was already under way.

Chapter 4 ⌒

BRITISH COLONISATION BEGINS: DERRY, COLERAINE, BELFAST AND NEWRY

KING JAMES I

On 24 March 1603 Robert Carey galloped out of London on the first of the many swift horses which would take him to Scotland. After 'a great fall by the way' he entered Holyrood Palace, 'bebloodied with bruises', to inform James VI that he was now 'King of England, Scotland, Ireland and France'. As proof he handed over a sapphire ring which James had sent south with orders that it be returned to him the moment Elizabeth died. 'It is enough I know by this that you are a true messenger', the King said in thanks.[1]

Only hours after the death of the Queen, her secretary, Sir Robert Cecil, with a clear voice read out a proclamation declaring James's 'undoubted right' to the Crown of England, first at Whitehall Gate, then at Cheapside and finally in the Tower of London, where even the prisoners were heard to participate in the rejoicing. The French ambassador was appalled by the noisy celebrations, the blowing of trumpets and the bonfires lit in celebration so soon after Elizabeth's death. As King James began his leisurely progress southwards, on 5 April, much uncertainty prevailed about what policies he would pursue. Lord Deputy Mountjoy made preparations to cross over to England, anxious for royal approval of the treaty he had made with the Earl of Tyrone at Mellifont; the servitors hoped the new monarch would tear up this treaty to their advantage, and many Old English Catholics had high expectation that James would allow them free exercise of their religion.

James had been King of Scots from the age of eighteen months, and during his minority he had endured an exceptionally harsh upbringing for a monarch, deprived of love, frequently whipped by his tutor, periodically locked up by his guardians and terrified by attempted assassinations and violent aristocratic feuds. His stern tutor, George Buchanan, nevertheless ensured that James grew up to speak good English and to be accomplished in Latin, French and Italian, as well as being thoroughly imbued with Protestant doctrine. Considering that his mother, Mary Queen of Scots, had lost her head at Fotheringhay, that his father, Henry Lord Darnley, had been blown up at Kirk o' Field, and that, as a five-year-old, he had seen the blood-stained body of his dying grandfather, James Stewart, Earl of Moray, being carried past him at Stirling Castle, James had proved a level-headed monarch, ruling Scotland rather well.

James had to wait until Elizabeth's body had been interred in Westminster Abbey. This gave him time to indulge in his obsessive passion for stag-hunting, which the English court and royal officials in Ireland (seeking urgent replies to correspondence) were to find often kept him from government business. As the King made his way towards London a reprint of his book *Basilikon Doron* sold in thousands. This treatise on the art of government, intended to guide his eldest son, Arthur, demonstrated that James had not accepted in its entirety the Presbyterianism taught him by Buchanan. He firmly believed in the divine right of kings—that he was God's chosen instrument—and he made it clear that he admired the liturgy of the established Church of England and the Anglican form of church government: 'No Bishop, no King', as he tersely informed a conference at Hampton Court soon afterwards.

Cecil knew the new King's intentions better than any other Englishman, the two men having conducted a detailed correspondence for years. They met when James reached York. 'Though you are but a little man, we will shortly load your shoulders with business'—this unflattering greeting to Sir Robert nevertheless demonstrated at once that James (quite unlike his unwise contemporary, Philip iii of Spain) did not intend a palace revolution sweeping away his predecessor's trusted and experienced personnel. Mountjoy got confirmation that he was still in post as Lord Deputy, and, indeed, he would shortly be given the elevated title of Lord Lieutenant of Ireland. Would the King's support for the Anglican establishment include a more tolerant attitude to his Catholic subjects? Here James gave out mixed messages. In a letter to Cecil in 1601 he had written: 'I will never allow in my conscience that the blood of any man shall be shed for diversity of opinions in religion, but I should be sorry that Catholics should so multiply as they might be able to practice their old principles upon us'. Did this mean that persecution might ensue if the number of Catholics increased? On the way down from Scotland, James had ordered the freeing of prisoners, except, he declared at York, 'Papists and wilful murderers'. Yet when he reached London he freed Father William Weston, who had languished in the Tower and other prisons for seventeen years, on the grounds that the gaol sentence had become 'obsolete with the passage of time'.[2]

LORD DEPUTY CHICHESTER

Sir Arthur Chichester was a surprise appointment as Lord Deputy. Usually when this post became vacant, leading English nobles would be found lobbying to be assigned to such an exalted position. However, when the elderly Sir George Carey decided to resign the post in 1604, following the unsettling accusations of peculation, the highest in the land were reluctant to be too far away from court at a time when the King of Scotland had been on the throne of England for a little more than a year. Chichester himself hesitated to accept the offer to become James I's royal governor in Ireland, partly because he was deeply in debt and feared that he might lack the resources to carry out the duties expected of him. He only agreed to make a temporary appointment permanent in February 1605.

Servitors, in particular army commanders who had seen to the crushing of the Gaelic lords of Ulster, had been appalled by the Treaty of Mellifont. Hugh O'Neill, Earl of Tyrone, had been restored to favour, and Rory O'Donnell had subsequently been created Earl of Tyrconnell. The dismantling of northern lordships and the granting of swathes of territory to men who felt they were fully deserving of the King's bounty had not happened. Now the servitors had their chief advocate—the man who had declared that his object was to 'cut the throat of the grand Traitor' Tyrone—securely placed in Dublin Castle.[3]

The new Lord Deputy had come a long way. Drawn from a minor landowning family in Devon holding strong Puritan beliefs, Chichester, probably because of lack of funds, had abandoned a degree course at Oxford to embark on a military career. In 1588, at the age of twenty-five, he had been in the English Channel as a captain of marines to help defeat the Spanish Armada. Four years later he became involved with his relatives in a faction fight with the servants of the Earl of Bath, and, after being dragged before the Privy Council to account for their behaviour, he and his kinsmen had been forced to flee to Ireland. Eventually restored to favour, Chichester joined Sir Francis Drake in 1595 on his last expedition to the West Indies; commanding five hundred men, he showed

outstanding bravery and set fire to a Spanish frigate. He played a prominent role in the Earl of Essex's attack on Spain in 1596; the following year
he was a sergeant-major-general in Picardy, taking part in the Siege of
Amiens so conspicuously that he was knighted by Henry of Navarre; then
he was transferred to service at Ostend; and in 1599 he returned to Ireland
in command of a large contingent accompanying the Earl of Essex during
his disastrous viceroyalty.[4]

Chichester's brother John had remained in Ireland, and, appointed
Governor of Carrickfergus, in 1597 he had rashly engaged James
MacDonnell, Lord of the Glynns and the Route, in the open, losing some
two hundred men and his own life. His severed head, sent to the Earl of
Tyrone, was reputedly kicked around the Irish camp like a football.
Burning with the desire to revenge his brother, Sir Arthur successfully
petitioned to be appointed Governor of Carrickfergus in his place. After
arranging the death of MacDonnell by poisoning, Chichester served under
Lord Deputy Mountjoy, launching daring attacks across Lough Neagh to
strike at the heart of Tyrone's country. He was the principal architect and
practitioner of the policy of laying waste the Ulster countryside to
extinguish the rebellion by famine. And he was completely unapologetic in
the regular despatches he wrote describing the slaughter, hunger and
destruction his forces inflicted.

MARTIAL LAW

Chichester could not immediately begin the process of dismantling the
settlement of Mellifont. The Irish government's budget was being slashed,
and most of the men in the Crown forces in Ireland were being
demobilised. The Earl of Tyrone had returned from the royal court in
London in the summer of 1603 to entice back to his lands those who had
fled the terror during the dying months of the rebellion. Chichester's
problem was that the earl appeared to have become a model subject of the
Crown, to have lent money to the government and even to have provided
victuals for garrisons placed on his lands. Carey, the previous Lord
Deputy, had felt no need to attempt to clip Tyrone's wings. In any case,
Lord Mountjoy, now Duke of Devonshire, retained his position as Lord
Lieutenant of Ireland. Though he never returned to the island, and
remained mostly on his English estate as his health declined, Devonshire
kept a close watch on Irish affairs. He remained a champion of the terms
of the Treaty of Mellifont, and it seems that he had become quite taken
with his former adversary.

One of the wisest of the King's early decisions was to recall the base coin which had been issued in Ireland from 1601 and return Irish coinage to its former standard.[5] The problem was that the servitors, along with their men, had been receiving pay which was almost worthless. If they returned to England they would be close to destitution. Mountjoy recognised the problem. 'If I discharge such old Captaines as I found here,' he wrote to the Privy Council in March 1602, 'I should onely returne unto her Majestie importunate suitors, armed with good justice to crave reward'. The simple resolution of paying them with good sterling was one that the London government shied away from. The war in Ireland, it was calculated, had cost just short of two million pounds sterling. The government was teetering on the brink of bankruptcy. Army officers in Ireland, most of them younger sons of gentlemen with no expectation of inheritance at home, opted to stay on in Ireland if they possibly could.

In April 1602 the number of soldiers in royal service in Ireland approached 17,500. By October it had been reduced to 9,000, and by October 1604 it was down to 4,300. By April 1606 Crown forces had been brought down to only 1,014 men.[6] As demobilisation got under way, in May 1602 Mountjoy urged the government not to cashier the officers as well as the men:

> If in that great cashering, there be not meanes to preserve the best Captaines, I would be loth to be the man, that should undertake the conclusion of the warre . . . Now the Captaines and the men thus discharged, thinking their fortunes overthrown by me . . . become so many enemies to me.

Most servitors managed to hang on. By 1608 twenty-five of the thirty-one army officers who had held a rank of colonel or higher in 1602 were still serving in the King's forces in Ireland.[7] In short, the servitors were determined to continue their careers in Ireland. So far, the amounts of land they had been able to acquire, either by outright grant or by lease, were comparatively small. But these modest holdings were to prove vital nuclei for British colonisation in the years to come.

Not only was Chichester eager to back the claims of the servitors but he was also certain that their presence and their accumulated military experience were vital to the island's security. Demobilisation of so many from the army, he believed, made it all the more important to keep the country under strict martial law. What is remarkable is that rigid enforcement of martial law was accomplished for years on end with so few men. The continued subjugation of Gaelic Ireland, Ulster in particular, was greatly assisted by the network of forts erected both during and after the war. Seventeen out of a total of forty strongholds were maintained in Ulster: Moyry, Mountnorris, Carrickfergus Castle, Toome, Fort Massereene, Mountjoy, Charlemont, Derry, Culmore, Ballyshannon, Enniskillen, Newry, Cloughoughter, Monaghan, Donegal Castle, Doe Castle and Loughfoyle. Each was manned by an English captain with a ward of forty or fifty—and sometimes a hundred—men.[8] These garrison captains continued to enjoy powers of summary execution, that is, to put to death any who opposed them, from the poorest peasants to leading members of the Gaelic gentry.

These powers were used liberally even after Mellifont; summary execution maintained an appropriate level of terror to ensure control, and it was cheap. Martial-law commissioners did not receive salaries; instead they were entitled to collect a third of moveable goods and possessions of those they executed. As commissioners were not generally required to render accounts, they often seized more than a third of their victims' possessions. The more a commissioner killed, the better off he became. In addition, he was in a good position to collect protection money from those he spared.

In the first year of the King's reign the Dublin government issued at least twenty new commissions of martial law. Chichester reorganised and tightened up this system on 20 February 1605, giving the title of Provost-Marshal to officials responsible for imposing martial law. County sheriffs were also invested with martial-law powers. More than any other province, Ulster possessed an elaborate infrastructure of English military control composed of forts, Provost-Marshals and roving martial-law commissioners. Here, too, the process of disarming the natives was especially assiduous. Early in 1605 the Dublin government issued a proclamation forbidding the bearing of arms 'to all persons travelling in Ireland' and authorised servants of the Crown to allow the compulsory collection of weapons.

O'Neill and O'Donnell and their allies had fought their war with four classes of men in arms: horsemen, drawn almost exclusively from the Gaelic gentry; gallowglass (pikemen re-trained to use the arquebus, musket and caliver); bonnaghts (men conscripted as warriors from their lordships); and kerne, drafted as skirmishers. Faced with the prospect of summary execution and dispossession, many of these warriors opted to go abroad to seek employment in Counter-Reformation armies. Spanish

Flanders was the most popular destination: it has been estimated that some ten thousand migrated there between 1586 and 1622. Philip iii issued a special order for a permanent Irish regiment there under the command of the Earl of Tyrone's sons, Henry and John. Other Irish soldiers served in the Holy Roman Empire, France, Bavaria and Poland. To those who opted to stay in Ulster, taking refuge on the mountains and in the forests, living largely by banditry, the English applied the general label 'woodkerne'. Before leaving Ireland, Mountjoy had recommended that these woodkerne be rounded up and sent to fight for Protestant rulers, particularly those of Sweden and Denmark. Chichester would later endeavour to implement this advice as the Plantation of Ulster got under way.[9] For the present, the haemorrhage of Gaelic fighting men overseas did much to assist the Crown authorities in maintaining tight military control in Ulster.

DISMANTLING THE TREATY OF MELLIFONT

How could the new Lord Deputy, as the servitors implored him to do, set about undermining the Earl of Tyrone and the Earl of Tyrconnell? Chichester turned for advice to the Solicitor-General, Sir John Davies. The third son of a Wiltshire tanner who had been expelled from the Middle Temple in London and gaoled for a time after smashing a cudgel over the head of a fellow-student of law, Davies became an admired poet at court and was appointed to his Irish post in 1603. After immersing himself in writings on Irish history and culture, Davies assured Chichester that there were sound legal ways to corrode the power of over-mighty Gaelic lords.

First, Davies believed, English legal institutions and Crown law officers must rapidly be introduced to undermine the arbitrary authority of the lords. He yearned to impose English law to the full on

> the Irishry in the Province of Ulster ... the most rude and unreformed part of Ireland, and the seat and nest of the last great rebellion, that the next generation will in tongue and heart and every way else become English; so as there will be no difference or distinction, but the Irish Sea betwixt us.[10]

Gaelic laws and customs repugnant to the Crown were to be set aside. Tanistry, by which property and position passed to the lord considered most worthy, was declared 'utterly void in law' and 'extinguished' between 1606 and 1608. Irish lords henceforth had to follow primogeniture and abide by English common law. Gaelic exactions and tribute were declared illegal.[11] At the same time lesser lords should be freed from their dependence on Tyrone, Tyrconnell and other Gaelic magnates to become independent freeholders with obligations directly only to the King. For example, the intention was to deprive the Earl of Tyrone of all jurisdiction over the *uirríthe* (his satraps, lords with the right to nominate the O'Neill) and especially the principal *uirrí*, Lord O'Cahan, who had the traditional right to inaugurate the O'Neill at Tullaghoge. This would severely erode Tyrone's economic base by depriving him of rent and traditional forms of tribute such as hospitality and the right to billet men without payment on the lands of dependent lords. The tribute levied by Gaelic overlords on their satellite lords before Mellifont had been burdensome. For example, the Lord of Inishowen—before Docwra succeeded in bringing the O'Dohertys over to his own side—had to supply the Lord of Tír Chonaill each year with 120 cattle, 60 mounted fighting men, 120 foot soldiers and the free maintenance of O'Donnell bonnaghts, 'be they ever so numerous for the space of nine nights'.[12]

There was nothing new in this proposal to create freeholders: it had been applied with striking success, for example, before the Nine Years' War in the county of Monaghan. What Davies did was to supply sheaves of legal precedents to justify the application of this type of the English form of subinfeudation. Davies and Chichester were also at one in their certainty that the process of anglicisation must include the full introduction of the Protestant religion, ensuring that the established church—the Church of Ireland—was the sole ecclesiastical authority throughout Ireland.

After overcoming fierce opposition to the establishing of freeholders in Co. Wicklow and Co. Clare, Chichester led a party of commissioners in Ulster during the summer of 1605. First, Co. Armagh was divided into baronies and hundreds and then similar action was carried out in Tyrone, Tyrconnell and Antrim. Coroners and constables were appointed, though the Earl of Tyrone succeeded in frustrating the Lord Deputy's plans for his estates by agreeing to have only trusted kinsmen nominated to these posts.[13] The aim was to transform Gaelic chieftains from warlords to landed gentlemen in order to promote demilitarisation and create political stability. Henceforth the principal lords would retain their demesne lands, but the heads of the other major landowning families—the 'ancient followers of the country'—would be redefined as 'freeholders' owing nothing more to the lords above them than fixed annual money rents.

Both the principal lords and the freeholders would be obliged to pay a yearly tax, or quit rent, to the Crown.[14]

Chichester in this tour of Ulster in 1605 was simply carrying out with more vigour the scheme of creating freeholders originally launched in 1603 by his predecessor, Sir George Carey. Carey had sent commissioners north to begin investigating land ownership there and record who the free-holders were. In January 1604 the first major step had been taken: two leading members of the Maguire family, Conor Roe and Cúchonnacht, had been brought to agree in outline a division of that 'country' between them. Now Chichester elaborated on this division and on the appointment of freeholders under them to be 'the free, natural and immediate subjects of the King'.[15] Chichester returned to Ulster in 1606 to set up gaols and session houses and to fine-tune the arrangements previously made for freeholders in Co. Monaghan. Then he moved on to Cavan and Fermanagh, his decisions in the latter county being particularly galling to Cúchonnacht Maguire.

The Treaty of Mellifont may well have confirmed the Earls of Tyrone and Tyrconnell in the possession of great territories, but the native Irish of every class were fast discovering that the new regime was bringing rapid alteration to their position. Well-provisioned forts, kept in good repair, stood as visible evidence of a new power in the land. Every part of Ulster was now within a few hours' gallop of a royal garrison. All were commanded by seasoned captains, now becoming familiar with the countryside, most of them veterans not only of many campaigns in Ireland but also of wars in the Netherlands and France, and some even of naval engagements across the Atlantic in the Spanish Main. These men were already laying secure foundations for the imminent British colonisation of Ulster.

DERRY: 'THE PLANTING OF CIVIL AND OBEDIENT PEOPLE IN THAT PLACE'

The servitors may well have been outraged on hearing of the terms of Mellifont, but they did not go empty-handed. Many of them had sub-stantial toe-holds in Ulster.

Sir Henry Docwra, Governor of Derry, had made fruitless appeals on behalf of his Irish allies during his meeting with Mountjoy in Dublin in 1603. Then he pressed his own case. He reminded the Lord Deputy of promises he had made in person to grant him the full fishing rights on the Foyle—until the mid-twentieth century the most prolific salmon fishery in Europe. Yet he had recently received an order that Tyrone's men were allowed to fish there. He records in his *Narration* that this was the Lord Deputy's response:

> Hee said Sr Henry Docwra, yow have deserved well of the kinge, & your service, there is greate Reason should be Recompenced, But it must be by some other meanes then this . . . Yow see what promise I have made to my lord of Tyrone . . . because I knowe it is for the Publique good.[16]

Not only did Docwra have to swallow this disappointment but he also had to bring the news of dashed hopes and broken promises to Niall Garbh O'Donnell, Donal Ballagh O'Cahan and Sir Cahir O'Doherty. Refused permission to travel with Mountjoy at the end of May 1603, when he took O'Neill and O'Donnell to London, Docwra followed later to put his own case at the court of King James. There he spent six months in a futile attempt to be appointed Lord President of Ulster (a post never created in the end) and in pursuit of more generous rewards.

Docwra may well have been bitterly disappointed, but he was rewarded handsomely enough. Certainly he was entrusted with highly responsible tasks and made a member of the Irish Privy Council. Above all, Docwra received in September 1603 a grant 'to him and his heirs' which effectually made him the founder of the city of Derry. This included the right to hold a market and fair at Derry with 'all the issues and profits arising out of the said markets' and also a market in the town of Lifford. The grant was clarified in May 1604: he was granted the demise of lands, without fine, the house he had newly built in the fort of Derry, the building of the dissolved chapel of nuns, the stone tower by the bog-side on the island of Derry, 'with the whole island of Derry and all other buildings, gardens etc. in the said Iland, but with exception of the store houses used for His Majesty's food supplies and munitions, woods, underwoods, and mines'. He was to pay a rent of 13s 4d each year and 'to pay yerely all proxies, synodalles, stipends of curates, etc.', maintaining the 'manses, chauncelles, etc.'

In March 1604 King James wrote to Mountjoy, still Lord Lieutenant and now Earl of Devonshire, stating that, because Docwra 'hath taken great pains in reducing those parts to our subjection; we are pleased that he shall have the chief government thereof, during life, by the name of our provost, mayor, or bailiff etc.' This was in preparation for the incorporation of Derry. Docwra also got the pension he had been seeking for some time:

twenty shillings a day for life for previous services given. The grant of a charter followed on 11 July 1604. The prologue stated:

> The town or borough of Derry is, by reason of the natural seat and situation thereof, a place very convenient and fit to be made both a town of war and a town of merchandise and so might many ways prove serviceable to the crown and profitable for the subject, if the same were not only walled, entrenched and inhabited but also incorporated and endowed with convenient liberties, privileges and immunities.[17]

The charter makes it plain that the King expected this to be a colonial nucleus:

> Sir Henry Docwra, Knt. in the reigns of Queen Elizabeth and King James, having by his extraordinary valour, industry and charge, repossessed, repaired, re-peoples, that town being utterly ruinated and laid waste by the late rebellion in those parts. And having begun and laid a good foundation there for the planting of a colony of civil and obedient people in that place, the king . . . did pursuant to letters dated at Westminster, 22nd March 1603, give, grant and confirm unto him and the inhabitants of the Derry and all the circuit and extent of land and water within compass of three miles to be measured from the circumference of the old church walls directly forth in a right line, every way round about, every miles containing 1000 geometrical paces, and every pace five feet in length entire and perfect City and Council of itself to be called the City and County of Derry and shall be a Corporation and body politic . . . Sir Henry to be Provost for life, as fully as the lord mayor of London.[18]

A council house was to be put up for the corporation's meetings, and a gaol house was to be built at the expense of the inhabitants. Sir Henry, as provost, was to nominate a recorder, a vice-provost and two aldermen to be justices of the peace for oyer, terminer and gaol delivery; and he was also to appoint two coroners, a town clerk, a treasurer, a water-bailiff, a sword-bearer and sergeants of the mace. His position as provost (or mayor) meant that he was the King's admiral, clerk of the market, escheator, and mayor of the staple.

Sir Arthur Chichester, by then Lord Deputy, visited Derry for the assizes in September 1605. He reported to the Council in Dublin that he had 'observed there many good buildings, and that, because it was a place of great importance', he hoped 'that so good a work may not be suffered to decay'. He advised that the city should be developed more speedily by bringing in more 'merchants, tradesmen, and artificers from England and Scotland which must be commanded by authority to come over and compelled to remain and set up their trades and occupations'. His anxiety was that Derry was surrounded by potentially dangerous Irish. When he travelled on to hold assizes in Omagh, where one of Docwra's officers, Captain Edward Leigh, had been granted the dissolved abbey and its lands, Chichester wrote that 'there are such wastes round that robbers harbour in them and rob and murder merchants and travellers going from Derry and Lifford to the Pale'.

Chichester was in Derry again the following year while Docwra was still there. It was evident that the city was not doing as well as he hoped. If 'the infant city' was not supported it was liable to decay, as it was situated 'among neighbours who long for nothing more than the ruin thereof'. The truth was that Docwra had now decided that his prospects would be improved if he moved closer to the centre of power. With the government's permission he sold his property interests in Derry to Sir George Paulet, a younger son of the Marquis of Winchester; in recommending him to Chichester, King James described Paulet as 'a gentleman of good sufficiency and of service in the wars'.

Why did Docwra leave Derry? Undoubtedly he was shaken by the surprise appointment of Chichester as Lord Deputy in October 1604. Docwra had played at least as important a role in subjugating Ulster as Chichester had, and perhaps he was hurt at not been asked to become the royal governor himself. Certainly, Docwra was aware that Chichester had little affection for him. Another irritant was the appointment of the King's confidant, George Montgomery, Dean of Norwich, as bishop of the combined dioceses of Derry, Raphoe and Clogher in February 1605. Montgomery was high-handed and grasping from the outset, and Docwra may well have concluded that his actions were certain to unsettle the whole north-west.

Chichester wrote to the Earl of Clanrickard, the hero of the Battle of Kinsale, in July 1606, just after Docwra had left Derry and before Paulet's arrival. The Lord Deputy expressed the view

that the city of Derry be cherished and countenanced in her infancy. The erection of it hath cost so much money and lost many men, and it is already greatly declining, albeit I support it the best I may. Some worthy and well-chosen man must be assigned with entertainment to lie there, if Sir Henry Docwra return not.[19]

Sir George Paulet was most certainly not the well-chosen man Chichester wished for. Arrogant and blundering, the new governor would ensure by his actions his own untimely death and that Docwra's infant city would be reduced to ashes.

SIR THOMAS PHILLIPS AND COLERAINE

When Sir Thomas Phillips came to Ireland during the winter of 1598/9 he had spent some twenty years soldiering in the French civil wars. He had gone over as a freelance to serve with English auxiliaries sent by Queen Elizabeth to support Henry of Navarre, and there he earned 'the special favour' of the man who would become Henry IV. He returned, aged about forty, to join the Crown forces in Ireland. Phillips successfully repulsed an attack on Kinsale as the Earl of Tyrone's Munster allies overwhelmed the Munster Plantation, and he was wounded in Leinster during fierce campaigning there. At the same time Phillips appears to have been acting as a kind of special agent for the Queen's principal secretary of state, Sir Robert Cecil.

Cecil ensured that Phillips was put in command of a company of foot at Carrickfergus, where Sir Arthur Chichester—impressed by his 'judgement and valour'—advised that he be promoted to positions of greater responsibility. In the summer of 1602 Phillips, using the old castle of Toome as his base, crossed the River Bann and seized the Earl of Tyrone's fort there. When the Treaty of Mellifont was being signed, Phillips commanded the garrisons of both the fort and the castle. The following year Cecil procured for Phillips custody of the abbey of Coleraine—a move strongly supported by Chichester, who feared the likely depredations of Scottish islanders there.

Over the next four years this veteran obtained from the Crown a lease of the customs of Portrush, Portballintrae and the Bann; fees earned from ferries across the Bann; a lease of the castle and fort at Toome, with thirty acres adjoining, 'for the better defence of those parts', at a rent of one pair of gilded spurs; a weekly market and an annual fair at Coleraine; and a licence to make *aqua vitae* in the county of Coleraine and the Route. (This last is the origin of Ireland's oldest licensed whiskey distillery, still flourishing in Bushmills.) He also bought the freehold of the abbey of

Coleraine with six townlands adjoining from James Hamilton, the Ayrshire laird then in the process of colonising north Down.

At a pinch Coleraine could be described as a town of the Earldom of Ulster in the thirteenth century, but when Phillips took it over it was no more than an ecclesiastical centre, and all previous urban traces had disappeared. On the left bank of the river stood O'Cahan's castle of Coleraine. On the right bank Phillips settled into the abbey and put up a house for himself there. He ordered the building of thatched houses for settlers with a water mill close by, and constructed fortifications. He brought in a clergyman of the reformed faith, who conducted services in the dilapidated church every day; according to Phillips, these were well attended. Merchants came over from Scotland for his markets. For Phillips and those joining him at Coleraine the chief attraction was the great forests of the interior. Phillips negotiated a deal with the restored Earl of Tyrone: in return for a tun of claret and a half tun of wine (presumably fortified) each year, he could fell and carry away timber from Killetra extending from the Bann-side to the Church of Tamlaght and from Lough Beg to the Church of Kilrea. The servitor set about exploiting this to the full, driving paths through the forest to take the timber to the river and then floating the logs downstream to the great waterfall at Coleraine.

Then, in September 1607, Phillips got news of the sudden departure of the Earls of Tyrone and Tyrconnell in a vessel sailing from Lough Swilly. Once again he was on active service during momentous events which would lead to the Plantation of Ulster. This would give Phillips a new role as the busy promoter of a new British colony by the River Roe at Limavady.[20]

BELFAST 'IS PLOTTED OUT IN A GOOD FORME'

Throughout the Nine Years' War, Carrickfergus had remained in the control of the Crown. In 1597 Sir John Chichester, governor of the castle, had rashly attacked the MacDonnells with inadequate forces in the open and paid for it with his life. Then, in June 1598, the MacDonnells returned to lay siege to it, as Captain James Byrt reported to the Irish Secretary of State, Sir Geoffrey Fenton: 'This toun is besieged by 800 Scots, and Belfast is in danger'. Three weeks later he wrote again that 'the enemi hath ever since they were here layd hard seage to Belfast . . . so that we doe greatly dowt that place will miscarry'. But the tide began to turn when Chichester's brother, Sir Arthur, took charge as the new Governor of Carrickfergus and of Upper and Lower Clandeboye. He proved himself the most ruthless of all the English commanders operating in Ulster. Indeed, it could be said that such was the devastation he inflicted that much of south Antrim and north Down was greatly depopulated by slaughter and famine.

Sir Ralph Lane, a Mustermaster-General famous for his exploits on the high seas, had been given the custody of the castle of Belfast. After his death, in 1603, the castle and the lands about it were granted to Chichester. The patent granted him the 'castle of Belfast, with the Appurtenants and Hereditaments, Spiritual and Temporal, situate in the Lower Clandeboye, late in the possession of Sir Ralph Lane Knt., deceased, dated 6th June, 40th Elizabeth'. In August 1603 King James wrote to the Lord Deputy, Sir George Carey, ordering him to invest Chichester with the government of Knockfergus (Carrickfergus), and of all other forts and commands in the district, including Lough Neagh, with a fee of 13s 4d per day for life. Also granted to him and his heirs for ever were 'the Castle of Belfast, the Fall, Mylone, Sinament, and the Fishery of the Lagan, to be holden as of our Castle of Knockfergus in free and common socage'.

Like Docwra and other servitors, Chichester regarded this as a niggardly reward for services rendered in the recent war. He made this clear when he wrote to the Irish Council concerning 'the letters wch the Kinge wrote heather in my behoufe tuchinge a Pattent for the Government of Knockfergus and lands of Belfaste', observing that 'albeyt when I have it att best perfection I wyll gladly sell the whole lands for the wch others sell, five poundes in fee simple in these partes of the Kyngdome'.[21]

Belfast in medieval times had been little more than a village clustering round a castle by the Farset River, guarding the crossing of the Lagan estuary at low tide. When Chichester was granted it, both the castle and the buildings about it were in ruins. In spite of the low value he placed on Belfast, Chichester saw that it had potential to generate an income. Its position at the mouth of the River Lagan, at the junction of several important routeways, indicated that profitable markets could be held here. In his letter making the grant, King James expressed the hope 'that his tenants in the lands may be better encouraged to plant and manure the same when they may have from him some certain estate therein'.[22] Though often absent from the area on government business, particularly after he had been sworn in as Lord Deputy in 1605, Chichester set about building a town at Belfast, ordering the firing of a million bricks. On the site of the ruined castle he constructed a Jacobean mansion, which he called Belfast Castle, which stood until it was destroyed by accidental fire in 1708.

In 1611, when the Plantation of Ulster was well under way, com-missioners reported on 'voluntary works' outside the scope of the scheme. They were particularly impressed by progress being made in Belfast:

> We came to bealfast where we found many masons, bricklayers, and other labourers aworke who had . . . layde the foundation of a bricke house 50 foote longe which is to be adjoined to the said Castle by a Stayrcase of bricke wch is to be 14 foot square . . .
> The towne of Bealfast is plotted out in a good forme . . . Neere wch town the sd Sr Arthur Chichester hath ready made above twelve hundred of good Brickes, whereof after finishing of the said Castle, house, and Bawne, there will be a good proportion left for the buyldinge of other tenements within the said Towne.[23]

Later, Chichester built himself another mansion on the eastern outskirts of Carrickfergus, which, in tribute to Lord Mountjoy, he named Joymount. By comparison with Galway in Connacht, and Waterford and Limerick in Munster, Ulster had no urban centre yet of any real size, but Carrickfergus was rivalled only by Newry. Carrickfergus itself had its long-established corporation with its own town fields farmed by its citizens.[24]

Chichester had been granted enough land in Lower Clandeboye to accommodate army officers who had served under him. He let the plains of Malone along the Lagan on a 61-year lease to Moses Hill, until recently lieutenant of his horse troop, who built a fort near the present Shaw's Bridge and a well-defended stone house at Stranmillis. Other officers getting access to land between Belfast and Carrickfergus were Cornet Thomas Walsh, Lieutenant Barry and Ensign Mitchell, who began erecting fortified houses on estates let to them by Chichester. Other retired army officers gaining a foothold in this part of Ulster included Sir Fulke Conway in Killultagh, who employed Major George Rawdon as his agent; John Dobbs, two miles out of Carrickfergus; Captain Hugh Clotworthy at Massereene; Lieutenant Humphrey Norton at Templepatrick; Captain Roger Langford at Muckamore; and Chichester's kinsmen Faithful Fortescue and Henry Upton, in the direction of Antrim.

They and their heirs were to remain here, being given many opportunities to extend their holdings in the years to come. Sir Henry Folliott, made governor for life of Ballyshannon, had not only a thousand acres attached to the fortress at his disposal but also valuable fishing rights at the falls of Assaroe on the River Erne. Captain Edmond Ellis was appointed Constable of Enniskillen in 1607; after he looked over 'the broken castle' there, the Master of Fortifications, Sir Josias Bodley, recommended its enlargement to make it on its own 'a sufficient bridle upon that country'.[25] But the man who was to develop Enniskillen and profit most from it was the soldier and seaman appointed to succeed Ellis in 1609, Captain William Cole.

Other constables ensconcing themselves in Ulster and developing the lands adjoining forts and castles included Captain Edward Leigh at Omagh, Sir Toby Caulfield at Charlemont, Captain Edward Blaney at Mountjoy, Captain Henry Hart at Culmore, Captain Basil Brooke at Burt and Sir Josias Bodley at Armagh. At first these army officers for the most part had only the lease of the acres assigned to fortifications, but the government soon saw the wisdom of turning leases into outright grants— if only because it relieved the exchequer of much of the expense involved in maintaining them. The lands they and other governors had in their possession were not inconsiderable, and, because they were generally fertile and in strategic positions, their loss was keenly felt by those native proprietors who had so recently lost them. Resident soldiers apart, these lands had few British colonists at this stage, but these garrisoned strongholds were to play a key role as the Plantation of Ulster got under way.

NEWRY

The Bagenals had been in Ulster longer than any other servitors. Fleeing from justice, Nicholas Bagenal had come to Ireland from Staffordshire in the reign of Henry VIII. He found employment as military adviser to Conn Bacach O'Neill, who, after he had been made the 1st Earl of Tyrone, successfully sought a pardon for Bagenal. By the time of Henry VIII's death, in 1547, Nicholas had been knighted and had risen to become Marshal of the King's Army in Ireland.

Monks of the abbey of Newry had been forced to accept dissolution in 1550. Bagenal was given the lease of these abbey lands for twenty-one years and, soon after, outright possession of the town and its hinterland. Edward VI's government realised that he was just the person to defend the northern extremity of the Pale. Bagenal also had additional income from the Lordship of Newry, the Lordship of Mourne, centred on Greencastle, and the Lordship of Carlingford and Newry. His income from these properties totalled £1,925 in 1575.[26] Newry was an English outpost, but it was not yet an English colony: the great majority of tenants were Irish. Sir

Nicholas in old age managed to get his son Henry appointed Marshal in his place. It was from Newry that Sir Henry Bagenal had set out in the summer of 1598 in an attempt to relieve the beleaguered garrison at Blackwater Fort, only to meet with crushing defeat and lose his life at the Battle of the Yellow Ford.

Sir Samuel Bagenal, Sir Henry's nephew, had led a fresh cohort of troops into Ireland after the Yellow Ford and was appointed Governor of Newry. Sir Henry's son, Arthur, came of age in 1603, and he was to spend the next decade seeing to the development of Newry. There was much to do. The town had to be largely rebuilt as a result of an accidental fire, caused by a whiskey distiller, in 1600. Nevertheless, Newry had claim to be as large a town in Ulster as Carrickfergus, and, like Derry and Belfast, it was to become a focal point for British colonisation in the years to come.

As in Belfast and Carrickfergus, demobilised soldiers hovered in Newry looking for opportunities to acquire access to land. Most of them had served with the Bagenals and hailed from Wales and its borderlands. Many had been involved in the abortive conspiracy of the Earl of Essex in 1601 and remained in Ireland to avoid discredit and possible prosecution at home.[27] They included Sir Edward Cromwell, Sir Richard Trevor (for a time Governor of Newry) and his kinsman Captain Edward Trevor, owner of a modest estate in Brynkinalt, near Chirk, in the marcher country of Wales and Shropshire. Also awaiting opportunities were Marmaduke Whitchurch, lieutenant of Sir Henry Bagenal's horse company at the Yellow Ford, and George Sexton, a secretary to the Lord Deputy, appointed a Crown escheator in 1605.[28]

These men looked just beyond Newry inland to the Lordship of Iveagh, the anglicised form of the old Irish kingdom of Uíbh Eacach Cobha. As the Earldom of Ulster had disintegrated in the fifteenth century, this Lordship of Iveagh, ruled by the Magennises, had expanded from west Down as far east as Dundrum Castle. The unity of this Magennis hegemony was constantly threatened by rivalry between the Rathfriland, Corgary, Kilwarlin and Castlewellan branches of the family. Nevertheless, as the authority of the Tudors increased in Ireland in the sixteenth century, the Magennises proved remarkably adaptable. When Conn Bacach O'Neill travelled to London to receive his patent and title of Earl of Tyrone in 1542 his companions were Donal Óg Magennis of Rathfriland and Art MacPhelim Magennis of Castlewellan, both of whom received knighthoods. The Magennises generally took care to be on good terms with the Bagenals in Newry. Indeed, Sir Henry Bagenal in 1587 went so far as to describe Donal Óg's son and successor, Sir Hugh Magennis, as 'the civillist of all the Irishry', who lived 'very civilly and English-like in his house and every festival day weareth English garments amongst his followers'.

Then the dispute between Sir Henry Bagenal and Hugh O'Neill, Earl of Tyrone, led directly on to the Nine Years' War.[29] Which side should the Magennises support? Neutrality was not an option. After the Yellow Ford the Magennises had little choice but to join the other Gaelic lords of Ulster in the war against the Queen. Sir Hugh Magennis had died in 1596, and his son Art Roe, who succeeded him, was tied closely to Tyrone, who married Art's sister Catherine (Caitríona) in 1597, who became the earl's fifth wife.[30]

The inhabitants of Iveagh endured famine and slaughter on a terrible scale as Lord Deputy Mountjoy's troops closed in on the rebel lords. To prevent the annihilation of his people Art Roe detached himself from O'Neill and submitted to Mountjoy. The promise that he could keep his lands seemed to be underlined by the Treaty of Mellifont in 1603. But the predatory servitors, who had been kicking their heels not only in Newry but also in Carrickfergus and Belfast, were circling. Their champion, Sir Arthur Chichester, was sworn in as Lord Deputy in 1605, and that year he set up a Commission for the Division and Bounding of the Lords' and Gentlemen's Livings—a body which immediately imperilled the security of every Gaelic landowner in Ulster.

The native lords were facing the consequences of military defeat: loss of their strongholds and profitable lands about them; martial law ruthlessly and arbitrarily applied; the often peremptory demands of sheriffs and other Crown officials; loss of income from lands taken over by the state-sponsored church; and insistence that they abide by an English law that they imperfectly understood. And now, as the commission began its probing, each one harboured acute anxiety about whether or not the government would uphold the title to his estate. At the same time they were confronted with another threat: punishment if they did not accept the reformed religion of the conquerors. The shock-waves of a vigorous drive to enforce conformity, beginning in the Pale, were not long in reaching Ulster.

A REIGN OF RELIGIOUS TERROR

Even at the height of his power the Earl of Tyrone had been unable to win over to his side the 'Old English'. These descendants of twelfth and thirteenth-century Norman conquerors, and of the people they had brought over the Irish Sea with them, were still proud to be called English, and many had fought against the Gaelic lords in the Lord Deputy's armies.

But the Old English also were Catholics, loyal to the Pope. Just before leaving Ireland at the end of May 1603, Mountjoy had given permission to Catholics—provided they did not use churches—to practise their religion in the privacy of their homes. How would this decision be viewed in London? It was not long before it became very plain that the new King would insist on strict religious conformity.

Mountjoy, by now Earl of Devonshire, himself encountered at first hand James's inflexibility on religious matters. Deciding to make an honest woman of his long-term mistress, Lady Penelope Rich, he obtained a divorce for her from her husband, Richard, Lord Rich. Then, in 1605, the Lord Lieutenant married Lady Penelope, persuading his private chaplain to perform the ceremony. The King was horrified and banished Devonshire from his court.

Soon the King's reckless religious policies for Ireland, implemented with savage enthusiasm by Chichester, threatened to drive the Old English into the arms of disaffected Gaelic Irish. During his sojourn in London, Tyrone had risked presenting a petition drawn up by lords of the Pale seeking religious toleration. Two years later the Old English were startled to find that the King was determined to make them Protestants. James issued a proclamation in July 1605 declaring that he would fight to his knees in blood rather than grant toleration. He would never

give liberty of conscience . . . to his subjects in that kingdom . . . or . . . confirm the hopes of any creature that they should ever have from him any toleration to exercise any other religion than that which is agreeable to God's Word.

Chichester launched a programme of religious persecution on a scale never witnessed before in Ireland. He now rigidly enforced an earlier law which fined ordinary Catholics a shilling for every Sunday they failed to attend a Protestant church. Letters were delivered to sixteen leading Catholic gentlemen in Dublin fining them a hundred pounds each.[31] A petition against this persecution was sent just when news arrived of the discovery of the Gunpowder Plot, a Catholic conspiracy, led by Guy Fawkes, to blow up the Houses of Parliament in London in November 1605. This was no time for Catholics in either England or Ireland to be demanding their rights.

The petitioners were put under house arrest. Sir Patrick Barnewall and other Old English Catholic leaders were cast into the dungeons of Dublin

Castle. In Drogheda, Chichester personally led the campaign to force Catholics to attend Protestant services. One Catholic gentleman went as far as the church door but would go no further, whereupon Chichester

> told him, blandly at first, and then savagely, to go in, and seeing he could not prevail on him, struck him a cruel blow on the head with his stick. Then the macebearer attacked him so savagely that he fell to the ground like a dead man, and the viceroy had him dragged into church, where he lay insensible and gasping all the time of the sermon, and no one dared to approach him. Some of his friends afterwards took him home, where he gave his blessed soul to God in two hours.[32]

Unpaid fines were violently collected:

> No doors, no enclosures, no wall can stop them in their course; they are unmoved by the shrieks of the females and by the weeping of the children. Everything is torn open, and whatever is of any value is set aside to be taken away, whatever is worthless is thrown in the streets, and devoted to the flames . . .[33]

Meanwhile Sir Henry Brouncker, Lord President of Munster, orchestrated a similar reign of terror in the south:

> They rush in crowds into the houses of these servants of God, break open doors, tear off locks, ransack shops, leave no corner unsearched, and carry off everything they can lay their hands on, besides taking the owners prisoners.[34]

Little wonder then that, on hearing that Sir Patrick Barnewall had been locked up in the Tower of London, some Old English lords began to plot a rising. And it seems that the man who was doing most to encourage them was none other than the Earl of Tyrone.

While this religious persecution was raging, native lords in eastern Ulster were witnessing the first major influx of Protestant British colonists. This was orchestrated not by resident servitors but by two of King James's trusted spymasters.

Chapter 5 ~

'CIVILIZINGE OF THOSE RUDE PARTES': DOWN AND ANTRIM

CONN O'NEILL'S GAOL BREAK

Hugh Montgomery, eldest son of Adam Montgomery, 5th Laird of Braidstane in Ayrshire, has claim to be the most successful planter in all of Ireland in the seventeenth century. After leaving the University of Glasgow he decided to seek his fortune as a soldier, serving as a captain of foot first in a Scottish regiment fighting for Henry IV in France and then for the Prince of Orange in the Netherlands. On hearing of the death of his parents he travelled to Edinburgh to kiss the hands of James VI to become the 6th Laird and then returned to Holland. Here he was gaoled following a duel with a fellow-Scot, a member of the rival Cunninghams of Ayrshire. A compatriot romanced the gaoler's daughter, who, with the help of a purse of gold, released Montgomery—a stratagem the laird was to employ again in Ireland.

Meanwhile Hugh Montgomery maintained a frequent correspondence with his brother George, a parson of Chedzoy in Somerset and later Dean of Norwich. As there was no regular post between Scotland and England the brothers employed a footman 'with letters of intelligencies and of business and advice, and in requittal he received more and fresher informations (touching the English Court and the Queen)'.[1] Hugh called on James VI to bring him the latest news from his brother George. Hugh was 'graciously received' but not without 'a severe check given him by his Majesty' about his quarrel with the Cunninghams. Hugh promised to bury the hatchet, 'and thus by his Majesty's care was the revival of the old bloody fewd between the Montgomeries and Cunninghams fully prevented'.[2] And now 'halcyon days shined throughout all Scotland, all animosities being compressed by his Majesty (who in a few months afterwards) having certain intelligence of Queen Elizabeth's sickness, and extreme bodily weakness, and not long thence of her death', after being proclaimed King of England, travelled to London.[3]

Hugh Montgomery journeyed with James's retinue and took lodgings at Westminster; he met at court, the Montgomery Manuscripts continue,

> the said George (his then only living brother), who with longing expectations waited for those happy days. They enjoyed one the others most loving companies, and meditated the bettering and advancing their peculiar stations. Forseeing that Ireland must be the stage to act upon, it being unsettled, and many forfeited lands thereon altogether wasted, they concluded to push for fortunes in that kingdom, as the Laird had formerly done.[4]

Hugh returned to Braidstane but was kept thoroughly informed by his brother. There 'the said Laird in the said first year of the King's reign pitched upon the following way (which he thought most fair and feazable) to get an estate in lands with free consent of the forfeiting owner of them'. Men from Ayr, trading regularly across the North Channel, brought him news that the Lord of Upper Clandeboye and the Great Ards was languishing in gaol in Carrickfergus. An elaborate scheme was hatched.

Towards the close of the year 1602 the Clandeboye O'Neills had detached themselves from the Earl of Tyrone and submitted to the local English commander, Sir Arthur Chichester. However, Conn Mac Néill O'Neill, Lord of Upper Clandeboye, failed to keep out of trouble 'on account of a quarrel made by his servants with some soldiers in Belfast, done before the Queen died'. The Montgomery Manuscripts explain:

> The said servants being sent with runletts to bring wine from Belfast aforesaid, unto the said Con, their master, and Great Teirne as they called him, then in a grand debauch at Castlereagh, with his brothers, his friends, and followers; they returning (without wine) to him battered and bled, complained that the soldiers had taken the wine, with the casks, from them by force. Con enquiring (of them) into the matter, they confessed their number twice exceeded the soldiers, who indeed had abused them, they being very drunk. On this report of the said servants, Con was vehemently moved to anger; reproached them bitterly; and in a rage, swore by his father, and by all his noble ancestors' souls, that not one of them should ever serve him or his family (for he

was married and had issue) if they went not back forthwith and revenge the affront done to him and themselves, by those few Boddagh Sasonagh soldiers (as he termed them).

Conn's men—'as yet more than half drunk'—returned to Belfast and killed a soldier. 'But the Teagues were beaten off and chased, some sore wounded and others killed; only the best runners got away Scott free'.[5] Accused of levying war again the Queen, Conn was incarcerated in Carrickfergus. The following year, 1604, Montgomery prepared a gaol break in collaboration with Conn's wife, Éilís; if the laird could free Conn from prison and gain him a royal pardon, she was prepared to arrange that Montgomery could acquire a substantial portion of Upper Clandeboye.

Montgomery sent a relative from Ayr, Thomas Montgomery of Blackstown, over to Carrickfergus:

> This Thomas had personally divers times traded with grain and other things to Carrickfergus, and was well trusted therein; and had a small bark, of which he was owner and constant commander; which Thomas being a discreet sensible gentleman . . . was now employed and furnished with instructions to the said Con.

The Montgomery Manuscripts continue:

> With full secrecy concerted, Thomas aforesaid (as the Laird had formerly advised) having made love to the Town Marshall's daughter, called Annas Dobbin (whom I have often seen and spoken with, for she lived in Newtown till Anno 1664), and had gained hers and parent's consents to be wedded together. This took umbrages of suspicion away, and so by contrivance with his espoused, an opportunity one night, was given to the said Thomas and his barque's crew to take on board the said Con, as it were by force, he making no noise for fear of being stabbed, as was reported next day through the town.[6]

According to another account, Conn's wife assisted by smuggling in rope in two big cheeses, 'the meat being neatly taken out, and filled with cords, well packed in, and the holes handsomely made up again'. Annas Dobbin opened the cell, and Conn lowered himself down the rope to a waiting boat, to be taken across the North Channel to Largs and freedom.[7]

THE TRIPARTITE DIVISION OF UPPER CLANDEBOYE

At Braidstane Castle the deal was finalised. In return for half his lands the laird would obtain for Conn a royal pardon:

> In this place the said Con entered into indenture of articles of agreement, the tenor whereof was that the said Laird should entertaine and subsist him . . . should procure his pardon for his and all their crimes and transgressions against the law . . . and the one-half of his estate (whereof Castlereagh and circumjacent lands to be a part) to be granted to himself by letters patent from the King . . . the said Con did agree, covenant grant, and assign, by the said indenture, the other one-half of all his land estate, to be and enure to the only use and behoof of the said Laird, his heirs and assigns.[8]

The agreement signed, Conn and Hugh travelled to Westminster, there to meet George Montgomery, who for some months had been serving as chaplain to the King. James received Conn graciously and knighted Hugh Montgomery. He gave orders that the arrangement should be confirmed by letters patent, 'under conditions that the lands should be planted with British Protestants, and that no grant of fee farm should be made to any person of meer Irish extraction'.[9]

Before the patents were issued, two Lowland Scots intervened. The King was approached by Sir James Fullerton, who suggested that 'the lands granted to Sir Hugh and Con were vast territories, too large for two men of their degree, and might serve for three Lords' estates'.[10] Fullerton, a native of the parish of Dundonald in Ayrshire, was a close associate of James Hamilton, son of a minister of the parish of Dunlop. After graduating in Glasgow, Hamilton had taught in a school there for a time until he decided to seek his fortune elsewhere. Though they may not have intended to go to Ireland, both men landed in Dublin in 1587 after their ship had been forced to seek shelter there in a storm.

Hamilton set up a school in Dublin and employed Fullerton as his assistant. They were to remain in the city for thirteen years. The University of Dublin, with Trinity College as its sole college, was founded in 1591, and its first provost was impressed by Hamilton, observing that he had 'a noble spirit . . . and learned head'. Hamilton was persuaded to become a fellow in 1595 and threw himself into the task of raising funds for the college, travelling to places as far apart as Tuam and York. He was an obvious choice to be appointed bursar in 1598.

Meanwhile both Hamilton and Fullerton were at pains to keep themselves well informed about developments across the Irish Sea and, crucially, acted as agents—secret or not—for James VI of Scotland. Indeed, Hamilton moved to London in 1600 to serve as the Scottish King's agent at Elizabeth's court.[11] On James's accession, Fullerton also made his way to London, where he was knighted and served at court as a gentleman of the bedchamber, master of the privy purse to the Duke of York and master of the court of wards and liveries.

Fullerton successfully 'begged his Majesty that Mr. James Hamilton who had furnished himself for some years last past with intelligencies from Dublin, very important to his Majesty, might be admitted to a third share of that which was intended to be granted to Sir Hugh and Con'.[12] Exactly how Fullerton succeeded in getting the King to let Hamilton muscle in on Montgomery's deal is not clear. It is certain, however, that King James had overlooked a letter he had issued in December 1604 in favour of a London merchant, Thomas Ireland. Ireland, in return for an advance of £1,678 6s 8d sterling, was to get sufficient Irish land to ensure an income of a hundred pounds a year, including 'so muche of the lands in the twoe Ardes, in the province of Ulster, as he or his nominee shall think fitt, to be parcel'.[13] Ireland then assigned his rights by this grant (for what reason is not known) to James Hamilton on 25 February 1605.

King James issued his letter patent on 10 April 1605 directly to Hamilton, but it specified a tripartite division, to include Conn O'Neill and Sir Hugh Montgomery. To mollify Montgomery the King agreed to add to his estate abbey lands in the area and to make sure that Montgomery and Hamilton would between them take possession of all of the Great Ards. The patent states:

That the aforesaid James Hamilton, his heirs and assigns, should have of our gift or grant the countries or territories of the Upper Clandeboy and Great Ards, and all castles, manors, lands, tenements, and hereditaments in the said country of the Upper Clandeboy and great Ards, of which Neal McBrian Fertagh O'Neale, or his father, Brian Fertagh O'Neale, in their lifetimes were possessed of ... rendering unto us, our heirs and successors, £100 good and lawful money of Ireland annually, at the receipt of our Exchequer there.

The land was to be held of the Crown by 'free and common socage' rather than by the more complicated and burdensome 'knight service', which had been usual in the past. For the first time in James I's reign a grant of Irish land was made conditional upon the introduction of Scottish or English tenants. For the first time, also, Scots settlers were put on an equal footing with English ones. The patent continues:

> The aforesaid James Hamilton should promise to inhabit the said territory and lands with English or Scotchmen; therefore, that the aforesaid James Hamilton may the better able to inhabit the said territories, depopulated and wasted, and to pay the rent aforesaid.[14]

The threefold division between O'Neill, Montgomery and Hamilton followed a few days later. The Irishman was to receive half of Upper Clandeboye, with Castlereagh at his estate's centre, while the two Scots were to divide the other half of Upper Clandeboye and all of the Great Ards between them. It was agreed that Hamilton and Montgomery would supply Scots and English tenants to settle a third of O'Neill's estate. The tripartite division was so arranged that 'the sea coasts might be possessed by Scottish men, who would be traders as proper for his Majestie's future advantage'.[15]

'THE PICKLE WHEREIN CON WAS SOUSED'

Sir Hugh and Conn left court for Edinburgh and Braidstane and, 'after a short necessary stay for recruits of money', made their way to Ulster.[16] According to the Montgomery Manuscripts,

> Con then returned home in triumph over his enemies (who thought to have had his life and estate), and was met by his friends, tenants and followers, the most of them on foot, the better sort had gerrans, some had panels for saddles (we call them back bughams), and the greater part of the riders without them; and but very few spurs in the troop, yet thereof they might have thorn prickles in their brogue heels (as is usual), and perhaps not one of the concourse had a hat; but the gentry (for sure) had on their done wosle barrads, the rest might have sorry scull caps, otherwise (in reverence and of necessity) went cheerfully pacing or trotting bare-headed. Con being so come in state (in Dublin equipage) to Castlereagh, where no doubt his vassals (tag-ragg and bob-tail) gave to their Teirne More, Squire Con, all the honour and homage they could bestow, presenting him with store of beeves, colpaghs, sheep, hens, bonny blabber, rusan butter (such as it was); as

for cheese I heard nothing of it (which to this day is very seldom made by the Irish), and there was some greddan meal strowans, with snush, and bolean, as much as they could get to regale him.[17]

Conn O'Neill had reason to conclude that he had done well in the circumstances. His lordship had been part of the Earldom of Ulster, which his ancestors had overrun in the fourteenth and fifteenth centuries. It had been granted by Queen Elizabeth first to Sir Thomas Smith and then to the Earl of Essex. Pardoned for past rebellions against the Crown, O'Neill now possessed a great estate by English law, which he could pass on to his heirs. His close relatives could argue that the two-thirds of his lordship alienated to Montgomery and Hamilton were not, by customary Gaelic law, his to give away. Certainly the author of the Montgomery Manuscripts was at pains to point out that

> Con's title was bad . . . being but a claim by tanestry, whereby a man at full years is to be chosen and preferred to the estate (during his life) . . . This being the pickle wherein Con was soused, and his best claim but an unquiet possession, usurpation and intrusion against the laws of the kingdom.[18]

O'Neill had swiftly to familiarise himself with English law and English practice in managing his estates. An early indication of his inability to cope in a new regime was his sale in August 1606 in Slut Neale (roughly between Ballylesson and Drumbo) of the valuable woods of four townlands to Montgomery.

Meanwhile Hamilton travelled to Dublin on 19 July 1605 and there presented the newly appointed Lord Deputy, Sir Arthur Chichester, with his letters patent. Chichester was appalled. As he wrote to Salisbury, 'if he have his desires, he will have more lands than the greatest Lords in that kingdom; and all is given in free and common socage, whereby His Majesty's tenures are lost and every where abridged'. Chichester not only had to accept the *fait accompli* but also had to swallow the news that, the following day, Hamilton was issued with further royal grants of priory lands in Coleraine, Kells and Massereene in Co. Antrim, and Newtown (now Newtownards), Holywood, Movilla, Black Abbey, Greyabbey and Bangor in Co. Down.

Chichester journeyed north in July 1605, almost certainly in Hamilton's company. Hamilton, after only four days, gave Massereene to Chichester, no doubt to mollify the Lord Deputy. Then, in September, he sold his lands in Coleraine to the servitor, Sir Thomas Phillips; and, in October, Montgomery bought—for £105 10s—Hamilton's abbey lands in Movilla, Newtown and Greyabbey.[19] In February 1606 Hamilton, as Thomas Ireland's assignee, received in Co. Antrim the fishery of the River Bann between Lough Neagh and the Salmon Leap above Coleraine; Magheramorne; Moylinny; Ballinlinny and Clandermot; the granges of the abbey of St Peter and St Paul; the friary of Inver and the abbey of Islandmagee; and lands around Toome Castle. The same grant awarded him in Co. Down the abbey of Comber and townlands in the vicinity of Dufferin.[20] Some of these new possessions in Co. Antrim Hamilton was to sell on (using the proceeds to buy the entire barony of Dufferin in 1610), but the salmon fishery would later become the focus of a bitter dispute. Hamilton would also lock legal horns with Montgomery; but for the present both men concentrated on making a success of their lands in Co. Down.

COLONISING 'THOSE PARISHES MORE WASTED THAN AMERICA'

Montgomery and Hamilton had received their grants on condition that they settle English and Scottish Protestants on their estates. Both set about meeting this obligation with considerable determination. During the winter of 1605/06 Sir Hugh returned to Braidstane with the purpose of inducing his neighbours to join him. He found many willing to do so. Initially they included John Shaw of Greenock, brother of his wife, Elizabeth; Patrick Montgomery of Blackhouse, married to Shaw's sister, Christian; Colonel David Boyd; Patrick Shaw, Laird of Kelso, Sir Hugh's uncle by marriage; Hugh Montgomery, a cadet of the Braidstane family; Thomas Nevin, brother of the Laird of Monkredding and Cunningham, and Lady Montgomery's nephew; Patrick Moore of Deugh, Kirkcudbrightshire; Sir William Edmonston, 7th Laird of Duntreath, of Stirlingshire; and John Neill of Mains-Neill, near Braidstane.

The surnames of Scots who took out letters of denization in 1617—the majority settling on Sir Hugh's estates—include Catherwood, Wyly, Boyle, Harper, Barkley, Moore, Hunter, Thompson, Logan, Crawford, Agnew, Adair, Wilson, Williamson, Cunningham, Cathcart, Maxwell, Allen, Fraser, Aiken, McDowell, Harvey, Semple, Anderson, Kennedy, Martin, Speir and more Montgomerys and Cunninghams.[21] Among those colonising on the Hamilton estates were families with such names as Maxwell, Rose, Barclay, More and Baylie.[22]

The Scots began to arrive in force in the spring of 1607. As surviving records for Hamilton's properties in eastern Ulster are sparse, it is to the Montgomery Manuscripts that we must turn for evidence of what was to become the most successful British colonising venture in Ireland in the seventeenth century:

> Therefore let us now pause a while, and we shall wonder how this plantation advanced itself (especially in and about the towns of Donaghadee and Newton), considering that in the spring time . . . those parishes were now more wasted than America (when Spaniards landed there), but were not at all encumbered with great woods to be felled and grubbed, to the discouragement or hindrance of the inhabitants, for in all those three parishes aforesaid, 30 cabins could not be found, nor any stone walls, but ruined roofless churches, and a few vaults at Gray Abbey, and a stump of an old castle in Newton, in each of which some Gentlemen sheltered themselves at their first coming over.

The author, of course, was concerned to demonstrate the extent to which his relatives and other Scots improved the lands to which they had migrated. There is little doubt, however, that ruthless and destructive tactics employed by Mountjoy and his officers at the close of the Nine Years' War had left much of Ulster in a ruined condition; though never the heart of Tyrone's rebellion, Co. Down suffered disproportionately. The best-known passage in the Montgomery Manuscripts does paint a rosy picture, but it is well supported by other contemporary evidence:

> But Sir Hugh in the said spring brought with him divers artificers, as smiths, masons, carpenters, &c. I knew many of them old men when I was a boy at school, and had little employments for some of them, and heard them tell many things of this plantation which I found true. They soon made cottages and booths for themselves, because sods and saplins of ashes, alders, and birch trees (above 30 years old) with rushes for thatch, and bushes for wattle, were at hand. And also they made a shelter of the said stump of the castle for Sir Hugh, whose residence was mostlie there, as in the centre of being supplied with necessaries from Belfast (but six miles thence), who therefore came and set up a market in Newton, for profit for both the towns. As likewise in the fair summer season (twice, sometimes thrice every week) they were supplied from Scotland, as Donaghadee was oftener, because but three hours sail from

Portpatrick, where they bespoke provisions and necessaries to lade in, to be brought over by their own or that town's boats whenever wind and weather served them, for there was a constant flux of passengers coming daily over.

I have heard honest old men say that in June, July, and August, 1607, people came from Stranraer, four miles, and left their horses at the port, hired horses at Donaghadee, came with their wares and provisions to Newton, and sold them, dined there, staid two or three hours, and returned to their houses the same day by bed-time, their land journey but 20 miles. Such was their encouragement from a ready market, and their kind desires to see and supply their friends and kindred, which commerce took quite away evil report of woodkerns, which enviers of planters' industry had raised and brought upon our plantations.

Now every body minded their trades, and the plough, and the spade, building, and setting fruit trees, &c., in orchards and gardens, and by ditching in their grounds. The old women spun, and the young girls plyed their nimble fingers at knitting—and every body was innocently busy. Now the Golden peacable age renewed, no strife, contention, querulous lawyers, or Scottish or Irish feuds, between clans and families, and sirnames, disturbing the tranquillity of those times; and the towns and temples were erected, with other great works (even in troublesome times) . . .[23]

Sir Hugh set about building himself a residence fitting for his status:

Some of the priory walls were roofed and fitted for Sir Hugh and his family to dwell in; but the rest of these walls, and other large additions of a gate-house and office-houses, which made three sides of a quadrangle (the south side of the church being contiguous, made the 4th side), with coins and window frames, and chimney-pieces, and funnels of freestone, all covered: and the floors beamed with main oak timber, and clad with boards; the roof with oak plank from his Lordship's own woods, and slated with slates out of Scotland; and the floors laid with fir deals out of Norway, the windows were fitly glazed and the edifice thoroly furnished within. This was a work of some time and years, but the same was finished by that excellent Lady (and fit helper mostly in Sir Hugh's absence) because he was by business much and often kept from home, after the year 1608 expired.[24]

SIR RANDAL MACDONNELL, THE GREAT SURVIVOR

Randal Arannach MacSorley MacDonnell (the son of Sorley Boy, so called because he had been fostered on the Scottish Isle of Arran) was unquestionably the most fortunate survivor of those who had waged war against Queen Elizabeth. He had fought with the Earl of Tyrone, married his third daughter, Éilís, and had marched the length of the island in 1601 to fight alongside him at the Battle of Kinsale. There almost his entire contingent of several hundred infantrymen armed with firearms, together with archers and horsemen, was slaughtered. While Randal was in Munster, Sir Arthur Chichester devastated the MacDonnell lands. Chichester reported that he

cominge unlooked for amonge them, made my entrance almost as far as Dunluce, where I spared neither house, corne, nor creature; and I brought from thence as much prey as we could well dryve, being greatlye hindered by the extreme snowe fallen in the tyme of my beinge abroade.[25]

Fortunate to escape the battlefield, Randal returned to his lordship, only to find that relatives, led by Sir James of Knockrinsay, had occupied Dunluce Castle to challenge his position as head of the MacDonnells. Tyrone supported his claim, however, and may have encouraged Randal to seek terms with the English so that he could act as a go-between should a negotiated peace be on offer.[26] In any case, seeing that further resistance to the Crown forces was futile, Randal had submitted in the autumn of 1602. During the final bloody stages of the campaign, MacDonnell had fought in Fermanagh with five hundred foot and forty horse, supplied at his own expense. At Tullaghoge, Chichester introduced him to Mountjoy, and there the Lord Deputy knighted him.

On 11 May 1603, only weeks after he had become King of England, James sent instructions to Mountjoy to pass all of the Route and the Glynns to the recently knighted Sir Randal. The first Scot to receive a grant of land in Co. Antrim, Sir Randal MacDonnell was duly confirmed on 28 May in his possession of a vast estate of 333,907 acres, which included lands he and his brother James had grabbed from the MacQuillans of the Route and their kinsman Angus MacDonnell of Dunyveg. In addition, Randal was not, in English eyes, even the rightful owner of the MacDonnell lands: when James, the Lord of the Glynns and the Route, had died, in 1601, he had been succeeded not by his eldest son, Alexander, but by his younger brother,

Randal Arannach—a usual enough occurrence in the Gaelic world, where the man with the strongest following was generally nominated successor, but not acceptable by English law. Elizabeth had consistently regarded these Gaelic-speaking and Catholic Scots as a grave threat to England's security, and she had launched numerous costly campaigns to subdue them even before the beginning of the Nine Years' War.

How can this sudden change in the Crown's attitude to the Antrim MacDonnells be explained? The whole situation had been altered by the accession of James VI of Scotland as James I of England. The fear that Scots would ally themselves with England's enemies had suddenly evaporated. More specifically, Randal had provided the Scottish Crown with vital assistance against his cousin Angus MacDonald of Dunyveg.[27] Indeed, one reason for James being so quick to confirm Randal in his Irish estates was to preserve this property 'from the violence of his bade kynsmen'.[28] Mountjoy had already advised the King that if he attempted to deprive MacDonnell of his lands he would lose Randal, 'who is rich, powerful, and, at present, loyal'.[29] The Lord Deputy, anxious to leave Ireland to be at the centre of power in London, seems to have drafted the grant to Sir Randal in some haste. Certainly he forgot to include the island of Rathlin, and the patent contained a clause stating that Sir Randal's estates would be forfeit if he fell behind in his rent to the Crown. Sir Randal in fact *was* in severe danger of falling behind in his rent payment, and he conducted a tenacious campaign to have this charge reduced. The King was not slow to make matters easier for MacDonnell. Sir Randal's 1603 patent was handed back, and on 6 July 1604 a fresh one was issued. Not only did it carry out the King's instructions but it also included a new clause—presumably inserted in Dublin Castle—which was to be of great significance in shaping the way Ulster would be colonised in the ensuing decades. It stated that Sir Randal was to have authority

> to divide the said territories into several precincts, each to contain 2000 acres at least, and to give different names to each division, so that they may become different manors—to set apart 500 acres in each for demesne lands, and to build a castle or mansion-house upon each, within seven years—to hold courts baron, and appoint seneschals.[30]

Though this clause made no mention of introducing British settlers, it was to serve as a draft template for the apportioning of estates in the Plantation of Ulster a few years later.

INVITING LOWLAND SCOTS TO SETTLE

In fact the astute Sir Randal, very soon after he had received his second patent, *did* set about inviting Scots of a variety particularly acceptable to the King—Protestants from the Lowlands—to settle on his lands on attractive terms. One reason for doing this was that he was acutely aware that the servitors thought that James had been far too indulgent to him, and these seasoned commanders had little reason to trust the Gaelic-speaking, Catholic MacDonnells. Randal's brother James, after all, had been responsible for the killing of Sir John Chichester in 1597, then Governor of Carrickfergus; when Sir Arthur Chichester, his brother and principal spokesman for the servitors, was appointed Lord Deputy, Sir Randal knew that he must do all in his power not to lose the King's favour. Almost as soon as he was appointed, Chichester was advising that no part of Ireland needed 'better looking unto' than the MacDonnell possessions.[31]

Sir Randal was quite open in admitting his difficulty in raising ready cash to pay the modest rent demanded of him by the Crown. The concluding years of the Nine Years' War had left his estates in a ruinous condition. 'The whole region of the county Antrim', a patent of 1604 began, was 'wasted by rebellion'.[32] In short, like much of the rest of eastern Ulster, Sir Randal's estates sorely needed more inhabitants capable of bringing the land into full production and, crucially, capable also of paying rent. There is little doubt that the early success of Montgomery and Hamilton in Co. Down encouraged Sir Randal to seek new tenants on the other side of the North Channel. A supply was immediately available: Lowlanders planted on Kintyre at King James's behest by the Earl of Argyll had been forced to take flight after ferocious attacks in 1607 by Angus MacDonnell of Dunyveg, former owner of the territory, who had already had his claim on the Glens of Antrim rejected by the King.[33] In a letter to Lord Salisbury, Chichester explained that

> the pretended Lord of Kintyre, has put himself into arms and done some annoyance to the Earl of Argyll's people seated in that promontory. Many of the poor people make means to fly to the Route, to Sir Randal MacDonnell, and Angus threatens to put over into those parts with his galleys for the spoil of that country and the subjects adjoining.[34]

For once the Lord Deputy did not insert a disparaging observation on Sir Randal: these 'poor people' were Presbyterians from Renfrew, Dumbarton and Ayr, planted in Kintyre seven years before. Angus then, after being crushed by the forces of King James, had been forced to agree to the removal of all his clansmen and adherents from the peninsula. The Earl of Argyll had offered to pay more rent to the Crown than the MacDonnells had done and to colonise Kintyre with respectable farmers from the Lowlands. When Angus rose in revolt again, in 1607, these Lowlanders did not wait to be expelled and crossed the North Channel. Sir Randal did not hesitate to welcome them as tenants—particularly as they had come over with their own cattle, seed corn and farm equipment. He knew also that his willingness to take in Protestants would be especially pleasing to the King.

Other Lowland Scots followed those driven out of Kintyre, but a shortage of evidence means that their progress in colonising Sir Randal's lands at this stage is somewhat uncertain. Sir Randal does seem to have been careful—unlike Montgomery, Hamilton and servitors in Co. Down—to prevent Scots incomers from bankrupting the natives on his Antrim estates. Grants were made to promote industry and the development of market towns, and to place settlers in places likely to encourage trade. Freehold leases were given to the Ó Gnímh bardic family, while further large grants on adjacent land were made to the Agnews of Loughnaw, their Galloway cousins. The Agnews were therefore able to give some protection to the Ó Gnímhs. Many Lowlanders settled at Glenarm, where the Presbyterian Donaldsons acquired leases to substantial holdings, including the right to reside in the old castle of Glenarm.[35]

Sir Randal also welcomed in Hebridean Scots ousted from Kintyre and elsewhere in the Isles. Their settlement in numbers helps to explain why most of the Glens remained Catholic. Muster rolls and later surveys indicate where they settled. Leading families included McAuleys in Glenarm and Carnlough and about Cushendall; Magills in Glenarm and Carnlough; McKays in Glencloy, Glenarm and Glendun; McNeills in Glenmakeeran, Cushendun and Carnlough; McAllisters in Glenaan and Glenariff; and a Highland branch of the Stewarts in Ballintoy.[36]

'A BEGGAR IS MADE GREAT AND YET RESTS UNTHANKFUL'

The Lord of the Glynns and the Route was often distracted from efforts to develop his estates by a prolonged dispute over valuable fishing rights on the Lower River Bann—a crucial source of income. Sir James Hamilton already had possession of the fishing rights from Toome, where the river flows out of Lough Neagh to the Salmon Leap, just above Coleraine. On

2 March 1606 a merchant named John Wakeman had received a grant of the fishing from the Salmon Leap to the sea, and the following day he sold his rights to Hamilton. This short stretch produced the greatest hauls of salmon, particularly in summer, when grilse wait to ascend below the falls in low water.

Sir Randal was outraged when he heard of Hamilton's acquisition: this fishing lay within his estates on both sides of the river and its estuary. Hamilton, he declared, had, by 'searching and prying curiously into his patent (as he doth into many other men's estates)', robbed him of his main source of income. Sir James, he continued, 'is now possessed of great countries, and yet is not contented therewith, but seeks to pull from him that little portion which His Majesty of his bounty hath been pleased to bestow upon him'. Hamilton could respond that he had been granted the abbey lands of Coleraine.

In any case Sir Randal's position was weakened further when, on 10 April 1606, Sir Arthur Chichester bought the fishing rights from Toome to the Salmon Leap and, on 14 May, 'the moiety' of Hamilton's portion from the leap to the sea. Chichester, of course, had not forgotten that his brother John had been killed by the Antrim MacDonnells. The Lord Deputy was warmly supported by Sir Thomas Phillips, commander of the garrison at Toome Castle. Initially, Phillips had got on well with Sir Randal, who gave the servitor 'a little neck of land called Port Rush . . . for 40 years, paying yearly one hogshead of claret wine', but then MacDonnell 'is sorry to let him have it'—indeed Sir Randal was with justice becoming alarmed at the Englishman's territorial ambitions in the vicinity.[37]

Chichester, enthusiastically supported by Phillips, did all he could to blacken Sir Randal's name, declaring to Salisbury that there was not 'a more cancred and malicious person than Sir Randal MacDonnell, who from a beggar is made great and yet rests unthankful'.[38] Phillips accused Sir Randal of treating his tenants badly and of the fact that this provoked 'stealths, robberies, and other evils' along the Bann. Sir Randal in turn wrote that Phillips had terrorised his tenants, forcing them to flee from their homes. The Lord of the Glynns and the Route did have the support of George Montgomery, who had arrived in Ulster in 1605 to take up his new position as Bishop of Derry, Raphoe and Clogher. Salisbury was informed by Sir Thomas Lake that 'the bishop of Derry, Montgomery, who is his neighbour, has received great commendation of his civil behaviour, he thinks good he be encouraged with any reasonable favour that may maintain him in his good disposition'.[39]

Sir Randal took care not to lose the King's favour and attended at court in London in the summer of 1607. Here he persuaded James that he was only too anxious to attract more approved Scots settlers to his estates. Chichester received orders on 22 August 1607 that he was to help MacDonnell make freeholders on his lands on English conditions 'as Sir Hugh Montgomery and other our fee farmers in those parts doe'.[40]

Less than three weeks later, news spread rapidly that the Earls of Tyrone and Tyrconnell had sailed with their kin and trusted companions from Lough Swilly, apparently never to return. The 'Flight of the Earls' would transform the King's plans to colonise the north of Ireland with loyal British subjects.

Chapter 6 ～

THE FLIGHT OF THE EARLS AND O'DOHERTY'S REBELLION

BEGGARING THE EARLS

Lord Deputy Chichester was convinced that Tyrone had never ceased to be a traitor and that he was assiduously plotting against the Crown. He was quite unable to prove that this was the case, however. In the meantime the Lord Deputy and Sir John Davies, freshly promoted to become Attorney-General, at the same time as they were heedlessly alienating the Old English gentry, whittled away at the earl's authority so that, Chichester reported, 'now the law of England, and the Ministers thereof, were shackles and handlocks unto him, and the garrisons planted in his country were as pricks in his side'.[1]

By any standard of the day Tyrone was still immensely rich: he had retained most of the vast estates which had enabled him to spend five hundred pounds a day funding military operations during the Nine Years' War. In contrast, the Earl of Tyrconnell's position was fast becoming desperate. Writing in April 1604, Sir John Davies concluded that

in Tirconnell Neale Garve O'Donnell . . . hath gotten many followers, hath possessed himself of the tenants and herds of cattle, and has grown so strong that the earl seems to hold it not safe to return thither, but lies here within the Pale very meanly attended.[2]

For a start, the patent Tyrconnell received for his lands ruled out any form of overlordship, which the O'Donnells had usually been able to exercise over much of north Connacht and Fermanagh. The patent included a specific 'injunction' that the earl and his successors 'should renounce and relinquish all claim or right which they had or might pretend to have over

O'Dohertie's and O'Connor Sligoe's countries'.[3] Much of Tír Chonaill was made up of igneous rock thinly covered with infertile acid soil leached by rains from the Atlantic, or, after the trees had been removed, clothed in blanket bog, which provided at best some firing and summer grazing for cattle. It took unremitting labour by the peasantry in the eighteenth and nineteenth centuries to bring fertility to the coastlands by spreading seaweed and shell sand over them. At the beginning of the seventeenth century, however, the naturally rich agricultural land was then largely restricted to lower river valleys. And now, as a subject of James I, the Earl of Tyrconnell had to pay two hundred pounds quit rent to the Crown and give the service of 60 mounted soldiers and 120 foot each year for the lands he did actually control.[4]

The problem for the Earl of Tyrconnell was that much of this fertile land was lost to him. It included all of the Inishowen Peninsula, now under the independent possession of Sir Cahir O'Doherty, confirmed by patent in January 1605 (including the agriculturally rich island of Inch, granted in 1607); Derry and the countryside about it (and its fishings), granted to Docwra; Castlefinn and the lands of the Finn Valley, given to his rival Niall Garbh O'Donnell; Lifford, in the possession of the sheriff of the day; Ballyshannon and its abbey lands, together with the valuable salmon fishery below the falls of the Erne, leased and later granted to Sir Henry Folliott; and other forts garrisoned with Crown forces usually accompanied by surrounding farmland.

The salmon fisheries had been a major source of steady income for the lords of Tír Chonaill, and their loss was keenly felt. Then the Earl of Tyrconnell had to endure further reductions in his authority and income. The commission appointed in 1605, 'for the division and bounding of the lords' and gentlemans' livings', had ruled that the O'Boyles, MacSweeneys and other families in Tír Chonaill did not have to pay rent to the earl. And, with Chichester's backing, other fertile O'Donnell lands were now being occupied by the newly appointed bishop of the united dioceses of Derry, Raphoe and Clogher, George Montgomery. His wife, Susan, wrote to her brother in May 1605:

> My Lord Bishop will be at home before Wednesday night. The King hath bestowed on him three Irish bishoprics; the names of them I cannot remember, they are so strange, except one, which is Derry: I pray God it will make us all merry.

A year later she wrote:

> We are settled in the Derry, in a very pretty little house builded after the
> English fashion . . . I think that Mr Montgomery hath many thousands
> acres of as good land as any in England; if it were peopled, it were
> worth many hundreds of pounds by the years.[5]

Bishop Montgomery's claim that this was all church land—which it was
not—was not disputed in Dublin Castle. The outcome was that the Earl of
Tyrconnell was left with only poor mountainous land. The same Bishop
Montgomery also laid claim to swathes of the Earl of Tyrone's territory.
This led Tyrone to write in complaint to King James in May 1607:

> Whereas it pleased Your Highness of your great bounty to restore me to
> such lands as I and my ancestors had and enjoyed . . . but now, most
> gracious Sovereign, there are so many that seek to despoil me of the
> greatest part of the residue which Your Majesty was pleased I should
> hold . . . for the Lord Bishop of Derry, not contented with the great living
> Your Majesty has been pleased to bestow on him, seeketh to have a great
> part of my lands, whereunto none of his predecessors ever made claim.[6]

When the earl met Montgomery in Dungannon he declared: 'My Lord,
you have two or three bishoprics, and yet you are not content with them,
but seek the lands of my Earldom'. The bishop replied: 'My Lord, your
Earldom is swollen so big with the lands of the Church that it will burst if
it be not vented'.[7]

With the full backing of Chichester and Davies, Montgomery also
encouraged Donal Ballagh O'Cahan, the young and reputedly drink-
sodden lord of what was then known as O'Cahan's Country, to set aside
his wife, who was Tyrone's daughter, to deny the earl's traditional
overlordship in his territory and to refuse to pay him any rent. The dispute
became very public when Tyrone declared his intention of taking his case
to the highest court in the land. Davies helpfully offered to act as
O'Cahan's legal counsel. Meanwhile, Chichester strove, through spies and
informers, to obtain evidence that Tyrone was a traitor.

PLOTTING WITH SPAIN

We now know that the Earls of Tyrone and Tyrconnell were indeed
engaged in treason against the Crown. Terms of peace had been agreed
between James I and Philip III in London in August 1604. The treaty

included a stipulation that neither monarch would give any help to the rebellious subjects of the other. Neither ruler adhered strictly to that stipulation. At the end of that same year, before Chichester took up his appointment as Lord Deputy, the earls had entered into traitorous negotiations with King Philip for a substantial Spanish annuity in return for promoting his cause in Ireland. O'Donnell travelled to London and, in the dead of night, met the Spanish ambassador. The deal was only completed early in 1607, when the Spanish authorities released a first payment of four thousand ducats.[8] It is likely, but impossible to prove, that Tyrone had connections with the Gunpowder Plot—he was in the Pale when it was uncovered.

The Lord Deputy had made a viceregal progress in Ulster during the summer of 1606. The Earl of Devonshire had just died, and so any restraining influence he might have had was now gone. Chichester's principal purpose was to question the property rights of Gaelic freeholders in Monaghan, Cavan and Fermanagh—and to keep a close eye on the earls. During this time Chichester received information that Cúchonnacht Maguire and the Earl of Tyrconnell were planning to flee Ireland without leave. Cúchonnacht was placed under temporary arrest, and Tyrconnell, made aware that the Lord Deputy had been forewarned, felt he had no choice but to stay.

Chichester certainly made no attempt to make life more comfortable for Tyrconnell. He refused to punish an army captain convicted of raping an eleven-year-old girl on Tyrconnell's property while her limbs were held down by two soldiers. Tyrconnell had, as a mark of good will, sent the Lord Deputy a cast of hawks every year. Chichester now seized Tyrconnell's remaining three casts, the earl declaring to the Lord Deputy that he 'found himself more grieved at their loss in that nature than all the injuries he had before received'.[9]

Meanwhile Davies was making assiduous attempts to question Cúchonnacht's legal title to his lands in Fermanagh. The Attorney-General seemed to relish the fact that he was loathed by so many of those who had dealings with him. Actually, the most contemptuous description of him was that of a fellow-Englishman, who remarked on how the corpulent Davies 'goes waddling with his arse out behind him as though he were about to make everyone that he meets a wall to piss against . . . He never walks but carries a cloakbag behind him, his arse sticks out so far'.[10]

Cúchonnacht Maguire could take no more humiliation. He succeeded in getting out of Ireland unnoticed by the Crown authorities, and by June 1607 he was in Spanish Flanders.

A DOUBLE AGENT

About thirty years before, Gráinne O'Malley, the legendary Granuaile, 'Pirate Queen of Connacht', had put in at Howth after a long voyage, to obtain water and provisions. Furious that Lord Howth kept his castle closed and refused her hospitality, Gráinne had seized his little grandson on the beach and taken him back to Mayo. When Lord Howth travelled west to find his grandson, Gráinne refused a ransom but handed over the boy on the promise that the gates of Howth Castle would never be closed and that an extra place would always be set at his table for anyone seeking hospitality.

The little boy, Christopher St Lawrence, grew up to be a dashing—if somewhat unhinged—soldier who served the Crown bravely in the Lord Deputy's armies. Renowned for his heroic feats, he had been involved in many skirmishes and several major engagements, had served as a garrison commander and had commanded the largest regiment in the Crown forces at the Battle of Kinsale.[11] He had, however, been involved in the Earl of Essex's conspiracy in 1601 and had been fortunate, unlike the earl, not to lose his head. St Lawrence was—like so many New English servitors— deeply disappointed that he received no better reward for his services than to be appointed governor of Monaghan Fort.[12] This Old English lord of the Pale seems to have spent the rest of his career as a double agent, acting for both the King of Spain and the Lord Deputy. He had spent several months in Spanish Flanders and was on good terms with Henry O'Neill, the Earl of Tyrone's son, who had become a colonel in the Spanish army. An English spy reported that the two were 'very familiar and inward friends and were oftentimes bedfellows'.[13]

St Lawrence was back in Flanders early in 1607, where he had talks with Father Florence Conry, who had come from Madrid with a grant of three hundred crowns from Philip III. In July, St Lawrence was in London, where he sought an urgent meeting with James I's Secretary of State, Sir Robert Cecil, now Earl of Salisbury. There he told the King's minister that there was a conspiracy in Ireland, 'a general revolt intended by many of the nobility and principal persons of this land . . . and that they will shake off the yoke of the English government, as they term it, and adhere to the Spaniard'.

St Lawrence then travelled to Dublin to repeat his accusations to Chichester, naming the Earl of Tyrconnell and Richard Nugent, Baron of Delvin, as leaders. He added that, while he lacked direct evidence, he was certain that the Earl of Tyrone 'is as deep in the treason as any'. The Lord

Deputy's problem was that St Lawrence flatly refused, even at the peril of his life, to give testimony in court. Salisbury and Chichester decided to keep these revelations to themselves for the time being.[14]

Until now, King James had been extremely cordial in his correspondence with the Earl of Tyrone. Rather suddenly, in the summer of 1607, his tone changed—clearly, he was reacting to St Lawrence's report, passed on to him by his Secretary of State. Tyrone and O'Cahan received peremptory orders to appear in London by September to have their dispute resolved in court.

Normally a man not easily rattled, Tyrone was now in a state of acute anxiety. Chichester wrote later that 'it is observed here by some that knew him best, that since he received His Majesty's letter for his repair thither, he did lose his former cheerfulness and grew often exceeding pensive'. The prospects of the case against O'Cahan going his way were rapidly ebbing away. Bishop Montgomery had stepped in to tell O'Cahan to set aside Tyrone's daughter and 'by order of law' to take back his first wife. At a preliminary hearing in May 1607 in Dublin, Tyrone lost his composure, 'snatching a paper out of O'Cahan's hand, and rending it' in front of Chichester.[15] He was beginning to fear that, once in London, his life would be in peril. Later, Tyrone and Tyrconnell wrote that 'the King of England summoned us to London with the intention of either beheading us, or putting us in the Tower of London for life'.[16] Certainly the Spanish ambassador thought so, observing soon after the Flight: 'I know that they wish to kill him by poison or by any possible means . . . their fear of him gnaws at their entrails'.[17]

Had King James been informed of his treasonable dealings with the Spanish court? It seems that the incorrigible St Lawrence—who had succeeded his father in May 1607 to become Lord Howth—had called to warn Tyrone that James had been told of his conspiratorial communications with Spain.

Still, the Earl of Tyrone had no immediate plans to flee from Ireland . . . not, that is, until he was given a message that a certain ship had sailed into Lough Swilly.

LOUGH SWILLY

Cúchonnacht Maguire masterminded the Flight of the Earls. Described by the Annals of the Four Masters as a 'rapid-marching adventurous man, endowed with wisdom and beauty of person', he was such a master of disguise that it was said his nearest friends would have found it hard to identify him.[18] Provided with silver and gold by the Spanish King, Maguire took great care to obtain a ship which would not immediately arouse suspicion. He leased an eighty-ton vessel in France, armed with sixteen cannon and manned by sixty heavily disguised soldiers. Maguire set sail in great secret from Nantes and made for Ulster. Near to its destination the ship was arrested by a Scottish warship and held for two days. Fortunately Maguire had put nets and salt aboard, and he convinced his captors that he had come to Ulster only to fish.

On 4 September 1607 the vessel sailed into Lough Swilly and anchored off Rathmullan. At nightfall a man came ashore with Spanish ducats and set out to bring the news to the Earl of Tyrconnell of the ship's arrival. Two days later a messenger reached the Earl of Tyrone, who was staying with Sir Garret Moore, foster-father to his son John, at Mellifont. Chichester, who had just had a meeting with Tyrone nearby at Slane, observed afterwards:

> The manner of his departure, carrying his little son with him who was brought up in Sir Garret's house, made me suspect he had mischief in his head; harm I knew he could do none, if they were upon their keeping, for he was altogether without arms and munition; and his flight beyond the seas I should never have suspected.[19]

Sir Garret himself reported that Tyrone 'wept abundantly when he took his leave, giving solemn farewell to every child and every servant in the house, which made them all marvel, because it was not his manner to use such compliments'.[20]

The earl made his way from Mellifont to Dundalk, and from there to Armagh and Dungannon. He stopped only when he reached 'the Craobh', a house on a lough in the wilds of Tyrone. The problem now facing the northern lords was finding all their children, fostered in the Gaelic tradition, over a wide area. For two days O'Neill stayed in Tyrone, frantically searching for his six-year-old son, Conn. But Conn could not be found, for he was with his foster-family rounding up cattle from their summer grazing in the hills. Then, at midnight, the earl and most of his family and servants set off across the Sperrin Mountains. According to Sir John Davies,

> he travelled all night with his impediments, that is, his women and children; and it is likewise reported that the Countess, his wife, being

exceedingly weary, slipped down from her horse, and weeping, said she could go no farther; whereupon the Earl drew his sword, and swore a great oath that he would kill her in the place, if she would not pass on with him, and put on a more cheerful countenance withal.[21]

A year before, Countess Catherine (Caitríona), sister of Art Roe Magennis, Lord Iveagh, and Tyrone's fifth wife, had told the veteran servitor Sir Toby Caulfield that she had been the victim of the earl's brutality and drunkenness, and that if she had two hundred cows she would leave him.

On their way through Derry the unsuspecting governor, Sir George Paulet, invited the party to dinner, which the earl refused as graciously as he could. When they got to Rathmullan a child with six toes on one foot, which was considered very lucky, was sent for, and they 'took the infant violently . . . which terrified the foster-father'.[22] By the shores of Lough Swilly all the indications were that the Flight had been prepared in extreme haste. The Earl of Tyrconnell was without his pregnant, seventeen-year-old countess. He had not dared to risk arrest by going to Maynooth where she— Brigid FitzGerald, the daughter of the 12th Earl of Kildare and grand-daughter of Charles Howard, Earl of Nottingham and Lord High Admiral of England—was staying with her grandmother. Though the ship had been at anchor in the lough for eleven days, it was not until the final day that Maguire felt he could risk arousing suspicion by taking provisions on board.

The two earls and their families crowded aboard the vessel. Though there were fewer than forty of them, they represented the cream of Ulster's Gaelic aristocracy. Altogether, including the soldiers and sailors that Cúchonnacht Maguire had brought with him, the ship's complement was ninety-nine. Far from being bidden *bon voyage* by the people of Donegal, there were angry MacSweeneys waving weapons on the shore, bitter that the earls had seized some of their cattle as food for the journey. The earls themselves reported to King Philip that, at noon on Friday 14 September, 'leaving their horses on the shore with no one to hold their bridles, they went aboard a ship to the number of about one hundred persons, including soldiers, women and principal gentlemen'.

For the Four Masters the Flight was an unparalleled disaster:

Woe to the heart that meditated, woe to the mind that conceived, woe to the council that decided on, the project of their setting out on this voyage, without knowing whether they should ever return to their native principalities or patrimonies to the end of the world . . . It is indeed certain that the sea had not supported, and the winds had not wafted from Ireland, in modern times, a party of one ship who would have been more illustrious or noble, in point of genealogy, or more renowned for deeds, valour, prowess, or high achievements than they.[23]

THE JOURNEY

Tadhg Ó Cianáin, who sailed with the earls, tells us in his chronicle that they planned to make directly for Spain. It was bad weather rather than ships of the Royal Navy which prevented them from reaching their destination, he informs us:

> They were on the sea for thirteen days with excessive storm and dangerous bad weather. A cross of gold which O'Neill had, and which contained a portion of the Cross of the Crucifixion and many other relics, being put by them into the sea trailing after the ship, gave them great relief. At the end of that time, much to their surprise, they met in the middle of the sea two small hawks, merlins, which alighted on the ship. The hawks were caught and were fed afterwards.[24]

Fierce contrary winds forced them to change course for France. They made landfall at Quilleboeuf at the mouth of the River Seine. Since they had neither passports from the King of France nor licences from their own monarch, the governor of the town viewed these Irish refugees with deep suspicion. The earls attempted to ingratiate themselves by presenting the pair of merlin to the governor.

As the Irish made their way to Rouen almost as prisoners, Sir George Carew, the former Lord President of Munster and now the English ambassador in Paris, demanded an audience with Henry iv to seek the extradition of the earls. King Henry—Henry of Navarre—the Protestant victor in the long and wasting civil war in France, had not long before become a Catholic—'Paris is worth a Mass', he had said. He had to take care now that his Catholic subjects did not regard his recently acquired faith as skin deep. So he went away to hunt until he was certain that the Irish exiles had arrived safely in Spanish Flanders.

The earls soon found that they were famous throughout Catholic Europe. They were champions of the faith against the heretics. Their long war against Queen Elizabeth had seemed like the struggle of David against Goliath. Henry iv described the Earl of Tyrone as being the third-greatest general in Europe (Henry being the top general, of course).

When the earls arrived in Spanish Flanders the governor, Archduke Albert of Austria, and his wife, Infanta Isabel, gave them luxurious apartments in their palace. Two days later they were given a military escort to Brussels, where the Marqués Ambrosio de Spínola, commander-in-chief of the Spanish army in Flanders, invited them to a splendid banquet. Tadhg Ó Cianáin was there:

> When greetings had been exchanged in abundance, they entered the hall of the Marquis . . . He himself arranged each one in his place, seating O'Neill in his own place at the head of the table, the Papal Nuncio to his right, the Earl of Tyrconnell to his left, O'Neill's children and Maguire next to the Earl and the Spanish ambassador and the Duke of Aumale on the other side . . . The rest of the illustrious, respected nobles at table, the Marquis himself, and the Duke of Osuna were at the end of the table opposite O'Neill. The excellent dinner which they partook of was grand and costly enough for a king, and nothing inferior was the banquet. Gold and silver plate was displayed inside that no king or prince in Christendom might be ashamed of.[25]

Back in Ireland, the Attorney-General was convinced that 'O'Neill and his train of barbarous men, women and children . . . will be taken for a company of gypsies and be exceedingly scorned . . . The formal Spanish courtier will hardly believe he is the same O'Neill which maintained so long a war against the Crown of England'.[26] Davies was quite wrong. The exiled Irish made a very favourable impression and were treated with great respect. The Governor of Tournai had cannons fired in salute as they entered his town. But what was to be done with the Irish lords and their families?

EXILE TO ROME

The Spanish government had just signed peace terms with the Dutch, who for long had been close allies of England. King Philip rapidly concluded that the continued presence of the earls in Spanish Flanders could imperil that peace. Teetering on the brink of bankruptcy, Spain could not risk another war with England. The exiled Irish nobles had become an embarrassment. Far from acceding to their request to be allowed to return to Ireland with a Spanish army to root out the heretics, Philip could not even risk giving them permission to come to Spain. And so it was decided to transfer the earls and their families to Italy under the protection of the Pope. The King's ambassador in Brussels, the Marqués de Guadaleste, was appalled when he heard of the decision. On 4 December 1607 he wrote to Philip:

> I do not know how the Earls will take this and I confess to Your Majesty that it seems to me His Highness has taken a harsh decision on this matter with regard to people who have given such service to God and to Your Majesty.[27]

So it was that the Flight of the Earls from Ulster had been for nothing. It was in vain that O'Neill and O'Donnell sent an appeal to King Philip on 17 December 1607:

> Señor
>
> Having arrived in these States, in safe haven as we thought, for our sins and God permitting, another misfortune has befallen us. His Serene Highness orders that we leave his States so that he may keep a promise he made to the King of England . . . This has caused us much sorrow and astonishment . . . As God is our witness, we would rather have chosen to die in our country than to see ourselves treated in this manner by a Prince in whom we placed our greatest trust . . . Our concern is the pleasure and satisfaction it will give the heretics to see us thus treated.[28]

Arrangements were made for the youngest children to stay in Flanders with nurses, tutors and servants. They included Tyrconnell's infant son Hugh, and O'Neill's sons John and Brian, both under ten years old. Then, on 28 February 1608, the earls and their party, thirty-two of them on horseback and the women following in a coach, set out from Louvain for Italy. As they passed through Lorraine the ruling Duke Charles gave them a hospitable reception at Nancy—so warm, indeed, that James I refused to send a representative to his funeral when he died shortly afterwards.

The Irish then pressed on through Colmar, Basel and Lucerne. Then, as they set out to cross the mountains, they lost most of their money, as Ó Cianáin tells us:

> The next day, Saint Patrick's Day precisely, the seventeenth of March, they went to another small town named Silenen. From that they advanced through the Alps. Now the mountains were laden and filled with snow and ice, and the roads and paths were narrow and rugged.

They reached a high bridge in a very deep glen called the Devil's Bridge. One of O'Neill's horses, which was carrying some of his money, about one hundred and twenty pounds, fell down the face of the high, frozen, snowy cliff which was in front of the bridge. Great labour was experienced in bringing up the horse alone, but the money decided to remain blocking the violent, deep, destructive torrent which flows under the bridge through the middle of the glen.[29]

After spending a full day in a futile attempt to retrieve the money, on they went through Andermatt, the St Gotthard Pass, Bellinzona and Lugano. They reached the shores of Lake Como on 22 March and then descended to the city of Milan. There the earls were received very cordially by the governor, Pedro Enríquez de Acevedo, Conde de Fuentes. He sent this report to King Philip on 13 April 1608:

The Earls of Tiron and Tirconel arrived here before Holy Week and, in accordance with Your Majesty's orders, I feasted them and treated them with care in as discreet and secret a manner as possible, in order both to assure them of the generosity and compassion of Your Majesty . . . I felt the greatest pity for them; one of them brings a sister of marriageable age, and another a wife and son; they bring also many persons who would not be parted from them. They arrived in great distress from the hardship of the journey and in such need that it was necessary to pay their hostelries and to give them money for the journey.[30]

But Milan was then a Spanish possession, and the Irish could not be allowed to stay. In Spain the English ambassador, Sir Charles Cornwallis, protested at their presence in the city: 'Having lately gathered amongst the Irish here that the fugitive Earls have been in Milan, and there much feasted by the Conde de Fuentes, I expostulated it with the secretary of state, who answered that they had not yet had any understanding of their being there.'[31]

Philip's minister was not telling Cornwallis the truth, but Fuentes had no choice but to send the earls on their way. Just before their arrival in Rome, on 29 April, the Spanish ambassador in Rome, the Marqués de Aytona, had an interview with Pope Pius v, as he informed Philip III:

I have represented to His Holiness, on behalf and in the name of Your Majesty, how fitting and proper it would be that His Holiness protect and help those who, for the Catholic Faith and in defence of our holy religion, have lost their possessions and country and everything they owned. I also told His Holiness that the Earls' presence here may act as a deterrent against the persecution of the Catholics in England. His Holiness replied that he would honour and favour them as much as he could. I think he will give them nothing, or very little, because the apostolic treasury is very low, and His Holiness is not very liberal.[32]

And so it proved. On 22 May the ambassador reported that 'the Pope gave them a house but nothing else', and, while he was exasperated by the earls' haughty demands, he did make this appeal to his monarch six months later:

I beg Your Majesty to give them extra financial aid. Their grant is barely sufficient for their food and in other respects they suffer great want. They are so poor that one must have compassion for them. The Pope gives them a house but not one stick of furniture and they have neither beds nor chairs. The unfortunates have not enough money to buy such bare necessities and, as there are many Irish with the Earl, a large sum would be necessary to buy even what would be needed so that they might not be forced to sleep on the floors.[33]

The ambassador's appeal was in vain. Meanwhile, the Flight of the Earls was precipitating momentous changes in Ireland, particularly in Ulster.

CONSIGNED TO THE TOWER OF LONDON

'The undutiful departure of the Earls of Tirone, Tirconnell, and McGwyre offers good occasion for a plantation,' an Irish Crown official observed to Lord Salisbury. Chichester quickly grasped the opportunity presented, though he knew of no plan to seize or poison O'Neill and thought 'it were strange that he should quit an Earldom, and so large and beneficial a territory for smoke and castles in the air'.[34] The Lord Deputy wrote to King James just after the Flight:

If His Majesty will, during their absence, assume the countries into his possession, divide the lands amongst the inhabitants . . . and will bestow the rest upon servitors and men of worth here, and withal bring in colonies of civil people of England and Scotland . . . the country will ever after be happily settled.

There was no time like the present, for 'the whole realm, and especially the fugitive countries, are more utterly depopulated and poor than ever before for many hundred years'.[35] Chichester was gratified that Tyrone had chosen to flee with so many members of his family. In his view the Flight was 'far better for the King and Commonwealth than if he were in the Tower of London, for by this course he had carried his children and kinsmen with him who were in remainder in the estate of his country, and I think unacquainted with his treasons before their departure'.[36]

Chichester's initial view that Ireland was well rid of the earls was not well received across the Irish Sea. Indeed it led to a suspicion that he had done much to force them to leave and that he had actually helped to smooth their way to Lough Swilly—a suspicion which has never been entirely removed. Near-panic prevailed at court in London. Would this end the peace with Spain? Would the earls return to Ireland with an imposing Spanish force? How much credence should be given to the revelations of Lord Howth? Were the Old English about to launch an uprising in collaboration with the disaffected Gaelic Irish?

The government had only 880 foot soldiers in all of Ireland. Its immediate response to the Flight was to get more troops to the island. Such was the financial predicament of the Treasury that those sent over were of very poor quality. Commissioners for Northumberland were instructed to 'select 100 men from any of the outlaws of Riddesdale and Tynedale, except the ring-leaders, taking from prison those accused of lighter crimes and to enlist them for the King's service in Ireland'. Two hundred men arriving from Workington 'were without arms and clothes, and an object of derision to the Irish'. Thirty men had to be sent back as unfit to serve, and Chichester wrote that others were 'old persons or otherwise disabled and insufficient, and who, for mere debility of body, will soon be consumed here without any other adversary'.[37]

Even Crown officers, including Thomas Jones (Archbishop of Dublin and Lord Chancellor) and Sir Garret Moore, were falling under suspicion. The principal informant, Lord Howth, was committed to custody, first in Ireland and then in England, where it was reported that 'he carried himself in his accustomed half-wild fashion'.[38] The young Baron of Delvin was also imprisoned and made a rather vague confession of treason. Delvin then escaped from Dublin Castle, climbing down a rope 35-yards long, and remained at liberty for the ensuing six months—the 'most unpleasing tidings' he ever had to tell since taking office, Chichester observed.[39]

And what about the Gaelic lords that Tyrone and Tyrconnell had left behind in Ulster? Perhaps to head off a general rising in the north, the Dublin government issued a proclamation immediately after the Flight to 'assure the inhabitants of Tyrone and Tyrconnell that they will not be disturbed in the peaceable possession of their lands'.[40] In reality all the Gaelic Irish of any standing in Ulster were now suspect. These included those who had changed sides to assist the Crown forces towards the end of the Nine Years' War and who had gone out of their way to become loyal and obedient subjects.

Relatives of the Earl of Tyrone were now in peril. Brian MacArt O'Neill, Tyrone's nephew, had been arrested before the Flight on a charge of murder. The immediate fear was that 'it is credibly thought he will attempt to restore the name of O'Neill again'. Because Brian was so popular, Chichester concluded that no jury in Armagh would convict him. He was therefore taken clandestinely—'for fear of rescue'—to be tried at the King's Bench in Dublin. There he was duly convicted and executed, to the delight of Davies, who wrote that 'the hand of justice has cut him off, which is a notable example to all the kingdom'.[41] Tyrone's young son Conn was an obvious victim. Taken into custody by Sir Toby Caulfield at Charlemont, he was transferred to England to be enrolled as a pupil at Eton. Then the government thought better of it, and, for fear that he would become a future rebel leader, he was incarcerated in the Tower, where he was to languish for the rest of his life. Conn was joined by Tyrone's brother Sir Cormac, and, despite Sir Oliver St John's opinion that he had 'little in him to make him dangerous', he too was to spend the rest of his days in the Tower.[42]

Sir Donal O'Cahan was now surplus to requirements. Bishop George Montgomery and Sir John Davies had both championed his case, which had been due to go to London, to be free of rent and other obligations to the Earl of Tyrone. Sir Donal was too confident. He quarrelled with Montgomery, who was 'demanding great quantities of lands within his country', and when he refused to take any part in the indictment of the earl he was summoned to Dublin to explain himself. When O'Cahan foolishly volunteered to be 'restrained' in gaol, Chichester could not resist the opportunity to do just that. Dismissing the man he had so recently knighted as 'a barbarous unworthy man', the Lord Deputy had Sir Donal cast into the Tower with his son, there to be joined by the man who had fought so valiantly under the command of Sir Henry Docwra, Niall Garbh O'Donnell.[43] These men had served their purpose, and they were never to be released.

Perhaps no Gaelic nobleman in Ulster was more deserving of the gratitude of the Crown than Sir Cahir O'Doherty, Lord of Inishowen. As a fifteen-year-old, O'Doherty had joined the Crown forces at Derry in 1600 and had received fulsome praise from Docwra, who wrote that he had been 'with me, alighted when I did, kept me company in the greatest heat of the fight, behaved himself bravely, and with a great deal of love and affection: so much so, that I recommended him at my next meeting with Lord Deputy Mountjoy, for the honour of a knighthood, which was accordingly conferred on him'.[44] He took particular care to abide by English law and to co-operate fully with the Lord Deputy and his officials. Even he, however, came under suspicion after the Flight.

Now O'Doherty fell out with Sir George Paulet, who in 1607 had replaced Docwra as Governor of Derry. Possessing none of his predecessor's diplomatic finesse, Paulet was contemptuous of the native Irish. Chichester thought him an 'ill exchange' for Docwra, observing that 'many dissensions have arisen since he came thither'.[45] When O'Doherty was on a wood-cutting expedition at Canmoyre Wood, near Kilmacrenan, Paulet jumped to the conclusion that he was raising a revolt and attempted to take the Inishowen lord's new castle at Burt. The fact that Lady O'Doherty was at home seemed to indicate that her husband was not up to no good.

O'Doherty travelled to Dublin, confident that he could clear his name. The problem was that he arrived there only days after Baron Delvin's dramatic escape. Chichester now felt inclined to 'mistrust many in whose care and honesty I could before that time have reposed my life and safety'—and that included the Lord of Inishowen, though the Lord Deputy found it difficult to 'give firm credit' to Paulet's allegations. O'Doherty was taken into custody and asked for a 'recognisance' of a thousand pounds, with two sureties of five hundred marks each. This was an outrageously large sum when it is remembered that the Irish government's entire budget for 1608—a year of exceptionally high expenditure—was no more than £100,000.[46]

Nevertheless, O'Doherty continued to co-operate and was foreman of the grand jury at Lifford, which found a true bill of treason against the Earl of Tyrconnell in January 1608. He lobbied to become a member of the household of the Prince of Wales, sending his representative with a pair of hawks and a letter of recommendation from Bishop George Montgomery. There was not much more Sir Cahir was prepared to endure, however.

THE REBELLION OF SIR CAHIR O'DOHERTY

On business in Derry, Sir Cahir became involved in a stormy exchange with the governor, Sir George Paulet. After insulting and abusing the Lord of Inishowen, the governor punched him in the face. According to the Four Masters, O'Doherty

> would rather have suffered death than live to brook such insult and dishonour, or defer or delay to take revenge for it; and he was filled with anger and fury, so that he nearly ran to distraction and madness. What he did was to consult with his friends how he should take revenge for the insult which was inflicted upon him.[47]

It is likely that Sir Cahir was encouraged to rebel by Niall Garbh O'Donnell. Affecting to be his friend, O'Donnell hoped that by co-operating with the Crown he could be granted Inishowen—indeed, he had been promised the peninsula at the time of the Canmoyre Wood incident if he brought Sir Cahir in. There is little doubt, too, that Sir Cahir's foster-father, Phelim Reagh MacDavitt, was eager for rebellion, and without Niall Garbh's duplicitous intent; O'Doherty had been asked to bring Phelim in to answer charges. According to Henry Dillon, a senior law officer, MacDavitt had been constantly harassed by Crown itinerant judges 'so that by this proceeding the fellow was impoverished and made desperate, and for revenge drew Sir Cahir to this rebellion'.[48] In short, this insurrection was brought about not by any grand plan to change Ulster's political future but by an accumulation of petty grievances largely the result of insensitive behaviour by Crown officers, usually at the local level.

On 18 April 1608 Sir Cahir invited his neighbour, Captain Henry Hart, governor of Culmore Fort, and his wife to dinner at Buncrana. There he seized them, threatening 'that if she or he did not take some present course for the delivery of Culmore into his hands, both they and their children should die'. To save her husband's life Captain Hart's wife agreed to a ruse to lure the warders into an ambush, and Culmore fell into O'Doherty's hands. The seizure of this fort's arsenal was vital, as O'Doherty and his men had few arms. Then, at two in the morning, O'Doherty made a surprise assault on Derry with about seventy men. As the watchmen were asleep, Sir Cahir was able to take the lower fort without a fight, but Phelim Reagh MacDavitt encountered resistance in the higher fort. MacDavitt shot Paulet dead. John Baker, a surviving defender, reported afterwards:

Lieutenant Gordon, lying within his chamber within the higher fort, and hearing the shot, issued forth naked upon the rampier toward the court of guard, with his rapier and dagger, where, with one soldier in his company, he set upon the enemy and killed two of them, using most comfortable words of courage to the soldiers to stand to it and fight for their lives; but the enemy being far more in number, one struck him on the forehead with a stone, whereat, being somewhat amazed, they rushed upon him and killed him and the soldiers also.

As dawn broke, the surviving townspeople barricaded themselves in the Bishop's House and adjacent dwellings but, Baker records,

> destitute of victuals and munition, and seeing a piece brought by the enemy from Culmore, and ready mounted to batter the said houses, and being out of all hope of relief at that time and wearied with lamentable outcry of women and children, after much parley and messages to and fro, yielded the said houses.[49]

The bishop's wife, Susan Montgomery, and her sister were amongst those taken prisoner. An offer of a hundred pounds to save Bishop Montgomery's library of two thousand volumes was turned down—no doubt because it was regarded as a heretical repository—and the books were destroyed as Derry was set aflame. All eighty-five houses in the 'infant city' were burned to the ground. Strabane was torched soon after by some Scots who had settled there before they took refuge across the river in Lifford. Doe Castle fell by a ruse: warders were enticed out by being told that wolves were attacking their cattle. Soon O'Doherty had about five hundred men in arms. Rumours spread that the Earls of Tyrone and Tyrconnell would return with a Spanish force in the autumn. Perhaps this is why O'Doherty declared that 'all he has done is in zeal for the Catholic cause'.[50]

The O'Gallaghers of Glenveagh, fosterers to the Earl of Tyrconnell, and some O'Cahans joined O'Doherty in arms. More alarming to the government, Eochaidh Óg O'Hanlon, O'Doherty's brother-in-law and the Earl of Tyrone's nephew, brought his people in south Armagh out in rebellion, putting Newry in immediate danger. Criticism of Chichester mounted on both sides of the Irish Sea. Had he been responsible for driving O'Doherty into rebellion?—a man, the Lord Deputy himself had admitted, that 'all men believed . . . had been wronged'.[51] Why had Derry fallen when its garrison actually outnumbered its attackers? To recover his reputation Chichester had to act quickly. Unlike so many of his viceregal predecessors, he did not wait for the arrival of reinforcements from England, though over the whole of Ireland he had the disposal of no more than 1,700 men. Chichester ordered a general hosting of the Pale on 24 May and sent north Sir Richard Wingfield, the King's Marshal, with some 800 men (described by Sir Josias Bodley as a 'small diminutive of an army') who had instructions to engage in a 'thick and short' military campaign. Other troops already in Ulster were diverted from an expedition planned against a rebellion in the Scottish Isles to join him. The Lord Deputy himself led a force towards Armagh.

From Coleraine, Sir Thomas Phillips wrote a frantic appeal for help, concluding with the words 'haist, haist, haist'. The need for haste was underlined by mounting fears that the return of the Earls of Tyrone and Tyrconnell was imminent. As Chichester observed: 'It may be taken as certain that every mother's son of them will go into rebellion if any foreign assistance . . . or but some of the principal fugitives shall arrive'.[52] Outflanked by experienced veterans, O'Doherty and his allies were quickly outmanoeuvred and crushed. Sir Cahir advanced southwards to seek further support. In case the Earl of Tyrone should return soon, Dungannon was left untouched, but allies of the Crown were not spared. Sir Henry Óg O'Neill of Kinard (now Caledon) was killed and his township burned. Soon, however, Wingfield was recovering the burnt shell of Derry and taking O'Doherty's town of Buncrana; his men, he reported, 'could not abstain from burning it as well as from anger as for example's sake'.[53] O'Doherty returned but not in time to save Burt. Here Lady O'Doherty and her infant son had taken refuge. Also lodged there were some prisoners from Derry, including Bishop Montgomery's wife, Susan. Not willing to offer terms to the defenders, the English commander ordered the firing of a cannon at the walls. The rebels responded by threatening to put Susan Montgomery into the first breach made in the walls. The response was that the 'King's honour was a fairer mark and to be handled more tenderly . . . than any woman in the world'. More cannon fire ensued until the defenders surrendered.[54]

On his return, O'Doherty made a last stand on 5 July with about a thousand men by the Rock of Doon, close to Kilmacrenan. According to a contemporary English account, this was hard-fought: 'Bravely was the onset given, and as bravely answered: you would have thought that thunder had been only upon earth, the guns did speak so loud, and with such dreadful voices'. Actually the engagement may have lasted no more than half an hour. Then, at the height of the battle, Sir Cahir was hit 'by a happy shot which smote him on the head'. As his men scattered, soldiers rushed forward to sever O'Doherty's head, and eventually John Trendor, a rank-and-file soldier, was awarded the five hundred pounds which the government had placed on his traitor's head.

Meanwhile Chichester put down the O'Hanlons, hanging many he captured, and moved from Mountnorris to Dungannon, executing dozens more by hanging, 'a death which they contemn more, he thinks, than any other nation living; they are generally so stupid by nature, or so tough or disposed by their priests, that they show no remorse of conscience, or fear of death'. The last O'Cahan rebels were pursued into the woods of Glenconkeyne, where, Chichester reported, 'the wild inhabitants wondered as much to see the King's Deputy, as the ghosts in Virgil wondered to see Aeneas alive in Hell'.[55]

Notwithstanding Sir Cahir's death, the revolt spluttered on. Sir Oliver Lambert besieged Doe Castle, 'the strongest hold in all the province which endured 100 blows of the demi-cannon before it yielded'.[56] Shane MacManus Óg O'Donnell retreated to the islands, pursued by Sir Henry Folliott, Governor of Ballyshannon, with a hundred men and five vessels. Folliott took the castle on Tory Island by treachery, cutting down the warders after promising them their lives. The rebellion concluded when Marshal Wingfield crossed the mountains to Glenveagh, where the O'Gallaghers made a last but futile stand in their island castle. Eochaidh (Oghy) Óg O'Hanlon managed to keep the rebellion alive in Armagh as late as September 1609.

The English were getting to know the province they had conquered from end to end, parts of which Chichester admitted had been only recently as inaccessible as 'the kingdom of China'. The highlands from Errigal to Muckish and Glenveagh repelled the Lord Deputy, being 'one of the most barren, uncouth, and desolate countries that could be seen, fit only to confine rebels and ill spirits into'.[57] This distaste, however, did not prevent Chichester from seeking and obtaining a grant of O'Doherty's lordship of Inishowen for himself almost immediately afterwards.

The Lord Deputy was at pains to strike fear into any Irish who contemplated remaining in arms in the hope of the earls returning with Spanish aid. O'Doherty's body was further dismembered and put on display in Derry as 'signs', and his head was taken to Dublin to be skewered on a pike at Newgate. Surviving rebels were rounded up and, rather than be hanged summarily as they could be by martial law, were sent on to be tried for treason. When duly convicted they could then be hanged, drawn and quartered in the usual grisly way. One of the first to endure this fate was Shane Carragh O'Cahan, brother of Sir Donal. Phelim Reagh MacDavitt, cornered in a wood, was taken with his men to Lifford, where they were all tried, condemned, dragged through the streets tied to horses, hanged, disembowelled, decapitated and cut into quarters.[58]

The government had already returned to the task of planning the colonisation of the escheated counties, the confiscated lands of the Earls of Tyrone and O'Connell. O'Doherty's rebellion, swiftly suppressed though it was, had transformed the situation. The scheme being perfected in London would soon be far more grandiose than that originally envisaged.

DEATH IN ROME

During the summer of 1608 the Irish in Rome got news of O'Doherty's revolt. The earls there quickly realised that the opportunity offered by the rebellion would be lost unless the Spanish sent immediate military aid. On 9 July they wrote to King Philip:

> Señor,
> By order of Your Majesty we wrote from Flanders saying what our requests were, how anxious the Irish Catholics were to show their zeal in defence of the Holy Catholic Faith and how they hoped that Your Majesty would deliver them from the intolerable persecution and tyranny they are suffering . . . Although up to the present we have waited patiently, believing that Your Majesty's delay was due to the great care and consideration being given to the matter, we can no longer disguise our feelings.
> We have been informed that in Ulster four thousand of our people have revolted and are causing great losses to the English. The rising is spreading to the other provinces for, knowing that we are here, all firmly believe that Your Majesty will not fail to send help with us to Ireland . . .
> The only wish of the Catholics of Ireland is to be free of their troubles and to become subjects of Your Majesty . . . If you were to send them some help now, and indeed the Irish wish to open all the ports to Spanish help, within a few days Ireland would belong to Your Majesty and the English and the Dutch would be held in check.[59]

Philip III did indeed toy briefly with the idea of joining forces with Pius V to send an expedition to Ireland, but by September he had dropped the idea. Realising this, Tyrone rather desperately made an approach to James I seeking some sort of reconciliation and a return to his lands. King James, however, was already making preparations for the Plantation of Ulster.

In January 1609 King James issued orders for the plantation, printed under the title 'A Collection of Such Orders and Conditions as Are to Be Observed by the Undertakers upon the Distribution and Plantation of the Escheated Lands in Ulster'. In Rome a copy came into the hands of Father Florence Conry, recently appointed Archbishop of Tuam, and he wrote in May to the Spanish Council of State:

> A small English pamphlet has come into my hands. It was printed in London a few months ago and contains the articles by which the King of England declares, without stating the reasons, to have confiscated the lands of the Earls of Tiron and Tirconnell to the extent of six counties. The English King offers these lands in perpetuity for themselves and their descendants to any English or Scots who may wish to take possession of them provided that they comply with the following conditions:
>
> They must first swear that the King is head of the Church; they may not sublease these lands to any Irish of the ancient race of Ireland; each county must have schools for the instruction of youth in the Calvinistic religion; instead all parish churches must have heretical ministers who will consume the income of the heretical church.[60]

Somewhat bitterly he remarked that the Earl of Tyrone

> believes that this would not have happened if the English had not seen that the King of Spain is not so inclined to help him now as was at first expected . . . With the help of God and the assistance of His Catholic Majesty, who will not consent to such an extraordinary and renewed extirpation and oppression of Catholics and of the Holy Faith, I hope that those iniquitous articles of the King of England will resolve themselves into air.[61]

The 'iniquitous articles' did not resolve themselves into air.

'This rumour of Tyrone's return has somewhat cooled men's affections to the Ulster plantation', Chichester observed in a letter to the Earl of

Salisbury in April 1609. In the same month the Solicitor-General, Sir Robert Jacob, reported on the condition of Ulster:

> There are great probabilities that all the people of that province would easily run into rebellion if Tyrone should return, or if any munition or aid should be sent to them from foreign parts; for they are generally diseased with the rumour of the new plantation that is intended . . . They want no men, notwithstanding the late wars, the famine and the great plague that was amongst them.[62]

With furious zeal Chichester rounded up as many native 'idle swordsmen' and 'woodkerne' in Ulster, shipping out thousands of them to serve in the armies of Gustavus Adolphus of Sweden, then campaigning in Poland. He need not have worried: there was no possibility that the King of Spain would fund an expeditionary force to Ireland. Besides, the unhealthy air of Continental Europe was reaping a fearful harvest in the Irish exile community, ridding the English Crown of detested adversaries.

In July 1608 the Earl of Tyrconnell, his son Cathbarr, Tyrone's son Hugh, Baron of Dungannon, and some others decided that they needed some relief from the summer heat of Rome. They stayed for two nights at Ostia, fifteen miles away on the coast—a bad idea, as Tadhg Ó Cianáin explained, 'for all are agreed that that particular place is one of the worst and most unhealthy for climate in all Italy'. He continued:

> Indeed, it was not long until it proved so to them, for the Earl took a hot, fiery, violent fever on the eighteenth of July in 1608 . . . On Saturday, the following day, Cathbarr, the son of O'Donnell, caught the same fever. On the Monday afterwards, the Baron was stricken with it, and Donal O'Carroll in a short time after him. The page and the footman who were with them both got the fever in a very short time.[63]

After eleven days in fever, Rory O'Donnell, Earl of Tyrconnell and brother of Red Hugh, died. Ó Cianáin described the funeral:

> Tuesday the twenty-ninth of July, the feast of Saint Martha, the Earl was buried in the monastery of San Pietro Montorio. A large and splendid funeral in grand procession was ordered by his Holiness the Pope, and on either side of the body there were large numbers of lighted waxen torches and sweet, sad, sorrowful singing. It was enwrapped in the habit

of Saint Francis, as he himself had ordered that it should be put about him.[64]

Five days later Muiris, Tyrconnell's page, died. Dr O'Carroll expired on 18 August. In the same month Cúchonnacht Maguire, who had brought the French ship to Lough Swilly less than a year before, and Séamus MacMahon, who had boarded that vessel with the earls, died within hours of each other in Genoa on 12 August. On 15 September, Cathbarr O'Donnell died in a palace on Monte Citorio and was buried beside his father.

In despair Ó Cianáin reflected:

It may well be believed that it was not through good fortune or the best of fate that it happened to Ireland that so many of the choicest descendants of Míl Easpáinne died suddenly, one after another, in a foreign and strange land, far removed from their own native soil.[65]

At least the Baron of Dungannon survived the fever, but a year later Ó Cianáin had to add this footnote to his narrative:

Bitter woe! . . . Yesterday, the twenty-fourth of September, 1609, the son and proper worthy heir of O'Neill, Hugh O'Neill, Baron of Dungannon, he who would have been lord of Cenél Eoghain and the northern half of Ireland without contention or opposition, was buried.[66]

Eleven months later King Philip himself wrote from his palace at Aranda de Duero to his ambassador in Rome, the Conde de Castro, asking him to tell the Earl of Tyrone of another untimely family death:

Don Enrique Oneil, eldest son of the Earl of Tiron, died of illness here three days ago. He had come from Flanders where he served me with an infantry regiment of his nation. His death has grieved me . . . because he had great qualities and served me well, for which I was well pleased with him. I have ordered that he be buried in a manner suited to his rank in a much honoured chapel of the Monastery of St. Francis . . .[67]

The Earl of Tyrone was now the only prominent survivor of those who had sailed out of Lough Swilly in September 1607. Many native Irish in Ulster yearned for his return at the head of a Spanish army. Frequent rumours and assurances given by Franciscan preachers allowed them to believe that their hope would soon become a reality. Indeed, Tyrone continue to shower Philip III and his courtiers with letters pleading for him to be allowed to make a triumphant return to his homeland. That homeland, however, was about to be transformed as a new era dawned in Ulster.

Chapter 7

THE 'PRINTED BOOK': PLANNING AND JUSTIFYING COLONISATION

'A GREATER EXTENT OF LAND THAN ANY PRINCE IN EUROPE HAS TO DISPOSE OF'

As soon as he had come to the throne of England, King James had set about ensuring that Scotland and England together, 'the Ile', should be considered one state: Great Britain. The 'Proclamation Concerning the Union of the Crowns', made on 15 November 1604, declared that the two monarchies of England and Scotland were united in the person of James VI and I to become 'the invincible monarchy of Great Britain . . . this grettist Iland of the world'.[1] The King tried to persuade Westminster that the union of Crowns should be followed by a proper Anglo-Scottish Union. Was he, the head, to preside over 'a divided and monstrous body'? Was 'so fair a Flock (whose fold hath no wall to hedge it but the four Seas)' to remain parted in two? Fearing 'an Effluxion of People from the Northern parts', the House of Commons rejected the King's proposal.[2] Nevertheless, James gradually persuaded others to use the term 'Great Britain', and servants of the Crown now routinely classed together English, Scots and indeed Welsh as 'British'.

That he was also King of Ireland was not at first a primary concern for James. The Flight of the Earls in September 1607 changed that. Rather unusually, he requested that during his frequent and protracted hunting expeditions he be interrupted to be informed about fresh developments across the Irish Sea. The King's anxiety became acute as news of O'Doherty's revolt arrived at court. James needed little convincing that his Lord Deputy, Sir Arthur Chichester, was right to advise that now was the unique opportunity for a plantation in the north of Ireland. When Sir John Davies, the Irish Attorney-General, wrote to him from the army camp in Coleraine on 5 August 1608 that he now had six counties in actual possession in Ulster, 'a greater extent of land than any prince in Europe has to dispose of', James threw himself energetically into plantation preparations with a belief that it could be the greatest project of his reign.[3]

The decision in principle to plant was made soon after the Flight of the Earls. While the King and his courtiers began discussions on the scale and nature of the colonising scheme, Chichester and Davies set out from Dublin in the spring of 1608 to survey the lands abandoned by the earls and to garner all the evidence they could to give legal justification for their confiscation. Before reaching Ulster the two men got news of O'Doherty's rebellion. The energies of the King's principal officers were then primarily directed towards crushing the revolt, but by the summer of 1608 they were able to return to the task of drafting ideas for a scheme of plantation.

The O'Doherty rebellion had changed everything, at least in the eyes of Davies and the Chief Justice, Sir James Ley. They were convinced that the breaking up of the great lordships to create freeholders should now be abandoned and that British colonists should be enticed over to clear the land of natives. In his letter to the King written at Coleraine, Davies wrote:

There have been sundry plantations in this kingdom, whereof the first plantation of the English pale was the best, and the last plantation of the undertakers in Munster was the worst. The plantations in Ulster, on the sea coast, by Sir John Courcy, the Laceys, and the Bourks; the plantation in Connaught by the Bourks and Geraldines; in Thomond by Sir Thomas de Clare; in Munster by the Geraldines, Butlers, Barrys, Roches, and other English families, are in part rooted out by the Irish; and such as remain are much degenerated; which will happen to this plantation if the number of civil persons to be planted do not exceed the number of natives, who will quickly overgrow them, as weeds overgrow the good corn.[4]

MAKING ULSTER VISIBLE

The creation of maps was a vital prerequisite of colonisation. Sixteenth-century maps demonstrate how little the administrations in London and Dublin knew of the geography of Ulster. The earliest English-derived map of Ireland, the map dating from the 1520s in the British Library's Cotton Collection, is described by the historical geographer William Smyth as a mainly egg-shaped island with some few indentations on its east side . . . Apart from a few dominant rivers shown as wide blue rivulets, and square blobs of red which mark the main cities and towns in the eastern half, the rest of the island is a pale, creamy shadow, full of silences and absences. It is an island in embryo—slowly leaving behind the dark shadows of the later Middle Ages to emerge out of the womb of the early modern revolution in art, government, science and technology.[5]

Soon after, Ireland steadily became more visible. The map created by Ptolemy of Alexandria in about AD 150, printed for the first time in 1477, pictured the island more accurately than Cotton was to do. Even though he never visited the country, the Dutch cartographer Mercator published a map of Ireland in 1564 which drew together the knowledge acquired from those who had. This was remarkably accurate for the south and east, but Connacht and Ulster in this map are still barely recognisable. Mercator's work was popularised and (particularly for eastern Ulster) improved in Ortelius's world atlas, *Theatrum Orbis Terrarum* (1570). No fewer than six thousand copies were printed. In the 1560s John Goghe located Ireland along specific lines of latitude and longitude (calculated from the Azores). He inscribed the location of Irish lordships and ruling families on his chart. The north-west, however, was still very inaccurately portrayed on all maps.[6]

Sir William Cecil, Lord Burghley, Elizabeth's Secretary of State, was so fascinated by maps that he kept a small atlas of Britain and Ireland in his pocket for quick reference. On his death, in 1598, he was succeeded by his son Sir Robert Cecil (later Lord Salisbury) in that post, who displayed an equal enthusiasm for cartography. They both saw maps as being crucial to planning the state's defences and the expansion of English power in Ireland and to locating England's principal friends and enemies on the island.

The man who must be credited with providing the first fully recognisable maps of Ulster is Richard Bartlett. He accompanied Lord Mountjoy during his campaigns and in a series of maps charted the Lord Deputy's advance from the Moyry Pass into the heart of Tyrone's territory, including vignettes of the newly constructed star-shaped and triangle-shaped forts. His finest achievement was his overview of the Blackwater Valley from Castle Benburb northwards to the junction with the River Callan, entitled *The Way to Dungannon by the Plains*. His maps eloquently illuminated the story of conquest and subjugation, culminating with a view of Tullaghoge, the home of the O'Hagans, with its stone inauguration throne of the O'Neills, which Mountjoy duly smashed to pieces.

Meanwhile the crew of the warship *Tremontana* was charting the rugged coastline of Co. Donegal, providing Bartlett with a faithful representation to include in his map *A Generalle Description of Ulster*. Mapping was a dangerous business. One cartographer, Francis Jobson, observed when he was mapping Ulster in 1590 that the province was 'inhabited with a most savage and rebellious people from whose cruelty . . . God only by his divine power delivered me being every hour in danger to lose my head'. Bartlett, indeed, *was* to lose his head while carrying out his cartographical duties in Donegal.[7]

SURVEY BY INQUISITION

The lands in Ulster that had been escheated (the feudal term for confiscation) in 1607 and 1608 realistically could be apportioned to grantees only if they were surveyed. To measure such a great amount of territory before patents (legal grants) were issued was quite impossible, at least in the time-scale envisaged. Therefore, 'to avoid His Majesty's further charge', the government decided to carry out a survey by inquisition, that is, by talking to the locals. Enquiries were made about the ecclesiastical and temporal lands in each barony (in some counties the subdivision of counties into baronies had been very recent) together with their fisheries, markets and fairs. A commission was appointed to sit in Dungannon, composed of Sir Thomas Ridgeway, Vice-Treasurer of Ireland; Sir Oliver St John, Master of the Ordnance; Sir William Parsons, Surveyor-General; and the Attorney-General, Sir John Davies.[8]

The problem facing these commissioners was that the native Irish did not measure their lands in acres or by anything equivalent. In ancient Ireland provincial kingdoms (each ruled by a *rí ruireach*) had been divided into overkingdoms (each ruled by a *ruire*), and in turn into petty kingdoms, or *tuatha* (each ruled by a *rí tuaithe*). The provincial kingdoms did not long survive the Anglo-Norman invasion, and the overkingdoms became lordships, such as Tír Chonaill and Tír Eoghain. The *tuath*, or petty kingdom, became a *baile biataigh* (literally, a territory that provided food), the landed territory of a local corporate kin-group or sept electing a sublord, the *uirrí*. The *uirríthe* had a strictly hierarchical relationship with their overlords; in the O'Neill lordship of Tír Eoghain, for example, the O'Cahans provided the most senior dependent lord.

The English Crown had shired Ulster in stages by creating counties: Antrim and Down in 1570, Armagh in 1571, Cavan in 1583, Donegal in 1585, Monaghan in 1587, Fermanagh in 1588, Tyrone in 1591 and Coleraine in

1603 (this, with additions, became Co. Londonderry in 1613).[9] As the subjugation of Ulster proceeded, the counties were subdivided into smaller administrative units: baronies. For convenience the Crown usually converted a *baile biataigh*—anglicised as 'ballybetagh'—into a barony. In some places ballybetaghs had been divided into quarters or sessiaghs (sixths). The basic land unit in each ballybetagh, quarter and sessiagh was what the English were to describe as 'townlands', known as 'ballyboes' in much of Ulster, as 'tates' in Co. Fermanagh and parts of Co. Tyrone, and as 'polls' primarily in Co. Cavan. The size of these divisions, each roughly capable of sustaining two families, was based on the productivity of the soil; in fertile areas they would therefore be small by comparison with those in mountainous or less fertile ones.

The rationale behind this Gaelic system of marking out land units was very imperfectly understood by the commissioners. They were anxious to give these territorial divisions equivalents in acres to make grants of estates intelligible to the government and the recipients. Rather too hastily they decided that a ballyboe, tate or poll was made up of 60 acres of 'profitable' land, except in the barony of Armagh, where it was believed to have 100 acres, and in the barony of Orior 120 acres. They found quarters in Co. Donegal especially confusing: they were variously listed as containing 128, 160, 180, 220 or 240 acres of profitable land. The commissioners also assumed that a ballybetagh of sixteen townlands was the equivalent of 1,000 acres.[10] Much trouble was to arise from these assumptions. Having made their survey, Davies and Ley made their way to London with their findings and proposals.

The Lord Deputy's initial reaction to the O'Doherty rebellion was to recommend 'removing of the inhabitants of Tyrone, Tyrconnell and Fermanagh beyond the rivers of Lough Erne, Blackwater and the Bann'.[11] He soon reverted to his earlier view that it would be politic to make a reasonably generous provision for the native Irish in the plantation scheme. Chichester clearly believed that the detailed recommendations the Attorney-General and the Chief Justice would be presenting to the King were going too far. In September 1608 the Lord Deputy sent over his own proposals, entitled 'Certain Notes and Remembrances'.

The natives, he argued, could be prised away from their disloyal inclinations 'if they might be induced by entertainment, or gifts of land, with some reasonable help to stock and manure it'.[12] The Gaelic Irish must be given a substantial allocation of territory; otherwise, he continued, they 'will kindle a new fire in those parts at one time or other, if they be not well looked to or provided for in some reasonable measure'.[13] The government had entered into many agreements with lesser lords in particular, he wrote, and warned that to disregard them could lead to bitter resentment and create dangerous instability. He listed for the King the many lords and freeholders who had valid legal claims. For example, Henry and Conn O'Neill, two surviving sons of Shane O'Neill, had behaved impeccably during O'Doherty's rebellion; in receipt of pensions from the Crown, they had been settled temporarily on Cúchonnacht Maguire's lands in Fermanagh. Chichester described them, 'especially Henry', as 'civil and discreet men' whom the King might consider 'worthy the cherishing' and who might be given permanent estates, either in Co. Fermanagh or Co. Armagh.[14]

He proposed that the counties of Cavan and Fermanagh be divided up amongst freeholders, just as Co. Monaghan had been in the reign of Elizabeth. For practical reasons Chichester felt that provision must be made in the plantation scheme for the lesser septs, if only because it would be 'hard and almost impossible to displant them'.[15] The Lord Deputy was sure that these Irish could be made into loyal subjects of the Crown if they were prevented from ranging across the countryside with their cattle herds and be made to run their estates on English lines, building houses on them 'like those of the Pale'.[16] Certainly he entertained high hopes that, if treated fairly, they could be persuaded to become Protestants.

Chichester also pressed the claims of the servitors, particularly those already in command of garrisoned forts and castles in Ulster. They should get grants in parts of the province of strategic military and naval importance and where trouble was most likely to erupt in the future. The Lord Deputy recommended that the servitors be given financial assistance to plant. Had not King James ordered a levy on landowners in the Borders to fund the transportation of the notorious Grahams from their 'Debateable Land' over to Roscommon in 1606? A striking feature of the Lord Deputy's 'Remembrances' is that there is no mention of segregation of British and natives on the forfeited lands. The Lord Deputy got news that the King was already making offers of large grants of land in Ulster to Scottish suitors at court. Reports of such royal intentions horrified the Lord Deputy. This approach would

altogether overthrow the expected plantation and reformation of that province . . . If the nobility and subjects of Scotland, having part of the escheated lands passed to them, be permitted to bring over the islanders or their neighbours of those northern parts, I think more trouble and less profit will arise from thence than if the Irish themselves held it as they do now.[17]

Actually, James shared Chichester's deep suspicions of the feuding and independent-minded Gaelic-speaking islanders. Nevertheless, he did intend generous grants to favoured Lowlanders.

Summoned by the King, Davies and the Irish Chief Justice, Sir James Ley, travelled over to London. Here James demanded that information should be furnished without delay

> respecting the lands to be divided; what countries are most meet to be inhabited; what Irish fit to be trusted; what English meet for that plantation in Ireland; what offers will be made there; and what is to be done for the conviction of fugitives, because there is no possession or estate to be given before their attainder.[18]

For the present, the King instructed Chichester to refrain from promising land to anyone until a final plan had been agreed:

> Now in order to prevent for the future that it shall be in the power (as it heretofore has been) of any rebellious companion that chooseth to make himself head of any sept by presuming on a rabble of his base followers, to disturb the peace, and put his Majesty to the cost and trouble of prosecuting a vagrant company of woodkerne, there must not be so great a facility for granting pardons and taking submissions. He is to abstain from making promises of any of the escheated lands, and to assure himself that not an acre will be disposed of till the survey and certificate of lands be returned over to them [the Council in London].[19]

A committee—the Commissioners for Irish Causes—was formed in London, made up for the most part of Irish privy councillors, to draw up a detailed scheme of plantation. It included Attorney-General Davies; Lord Chief Justice Ley; Sir Anthony St Leger, Master of the Rolls; Sir Oliver St John, Master of the Ordnance; and two other Irish privy councillors, Sir Henry Docwra and Sir James Fullerton. The Lord Deputy was therefore not involved in this detailed planning process. This planning committee's draft proposals would then be submitted to the King's Council, which in turn would make recommendations after a further close study of the survey brought over by Davies and Ley.

Letters from Ireland began to pour in urging claims for land in Ulster on the part of the writers. Most of these were from servitors, for, as Chichester wrote on 14 October, 'all men are in expectation thereof'.[20] Sir Thomas Ridgeway wrote to Salisbury on 30 November warning that delay 'will become so prejudicial to his Majesty's rents or duties there, especially in Tirconnell . . . Suggests also the danger that may arise by distraction of the mind of a rude and savage people when they are not subject to the control of any near hand'.[21]

Salisbury was putting his mind to the best way to allocate Ulster lands to undertakers. On 16 December he produced a paper entitled 'Lottery Suggested for Proportions in the Ulster Plantation'. He proposed that English and Scottish colonists should be 'placed both near and woven one within another' and should be next to rivers. The Irish permitted to remain should be located 'on the plains', and the 'captains and servitors on the borders, and near the Irish'. There should be 'several sorts of proportions' appropriate to the means and standing of the undertakers. This was how he suggested that the estates should be allocated:

> The manner to be by lottery, viz., all the lands proportioned to be put in several scrolls. Those scrolls to be wrapped in wax balls of three bigness. In the big the best proportion, and so on in order. All these balls to be put in one box . . .[22]

Meanwhile, Chichester was becoming ever more anxious about what was being decided in London.

The Lord Deputy was right in thinking that control of the plantation was slipping out of his control. Apart from the fact that he was not in England to advise the planning committee, the problem was that—unlike Davies—he had not submitted a detailed project, only 'remembrances touching the plantation'. To submit a detailed project, he felt, rather than notes, would have been 'too great a presumption'. He feared that Scottish suitors at court, who had neither fought in Ireland nor helped to pay for the war, would be generously provided with estates in Ulster.[23] When he received the scheme drafted by the Commissioners for Irish Causes in the spring of 1609, Chichester found to his chagrin that much of his advice had been ignored. 'Either it was not perused or not understood', he complained to the Earl of Nottingham about one important letter he had sent.[24] The Lord Deputy, after receiving the scheme, 'published it every-where, to as many as may best impart his Majesty's intentions therein, and to all others to whom it may appertain'. He added: 'What this will work in the minds of many here is not yet known', and he observed that he 'foresees great difficulties likely to arise to hinder this plantation'.[25]

The London committee published a comprehensive plan by the end of January 1609, embodied in two documents. The 'Orders and Conditions', the document that had come into the hands of the Archbishop of Tuam, Florence Conry, opened by declaring that

> His Majesty by his princely bounty, not respecting his own profit, but the public peace and welfare of that Kingdom, by the civil Plantation of those unreformed and waste countries, is graciously pleased to distribute the said lands to such of his subjects, as well of Great Britain as of Ireland, as being of merit and ability shall seek the same, with a mind not only to benefit themselves but to do service to the crown and commonwealth.

The estates to be distributed to the undertakers were to be 'of three different quantities, consisting of sundry parcels or precincts of land, called by certain Irish names known in the several counties, viz., Ballybetaghs, Quarters, Ballyboes, Tates, and Polls'. The three classes of proportions—great, middle and small—would contain 2,000, 1,500 and 1,000 English acres, respectively, 'to every of which proportions shall be allowed such quantity of bog and wood, as the country shall conveniently afford'. There were to be three classes of grantees: English and Scottish undertakers, 'who are to plant their portions with English or inland Scottish inhabitants'; servitors 'of the kingdom of Ireland, who may take mere Irish, English, or inland Scottish tenants at their choice'; and 'Natives of Ireland who are to be made freeholders'.[26]

The King would 'reserve unto himself the appointment in what county every undertaker shall have his portion', but

> to avoid emulation and controversy, which would arise among them, if every man should choose his place where he would be planted, his Majesty's pleasure is that the sites or places of their portions in every county shall be distributed by lot.

There followed, under the heading 'Articles', further details. Undertakers were to pay the Crown rent of £5 6s 8d (English) for every thousand acres, 'and so rateably for the greater proportions'. No rent had to be paid for the first two years, 'except the natives of Ireland who are not subject to the charge of transportation'. Undertakers receiving great and middle proportions were to hold their estates by knight's service (a feudal form, requiring military service when needed), but those with small proportions held their estates by common socage (that is, demanding only civil obligations such as jury service, which explains why this was called a 'civil plantation').

All had building obligations: each undertaker with 2,000 acres had to 'build thereupon a castle, with a strong court or bawn about it'; each with 1,500 acres to 'build a stone or brick house thereupon, with a strong court or bawn about it'; and each with 1,000 acres to 'make thereupon a strong court or bawn at least'. All 'shall draw their tenants to build house for themselves and their families near the principal castle, house or bawn, for their mutual defence or strength' and 'shall have ready in their houses at all times a convenient store of arms'.

Each undertaker 'before the ensealing of his Letters Patents shall take the Oath of Supremacy [to the King as head of the Church of England] ... and shall also conform themselves in religion, according to his Majesty's laws'. In short, all undertakers had to be Protestants. In addition, they could not 'alien or demise their portions, or any part thereof to mere Irish' or to those who had not taken the oath. Every undertaker was, within two years, to 'plant or place a competent number of English and Scottish tenants upon his portion', and 'for the space of five years next after the date of his Letters Patents shall be resident himself upon his portion, or place some other person thereupon as shall be allowed by the State of England or Ireland'. Undertakers could 'alien' or sell their portions after five years, but not to the native Irish or to those who had not taken the Oath of Supremacy. Irish customary practices of landholding were strictly forbidden:

> No uncertain rent shall be reserved by the Undertakers, but the same shall be expressly set down without reference to the custom of the country, and a proviso shall be inserted in the Letters Patent against cuttings, cosheries, and other Irish exactions upon their tenants.

Undertakers could bring into Ireland 'out of Great Britain, victuals, and utensils for their households, materials and tools for building and husbandry, and cattle to stock and manure the land as aforesaid, without paying any custom for the same'.

The same terms and conditions applied to the servitors, except that they were to pay a quit rent of eight pounds (English) for every thousand acres, and they were permitted to have as tenants native Irish and those who had not taken the Oath of Supremacy. However, if they planted their portions with English and Scots Protestants they would only pay rent at the same rate as the undertakers.

Native Irish receiving estates were to pay £10 13s 4d for every thousand acres, but they were only allowed one year free of rent to enable them to meet their building obligations—and, for many of them, the cost of moving from one part of Ulster to another. They were to 'use tillage and husbandry after the manner of the English Pale'. Their tenures were to be the same as for undertakers and servitors, 'with a proviso of forfeiture of their estates, if they enter into actual rebellion'.

All church lands—erenagh, termon (where sanctuary could be sought) and monastic—were taken to be the same, though those who held them were by now much more secular than ecclesiastical, and were to be assigned to the established church, the Church of Ireland. Bishops appointed by King James had already taken over diocesan lands. There was to be a 'convenient number of parishes and parish churches with sufficient incumbents in every county', and tithes were to be paid 'in kind to the incumbents of the said parish churches'. Land was to be set aside for Trinity College, Dublin, and for the maintenance of a 'Free School' in every county planted.[27]

The second publication followed the Orders and Conditions about a month later. Entitled 'A Project for the Division and Plantation of the Escheated Lands in ... Ulster', it provided more specific information for the benefit of prospective planters, giving more substance, for example, to the word 'convenient' used in the earlier document. It specified how in each county half the land was to be divided into small proportions, a quarter into middle and a quarter into great proportions. Every proportion was to be made a parish, a parish church was to be erected on it, and sixty acres of glebe land were to be assigned to each incumbent.[28]

Detailed provisions were made for each county. In Co. Tyrone, for example, 28 proportions (13 great, 5 middle and 10 small) were to be assigned to English and Scottish undertakers; 17 (2 great, 8 middle and 7 small) to servitors; and 8 (1 great, 2 middle and 5 small) to natives. There were to be five corporate towns with the power to send burgesses to Parliament: Dungannon, Clogher, Omagh, Loughinsholin and Mountjoy. For 'the maintenance of a Free School to be erected at Mountjoy', 750 acres were assigned. 'Swordsmen' (another word used for woodkerne on the run) were to 'be transported into other such parts of the Kingdom, as by the reason of the waste lands therein are fittest to receive them, namely, into Connaught, and some parts of Munster, where they are to be dispersed, and not planted together in one place'.[29]

In Tyrone and Coleraine a ballyboe was calculated to contain 60 acres (English) 'or thereabouts'. In Fermanagh, 'commonly called MacGwyer's County', the land was 'divided into small precincts called tates, every tate containing by estimation 30 acres, or thereabouts'. Here 1,070 tates were thought to make up a total of 33,437½ acres, excluding forty-six lough islands—'what number of acres the said islands do contain is not set down in the survey'. In this county 'Connor Roe Maguire hath his Majesty's word for the whole barony of Magherastephana' and other lands, in total 390 tates, which 'are to be passed unto him according to his Majesty's royal word . . . Howbeit, we think it convenient, that he do keep in his possession only one great proportion of 2,000 acres, and do make estates of freehold in the rest'. In Cavan the 'small precincts called polls' were reckoned to be 24 acres each. Territorial divisions in Co. Donegal—'certain parcels of land called Quarters'—proved too confusing to the commissioners. Because 'they are not equal in quantity . . . we are to make our division by acres'.[30]

Men were now coming forward in ever-rising numbers, with their sureties, to put their names down for proportions of land in Ulster. It soon became obvious to King James's Council that, in order to make clear grants, the survey of escheated lands supplied to the planning committee did not contain enough information. And so Sir Josias Bodley was asked to lead a second and more detailed survey.

THE BODLEY SURVEY

Bodley certainly was well qualified for the task. A veteran 'trenchmaster' at Kinsale in 1601, he had commanded the garrison in Armagh and was now Inspector of Fortifications in Ireland. Bodley and his fellow-commissioners were given 'full power and authority to enquire as well by the oaths of good and lawful men, as by all such other good ways and means, as you shall seem fit and convenient' to make 'an exact survey' of the lands which 'are escheated and come to our hands by the attainder of sundry Traitors and Rebels, and by other just and lawful titles'. Chichester was instructed to ensure 'a sufficient store of bread to be sent before them to the Newrie'.[31]

This second survey, begun in the summer of 1609, was to be accompanied by maps which were to name all the townlands and their boundaries within each ballybetagh. Altogether eight men, including the talented cartographer Thomas Raven, were involved in this exercise. Apart from an occasional 'treading out', time did not permit a measurement of the lands. The surveyors, accompanied by key local informants, Davies explained, 'were sent forth into each barony . . . and in their perambulation took notes . . . These surveyors, being returned to the camp, out of their notes drew up cards or maps wherein every ballibo is named and placed in his proper situation'. Bodley further explained:

> We thought it our readiest course that . . . we should call unto us out of every barony, such persons as by their experience in the country could give us the name and quality of every ballibo, quarter, tate or other common measure in any of the precincts of the same; with special notice how they butted or mered interchangeably the one on the other. By which means and other necessary helps, we contrived those maps.[32]

The assistance Bodley and his team received from local people— described by Davies as 'the ancient natives, especially such as had been rent gatherers and sergeants to the Irish lords'—was vital. They made it possible to name each townland and determine its boundaries. The 'mears and bounds' of each ballyboe had not been mapped by the Irish: instead they used markers such as venerated trees, streams, fords, wells, the remains of Neolithic portal tombs and stone circles. The commissioners called up the most prominent men in each barony to confirm and add to the information gathered. Davies observed that the local jury in Limavady was made up of fifteen sworn men, thirteen of whom 'spoke good Latin and that readily . . . They conceaved their verdict or praesentment in a singular goode forme and methode'.[33] These were most likely former *críochairí* (boundary surveyors), *maoir* (bailiffs) of the Gaelic lords and members of the erenagh class, hereditary guardians of church lands. The degree of helpful co-operation from local native dignitaries was remarkable, particularly at a time when rumours were circulating that the Earl of Tyrone would soon return with a Spanish army. Peaceful collaboration was not universal, however. It was while surveying in Co. Donegal at this time that Richard Bartlett was murdered.

Even while Bodley was at work, the details of the plantation scheme were being agreed. Not all of Chichester's recommendations would be ignored. The experience of the Munster Plantation had confirmed the view that excessively large estates should not be granted. Lord Audley,

Davies's father-in-law, put in a proposal that he plant 100,000 acres—all of Co. Tyrone. This was swiftly turned down. Sir Francis Bacon, James I's Lord Chancellor, though not intending to apply for land himself, had long been an advocate of plantation and—strongly influenced by classical texts on colonisation—had written on the subject. He was certain that dispersed settlement should be avoided: tenants should dwell in villages and corporate towns, clustered around manor houses, and this view was to be incorporated in the final scheme.[34] Chichester did manage to get the planners in London to set aside their scheme to transplant 'swordsmen' from Ulster to Connacht and Munster. The Lord Deputy had warned:

> The very report of transplanting the swordsmen was like to have brought new work upon us. That course is not to be thought upon, unless the King be at the charge of an army as great as any in the last rebellion.[35]

Perhaps the most original proposal made by Chichester was that Scottish as well as English Protestants should be invited to become undertakers in Ulster. This immediately appealed to King James. Chichester had been impressed by the pioneering colonisation of north Down by Hugh Montgomery and James Hamilton. In 1608 he had written that the Scots were particularly suited to plant a town in Strabane and to 'make it pretty although it was all but burnt to the ground by O'Doherty'. Back in 1605 Chichester had recommended that Lifford, Derry and Coleraine should be taken away from Gaelic lords and be 'replenished . . . with merchants, tradesmen, and artificers from England and Scotland who must be commanded by authority to come over and compelled to remain'.[36]

Soon after he had news of O'Doherty's rebellion, James ordered that the recruitment of Scottish soldiers for service on the Continent should stop immediately, as they were needed for the 'intended subduing of the Isles' and the 'suppressing of our rebels in Ireland'. Andrew Stewart, Lord Ochiltree, Lieutenant of the Northern and Southern Isles, had been putting together an expedition with the assistance of the English navy to bring the Western Isles to order and to create there a 'civil society'. Now he was commanded to redirect this force to assist in the suppression of O'Doherty. The towns of western Scotland were instructed to arrest any Irish found there fleeing from justice, especially Phelim Riabhach MacDavitt, described as a man 'of mean stature, strongly made, a great hairy black beard, his head inclining towards baldness, and about the age of forty years'.[37] Some two hundred of Ochiltree's troops landed at Carrickfergus and got to Dungannon. Chichester had a low opinion of them, considering them to be 'young lads, and all for the most part so badly clothed and armed as lichtelie the like [had] never been suffered to pass in any former musters here'.[38] Nevertheless, in gratitude once the rebellion had been put down, he sent Captain Richard Bingley with a galley to reinforce Ochiltree's postponed expedition to the Isles.

Those Protestants in Ireland who expressed opposition to Scots involvement—most notably Matthew de Renzy, a German adventurer there who had become a naturalised Englishman—were ignored in both London and Edinburgh. Even before his accession to the throne of England, James had sanctioned projects to 'reforme and ciuilize the best inclined' of the inhabitants of the Isles, who were 'alluterly barbares', by 'planting colonies among them of answerable In-Lands subjects' and by 'rooting out or transporting the barbarous or stubborne sort, and planting ciuility in their rooms'. Despite embarrassing setbacks, this policy was resumed in 1608 when Lord Ochiltree was appointed to his mission in the Isles. Ochiltree was provided with extraordinary powers, and those who failed to answer his summons he had authority to 'hunt, follow, and pursue with fire and sword and all kinds of extremity and to repel and hald them, their wyffis, and bairnis out of the country'. Andrew Knox, Bishop of the Isles, assisted this process energetically. Because he had been responsible for 'reducing of the ignorant and wicked people of our Isles to the acknowledging of God and obedience of the King's Majesty', he was to be translated to the diocese of Raphoe in 1610 in order to have the 'ignorant multitude . . . reclaimed from their superstitious and popish opinions and reduced to the acknowledging of God and his true worship'.[39]

Towards the end of 1608 Sir Alexander Hay, secretary to the Scottish Privy Council, gave enthusiastic backing for the active participation of his fellow-countrymen in bringing about the Plantation of Ulster. His colleagues agreed, and the Council issued a proclamation, to be published in 'all places needful', on 28 March 1609. The response to the proclamation was so immediate that, within a very short space of time, the Council was able to draw up a list of 77 persons, with sureties, who advanced claims to a total of 141,000 acres of land in Ulster. Perhaps fearing that not enough land would be left for Englishmen, the Council in London decided that the King himself should take personal charge of allocating estates—grants would therefore require the Great Seal of England. Only 18 of the original

77 Scottish applicants appeared on the list of 'British' undertakers, but there were to be 59 Scots names placed on this composite list of undertakers, and full Scottish involvement in the plantation was guaranteed.

The fact that the King himself was directing and supervising the entire scheme of plantation indicated that a strictly hierarchical approach was being adopted: those who would top the list of grantees (who had registered an interest) would be the highest in the land and, therefore, those with most resources. This certainly reflected the opinions of those who wrote to justify colonisation and to give their views on the best way to ensure successful settlement.

BIBLICAL, FOREIGN AND NEW ENGLISH SIGNPOSTS TO COLONISATION

Those at the centre of working out a strategy for the Plantation of Ulster sought, first, to justify the colonisation scheme on political and moral grounds and, second, to put together practical directives to ensure the success of the plantation. Classical models were studied closely, especially histories of Roman colonies in Europe, Africa and Asia. Though previously available in Latin, a key work by Appian (c. AD 95–165) was published in English in 1578 with the title *An Auncient Historie and Exquisite Chronicle of the Roman Warres.* Livy (c. 59 BC to AD 17) was translated into English and published as *The Romane Historie* in 1600. Seneca (4 BC to AD 65) appeared in print in 1602, his *De Consolatione ad Helviam* being published in Louvain. Despite the ignominious failure of his attempt to colonise the Ards in 1572, Sir Thomas Smith was still regarded as an authority to be respected. *Brevíssima Relación de la Destruyción de las Indias,* a critical account of the Spanish treatment of native Americans by Bartolomé de las Casas, first published in 1552, appeared in an English translation with the title *The Spanish Colonie* in 1583. *Les Six Livres de la Republique* by Jean Bodin, published in Paris in 1576, became available in English in 1606 with the title *The Six Books of the Commonweale.*

Since it was by far the most widely read book in England (with the likely exception of Foxe's *Book of Martyrs*), the Bible was consulted carefully to provide both ideological justification and practical advice.[40] John Hooker, in a commentary on the writings of Giraldus Cambrensis, referred to the lands devastated after the Desmond Rebellion as

> a notable and rare example of Gods inst judgement and seuere punishment, vpon all such as doo resist and rebel against the higher

powers and his anointed . . . For as it is written (Romans 13), Who resisteth against the higher power, resisteth against God's ordinances, and he shall receiue judgement. And the Lord shall root him from out of the earth that shall blaspheme his gods, and curseth the prince of the people.

In 'Opinions or the Suppressing of the Rebellion and the Well-Government of Ireland', an unpublished document written in 1582, Sir John Perrott states that 'the reformation must therefore begin at God. His Will and Worde must be duely planted and Idolatorie extirpated. Next lawe must be established and licentious customes abrogated'. An anonymous manuscript of 1598, 'Discourse for Reformation of Ulster by Collonies', concluded that the lesson to be learnt from the plantation of Laois and Offaly was that only English, Welsh and Flemish settlers should be allowed to become tenants. He added a warning that 'the mere Irish doe as dewlie expect the restoring againe to their olde Pentarchie, as the Jewes did the Restitution of Israell'.[41]

Edmund Spenser had come to Ireland in 1580 to serve as Lord Deputy Grey's secretary and obtained a grant of an estate at Kilcolman, Co. Cork, in the Munster Plantation. His verse epic *The Faerie Queene* was in part an allegorical demand for more forceful policies in Ireland. *A View of the Present State of Ireland*, written in the early stages of the Nine Years' War, was a direct appeal to policy-makers, written in the form of a dialogue with this subject under discussion: how Ireland with its rich resources can be turned from waste to 'good uses', and how 'the savage nation' can be reduced to better government and civility. Spenser was driven off his estate by those in alliance with the Earl of Tyrone, and he died in penury in London in 1599. Though *A View* was registered with the Stationers' Company in 1598 it was not published until 1633; however, it appears to have circulated in manuscript and was certainly consulted by some of those planning the Plantation of Ulster.[42] The dialogue is between Eudoxus (a person of good repute), a senior English official, and Irenius (man of Ireland), an Englishman with experience of Irish affairs. Essentially, the book puts forward the view, through Irenius, who has the overwhelming weight of evidence on his side, that what seemed reasonable at court in England was neither wise nor practical when applied in Ireland.

The native Irish, Irenius explained, were descended from 'sundry manners' of nations, including the Gauls and Scythians—the forebears of the inhabitants of Ulster being almost exclusively Scythians, the most barbaric people known to the ancient world. Common law had been introduced before the island had been properly subdued, with the result that the descendants of the first conquerors were 'for the most part . . . degenerated and become Irish, yea and more malicious to the English than the Irish themselves'.[43] The involvement of the Old English in the running of the country should end, the existing commonwealth should be razed to the ground, and a perfect, new one should be built on its foundations. Surrender and regrant had failed: before new laws could be applied, the country had to be ruthlessly suppressed by ten thousand foot and a thousand horse, campaigning in winter as well as summer and destroying the natives' cattle until 'he shall have no heart nor ability to endure his wretchedness'; there must be 'no remorse nor drawing back'.[44] Once subdued, the people would be taxed to pay for martial government, which would oversee the settling of English colonies on the confiscated property of defeated rebels. The existing septs and kinship groups must be broken up, and these Irish were to be resettled either in towns close to military garrisons or on the estates of English colonists.

Spenser did not advocate the separation of planters and natives: trans-plantation played a part in his scheme to erect 'that perfect establishment and new commonwealth', but he envisaged the Irish being taught superior farming and technical skills as they lived and worked alongside the English. Spenser's view was that, once the ordinary Irish had been freed from the tyranny of their lords, they would become good subjects of the Crown and assist in the growth of the colony. Once kinship groups had been dissolved, the Irish could adopt new surnames associated, for example, with their skills and trades. Regular musters of the people should be ordered so that every Irishman would 'not only not depend upon the head of [his] sept as now they do but also in short time learn quite to forget his Irish nation'. The young Irish should then be given a good English education

in grammar and the principles of sciences . . . whereby they will in short time grow up to that civil conversation that both the children will loathe the former rudeness in which they were bred, and also their parents will, even by the example of their young children, perceive the foulness of their brutish behaviour compared to theirs, for learning hath that wonderful power of itself that it can soften and temper the most stern and savage nature.

This would clear the way for the promotion of true religion, preferably by 'some discreet ministers of their countrymen'.

Irenius and Eudoxus were agreed that the creation of a new, perfect commonwealth would be justified only if Protestantism was firmly established on the island. Unlike most of his New English contemporaries, Spenser felt that the process of conversion could wait until they were educated out of their barbarism, because, as Irenius puts it, 'the most of the Irish are so far from understanding of the popish religion as they are of the protestants' profession'. Irenius was contemptuous of the established Church of Ireland because the clergy relied solely upon 'terror and sharp penalties', which made Protestantism 'hated before it be understood'. In any case the clergy were English without any knowledge of the Irish language. They were 'generally bad, licentious and most disordered' and 'could not be brought forth from their warm nests and their sweet love's side to look out into God's harvest which is even ready for the sickle, and all the fields yellow long ago'.[45] What distinguished Edmund Spenser's views from most of those of his contemporaries was that Irish society was not to be reformed but totally broken up and reconstructed.

'OBSERVATIONS TOUCHING THE ... PLANTING OF COLONIES'

The most detailed paper immediately preceding the Plantation of Ulster was written towards the end of 1608, entitled *Certeyn Notes and Observations Touching the Deducing and Planting of Colonies*.[46] The anonymous author, who addressed this document to the Earl of Nottingham, almost certainly was Sir John Davies. He began:

> There are now six entire counties escheated to the crowne in Ulster, which is so great a scope and extent of land as none of our King since the Norman conquest has had so much in demesne at one tyme, although there have fallen since that tyme both in England and Ireland manie great Estates and forfeitures.

Colonisation was justified

> bycause those countries are so depopulated, as there is not a sufficient number of natives to inhabit and manure the third part thereof. And the Irish, besides their fickleness and disloyalty, are at this time soe poore, and withal soe rude and unskillfull in husbandry, as they are very unfit tenants for this makes them being altogether unable to build

castles or good houses, or to stock and improve that wast land as that ought.

The author believed that much could be learnt by comparison with past colonies outside of Ireland.

Looking first at the Bible, he analysed the conquest and settlement of the land of Canaan by the children of Israel:

> This colony consisting of six hundred thousand men (a number farr exceeding the greatest colonie of the Romans in the tyme of the spreading of their Empire, or of the Spaniards in this later age, wherein they have made manie plantacions in the west Indies) this colonie or rather huge army of the Jewes was brought by Moses out of Egypt . . . After manie conflicte and battails they made a full conquest of the whole land, possessed by one and thirty little kings or lords of countries, which were not protected or put under tribute as the Irish Lords were upon the first conquest, but were all strangled and put to the sword. As for the natives they were commanded by the oracle of God to root them all out.

In spite of this instruction from God, 'they suffred divers septs of the natives to remaine among them in every severall tribe . . . as the next age they corrupted the religion and manners of that people'. Approvingly, the author explains that in Canaan a survey was first carried out:

> Joshua sent out surveyors, who first laid downe the utmost limit and borders of the land, and meared and bounded the same from the foreign countries adjoining. Then there were divers Triumvirate chosen, viz. three commissioners out of every tribe to make a division of the whole land that into twelve countries or territories according to the number of the tribes, and after that a subdivision into many particular portions for the several septs and families.

This survey 'being exactly made was reduced to writing and engrossed in a book'; the portions of land were not simply distributed at will but

> according to God's expresse commandment they all drew lots at the door of the tabernacle, and as the lot fell, the land was divided to every tribe . . . The wisdom of God foresaw this course of apportion the lands

by lot, to be the only means to give contentment to his people . . . This partition by lot bred peace and took away all occasion of envy, annihilation and controversy.

The land of Canaan was fairly distributed in manageable lots, and only 'extraordinary portions' were given out to the leaders, Caleb and Joshua.

After observing that 'this plantation made one of the first and best that ever was established upon the face of the earth', the author then turned to classical examples and, in particular, to Roman colonies—more than five hundred in total—in Africa, Europe and Asia. The first colony in the time of Romulus 'consisted only of 300', but 'when the empire was grown almost to the fullness Julius Caesar sent fourscore thousand to repeople Corinth and Carthage, and Augustus sent one hundred and twenty thousand into Germany'. With approval the author observed that the 'quantity of land allotted to particular persons were not very great, for Livy reports of a colony in Italy in the plantation whereof the Triumvirate or three commissioners assigned only duo Jugera to every soldier, which I take to be two plowlands'. By this approach the Romans 'filled the whole world with the glory of their Justice, wisdom and power'. Having read Jean Bodin, the author added that if Charles VIII of France had 'planted colonies of his own nation' in Milan and Naples, the French would not subsequently have lost control of those cities. His reading of Livy and Seneca demonstrated that, following conquest, the Roman approach was to confiscate a seventh, and later a quarter or a third, of the lands and grant them in small parcels to Roman citizens for colonisation. Care was taken to erect forts and plant garrisons to ensure security from outside attack. He pointed out that natives were on occasion transplanted to reduce the danger of future rebellion by those dispossessed—the author referred to the recent exiling of the Grahams from Scotland to Ireland.

The author of *Certeyn Notes* chose as his 'third example of deducing colonies' the Spaniards, 'who in this last age of the world have made many scattered plantations in the West Indies'. Clearly he had read de las Casas and his account of Spanish 'cruelty towards the poor naked natives in destroying infinite numbers of them and in oppressing them that did survive with intolerable slavery'. This approach 'is not to be proposed for an example'. Nevertheless, the author approved of the way land was given out to colonists (who could not be Jews or Moors) by three impartial commissioners—'to take away strife and emulation'—and of the fact that grants included detailed instructions on 'the forms of their towns, measuring out the circuit and compass thereof with the length and breadth of the street, of the market place, and place of the houses, with the like'. The author also noted that a tithe was levied, as in the Old World, to ensure the upkeep of the Church.

The author headed his final section 'Now to Apply Some Parts of These Notes and Observations to the Business We Have in Hand'. First, he concluded, 'here is place enough for 4000 English and Scottish inhabitants of all sorts', even if no native Irish were removed in Ulster. However, he did feel that it was necessary to transplant some natives, though 'we have not so hard hearts as the Spanish to destroy all the churls and native people. Neither have we express commandment from god to root out Canaanites and Jebusites as the people of the Jews had'. In the past, English families in Munster, Connacht and Ulster were 'either extinguished or utterly degenerated' as a result of living side by side with the Irish. Therefore, he recommended, apart from a very few native lords to whom firm promises had been made, such as Conor Roe Maguire, the remaining lords should be removed 'together with all their horsemen, swordsmen and idle followers', especially those in the fastnesses of Killetra and Glenconkeyne and those who had served the Earl of Tyrone. However, 'the husbandmen and such as follow creaghts or heards of cattle, whoe would gladly live in peace, may be retained as under tenants to our civil undertakers, not only to manure the land as churls but to keep that and stored the cattle as that is'.

The author recommended that the land to be colonised should be divided into portions of two ballybetaghs (2,000 acres), one ballybetagh (1,000 acres) and half a ballybetagh (500 acres). How should the King distribute these estates to be planted? All those considered worthy to receive land should be written into one roll; when this was done the names of the ballybetaghs

> may be written in sundry other little scrols of parchment in some two, in the other one, in others half a ballibetagh, which being put in several boxes may be severally drawn as lot by such as are enrolled for this plantation; every man drawing his lot out of that box as shall be appointed for his rank and degree.

This 'course of division or distribution of the land by lot', he concluded, 'will assuredly give contentment to very man'. As in the case of Caleb and Joshua in the land of Canaan, 'the lord deputy may be thought worthy of a special portion by assignation and not by lot'. Generous provision should be made for the Church, and all planters must be obliged to build strong houses and live together in towns. 'And if the undertakers should be bound to be resident in person for five years as the Spaniards were in the Indies, this colony would be the securer and the better planted and settled'. Those 'Irish gentlemen which have continued in their obedience and expect some portions of land' should not get estates 'lying together but scattered or distant from another' so that they and their followers would find it more difficult to conspire with each other and rebel.

The paper ends with a summary of the benefits which will accrue to the Crown 'by the well planting of this colony'. It would bring 'wealth, civility, and the form of tru religion into that province'. This 'ancient inheritance of his Majesty being the right heir in blood to the Earls of Ulster' had been 'suffered to ly in the hands of barbarous and irreligious people for the hundreds of years past . . . The present recovery and reformation thereof will bring far greater good to his majesty and to these times' than 'the planting of ten times as much land in Virginia'. The enterprise would strengthen Great Britain's defences and 'will save an infinite expense of treasure because this plantation will extirpe the very root of rebellion'. Finally, the plantation would 'increase the public revenue, and reward the public servitors' and give a fresh start to artisans, husbandmen and others 'which may well be spared in Great-Britain', who in turn would 'encourage many more to come over into other wast lands of that kingdom', bringing 'great felicity and security to all his Majesty's dominions'.[47]

Clearly, *Certeyn Notes* did much to guide the committee drafting the plantation scheme.

VIKINGS, NORMANS, SZEKLERS AND SAXONS

Those who planned and sought to justify the plantation looked to the Old Testament, the classical world and Spanish colonisation across the Atlantic. No attempt was made to see if parallels could be found in the Old World, at least since the fall of the Roman Empire. This was largely because they were generally not there to be found. Certainly examples could be found in every part of Europe where, as a result of conquest, ruling elites had been swept away and replaced by victorious ones. In the case of eleventh-century England this had occurred very rapidly, and the Domesday Book records the almost complete removal of the Anglo-Saxon nobility. The Norman conquerors in many cases brought in their own tenantry as a layer to be slotted in between them and the English peasantry. Though a new feudal regime was applied, they did not, however, colonise to a strict pattern laid down by central government.

The complete expulsion or extermination of a people to make room for newcomers was much rarer. There is overwhelming archaeological and documentary evidence that the Vikings completely wiped out the indigenous Pictish inhabitants of the Shetland Islands and Orkney in the eighth and ninth centuries to make way for Norse settlers. In the sixteenth century the Spanish monarchy expelled the Moors and the Jews. Most conquerors in the Old World found that they needed to retain the peasantry to keep the land in production.

Perhaps the closest parallel to the Plantation of Ulster was the 'Saxon' colonisation of Transylvania. This province, the 'country beyond the woods' inhabited by Romanians, had been conquered by Hungary, but it was under constant threat of being lost to invaders from the east and the south. Hungarian nobles, known as Szeklers, who had been attempting to exercise control on the King's behalf, needed support. In the middle of the twelfth century King Géza II invited Germans to colonise this land. They came from the west, where access to good arable land was becoming more difficult, principally from Luxembourg and the Moselle Valley. In particular the King appreciated their mining expertise and town-building prowess. The area they took over, based around Sibiu, became known as Altland or Hermannstadt Provinz. A second cohort of colonists arrived in the early thirteenth century from the Rhineland, Thuringia, the southern Low Countries and Bavaria. They settled along the Someş River and built a town they called Nösen (now Bistraşa). Immigration continued—to Unterwald in the east (centred on Sebeş) and further north to Weinland, near Mediaş. In 1211 the Knights of St John were invited by Béla IV to settle the south-east to guard the passes in the Carpathian Mountains. They were assiduous town-builders and founded the city of Kronstadt (now Braşov).

These arrangements were highly regulated, with strict obligations laid down in a 'Diploma' by King Andrew II for town-building, for the erection of castles and fortified churches and for other feudal and colonial duties. The administrative areas were known as 'seats' (*sedes*), with special privileges. With the assistance of the Cistercian Order, the Orthodox Church was to be replaced with the Catholic Church. Native Romanians were completely excluded from public life, and the functions of judges, operating Hungarian law, and members of the nobility were laid down in detail. Indeed, the Knights of St John were expelled in 1226 because they attempted to act too independently. Most of the people they brought with them remained, however, and were able to rebuild the colony after the Mongol invasion of 1241–2. In most of the areas settled, Romanian peasants remained, but where colonisation was most successful the population was overwhelmingly German-speaking. Indeed over the entire Kingdom of Hungary all 150 towns were predominantly German by the middle of the fourteenth century.

The privileges of the colonists were further documented and revised in 1438, but, soon after, the situation was transformed by the Ottoman invasions following the fall of Byzantium.[48] There were still more than 745,000 'Saxons' in Transylvania in 1930, but thereafter their fortunes were adversely affected by the advance of the Red Army in 1944–5 and by the establishment of an unsympathetic communist regime. Germany recognised these people as eligible for citizenship, and those who had not already emigrated to Idaho, Colorado and southern Ontario were invited in. Their numbers dropped from 119,462 in 1992 to 60,088 in 2002.

THE 'PRINTED BOOK'

After reading the Orders and Conditions and the Project, Sir Francis Bacon, England's Solicitor-General, wrote directly to the King to offer his enthusiastic support for the scheme. For Bacon the plantation of Virginia (the first colonists had left the Thames to cross the Atlantic only weeks after the Flight of the Earls) was as little to be compared to the Ulster project as Amadis de Gaul to Caesar's Commentaries. It deserved the full backing of Westminster:

> I will never despair but that the Parliament of England, if it may perceive that action is not a flash but a solid and settled pursuit, will give aid to a work so religious, so politic and so profitable.[49]

Britain was becoming overpopulated, and the export of surplus people across the Irish Sea would help to reduce tensions at home:

> An effect of peace in fruitful kingdoms, where the stock of people receiving no consumption nor diminution by war doth continually multiply, must in the end be a surcharge and overflow of people, more than the territories can well maintain which . . . doth turn external peace into internal troubles and seditions. Now, what an excellent diversion of this inconvenience is ministered by God's providence to your Majesty in this plantation of Ireland—wherein so many families

may receive sustentations and fortunes, and the discharge of them also out of England and Scotland may prevent many seeds of future perturbations.

He assured the King that 'great profit and strength . . . is like to redound to your crown, by the working upon this unpolished part thereof'—an island which would become another Britain,

> endowed with so many dowries of nature (considering the fruitfulness of the soil, the ports, the rivers, the fishings, the quarries, the woods, or other materials, and especially the race and generation of men, valiant, hard and active), as it is not easy, no not upon the continent, to find such a confluence of commodities, if the hand of man did join with the hand of nature.[50]

Bacon's main reason for writing to the King was to counter the argument, advanced principally by servitors in Ireland, that plantation was best left to men like themselves with experience and knowledge of that island. The best colonists, he argued, would be men possessing the necessary resources:

> If your Majesty shall make these portions of land which are to be planted as fortunes for those who are in want, and are likeliest to seek after them, they will not be able to go through with the charge of good and substantial plantations . . . So that this must be an adventure for such as are full, than a setting up of those that are low of means.[51]

Bacon was not alone in putting forward this view, and it was one which found favour with the King.

The realisation in the spring of 1609 that a second survey of the escheated lands was required meant that the timetable agreed with King James was slipping. For the benefit of those already applying for estates, the planning commissioners published a paper in May 1609 entitled *Reasons Proving that the Deferring of the Plantation of Ulster until the Next Spring Is the Most Convenient for the King's Majesty, for the Undertakers, and for the General Service*. The timetable would slip further. The results of Bodley's survey did not arrive in London until February 1610.

In April 1610 the commissioners published a revised and final scheme with the title *Conditions to Be Observed by the British Undertakers of the*

Escheated Lands in Ulster, Imprinted at London by Robert Barker, Printer to the King's Most Excellent Maiestie. Anno Dom. 1610—usually referred to as the 'Printed Book', and sometimes as the 'Articles of Plantation'.[52] This document refined the terms set out in the Orders and Conditions issued the year before, and made a few, relatively minor, changes. Instead of knight service, agreed in 1609, tenure was now replaced in all cases by 'free and common socage as of the castle of Dublin'.[53] Payment of rent was not demanded until 29 September 1614. The time limit for building and settling tenants was altered to three years from Easter 1610. Proportions would not be given out by lot. The commissioners had listened to the request urgently made by prospective colonists that their relatives, neighbours and acquaintances should be allowed to band together. Now whole precincts, the major units of plantation within each county, would be assigned either to English or Scottish undertakers. These settlers would form 'consorts' headed by a chief undertaker, and each undertaker had to undertake to plant twenty-four English or 'inland' Scots who had taken the Oath of Supremacy—that is, Protestants—from at least ten families on every 1,000 acres. The grantee of 1,000 acres was to settle himself on a demesne of 300 acres, and the rest was to be colonised by nine other families, to be made up of two freeholders each with 120 acres, three leaseholders on 100 acres each (leases to last either for twenty-one years or for three 'lives') and four families 'or more' of husbandmen, artificers or cottagers on the remaining 160 acres.

The reservation of certain precincts for either English or Scottish undertakers led in turn to the grouping of servitors and native Irish in precincts together. This had major implications for the native Irish. Undertakers were required to clear natives of all classes completely from their estates. Assigning entire precincts to them meant that those 'deserving Irish' fortunate enough to receive grants were likely to get estates *outside*—and often far from—the areas where they lived. Since undertakers must not 'alien', that is, let, any land to Irish tenants, this meant that natives—everyone from the humblest labourers to Irish grantees—would have to uproot themselves and squeeze into those precincts set aside for servitors and native Irish.

The commissioners reckoned that 459,110 acres in the six escheated counties were at the Crown's disposal. They assigned 162,500 acres to the undertakers (36 per cent); 54,632 to the servitors (12 per cent); 74,852 to the Church (16 per cent); 94,013 to Irish natives (20 per cent); 12,400 to the University of Dublin (3 per cent); 15,193 to schools, towns and forts (3 per cent); and, by an arrangement being finalised in the capital, 45,520 to the City of London (10 per cent). These were described as 'profitable acres' and did not include 'waste'. Nevertheless, the area thought to be available for the Plantation of Ulster had been wildly underestimated: the amount of land in the six confiscated counties is actually 3,690,714 statute acres.[54]

TRANSPORTING SWORDSMEN 'FULL SORE AGAINST THEIR WILLS'

As Lord Deputy, Chichester had to busy himself to prepare the province of Ulster for the impending plantation. Over much of the countryside, Irish warriors, veterans of the Nine Years' War and some also of O'Doherty's rebellion, were still at large. Some of these swordsmen had turned to banditry, and all would pose a danger to colonists as they arrived with their families. They appeared to be particularly numerous in Co. Armagh, especially in the wooded uplands in the south of the county, known as the Fews, where O'Doherty's ally, Eochaidh Óg O'Hanlon, had only just been forced to capitulate. Here Chichester attempted to impose a 'round' fine on citizens and issued a proclamation that those who submitted would not only be pardoned but would also receive the property of any former comrades they managed to deliver up 'dead or alive'. Davies reported in August 1608 that this approach had 'taken effect beyond expectation among this viperous generation of rebels, who are become like the armed men of Cadmus, who sprang from the teeth of a serpent sown in the earth, but presently fought and utterly destroyed one another'.[55]

This assessment proved premature. The government then, in February 1608, imposed a fine of a thousand marks on several northern counties to force local communities to deliver up the swordsmen. Chichester reported that, as a result, the 'principal rebels are grown to great necessities and misery'. The fine was so burdensome that leading inhabitants of Co. Armagh petitioned the government to propose that if such swordsmen could not be pardoned they could instead be enticed to go abroad to serve in a foreign army. No doubt the petitioners intended a Catholic destination, such as the Spanish Netherlands, but Chichester—after briefly considering Florida—chose Protestant Sweden. Ulster must be cleared of these swordsmen, the Lord Deputy believed, as they were 'but an unprofitable burden of the earth, cruel, wild, malefactors, thieves'.[56]

The first shipload of 240 men was being mobilised in July 1609. At the end of the summer, plans were in place to transport another thousand swordsmen to Sweden, kitted out 'after the English fashion'. The Lord

Deputy recommended 'the most factious and stirring men to take the charge and command of the soldiers to be levied, who will soon gather idlers together, and there will be a good riddance of them all when they are gone'.[57] He even agreed that Eochaidh Óg and his 'wicked crew' could be included in this transportation.

King James and his Council were most anxious that the Lord Deputy should succeed in this scheme of transportation—the return of the Earl of Tyrone from the European mainland was a constant anxiety. The scheme proved difficult to implement. Three ships sent to Derry and one to Carlingford to pick up the swordsmen were scattered by storms in October 1609. Sir Thomas Phillips wrote from Coleraine that swordsmen being rounded up had gone into hiding, 'for they are very fearful' of being sent to Sweden. Assize judges ordered the execution of some swordsmen as they toured Ulster that summer, but in general they preferred to have them rounded up for Swedish service.

Nevertheless, 'certain furies and firebrands of sedition' were succeeding in persuading some of those who had volunteered to go to pull back. At last the Lord Deputy arrived in person at Carlingford to supervise the boarding of some three hundred, including some of the 'notablest outlaws upon all the borders . . . full sore against their wills'. Plied with drink to make them more amenable, about 160 men on one ship mutinied, seized the crew, 'stowed them under hatches', slipped the cables and attempted to sail away. Contrary winds frustrated their escape, and after the vessel had been recaptured Chichester ordered the execution of half a dozen of the 'principal mutineers'. The Lord Deputy ruefully observed that once the swordsmen got to their destination the Swedes would find that 'they will run to the adverse side and thereby discover the perfidy of their nation'.

The transportation scheme continued to run into trouble. In November 1609 several ships were forced by storms to take refuge in the Thames estuary: 'There the men were landed to refresh themselves in Kent, and could not be gotten on board again, but spread all over the country'. Other swordsmen escaped from their vessels in Scotland; the Privy Council there had to issue a proclamation that the absconding Irishmen should return to their English captains on 'pain of death'. The ship which had been delayed by the mutiny at Carlingford was also driven by bad weather into the Tyne in December. Captain Lichfield, in charge of the transportees there, reported to Salisbury that some of 'these most wicked and ungodly creatures' managed to escape to Newcastle and beyond. They included Hugh Boy O'Neill, son of Sir Turlough MacHenry O'Neill, who had fought with the Crown against O'Doherty. Then the Tyne froze over, and the ship, with its reduced complement, did not get a 'fair wind' to Sweden until February 1610. The vessel affected by mutiny in 1609 sailed again from Carlingford in 1610, only to be 'cast upon the Isle of Man, in extreme danger of drowning there, after she had spent her masts, with all her sails she had'. The swordsmen had to be transferred to a Scottish vessel.[58]

It seems from the lack of reports of further mishaps that later transport vessels safely reached Sweden. Chichester claimed that he eventually 'vented' a total of 6,000 swordsmen 'to the wars in Sweden'. However, his prediction that these fighting men would change sides proved only too correct. Some of these swordsmen eventually reached Rome and got in touch with the Earl of Tyrone. 'Like another race of gypsies', the earl wrote, 'they now wander through the world, lost'.[59]

The most detailed account of their adventures is to be found in a letter, written at Tyrone's request to Philip III of Spain in February 1613, by the Spanish ambassador in Rome, Don Francisco Ruiz de Castro. The ambassador's purpose was to urge the King to enlist these Irishmen in his army. He began:

> The Earl of Tiron has told me that, since he left the kingdom of Ireland and fled to these parts, the English who appropriated his lands and estates have also persecuted his vassals particularly those who followed him in the wars of Ireland. Under pain of death they were forced by the English to go to various foreign lands and kingdoms to serve in the armies of heretics. In this manner, during the year following the Earl's flight from the kingdom of Ireland, the English forcibly sent, like slaves, as many as one thousand two hundred soldiers to serve the heretics of Moscow and Sweden in their wars against the King of Poland. During a battle against the King, seven companies of Irish in the service of the heretics passed over to the catholic army. In reprisal for this, the heretics killed two other companies of Irish who had been left in garrison, among whom, and also among those who are still living, are nephews and close relatives of the Earl.
>
> The seven companies who escaped served the King of Poland for three years until recently, when he dismissed them without paying them anything for their services. As a result of this, the poor men go begging from door to door and many of them have come to the Earl for they feel that he has an obligation towards them; this is true for, in his cause they were exiled. The hardship they suffer is a cause of great

sorrow to the Earl, all the more as he knows that, if they return to their country, all of them will be beheaded. Although they are men of great courage and would be most faithful to the service of Your Majesty, the Archduke Alberto refuses to have them enlisted as soldiers among those of their nation who serve Your Majesty in the States of Flanders. I beg Your Majesty to order that their case be examined for, if there is need of soldiers in those parts, the Earl affirms that none better could be found.[60]

It seems that many of these indigent Irish soldiers did make their way to join their compatriots in the Spanish Netherlands. And while the Earl of Tyrone did not live to see them fight in his cause, some of these men would later return to Ireland to renew the fight against the British Crown.

Chapter 8 ∿

'GREAT THINGS MOVE SLOWLY': THE PLANTATION OF ULSTER BEGINS

'MAKE SPEEDE, GET THEE TO ULSTER, SERVE GOD, BE SOBER'

For King James the Plantation of Ulster had become the greatest project of his reign; such was his interest that he personally took over much of its direction. The Scottish Privy Council issued its proclamation, to be published in 'all places needful', on 28 March 1609:

> Forasmeikle as the Kingis Maiestie haveing resolued to reduce and setle vnder a perfyte obedience the north pairt of the Kingdome of Ireland . . . his Maiestie, for this effect, hes tane a verie princelie and good course, alswell for establischeing of religioun, justice, and ciuilitie within the saidis boundis, as for planting of colonies thairin, and distributeing of the same boundis to lauchfull, ansuerable, and weill affected subjiectis, vpon certane easie, tolerable, and profitable conditionis, and although thair be no want of grite nomberis of the countrey people of England, who, with all glaidnes, wald imbrace the saidis conditionis, and transport thame selfiss, with their families, to Yreland, and plenische the saidis hail boundis sufficientlie with inhabitis, yit, his sacred Maiestie, out of his vnspeikable love and tender affectioun towards his Maiesties antient and native subiectis of this kingdome . . . hes bene pleasit to mak chose of thame to be Pairtnairis with his saidis subjiectis of England, in the distribution foirsaid . . .[1]

'Answerable' Scottish subjects responded so well to the King's invitation to become colonists that Sir Alexander Hay soon found that he had far more applicants than there was land available to grant. James's English subjects had already been given the opportunity to plant Virginia—would Ulster have the same appeal?

In 1610 Thomas Blennerhasset, an undertaker from Norfolk granted a proportion of two thousand acres in the barony of Lurg and Coolemakernan, Co. Fermanagh, published a pamphlet to exhort his fellow-Englishman to join him. This 'fourth parte of Ireland, depopulated Ulster, but now redeemed, delivered and quite acquitted . . . from the usurping tyrannie of traytors, and from a long and a most lamentable captivitie' offered untold opportunities:

> Dispoyled, she presents her-selfe (as it were) in a ragged sad sabled robe, ragged (indeed) there remayneth nothing but ruynes and desolation, with very little showe of any humanitie: of her selfe she aboundeth with many the best blessings of God: amongst the other provinces belonging to great Brittaines Imperial Crowne, not inferior to any . . . Fayre England, she hath more people than she can well sustaine: goodly Ulster for want of people unmanured, her pleasant fields and rich groundes, they remaine if not desolate, worse.

He assured his readers that His Majesty would give them clear title to estates—'thou needest not trouble thy head therwith, there hath bene already two survaies to know the parcels and precincts exactly'. Of course, British colonists could not expect to become prosperous in Ulster without effort,

> for discoursing will not doe it, it must be a paineful hand, and a discreet minde furnished with knowledge and much experience: we cannot enioy the happy Elizian fields, but by passing over the blacke river Stix: for heaven wil not be had without some tribulation . . . Great thinges without much labor can not be obtained: Rome was not built in one day.

To those who might be anxious about settling in a dangerous conquered land he gave assurance that there 'be fortes and garrisons in paye', and 'to comfort thy fearfull spirit, there thou shalt have many good neighbours . . . They have a sword always ready to maintain truth and equity . . . and in time of need violently abate the violence of any that shal intend thy trouble'.

If you are an Englishman who has suffered misfortune, Blennerhasset continued, then cross the Irish Sea, 'make speede, get thee to Ulster, serve

God, be sober, if thou canst not governe, or be governed, thou shalt recover thy selfe, and thy happiness there will make thee reioyce at thy former fortunes'. Britons of any standing in life would prosper in this plantation:

> Are thou a tradesman? a smith, a weaver, a mason, or a carpenter? goe thither, thou shalt be in estimation, and quickely inriched by thy indeavours. Art thou an husbandman, whose worth is not past tenne or twenty pounds? goe thither, those new manor-makers will make thee a coppy holder: thou shalt whistle sweetely, and feede thy whole family if they be six for six pence the day. Art thou a gentleman that takest pleasure in hunt? The fox, the woolfe, and the wood-kerne doe expect thy coming: and the comely well cabbazed stagge will furnish thy feast with a full dish . . . Art thou a Minister of Gods word? make speede, the harvest is great, but the laborers be fewe: thou shalt there see the poore ignorant untaught people worship stones and sticks: thou by carrying millions to heaven, maiest be made an archangell . . .

However, if you are 'a poore indigent fellow . . . goe not thither' for 'thou shalt starve there'. He was certain that 'Ulster which hath bene hitherto the receptacle and very denne of rebels and devowring creatures, shall farre excel Munster . . . and peradventure in civility and sincere religion, equal even faire England herselfe'. He concluded with this 'exhortation to England':

> Fayre England, thy flourishing sister, brave Hibernia; (with most respective termes) commendeth unto thy due consideration her youngest daughter, depopulated Ulster: not doubting (for it cannot but come unto thy understanding) how long continuance of lamentable warres, have raced and utterly defaced, whatsoever was beautiful in her to behold . . . Goe on, worthy gentlemen, feare not, the God of heaven will assist and protect you . . . And the successors of high renowned Lud, will there reedifie a new Troy . . .
>
> And thus (faire England) having laid before thy amiable eyes, how naked Ulster may be relieved, deckt, and richly adorned, and thy selfe certainely disburdened of much charge: I referre the effecting thereof to the kings most excellent Maiestie, who hath power to command, and will no doubt provide for Ulsters prosperity.[2]

That England was overpopulated was widely held; in 1619 another English writer urged the transport to Ulster 'of the superfluous multitudes of poor people which overspill the realm of England to the weal of both kingdoms'.[3] Underpopulated and underdeveloped, Ulster offered prospective colonists a secure title to cheap land, bountiful fisheries and great tracts of valuable woodland. Apart from Iceland, England and Scotland were probably the first countries in Europe to have their forests seriously depleted. In 1633 the Scot William Lithgow wrote:

> Ah! what makes now, my Countrey looke so bare?
> Thus voyd of planting, Woods and Forests fayre.[4]

Stands of sessile oak, ash, elm, holly, willow and alder in Glenconkeyne, Killetra, Killultagh, the Dufferin and about Lough Erne offered a quick return on investment when converted into barrel-staves, ship timber, rafters and charcoal for smelting.

And come to Ulster they did. The great migration began, drawn from every class of British society: the families of servitors who had long sought a share in the province they conquered; younger sons of gentlemen eager for lands to call their own; Scottish nobles like the Earl of Abercorn, 'induced' to plant Tyrone 'for a countenance and strength to the rest'; equerries, park-keepers, spies and other servants of the King's household; men accepting estates in lieu of arrears of pay from the Crown; London merchants and 'indwellers' of Edinburgh; sea captains who had fought the Spanish at Cádiz and in the Caribbean; Protestant clergy seeking harvests of corn from glebe land and harvests of the natives' souls; English and Scottish veterans who had served in the armies of King Gustavus Adolphus of Sweden, Henry of Navarre of France and Maurice of Nassau, Stadholder of Holland; relatives, neighbours, artisans and dependants of undertakers; 'artificers', both journeymen and apprentices, who had learnt their crafts with the London Companies; rack-rented and evicted Lowland Scots farmers; and horse thieves and other fugitives from justice. The English had more capital, but the Scots were the more determined planters, for, as Sir William Alexander observed,

> Scotland by reason of her populousnesse being constrained to disburden her selfe (like the painfull Bees) did every yeere send forth swarmes.[5]

Apart from those from London, the English came from the shires where undertakers and servitors (or their relatives) had their estates. Because so many servitors hailed from there, the West Country provided many colonists in spite of the counter-attraction of Virginia. The northern counties, East Anglia, the Welsh marches and Oxfordshire were also strongly represented. A great many of the Scots came from south-west Scotland, Lanark, Renfrew, Stirlingshire and the countryside in the vicinity of Edinburgh. Here land was hard to come by, and lairds often evicted tenants unable to make the down payments required under the 'feueing' land-letting system.

Later in the century the Rev. Andrew Stewart of Donaghadee claimed that 'from Scotland came many, and from England not a few, yet all of them generally the scum of both nations, who, for debt or breaking and fleeing from justice, or seeking shelter came thither'. It is likely that he had in mind immigrants principally from the Borders.

BORDER REIVERS: 'A FRACTIOUS AND NAUGHTY PEOPLE'

For centuries the wild frontier between England and Scotland, the 'Debatable Land', had been lawless and violent. Riding nimble unshod ponies, known as 'hobblers', wearing steel helmets and 'jacks' (quilted leather sewn with plates of metal or horn), and armed with lances, bills, cutting swords and hand guns known as 'dags', these Border reivers brought their reign of terror to a climax in the sixteenth century. Gavin Dunbar, Archbishop of Glasgow in Henry viii's reign, excommunicated them in what must be the longest curse in history, running to more than 1,500 words:

> I curse their heid and all the haris of their heid; I curse their face . . . their armes, their leggis, their handis, their feet, and everilk part of their body . . . I denounce, proclaimis, and declares all and sindry the committaris of the said saikles murthris, slauchteris . . . theiftis and spulezeis, oppinly apon day licht and under silence of nicht . . .
>
> I condemn thaim perpetualie to the deip pit of hell, the remain with Lucifer and all their bodies to the gallowis, first to be hangit, syne revin . . . with doggis, swine, and other wyld beasts . . .

It did no good. From Nithsdale, Annandale, Eskdale, Ewesdale, Liddesdale, Teviotdale and Tweeddale the reivers continued to feud with one another and inflict slaughter, destruction and misery on their more peaceful neighbours.

During the first days following the death of Queen Elizabeth, riders broke out all along the Borders, killing, looting and burning in search of plunder and driving deep from the West March into Cumbria, and from the East March into Northumbria. This would be long remembered as the 'Ill Week'. But in that spring of 1603 James VI of Scotland was now also James I of England. The Borders, which he henceforth referred to as the 'Middle Shires' of his kingdom, must be thoroughly pacified. He had, he declared, 'special regard to the Marchis and Bourdouris' and ordered ruthless repression so that 'the verie hart of the cuntrey sall not be left in ane uncertaintie'. A special force, known as the Armed Guard, set up in Dumfries and began the purging process by sending thirty-two Elliots, Armstrongs, Johnstons and Battys to the gallows and outlawing 140 more. 'Hard-trot' pursuits were launched repeatedly from both sides of the border. Mass hangings followed in Dumfries and Carlisle. The pacification would take seven bloody years.[6]

The most recalcitrant reivers, the Grahams of Eskdale, Leven and Sark, paid a particularly heavy price. The Border Commission, set up by the King in 1605, with special instructions to deal with 'the malefactors of the name of Graham', confiscated the lands of 150 of them, relentlessly carrying out orders to hunt them down forthwith, burn their homes and expel their families. Then, to the government's astonishment, Sir Ralph Sidley, an English landowner in Co. Roscommon, offered to settle the Grahams on his estate. King James was delighted and compelled local property-owners to subscribe to a fund to transport large numbers of them there. In September 1606, after a 'prosperous voyage' to Dublin, they made their way to the west of Ireland. Sidley seems to have pocketed most of the money raised. Soon these Grahams were complaining that they could not understand the language, that the land was waste and that 'we . . . cannot get a penny to buy meat and drink withal'. They scattered and drifted north to Ulster. As Lord Deputy Sir Arthur Chichester reported,

> they are now dispersed, and when they shall be placed upon any land together, the next country will find them ill neighbours, for they are a fractious and naughty people.

Meanwhile the pacification of the Borders was becoming so ferocious that even the King, who had ordered it, observed in January 1606 that it was 'savouring altogidder of barbarisme'.[7] Other Borderers began to join the Grahams in Ulster, fleeing from harsh justice and repression in their homeland. Fearful of arrest, many went as far west as they could, seeking out landlords who would give them farms in Donegal and Fermanagh. Once the Plantation of Ulster got under way undertakers were eager to entice as many British as they could to become their tenants in order to fulfil the conditions of their patents. Most were happy to settle Border families. Though their family had served the Crown for generations in organising hard-trot pursuits of the reivers, two brothers who were undertakers in Fermanagh, Sir John and Alexander Home, gladly settled them on their estates. The surnames of these Borderers—Johnston, Armstrong, Elliot and Beattie—in that order dominated the 1630 muster roll for Co. Fermanagh.

The suppression of the West March had not yet been achieved as the plantation got under way. There the Johnston family alone faced seventy-seven charges of slaughter in 1609. Soon those who had lived by plunder had no work, the King being assured that in every Border parish there was 'ane grit number fund of ydle people without any calling, industrie, or lauthfull means to leif by'.[8] Many chose to seek their fortune as mercenaries in the Netherlands, Scandinavia and Poland; but many also looked west to Ulster to seek a new livelihood there. Few Borderers were to become members of the landed class, but they continued to arrive in Ulster— eventually in great numbers—to become diligent farmers.

The turbulent marchlands of England and Scotland had not been known for their piety. Here families had hardly been touched by the Reformation. Arriving in Ulster in search of land to rent, they quickly found it politic and economically advantageous to be Protestants. Barely aware of Presbyterian or Puritan theology, they conformed to the state-sponsored church. This explains why such a large number of Protestants in Co. Fermanagh became, and remained, members of the Church of Ireland (though, like many Anglicans elsewhere, some of their descendants became Methodists).

The contribution of Border families to the British colonisation of Ulster in the seventeenth century almost certainly has been underestimated—if only because the great majority arriving had humble origins. A perusal of Ulster's telephone directories would reveal how many Border surnames crowd their pages. They include Johnston (the most common surname in Co. Fermanagh until the census of 2001), Maxwell, Beattie, Elliot, Armstrong, Scott, Kerr, Graham, Crozier, Irvine, Bell, Crichton, Douglas, Robson, Nixon, Young, Davison, Hall, Tait, Dixon, Trotter, Oliver, Rutherford, Little, Carruthers, Carlisle, Storey, Noble,

Forster, Musgrave, Hetherington, Dunne, Dodds, Charlton, Burns, Turnbull, Routledge and Pringle.[9]

The movement of British settlers to Ulster, however momentous for the future history of Ireland, was slow to get going. The major grantees had to be given their patents and escorted to their allotted lands before large numbers of ordinary people could be persuaded to risk crossing the North Channel and the Irish Sea to become colonists in an unfamiliar land.

ALLOCATION OF PROPORTIONS IN PRECINCTS

There appeared to be no shortage of British applicants seeking grants of lands. The principal anxiety of the King and his ministers was whether or not there were enough men of substance with the resources needed to implement the plantation conditions. James insisted on an impossibly tight schedule. There was so much to be done in so short a time. The 'Printed Book' specified that the accepted undertakers were to take out their letters patent and present themselves, either in person or through their representatives, before the Lord Deputy and the plantation commissioners before 24 June 1610. This meant that selected members of the English Privy Council and the Privy Council of Scotland were busy assigning estates to undertakers in the 'precincts' (baronies) allocated to them.

King James appointed a commission to apportion the land. Two Scots sat on this commission: George Montgomery—who, as bishop of the combined dioceses of Derry, Clogher and Raphoe, was expected to look after the Church's interest—and Sir James Fullerton, who was there probably to speak for the Scots. The commission began in November 1609 by drawing up a scheme for Co. Tyrone. The King's Council approved this draft and recommended that the same should be applied to the other five escheated counties.

On 19 June 1609 Sir Alexander Hay wrote from London to the Council in Edinburgh giving official notification that Scots were to be included in the plantation scheme. The original plan to have all the planters in Ireland by 24 June 1609 had already been revised: the Scots did not have to be in the island until 1 May 1610. Soon this date was seen to be far too ambitious.

The King's original wish was to have the land distributed by let 'so as the hole people of the one natioun sall not be cast together all in one place'.[10] Instead the escheated counties were to be divided into precincts, some for Scots undertakers, some for English undertakers and some for servitors and natives, with appropriate provision for the Church, Free Schools, the University of Dublin, forts and towns. The chief undertakers were to cast lots for the precincts and then each of them was to be responsible for distributing the proportions within his precinct. This met at least one of the criticisms Lord Deputy Chichester had made of the original scheme and allowed relatives, tenants and neighbours to group together and get access to estates in the same barony. The King wanted to retain some mixing of English and Scots, and for this reason not all the precincts in each county would be assigned to one or the other.

More specific Orders and Conditions followed on from the Bodley report. All the undertakers had to be in Ireland by 24 June 1610, and either they or their agents were supposed to be on the estates by 30 September. English undertakers were assigned the following baronies: Oneilland (Co. Armagh), Lifford (Co. Donegal), Loughtee (Co. Cavan), Clogher (Co. Tyrone), Omagh (Co. Tyrone), Clankelly (Co. Fermanagh) and Lurg and Coolemakernan (Co. Fermanagh). The temporal lands of these seven baronies totalled fifty-one proportions: two of 3,000 acres, twenty-one of 2,000 acres, eleven of 1,500 acres and seventeen of 1,000 acres—an area estimated to be 81,500 acres. Scottish undertakers were assigned the following: the Fews (Co. Armagh), Strabane (Co. Tyrone), Mountjoy (Co. Tyrone), Boylagh and Banagh (Co. Donegal), Portlough (Co. Donegal), Knockninny (Co. Fermanagh), Magheraboy (Co. Fermanagh), Clankee (Co. Cavan) and Tullyhunco (Co. Cavan). The temporal lands of these nine baronies amounted to fifty-nine proportions: five of 3,000 acres, seven of 2,000 acres, ten of 1,500 acres and thirty-seven of 1,000 acres— an area thought to be 81,000 acres.[11] What is now the county of Londonderry was not included, as plans were already well advanced for granting all of the county of Coleraine, with the addition of Loughinsholin and slices of Donegal and Antrim next to Derry and Coleraine, to the City of London.

ENGLISH UNDERTAKERS
Lists of English applicants for undertaker proportions had been drawn up by the beginning of 1609. Applicants generally arranged themselves into 'consorts', often from one region, led by the man who held the highest rank. They had to provide evidence of their wealth and annual income to determine whether or not they could meet the costs involved. Servitors, who had been complaining bitterly about the small amount of land allocated to them, managed to get grants to no fewer than fourteen English undertaker proportions, either for themselves or their kin. No doubt to the King's disappointment, only a minority of applicants were

made up of peers of the realm. Those receiving grants had an annual income on average of about two hundred pounds.

The most coveted precinct in the whole plantation was Oneilland in Co. Armagh. This was allotted to ten English undertakers in 1610. Here the chief undertaker, Sir Richard Fiennes, Lord Say and Seale, got a proportion of three thousand acres. Owning an extensive estate at Broughton in Oxfordshire and a house in London, he was clearly fit to fill a leadership role in the barony. In his application he promised to build a new town, to be rented to tenants and to be named after Sir Robert Cecil, Lord Salisbury, the King's secretary. Actually, Lord Say was becoming frail with age and passed it on to his neighbour in Oxfordshire, Sir Anthony Cope, in 1611. His son, also named Anthony, was to do most to promote the colony here.

Having property or regular business in London proved to be a distinct advantage for successful applicants. In Oneilland these included a father and his son, John and William Brownlow, from Nottingham and Lincolnshire, with legal business in the capital. William was to marry a daughter of the dead rebel leader Sir Cahir O'Doherty. Other undertakers in this precinct included the Rev. Richard Rolleston from Staffordshire, inventor of a power-driven sawmill; Francis Sacheverell from Leicestershire, a member of a consort headed by Sir Francis Anderson of Bedford; the Rev. James Matchett, a parish clergyman from Norfolk; and John Dillon from Aggardsley Park in Staffordshire.[12]

One barony, Omagh, was almost entirely taken over by one family. George Tuchet, Lord Audley, had put forward a grandiose scheme to establish thirty-three estates—each with a castle, a town and thirty British families planted there—on 100,000 acres in Co. Tyrone. Lord Deputy Chichester was particularly contemptuous of this proposal, but Audley seems to have impressed the commissioners. His consort got four estates in this barony, totalling 9,000 acres. In addition, Audley, as a servitor, had an estate of 500 acres in the barony of Orior in Co. Armagh, and the 2,000-acre proportion held by Art MacBaron O'Neill in the same precinct was for life only and was to revert to Audley on his death. By 1619 all but one of the undertakers' estates in the barony of Omagh were owned by Audley's son and heir, the Earl of Castlehaven.

Sir John Davies, the Attorney-General and Audley's son-in-law, got two 'great' undertaker proportions of two thousand acres each in the barony of Loughtee in Co. Cavan—these in addition to his great proportion in Omagh precinct. This left room in this fertile Cavan barony for only four other English undertakers: John Fishe from Bedfordshire, a member of

Anderson's consort; Sir Stephen Butler, part of a consort from Yorkshire; Sir Richard Waldron, a notorious 'discoverer' who had managed to grab estates in the south from those thought to lack proper title; and John Taylor from Cambridgeshire, the very first undertaker to be given possession of his estate by the sheriff in this plantation—probably because he actually appeared when he was supposed to. Those servitors who were still in the Crown's service, in touch with the latest developments in Dublin and London and not dependent on modest pensions, were in a particularly good position to do well out of this plantation.

The fertile precinct of Clogher was almost as attractive to applicants as Oneilland. The government Vice-Treasurer, Sir Thomas Ridgeway, made sure he got a productive great proportion, and one for his brother George from Devon, a veteran with a modest pension, one of those recommended by Chichester 'who may and will undertake of themselves with some helps and encouragement'. Here the brothers Walter and Thomas Edney had been agents of Sir George Carew when he was Lord President of Munster: Walter had been sent as a spy to Spain, possibly to poison Red Hugh O'Donnell there (unnecessary, as it happened, as the Lord of Tír Chonaill died of a fever in 1602). John Leigh was one of three brothers who had served in Ireland for many years. William Parsons, an Englishman who had worked in Dublin Castle, and a nephew of the Secretary of State in Ireland, Sir Geoffrey Fenton, got the thousand-acre proportion of Ballyclough.

In the Co. Fermanagh baronies of Clankelly and of Lurg and Coolemakernan all the undertakers were from Norfolk and Suffolk. They included Thomas Blennerhasset, author of the pamphlet exhorting Englishmen to plant, and Sir Edward Blennerhasset of Horseford, Norfolk, each receiving a proportion of two thousand acres; Thomas Flowerdew, who got two small proportions; Thomas Barton of Norwich; and three men from Suffolk: John Edward Archdale (who also had a London mercantile connection) and Henry Hunnings, both of Darsham, and Edward Warde, a member of Lord Say's consort.

It proved particularly difficult to persuade Englishmen of substance to apply for land in Lifford, the one precinct in Co. Donegal assigned to them. Perhaps this territory was considered too wild and remote. Servitors, who in any case had many demands on the King's patronage, were to form the majority of undertakers there. One of these was Sir Henry Docwra, former Governor of Derry, who swiftly passed on his proportion to William Wilson, a lawyer and landowner from Clare in

Suffolk. Others were seasoned veterans, including Captain Ralph Mansfield; Captain Edward Russell, related to the former Lord Deputy, Sir William Russell, who had campaigned in Newry; Sir Thomas Coach, placed in command of men levied in Leicestershire in 1598 and subsequently in the thick of fighting in Connacht and Ulster; Sir Robert Remington, knighted by the Earl of Essex for his courage in the naval assault on Cádiz in 1596; and Sir Henry Clare of Norfolk, who had been in command of the garrison in Galway and had engaged the Earl of Tyrone at the Blackwater in 1597. Sir Thomas Cornewall, a gentleman of Prince Henry's privy chamber and son of the Baron of Burford, a substantial Shropshire landowner, got the proportion of Corlackey with two thousand acres. Sir William Barnes got the 'middle' proportion of Monaster; son and grandson of two Lord Mayors of London, he was a merchant from Woolwich with trading interests which reached as far as Russia.[13]

SCOTTISH UNDERTAKERS

The King chose the chief undertakers for the nine Scottish precincts with particular care. He had to be sure that the men he picked had the resources required, heeding Chichester's advice that only men of 'rank and quality' should receive such grants. Some were the cream of Scotland's aristocracy, and the first to be chosen were the King's cousins Esmé Stewart, Lord Aubigny, and his brother Ludovic Stewart, Duke of Lennox. Lennox had served King James as ambassador to France and had been involved in the abortive attempt to plant the Isle of Lewis in 1598. Aubigny had helped to negotiate the union of the Crowns of Scotland and England. Another senior noble, James Hamilton, Earl of Abercorn, it was observed, was persuaded by the King to become a chief undertaker to encourage other men of standing to commit themselves to the enterprise. A privy councillor and a former gentleman of the bedchamber, Abercorn was given the right to press any ship on the west coast of Scotland to supply him with transport to Ireland.

Once the chief undertakers had been selected, the business of choosing the fifty ordinary ones could begin. The Scottish Council began enrolling Scots making application from 13 June 1609. By the end of July, Hay had received a preliminary roll of names with sureties. Most of them had applied for large proportions, and, as he informed Lord Salisbury, the total area asked for amounted to 75,000 acres. In short, far more had applied for estates than were available. Indeed, Lord Balfour, one of the chief undertakers, commented that in making his selection he had to reject 'divers famous and ansuerable gentilmen'. Even after the Scots had already applied for their full quota, the Council continued to enrol fresh applicants. Hay wrote to Salisbury on 6 August to say that he had just received from Scotland a 'roll of new undertakers for Ireland, being men of greater stuff and ability than those in the first roll'. The Scottish Council had decided that most of those on the first list who had applied for 'great' proportions would only be given small proportions. This, in his opinion, would be 'a good means for peopling of these bounds'.

Most of the applicants were from the most prosperous parts of Scotland, the majority, of them living within twenty-five miles of Edinburgh. There were no members of the nobility and only one knight, Sir George Livingston of Ogilface; most were small lairds or gentry, including Henry Acheson, whose family owned an estate at Gosford in Haddingtonshire (now East Lothian). There was one clergyman, Timothy Pont, minister of Dunnet in Caithness-shire. A great many were sons or younger brothers of the gentry and town merchants—burgesses such as the two goldsmiths Daniel and James Crawford. Only sixteen applicants from these lists were to get land in Ulster. Three more were cautioners (or guarantors) who eventually became undertakers. The flood of applications nevertheless demonstrated the enthusiastic interest in the whole project.

Much of this process of application had been under way before the scheme had been revised to divide the confiscated lands into precincts. The King would choose the chief undertakers. In this he was advised by Scots at the English court, including Sir Alexander Hay, the Duke of Lennox and the Earl of Dunbar. The final selection was as follows: Michael Balfour, Lord Burley, of Kinross, assigned Knockninny in Fermanagh; Sir James Douglas of Spott, Haddington, assigned the Fews in Armagh; Sir Alexander Hamilton of Inerwick, Haddington, assigned Tullyhunco in Cavan; James Hamilton, Earl of Abercorn, Renfrew, assigned Strabane in Tyrone; Sir John Home of North Berwick, Haddington, assigned Magheraboy in Fermanagh; Sir Robert McClelland of Bomby, Kirkcudbright, assigned Boylagh and Banagh in Donegal; Andrew Stewart, Lord Ochiltree, Ayr, assigned Mountjoy in Tyrone; Esmé Stewart, Lord Aubigny, Stirling, assigned Clankee in Cavan; and Ludovic Stewart, Duke of Lennox, Stirling, assigned Portlough in Donegal.

Not surprisingly, the Earl of Abercorn was allowed to take first pick, and he chose the proportions of Strabane and Dunnalong, totalling three thousand acres, with fertile land and easy access to the sea. Amongst those who got estates here were Sir Claude Hamilton, the earl's next brother (known in Scotland as *lerle previche*); Sir Thomas Boyd of Bedlay, brother-in-law of the earl; Sir George Hamilton of Greenlaw, brother of the 1st Earl of Abercorn and son of Lord Claude Hamilton; George Hamilton of Bynning, Renfrew, who had served in the Swedish army; and James Clapham, owed money by the King, who carried a note with him stating that 'inasmuch as he is an old servant, whom the King desires to favour, his Majesty has bestowed on him the castle of Newton, in Tyrone, and commands him to be kindly used and furthered in his settling'.

Sir James Douglas, of Spott in Haddington, the chief undertaker in the barony of the Fews in Co. Armagh, the natural son of the 4th Earl of Morton, Scottish regent between 1572 and 1578, had been page to the King's eldest son, Henry. His fellow-undertakers here included Sir James Craig, assistant to the Clerk of the King's Household, who had accompanied James to England in 1603, and Henry Acheson of East Lothian. Andrew Stewart, Lord Ochiltree, took charge of Mountjoy in east Tyrone. He was so financially embarrassed that he was forced to sell all his lands in the barony of Ochiltree in Galloway, which technically meant that he could no longer use his title; the King, in sympathy, made his son Lord Castle-Stewart. Sir Robert Hepburn, receiving the middle proportion of Ocarragan, had served the King well: in 1605 he took the surrender of the castles of Dunyveg in Isla and Dowart in Mull, seizing all the boats in case any of the MacDonalds and their rebellious allies tried to escape. Here two brothers got estates: Bernard Lindsey from Haddington, a servant in the King's household, and Thomas Lindsey, the Searcher-General of Leith, whose proportion included the O'Neill inaugural site of Tullaghoge.

As the chief undertaker of Portlough in Co. Donegal, the Duke of Lennox, from Stirlingshire, was granted an estate of three thousand acres. A former High Admiral of Scotland and ambassador to the court of Henry IV of France, he married three times but failed to produce any heirs; his estates were eventually passed to his brother Esmé Stewart, Lord Aubigny. One undertaker here, Sir Walter Stewart, seems to have chosen to come to Ulster to escape a decades-long dispute with the Turnbull family over his Lanarkshire estates of Minto. Five of his neighbours in this precinct were from Ayrshire: Sir James Cunningham, Laird of Glangarnocke; John Cunningham of Kilbirnie; Cuthbert Cunningham, also of Glangarnocke; William Stewart of Maybole; and John Stewart, who was to fall out of favour with Charles I.

Sir Robert McClelland, Laird of Bomby in Kirkcudbrightshire, led the undertakers in Boylagh and Banagh in Co. Donegal. A man with a quarrelsome past (including an assault on a clergyman), he had to be given a letter of remission from the King absolving him of past offences. McClelland was to advance his fortunes greatly by marrying the daughter of Sir Hugh Montgomery, who became the 1st Viscount Ards. Five of his fellow-undertakers were from Wigtownshire: George Murray, Laird of Broughton; James McCullogh; his kinsman Alexander Dunbar; Alexander Cunningham of Sorbie; and Patrick Vans of Kirkinner. Michael Balfour, Lord Burley of Kinross-shire, was chief undertaker in the barony of Knockninny in Co. Fermanagh, granted three thousand acres; he had survived involvement with the Earl of Bothwell (almost certainly the murderer of the Earl of Darnley, husband of Mary Queen of Scots) to serve as Scotland's ambassador to the Duke of Tuscany and Lorraine. Sir John Wishart, Laird of Pettaro, from Kincardineshire, seems to have joined Burley because he had been forced to mortgage or sell off most of his Scottish estates.

Other undertakers here soon sold their interests. A magnate of the Borders, Sir John Home of North Berwick, described by the Scottish Council in 1610 as a gentleman 'of good qualitie and one of his Majesties servandis', led the consort of undertakers in the barony of Magheraboy in Co. Fermanagh. There he was joined by his brother, Alexander Home of Crofts; Robert Hamilton of Stanehous, a younger son of a Lanarkshire laird; William Fowler, a merchant burgess of Edinburgh; David Lindsay of Leith; John Dunbar, possibly from Wigtownshire; and James Gibb of Carribber, a servant to the King. (In Ireland the spelling of the surname Home changed to Hume, the way it was pronounced.)

The Scots had two precincts in Co. Cavan. Lord Aubigny, the chief undertaker in the barony of Clankee, began negotiations to pull out of the plantation very soon after being given his grant, and he was to sell his interests to Sir James Hamilton of Clandeboye in 1611. Here the other undertakers were John Ralston, son of a Renfrewshire laird; William Baillie, probably from Finlayston in the same county; and William Dunbar of Enterkin, Ayrshire. Sir Alexander Hamilton of Inerwick, East Lothian, may have been chosen chief undertaker in the barony of Tullyhunco—despite his involvement in numerous quarrels—because he was bondsman for the Earl of Dunbar's debts. With him here were Sir Claud Hamilton of Cochno, Dumbartonshire; John Achmutie, a groom of the bedchamber from East Lothian; his younger brother Alexander; and John Brown of Georgiemill, constable of the sheriffdom of Edinburgh.[14]

SERVITORS AND NATIVE IRISH

The task of choosing servitors fell principally to the Lord Deputy—a task Chichester did not relish. Not nearly enough land had been assigned to them to satisfy them all. He was appalled to find that great estates had been allocated to court favourites and to men he thought might lack the commitment and resources to colonise such extensive territories. He certainly could have given himself more than the proportion of 1,300 acres he acquired in Dungannon precinct—but then he had already been granted almost the entire peninsula of Inishowen and a tract of Clandeboye.

The Lord Deputy disliked having to find room for two Scottish servitors. Captain Patrick Crawford, who, at the head of a hundred men stationed in Lifford, had helped to suppress O'Doherty's rebellion, got a thousand acres in the barony of Kilmacrenan. Called on to suppress rebellion on Isla, he was killed there in 1614. Captain William Stewart, a veteran who had served in the armies of both Denmark and Sweden, also came over to Ulster in 1608; when the rebellion there was over he was stationed in Dundalk with his company of two hundred men—he carried a letter with him from the King asking Chichester to give him 'extraordinary respect'. He got a thousand acres in the barony of Kilmacrenan.

While some of the servitors were government officials based in Dublin, the majority were seasoned captains who had campaigned across Ireland, completing the conquest of the island. Those who had already ensconced themselves in Antrim and Down, principally in Clandeboye, Lecale, the Dufferin and Newry, were for the most part to be disappointed in adding to their possessions. One of the few was Marmaduke Whitchurch, who got a modest proportion of 120 acres in the barony of Orior in Co. Armagh. Davies was able to augment his acquisitions as an undertaker: he took a fancy to Lisgoole in the barony of Clanawley when visiting Co. Fermanagh as a commissioner and got a servitor's middle proportion; but to obtain it he had to buy out the late Sir Henry Brunker's interest in it.

Sir Oliver St John had come a long way since being forced to flee England after killing a man in a duel. The second son of a landowner at Lydiard Tregorze in Wiltshire, he had served in Flanders before coming to Ireland with Mountjoy to distinguish himself at the Battle of Kinsale. In 1605 he became Master of the Ordnance and a member of the Irish Privy Council. Now he received 1,500 acres of land taken from Oghy O'Hanlon in the barony of Orior. As Lord Grandison, he would succeed Chichester as Lord Deputy.

Sir Richard Wingfield had also been in the thick of combat at Kinsale.

A native of Hampshire, he had come over with his uncle Lord Deputy Sir William Fitzwilliam, served with Sir John Norris in the Netherlands, fought in Brittany, taken part in Essex's expedition to Cádiz in 1596 and returned to Ireland with Mountjoy to take up his appointment as Marshal of the Queen's Army in Ireland in 1600. Now he was granted two thousand acres around the O'Neill castle of Benburb in the barony of Dungannon. Sir Oliver Lambert no doubt thought that he well deserved his 2,000-acre estate in the barony of Clanmahon in Co. Cavan. He had been soldiering in Ireland since 1580 and had been badly wounded in Clandeboye in 1584. He recovered sufficiently to serve under Norris in the Lowlands, to accompany Essex to Cádiz and to answer a summons to give up his command in the Netherlands to join Essex's disastrous campaign in Ireland in 1599.

Chichester usually neglected to mention that a good sprinkling of servitors, like himself, had already obtained considerable toe-holds in Ulster. None was more energetic in colonial enterprise here than Sir Thomas Phillips. He was to exchange his property in Coleraine for a fresh grant at Limavady to accommodate the Londoners in their plantation. Other servitors were constables of forts with generous acres surrounding them; in time, they obtained outright possession of those lands. Some got an additional proportion to add to these. A veteran from Oxford, Sir Toby Caulfield, who had fought in the Lowlands and against Spain as well as in Ireland, got the thousand-acre estate of Ballydonnell to add to his lands at Charlemont. Captain Henry Hart survived the embarrassment of being forced to surrender Culmore Fort to Sir Cahir O'Doherty and got an estate in the barony of Kilmacrenan. William Cole, who had served as a lieutenant under Captain Richard Hansard, ended the war in 1603 as captain of boats and barks at Ballyshannon, where Sir Henry Folliott was in command. He was given a thousand acres adjacent in the barony of Coole and Tirkennedy. Cole's commanders also received estates. Folliott got 1,500 acres about Ballinamallard in Coole and Tirkennedy. Hansard, now Sir Richard, an expert in fortifications, was granted 1,000 acres at Ramelton in the barony of Kilmacrenan. Captain Paul Gore, son of a merchant tailor and alderman of London, had served under Folliott and got 348 acres in Coole and Tirkennedy.

Other servitors included John Bourchier, who probably got his estate in the barony of Orior in lieu of pay owed by the Crown to his father, Sir George Bourchier, who had been Master of the Ordnance; Charles Poyntz from Gloucestershire, who, as an energetic settler, was to give his name to Poyntzpass in Co. Armagh; Captain Henry Adderton, who had been constable of Mountnorris Fort; Captain Basil Brooke, who for a time had charge of the O'Donnell castle of Donegal, with a grant in the barony of Kilmacrenan; two brothers, John and Henry Vaughan, who got estates in the same precinct; and Sir Thomas Chichester, youngest brother of the Lord Deputy, who received five hundred acres in Kilmacrenan.[15]

Philip Robinson provides comprehensive tables in his appendices of *The Plantation of Ulster* (1984), listing all the grants made to servitors, undertakers, the established church, the London Companies, towns and forts, major 'deserving Irish' recipients and Irish clans. Michael Perceval-Maxwell gives biographies for all the Scottish grantees in his appendices of *The Scottish Migration to Ulster in the Reign of James I* (1973). The writings of Theodore W. Moody, Robert J. Hunter, William Roulston, John McCavitt, Nicholas Canny and others have over the years provided further rich biographical detail on many of the major players in the plantation. The first and last time that every single grantee, including minor native Irish recipients, was listed (with extensive footnotes) in print was by the indefatigable Rev. George Hill in *An Historical Account of the Plantation in Ulster at the Commencement of the Seventeenth Century, 1608–20* (1877). Many of the estates granted to undertakers, and some given to servitors, changed hands very soon after patents had been issued. A considerable number of estates did not remain in the possession of the direct descendants of planters beyond the end of the seventeenth century, because of the failure of many grantees or their sons to provide male heirs. Others, and their descendants, were to play a leading role in Ireland's affairs for centuries to come.

The native Irish were granted 94,013 acres, or about 20 per cent of the escheated territory. However, some of the largest estates were only to be held for the duration of grantees' lives. For example, Art MacBaron O'Neill's estate of two thousand acres in Orior was to pass on to Lord Audley when he and his wife died. A great many of the 'deserving Irish' had to uproot themselves from their family homelands to unfamiliar territory. After the first winter, all the native Irish dwelling on the proportions granted to undertakers were expected to clear out and find access, if they could, to land elsewhere. In the view of men such as Sir John Davies, this was nevertheless a generous allocation to a conquered people. Lord Deputy Chichester remained convinced that not enough land had been left to them to ensure the peace and stability of the province. He was to be proved right. How the native Irish were treated, and how they fared as the plantation got under way, is the subject of a later chapter.

THE PLANTERS TAKE POSSESSION

In May 1610 Sir John Davies and Sir Thomas Ridgeway came back to Ireland with instructions for the transference of proportions to the accepted undertakers. In accordance with the English Privy Council's instructions, a commission was appointed to carry out this in June, and Lord Deputy Chichester and his colleagues set out for Ulster in July. This kept them very busy until September. A proclamation had to be made in each county detailing the proportions granted to British undertakers, servitors and natives, with a warning to the native Irish that they had to remove themselves completely from lands assigned to undertakers by May 1611.

The commission to draw up and issue patents had only begun work at the end of April 1610. Could the deadline be met? In the case of the Scots— all born before the union of Crowns in 1603—they were foreigners who could not enjoy full property rights in either England or Scotland. The King directed that all patents being issued to the Scots should contain a clause (at no extra cost) making them 'denizens', a half-way house towards full naturalisation, which secured their rights, and the rights of their heirs, to tenure of the estates being granted to them.

The schedule began to slip. Scots undertakers received notice from the Privy Council in Edinburgh, dated 22 May, that they should appear there to make sure that they met all the plantation conditions 'upoun Tyisday nixt'.[16] This meant that they had to have their 'cautioners' (guarantors) with them within a week. The majority of Scots did not get their patents until July or August. Undertakers at the same time had to attempt to persuade suitable persons to lease some of their lands to keep down costs and to fulfil the stipulated quota of colonists. Sir James Hamilton, the pioneer settler in Clandeboye, had bought Lord Aubigny's proportion in May. He was a seasoned recruiter, knowing well that men with the necessary resources might be hesitant about risking so much in Ulster, while to take on 'beggars and lean people without money' would be extremely foolhardy.[17]

On 9 June the King ordered the creation of yet another commission, this one headed by the Lord Deputy, to accompany the undertakers to their estates. Chichester was already fretting about delays and spent another month ensuring that, to evict the Irish to make way for the British colonists, his army was well supplied. He expressed his anxieties in a long letter to Salisbury on 27 June, stating that he was 'ignorant of what is resolved touching the plantation of the escheated lands in Ulster', and—

even though it was still high summer—remarking that the 'season of the year is far spent; winter in that province is at hand; and no undertakers are yet arrived here'. The Lord Deputy was to issue the undertakers with warrants of possession, preside over the swearing of the Oath of Supremacy, give licences to any agents sent by the undertakers and assign an area of wood and bog to each proportion.

Chichester faced the awesome task of informing many indigenous proprietors that they lost title to lands their people had occupied for generations and that they would have to leave them. A great many of the 'deserving Irish' would have to uproot themselves from precincts assigned to undertakers and settle on estates allotted to them alongside baronies assigned to servitors. This was bound to 'disquiet the people', who 'will not be removed from one place to another, though it be from the worse to the better, without trouble and disturbance'. He was therefore making sure that the commissioners 'must go provided to withstand and suppress them if they will not otherwise be brought to reason'. He worried that some of the commissioners might not be up to the task: some 'will hardly endure the winter tempests of those parts in the open field, where no houses or other shelter is to be had, but such tents as they carry with them'. Indeed, some of the commissioners refused to go north, and the Lord Deputy expressed his gratitude that the Marshal of the Army and some hardier men of the Council agreed to accompany him—men he was 'sure will never refuse any travel, hazard, or danger, which is fit for them to undergo for the furtherance of his Majesty's service and directions'.

Still, Chichester was clearly aware of the historic importance of this mission. On 19 July he informed Salisbury that he intended

> by God's permission to be at the Cavan on St. James's Day, the 25th instant, there to begin that great work on the day of that blessed saint in heaven and great monarch on earth; to which he prays God to give good and prosperous success, for they shall find many stubborn and stiff-necked people to oppose them and to hinder the free passage thereof, the word of removing and transplanting being to the natives *as welcome as the sentence of death.*

He decided to begin in Co. Cavan because 'the people there are more understanding and pliable to reason than in the remoter parts, and because there is more land to dispose towards the contentment of the natives in that county than in any of the rest'. He added that he had 'in readiness some dogs and mewed hawks' to send to Salisbury, 'poor presents for so rich a benefactor'.[18]

It was early August before the Lord Deputy led the commission into Cavan. As Davies pointed out, dealing with this county was not as easy as Chichester expected:

> They began at the Cavan, where . . . they found the first access and entry into the business the most difficult: for the inhabitants of this country bordering upon Meath, and having many acquaintances and alliances with the gentlemen of the English Pale, calling themselves freeholders, and pretended they had estates of inheritance in their lands, which their lords could not forfeit by their attainder; whereas, in truth, they never had any estates, according to the rules of common law, but only a scrambling and transitory possession, as all other Irish natives within this kingdom.

Though they engaged the services of a lawyer from the Pale, they were overruled. Davies continued:

> Whereupon his Lordship and the commissioners signed a warrant to the sheriff to give possession to one Taylor, an English undertaker, who was then arrived and present in the camp, which warrant was executed without resistance.

All in all, Davies reflected later in the year, the natives were being treated reasonably, even if they had to move to receive what lands were being allocated to them, for

> this transplantation of the natives is made by his Majesty rather *like a father* than like a lord or monarch. The Romans transplanted whole nations out of Germany into France; the Spaniards lately removed all the Moors out of Grenada into Barbary, without providing them any new seats there . . . but these natives of Cavan have competent portions of land assigned to them . . .[19]

Having finished with Cavan, the commission moved on to Devenish in Fermanagh, then to Lifford, reaching Dungannon on 4 September. Led by Lord Burley, one band of Scottish planters made their way to the port of Ayr, where the burgesses entertained them with 'sweetmeats, *confeittis* and sugar'.[20] They joined up with the commission in Fermanagh on 13 August. Bernard Lindsay, a groom of the bedchamber, met the commissioners the following day and accompanied the party to Co. Tyrone, where he received his proportion.

Lord Burley was delighted with his grant and returned to Scotland, where he wrote a glowing account of Ulster to Sir Alexander Hay. By the early autumn of 1610 forty-five of the fifty-nine Scottish undertakers or their agents had arrived. Many were shocked to find that the countryside was still ravaged by the recent wars. Everywhere buildings were in ruin, and there was scarcely one church with a roof intact. After a visit of only a few days, both Alexander and John Achmutie, court servants from Edinburgh, sold their proportions in Tullyhunco precinct in Cavan to the Purveyor of the King's Mines in Scotland, Sir James Craig. George Smailholm of Leith took one look at his estate in Fermanagh and went straight home, never to return.

The whole business of the commission was accomplished more peaceably than the Lord Deputy had dared to hope. In Fermanagh, Conor Roe Maguire 'seemed ill contented with his allotment' but surrendered two out of the three baronies he possessed to the sheriff, assuring him that he intended to go to England 'and there become a suitor for better conditions'.

'Divers of Tyrone's horsemen, namely the O'Quins and Hagans' refused to accept the estates offered to them, because as freeholders they would have the expense of serving on juries and other obligations. They intended to take their chances and seek to become tenants at will.

Davies reflected with some optimism on the government's decision that the great majority of the native Irish would have to move. He was

of opinion that, if they were once settled under the bishops or others who may receive Irish tenants, they would follow them as willingly, and rest as well contented under their wings, as young pheasants do under the wings of a home hen, though she be not their natural mother; and though the transplantation be distasteful to them (as all changes and innovations are at first unpleasant), yet . . . when they are once seated in their new habitations, they will like the new soil, as well as prove better themselves, like some trees which bear some harsh and sour fruit in the place where they naturally grow, but being transplanted and removed, like the ground better, and yield pleasanter and sweeter fruit than they did before.

The Lord Deputy and his commissioners also had to allocate estates to servitors. As Davies observed,

> now there were so many competitors for the land assigned to servitors, that it was not possible for the commissioners to give contentment to all; therefore many of them returned home unsatisfied.[21]

The best that Chichester could do was to give them some hope that they would be provided for on the lands granted to the Londoners in the county of Coleraine or elsewhere on the island.

THE LORD DEPUTY'S ANXIETIES: THE NATIVES 'ARE INFINITELY DISCONTENTED'

The Lord Deputy was altogether less upbeat than the Attorney-General on how this great colonising enterprise was taking shape. He wrote to Salisbury from Ulster on 27 September expressing some of his anxieties. He thought

> he shall not live to see the plantation performed according to the project laid down, of which opinion he was when he first beheld it and began to be informed of the quality and condition of the undertakers; and would gladly have stayed his journey thither this summer, had he not doubted the same would have displeased his Majesty . . . For to plant almost five counties in so barren and remote a place, with new comers, is not a work for such undertakers as those that, for the most part, are come unto them . . . Considering the greatness and difficulty of the work . . . he conceives these are not the men who must perform the business; for to displant the natives, who are a warlike people, out of the greatest part of six whole counties, is not a work for private men who seek a present profit.

A month later he wrote again on the same theme.

> Those from England are, for the most part, plain country gentlemen, who may promise much, but give small assurance or hope of performing what appertains to a work of such moment. If they have money, they keep it close, for hitherto they have disbursed but little; and if he may judge by the outward appearance, the least trouble or alteration of the times will scare most of them away.

He did admit that the 'Scottishmen come with greater port, and better accompanied and attended, but it may be with less money in their purses'. However, from the outset they were in cahoots with the local Irish and not clearing them from their estates: 'Some of the principal of them, upon their first entrance into their precincts, were forthwith in hand with the natives to supply their wants', promising to apply to the King to get permission to allow them to stay. The Irish 'are content to become tenants to any man rather than be removed from the place of their birth and education, hoping, as he conceives, at one time or other, to find an opportunity to cut their landlord's throats; for sure he is, they hate the Scottish deadly'.

As for the natives, Chichester believed that they were seeking 'by all means to arm themselves, and have undoubtedly some pieces in store; and more pikes, and thereof can make more daily; but powder and lead are scarce with them'. He concluded by assuring Salisbury: 'Will do his best to prevent their revolt, but greatly doubts it, for they are infinitely discontented'.[22]

The chief undertakers, in charge of each precinct, had the first choice of land, and they picked estates with fertile soil and close to rivers and loughs for easy access. Though his great proportion of Strabane included much mountainous land, the Earl of Abercorn had good arable soil on the east bank of the Foyle, easily reached form the sea. The King also lent him the services of twenty-five men from the army to help him get started. Lennox also had rich soil along the opposite bank of the Foyle. Scots from Wigtownshire, given estates in the precinct of Boylagh and Banagh in Co. Donegal, had to cope with thin acid soil blasted by storms; the chief undertaker there, Sir Robert McClelland, made sure he got an estate well protected from the Atlantic. However, their neighbours in the Scottish precinct of Raphoe had better land, convenient to safe anchorages in Lough Swilly and Lough Foyle.

Because they were arriving in the late summer and the autumn, the planters had to bring enough food with them to tide their tenants over the first winter. The devastated lands of Ulster could not be expected to supply them, so cattle and grain had to be brought in at great cost across the Irish Sea and the North Channel. This may have been a greater burden on the Scottish undertakers, as they appear to have brought over more families than the English. Indeed, Sir Alexander Hay wrote that the 'cuntrey people of the coomon sorte do flock over in so greit nowmeris that much landis ar lastin waste for lacke of tennentis'.[23]

Undertakers had to erect fortified castles or bawns, and their tenants had first to build homes for themselves. The land had to be ploughed for next year's crop. Breaking the condition of their grants that they were to remove all the natives from their proportions, the British undertakers were not slow to let the humbler Irish stay on and to employ them surreptitiously as labourers to help them with building and farming. In fact the plantation commissioners—seeing that some of the colonists could starve to death over the winter—were to allow the Irish to stay until May 1611, provided they paid rent to the undertakers.

Meanwhile, King James was fretting that his plantation of Ulster was falling far behind schedule. Chichester assured him in October that 'great things move slowly'. Nevertheless, it was the Lord Deputy's letters to Salisbury which had so alarmed the King. Some undertakers still had failed to turn up. Some who had appeared or sent their agents had not yet provided British tenants. The King ordered all undertakers to be present in Ireland by 1 May 1611 on pain of forfeiture. This did result in more tenants being sent over. Even in January, Sir John Davies reported from Dublin, Englishmen were arriving by every passage. One Scot who had leased land from an undertaker had made seven voyages to collect families between Ballintrae and Ulster by April 1611.

Despite the occasional encouraging despatch, King James was becoming ever more impatient. So when he was approached by the seasoned servitor Sir Thomas Phillips with a scheme to involve the City of London in colonising one of the most disturbed parts of Ulster, O'Cahan's country, the King responded with alacrity.

THE LONDONDERRY
PLANTATION

THE CITY OF LONDON: 'THE ABLEST BODY TO UNDERGO SO BRAVE AND GREAT A WORK'

In 1603, when King James set out from Edinburgh southwards, he was riding to a capital which embraced 130 parishes, inhabited by an estimated 250,000 people, at least a twentieth of the population of England. Though only a quarter the size of Rome at the zenith of its imperial greatness, London was a vibrant, fast-growing city. Wool still accounted for four-fifths of England's exports, the trade with Flanders in the hands of the city's chartered Company of Merchant Adventurers; but, as Europe's economic centre of gravity was moving away from Florence and Venice westwards to the Atlantic seaboard, London's entrepreneurs were beginning to reach out to new markets in the Baltic and across the oceans. Medieval guilds of craftsmen had developed into prosperous livery companies headed by men now seeking to invest their capital in profitable, innovative schemes. Thomas Gresham, a member of one livery company, the Worshipful Company of Mercers, had been the driving force behind the creation of the Royal Exchange in 1560, enabling London to challenge Amsterdam's domination of the money markets.

The economic and financial strength of London had been vital to the Crown during the Nine Years' War. In addition to recruiting substantial numbers of men in the capital, Elizabeth had raised eighty thousand pounds in loans there in 1598–9.[1] In turn, merchants in the city had received valuable contracts to supply victuals, munitions and other equipment essential for her armies campaigning in Ireland. Then, soon after he had launched the Plantation of Ulster, King James began to fret that not enough men of substance would come forward to ensure the success of the enterprise. The county which caused most concern was Coleraine, still widely known as O'Cahan's Country. Here great numbers of swordsmen had evaded Chichester's sweeps and held out in the dense forests and on the slopes of the Sperrins. The iniquitous treatment of Donal O'Cahan had created deep resentment and fear amongst the native Irish living there. This part of Ulster looked as if it would be the most dangerous area and therefore the most difficult and costly to colonise. The government feared that Tyrone would return with foreign support and attempt to disembark at either Lough Swilly or the Foyle. There seemed to be sound strategic reasons for making a special effort to ensure the success of the plantation in the county of Coleraine.

The most energetic and determined servitor here was Sir Thomas Phillips. Lord Deputy Chichester appreciated his energy in developing Coleraine and his ability as a soldier; he saw to it that Phillips was knighted in 1607 and made military superintendent of Coleraine and the area of Glenconkeyne. Coleraine proved a vital sanctuary in 1608 during the rebellion of Sir Cahir O'Doherty, particularly for fugitives from Derry. Here Sir Thomas had built fortifications, a water mill and thirty thatched dwellings, and had attracted Scottish merchants seeking timber and agricultural produce. In April 1609 he travelled to London from Dublin to petition Lord Salisbury for a grant of O'Cahan's ruined castle of Coleraine and three or four thousand acres adjoining. Meanwhile in the capital a tentative list of undertakers was being made for the county. In March 1609 the names Lord Clifton, Lord Aubigny and the Duke of Lennox were being put forward as suitable chief undertakers here. But Salisbury was already drafting a scheme to involve London in this most disturbed part of Ulster, and he outlined it to Sir Thomas. Salisbury, Phillips later recalled,

> conceiving the Londoners to be the ablest body to undergo so brave and great a work as the plantation of that county, and well knowing the experience I had in those parts was well pleased to grace me with the trust of his thoughts and made me acquainted with his purpose herein, the apprehension whereof breeding in me a most savoury estimation of the design, I forthwith applied to labour it by the fairest and best means I could.

It is likely that it was not Salisbury but the King himself who first came up with the idea that London should be persuaded to become involved— Phillips added a marginal note that 'His Majesty having first imparted his purpose touching the Plantation to the late Earl he propounded it to the Author'.[2] Phillips followed up his interview with the King's secretary by writing a paper outlining the county's natural resources, the fortifications required and his calculation that the City would need to find fifty thousand pounds to undertake the project. With Salisbury's help, Phillips then drafted a less ambitious and more tightly written document, dated 25 May 1609, to be presented to the city fathers, entitled 'Motives and Reasons to Induce the City of London to Undertake the Plantation in the North of Ireland'. It suggested that Derry (which could be made 'almost impregnable') and Coleraine would be the most suitable places to plant; that the King would be willing to create corporations in both towns and grant them the whole territory bounded by the Foyle, the sea and the Bann; that both towns would get a thousand acres rent-free and the rest at 'easy rent'; that the city could exploit 'the sea and river commodities' (including timber from Glenconkeyne) to establish a flourishing overseas trade; and that unemployment and the risk of plague in overcrowded London would be relieved. The example of the men of Bristol who repopulated the desolated city of Dublin in the reign of Henry II, to their great advantage, was given to whet the Londoners' appetite.

'IT WIL BE EXCEEDING CHARGEABLE': THE CITY CONTEMPLATES COLONISATION

This first overture was given to the City Remembrancer, Clement Edmonds, who then set up a meeting between Phillips and the Lord Mayor, Sir Humphrey Weld. Weld, initially impressed, consulted Sir John Jolles and William Cockayne. Jolles, a merchant and draper, had in the previous reign supplied English forces in Picardy and the Low Countries with victuals and clothing and, in December 1598, food supplies for three months to ten thousand men in service in Ireland during the Nine Years' War. These contracts were renewed, and he was joined by Cockayne, who had a flourishing trade with the Baltic and was a freeman of the Skinners' Company.[3] By July 1602 both men were supplying all the Crown forces in Ireland outside Munster. By 1609 Jolles had been knighted, was Master of the Drapers' Company and an alderman, and had been Sheriff of London from 1605 to 1606; Cockayne was Master of the Drapers' Company and had just been appointed Sheriff of London. Clearly the recommendations of these two men would carry great weight. Duly won over, they summoned a special court of aldermen, to which 'divers selected commoners' were also invited, to meet on 1 July, and here the document 'Motives and Reasons' was publicly read. The special court ordered that a 'precept' (a command from the Lord Mayor) be sent to all the city companies to send their 'gravest and most substantial members' to meet in conference and set down in writing their opinions on the proposal. Sir Thomas Phillips was summoned several times to answer a stream of queries put to him by representatives of the companies. Then they produced the written report, which arrived at the court of aldermen on 14 July.

The court of aldermen appointed a deputation of fifteen aldermen and liverymen (including Jolles and Cockayne) to meet the Council of Ireland. Following this, the Londoners committed themselves to the plantation. The companies were asked for contributions to fund an expedition to view the area to be colonised. Some of the companies now began to worry that this could prove a costly, unprofitable enterprise. At the Fishmongers' court of assistants some members declared that 'it were best never to entermeddle at al in this busyness . . . for that it is thought it wil be exceeding chargeable'.[4] After all, the companies were already being levied for contributions to support colonisation across the Atlantic. Had they not been informed recently by the Lord Mayor of a 'great mischief that was like to happen and come to this kingdom for want of sufficient means to plant Virginia'? The Fishmongers alone had given £816 to the Virginia enterprise.[5] A considerable number of members of companies protested that they had not the means to contribute. Only one member of the Barber-Surgeons, for example, gave anything, and his was a contribution of one pound only. On 30 July it was agreed that four 'wise, grave and discreet' citizens should be appointed to view the lands to be planted. Next day the following were chosen: John Broad (Goldsmith), Hugh Hamersley (Haberdasher), Robert Treswell (Painter-Stainer) and John Rowley (Draper).

With three hundred pounds to cover expenses, the party arrived at Carrickfergus on 22 August and travelled overland to Limavady, where they met Lord Deputy Sir Arthur Chichester and his company. They spent four days there, held the assizes for the county and made a sworn inquest of the escheated land. Chichester, who had been making a survey, as instructed by London, then took the party to Lifford, where they spent another four days. Phillips met the visitors at Derry and took them to the forest of Loughinsholin and to Toome, where a smith made steel from local ore within an hour—a feat which much impressed John Broad. From there they were conveyed down the Bann by boat to Coleraine. No attempt was made to show them the less hospitable parts of the territory—the Sperrin Mountains in particular. By the end of September, when they were making ready to return, they had seen all the most attractive areas of the country. Phillips was so sure of the mission's success that he ordered the felling of ten thousand trees so that the timber would be seasoned by the following spring. Chichester got for them samples of the country's products at knock-down prices, including salmon, eels, herrings, iron ore, raw hides, tallow and pipe-staves (wood cut for coopers to make barrels and pipkins). The visitors had to hire a ship to convey these goods back to London.

'THE HONOURABLE THE IRISH SOCIETY' AGREES CONDITIONS WITH THE CROWN

The Common Council, having heard the report of the four men on 2 December, appointed a committee to draw up conditions on which the City should undertake the plantation. The decision to raise twenty thousand pounds by a levy on the companies to fund the enterprise demonstrated full commitment. The King once again involved himself directly, personally attending three conferences in January 1610 to discuss the demands of the City at length. The main sticking point was that the City asked for Glenconkeyne and Killetra, with their extensive woods, arguing that stands of trees needed to be preserved for shipbuilding in the future. In the end the King was so impatient to get the plantation under way that he met virtually all the Londoners' demands. The City had not sought to be part of this colonising scheme, and now they had driven a hard bargain with the Crown.[6]

The twenty-seven articles of agreement agreed at the end of January 1610 made this plain. The City was to have not only the county of Coleraine (estimated at 20,000 acres, 'more or less') but also the whole barony of Loughinsholin detached from Co. Tyrone (4,000 acres, not counting bog and barren land—'waste'), territory on the left bank of the Foyle to be detached from Co. Donegal, and a slice of Co. Antrim (estimated at 2,000 acres and including Coleraine abbey lands). Provision was made to buy out existing private interests, most notably the nine townlands held by Sir Randal MacDonnell on the right bank of the Bann and by Sir Thomas Phillips at Coleraine and Toome. The City was to have all the fishing in the Foyle and the Lower Bann up to Lough Neagh, and, for six shillings and eight pence annually for ninety-nine years, tonnage and poundage and other customs within its territories and in Portrush. As it had the office of admiral on the coasts of Donegal and Coleraine, the City had the right to ships and cargoes suffering shipwreck all the way round from Ballyshannon to Larne. Sixty houses were to be erected in

Derry and forty in Coleraine 'with convenient fortifications'. The City would put up twenty thousand pounds, five thousand of which had already been levied to buy out private interests.

No mention was made as yet of the number of British to be settled or whether the native Irish had to be cleared out of lands granted. Many details had still to be worked out. To direct the affairs of the plantation the City set up a company consisting of a governor, a deputy governor and twenty-four assistants. This was a standing committee very similar in composition and constitution to the East India Company (December 1600), the Virginia Company (May 1609) and, later, the Newfoundland Company (May 1610) and the Bermuda Company (June 1615). The company's full title was the Society of the Governor and Assistants, London, of the New Plantation in Ulster, within the Realm of Ireland. After the Restoration of 1660 it was known as the Honourable the Irish Society or simply as the Irish Society.[7]

The Society acted promptly once the articles of agreement had been signed. It appointed John Rowley, a merchant-draper of London, as its chief agent. First, the City sent over to Derry about 130 masons, carpenters and other workmen, with tools and building materials, under the direction of William Gage, Rowley's brother-in-law. Chichester, who knew Rowley well, was instructed by the Privy Council to provide all the help he could by supplying food at normal prices and making labourers available to burn lime, quarry stone and fell trees. Rowley, accompanied by his assistant, Tristram Beresford, arrived at Larne on 20 May 1610 with further instructions for the Lord Deputy to hand over the fort of Culmore and to authorise the demolition of houses in Derry and Coleraine to make way for fresh building. Meanwhile public proclamations were posted on the corners of the Royal Exchange in London promising that persons who would go to Ireland to inhabit and plant on the City's estates would have land at four pence an acre.

Even at this early stage the City fathers had doubts about the prospects for their colony. Barnaby Rich, who knew Coleraine and its district, had just come over to London from Dublin. No fewer than sixteen times over six days he was asked whether or not he expected that the workmen sent over would keep their heads on their shoulders long enough to finish the building work. Rich, an ardent supporter of the plantation, was not about to dampen enthusiasm in the capital. He wrote a paper for Alderman Cockayne entitled 'A New Description of Ireland . . . No Lesse Admirable to Be Perused than Credible to Be Believed: Neither Unprofitable nor

Unpleasant to Bee Read and Understood, by Those Worthy Cittizens of London that Be Now Undertakers in Ireland'. This extolled the benefits awaiting English colonists and assured Cockayne that, provided no papists (whether English or Irish) were allowed to plant among them, the dangers were minimal.

In Derry work was stalled by the discontent of the workmen, who complained about their wages and discovered that the assurance that all they would need would be available was false. In any case, no money had arrived as yet to pay them. In addition, owners of the houses about to be demolished refused to move until compensation had been paid. In Coleraine work began with the arrival of Rowley and Beresford, carrying with them four thousand pounds, and when the Lord Deputy and his party called in, during August, they were agreeably surprised by the progress made. Sir John Davies, indeed, extravagantly compared the Londoners' operations there to Dido's building of Carthage. All this was preparatory work: it would not be until the end of 1613 that the territory granted to the City would be divided into proportions and assigned by lot to its livery companies.

Meanwhile, King James had become so frustrated by reports of further delays that in the summer of 1611 he sent over Sir George Carew, a former Lord President of Munster and now Lord Carew, to head a commission of inquiry into the plantation.

CAREW'S 'PERAMBULATION ABOUT ULSTER', 1611

Carew and his commissioners, accompanied by the Lord Deputy, set out from Dublin at the end of July 1611. Proceeding from Dundalk, they advanced north to Carrickfergus and Dunluce, and arrived in Derry on 14 August. Making what Carew described as a 'perambulation about Ulster', they made their way into Donegal and then turned south to Enniskillen, reaching there on 25 August. Then they went to Dungannon and Armagh, and returned to Dublin on 5 September.

It was a perfunctory perambulation and relied for the most part on reports by sheriffs and governors of forts. This rapid survey nevertheless demonstrated clearly that the grand scheme of colonisation had made a very slow start. In many cases there was no sign of any activity. In the precinct of Clankee, Co. Cavan, Lord Aubigny 'appeared not, nor any for him; nothing done, the natives still remaining'. In Knockninny precinct in Co. Fermanagh, Thomas Moneypenny, Laird of Kinkell, also had 'not appeared, and none for him; nothing done'. In the same barony George

Smailholm, Laird of Leith, 'had taken possession, returned into Scotland, left no agent, nothing done'. In the Co. Fermanagh precinct of Clankelly, 'nothing done' was Carew's verdict on six English undertakers. In the precinct of Magheraboy, allotted to Scottish undertakers, Sir John Home, granted 2,000 acres, 'has taken possession, returned into Scotland, nothing done, nor any agent present'; and Jerome Lindsay, granted 1,000 acres, 'took possession by attorney, did nothing else'. In the precinct of Boylagh and Banagh in Co. Donegal the chief undertaker, Sir Robert McClelland, Lord Bomby, 'took possession in the summer 1610, returned into Scotland; his agent, Andrew Johnson, resident, hath prepared no material for building'. James McCullough, '1,000 acres; not appeared; agent resident; nothing done'. On the precinct of Portlough in Co. Donegal the chief undertaker, the Duke of Lennox, had made 'no preparation for building, save some timber trees felled and squared'. His neighbours Sir Walter Stewart, Laird of Minto, Alexander McAuley, Laird of Durlinge and John Crawford, Laird Kilberry, had 'nothing done' against their names.[8]

Servitors who were governors of forts had made good progress, but only with the help of grants from the Crown. Sir Richard Hansard got two hundred pounds from the King to construct a fort at Lifford. When Hansard was appointed, in 1607, Carew reported, there was only one house there:

> There is another small fort in the town rampiered and ditched, about which there are certain houses built of good timber after the English manner, which serve for the use of a gaoler, and to keep the prisoners ... Upon view of the town we found it well furnished with inhabitants of English, and Scottish, and Irish, who live by several trades, brought thither by Sir Richard, who built 21 houses for tenants who are to give entertainment to passengers. Thirty-seven houses were built by others.

Captain Basil Brooke was praised for the work he had completed in the town of Donegal, where the commissioners 'found a fair bawn built, with flankers, a parapet, and a walk on the top 15 foot high. Within the bawn is a strong house of stone'. Brooke had been given £250 for this work of repairing and upgrading this O'Donnell castle. A couple of miles from there Captain Paul Gore 'has erected a fair stone house out of the ruins of O'Boyle's old castle upon the sea side ... He demands some consideration for his charges, which we think him worthy of'.

In Kilmacrenan precinct, Captain William Stewart, granted a small proportion, had built 'a fort or bawn of lime and stone, with two flankers' and 'three houses English fashion, and is in hand for more, which will serve for tenants'. But the 'rest of the servitors have done nothing by reason of the wildness of the land, being the worst in all the country, insomuch that the natives are unwilling to come to dwell upon it until they be forced to remove'.

In the precinct of Strabane the chief undertaker, the Earl of Abercorn,

> has taken possession, resident with lady and family, and built for the present near the town of Strabane some large timber houses, with a court 116 foot in length and 87 foot in breadth, the grounsells of oaken timber, and the rest of allor [alder] and birch, which is well thatched with heath and finished. Has built a great brew house without his court 46 foot long and 25 foot wide. His followers and tenants have, since May last, built 28 houses of fair coples; and before May, his tenants, who are all Scottishmen, the number of 32 houses of like goodness. Is preparing materials for building a fair castle and a bawn, which he means to put in hand for the next spring.

Sir George Hamilton 'is resident with his wife and family. Has built a good house of timber for the present, 62 foot long and thirty foot wide. He brought over some families of Scots, who have built them a bawn and good timber houses.'

In the precinct of Clogher, Sir Thomas Ridgeway, Vice-Treasurer and Treasurer at Wars in Ireland, on 4 May 1610 brought over from London and Devonshire

> 12 carpenters, mostly with wives and families, who have since been resident, employed in felling timber, brought by Patrick McKenna of the Trough, county Monaghan, none being in any part of the barony of Clogher, or else where nearer him, viz., 700 trees, 400 boards and planks, besides a quantity of stone, timber for tenements, with timber ready for the setting up of a water-mill. He is erecting a wardable castle and houses, to be finished about the next Spring. Ten masons, work upon the castle, and two smiths.

In the precinct of Mountjoy, Lord Ochiltree, the chief undertaker, being stayed by contrary winds in Scotland, arrived in Ireland (at the time of our being in Armagh, upon our return home) accompanied with 33 followers, gent. of sort, a minister, some tenants, freeholders and artificers, unto whom he hath passed estates; and hath built for his present use . . . within an old fort, about which he is building a bawn. He has sundry men at work providing materials, and there are in readiness 240 great trees felled and some squared; and is preparing stone, brick, and lime for building a castle, which he means to finish next Spring. There are two ploughs going on his demesne, with some 50 cows, and three score young heifers landed at Iland Magy, in Clandeboy, which are coming to his proportion, with some 12 working mares.

Sir Robert Hepburn, with a middle proportion,

sowed oats and barley the last year upon his land, and reaped this harvest 40 hogsheads of corn; is resident; hath 140 cows, young and old, in stock, and 8 mares. Hath 7 householders, being in number 20 persons; is building a stone house 40 foot long and 20 high, already a story high . . .

In Dungannon precinct Sir Arthur Chichester had 'now masons and workmen to take down such remains of the decayed ruins of the old castle as are yet standing'. Sir Richard Wingfield, Marshal of the Army, 'has a great store of timber for buildings, and will have other materials ready by the beginning of Spring'. Turlough O'Neill 'has removed', but 'none of the rest are removed, nor have made any preparations for building'.[9]

The precinct of Oneilland, reserved for English undertakers, was arguably the most fertile one in the plantation. Carew reported good progress here. The Lord Say and Seale, the chief undertaker, with three thousand acres, had made over his portion to Sir Anthony Cope. His men had 'begun a fair castle of freestone, and other hardstone, 14 or 15 workmen, and 9 carpenters employed'. John Brownlow, with a middle proportion, and his son John, with a small proportion, were 'both resident, and dwelling in an Irish house. Have brought over six carpenters, one mason, a tailor, and six workmen; one freeholder and six tenants upon their land'. Francis Secheverell, with a large proportion, was resident and 'has brought over three masons, one carpenter, one smith, nine labourers, and two women; four horses and a cart'.[10]

THE LONDONERS BEGIN

Though they were the last to be involved in the plantation, and the proportions had yet to be allotted to the companies, the Londoners had made a good start in Coleraine and Derry. Carew, visiting Coleraine in 1611, found more progress here than perhaps anywhere else in the escheated counties.

The plan for Coleraine was roughly hexagonal, with the River Bann on its west side and the other five sides by an earthen rampart, twelve feet high, strengthened by seven bastions and pierced by gates on the south and the east and by a ditch up to forty feet wide and three feet deep. At the centre of two intersecting parallel streets, room was left for a spacious market-place. Forty-three one-storey tenements with dormers were erected, framed with oak and birch, fitted with brick chimneys and roofed with slate. Work was well advanced on fifty other two-storey tenements, and some larger houses had been put up. The largest was already there, put up by Sir Thomas Phillips as his residence. The old church was being given a new roof, and the town also had a water mill, a brew house, a smithy, three lime kilns and a pound for cattle.

On the river a quay had been constructed and, just upstream of it, a small shipyard and a house for a shipwright. Carew found that there were 243 workmen in all, with thirty-four horses and four oxen, equipped with carts, tumbrils, wheelbarrows and quarrying and woodcutting tools. He saw large stores of bricks, tiles and timber; cables, canvas, anchors and other ship equipment; and arms with match and lead. Two miles upstream a quay had been built by the river, with workmen busy hewing the rock to ease the floating of timber downstream. Here there were two barges and four boats on the river; at Portrush four or five Irish cabins for workmen burning local lime in large quantities.

At Derry, however, little progress had been made in putting the plan on paper—similar in design to Coleraine but considerably larger—into effect. Carew reported that the old Church of St Augustine, in Docwra's upper fort, had been repaired and slated, with two stone houses close by, one of them intended for the Bishop of Derry. Though there were large quantities of stone, timber and slate in the vicinity, few other houses had been built. On the river, near Docwra's lower fort, a large quay had been constructed, three hundred feet long and fourteen feet wide. Here a barque of some eighty tons was being built. Altogether 150 men, assisted by twelve horses, were employed here.

Construction at Coleraine and Derry was possible only with a large supply of timber. The woods of Glenconkeyne provided vast quantities. Here, in 1611, eighty-four men, both English and Irish, were engaged in felling, squaring timber and making laths, scaffold poles, the frames of houses and even the frames of two ships. Fifty men, with thirty-three oxen and three horses, hauled this timber to the River Bann, where it was floated downstream to Coleraine, and much of it was shipped along the north coast to the Foyle and Derry.

Though the City of London had been enticed into the plantation of the escheated counties later than most other undertakers, it had actually made an earlier and more respectable start than the great majority of them. And the City, just like almost all undertakers, had made very little progress in removing the native Irish from the countryside and replacing them with British tenants.

Meanwhile, what of Sir Thomas Phillips? How he was to be compensated for surrendering his interests in Coleraine had still to be worked out when the City's articles of agreement had been signed with the King. In July 1610 the City had very reluctantly agreed to let him have two thousand acres in Killetra, in the barony of Loughinsholin. The reluctance was that this was in the heart of valuable mature woodland, urgently needed for building. Taking note of this, the Privy Council in April 1611 decided instead that Phillips should have the castle of Limavady, with three thousand acres adjoining and another five hundred acres around the River Moyola, close to his castle at Toome.

Though the relationship between Phillips and the City had already begun to deteriorate, Sir Thomas began with energy to develop his grant at Limavady. Stone was quarried at Limavady itself, and up to thirty tons of shells were gathered from the shores of Lough Foyle and taken on horseback to Limavady, there to be burned to make mortar. By the time Carew was making his survey, only a few months later, Phillips had built a water mill at Limavady (now called Newtown Limavady, a name it retained for a century and more) and a two-storey inn for travellers between Coleraine and Derry. Other enclaves of property inside the area granted to the City included Captain Edward Doddington's property at Dungiven, scattered church lands and lands granted to a number of native Irish. Carew observed that Doddington had built a strong four-storey structure with a bawn at Dungiven using the ruins of O'Cahan's castle there and put up a number of houses. The Archbishop of Armagh and the Dean and Bishop of Derry had done very little to develop their lands. Both Rowley and Beresford leased portions of this land with much profit to themselves.

As in the other escheated counties, some provision had to be made for native Irish considered deserving enough to receive grants of land. Sir Donal O'Cahan was languishing in prison without a charge being brought against him, but it was considered politic to assign 1,000 acres in total to his wife, Lady Honora, and her two sons, Rory and Donal Óg. Captain Manus O'Cahan got a great proportion of 2,000 acres; Manus McCowy Ballagh O'Cahan and Cowy Ballagh McRichard 1,000 acres each; Owen Keogh O'Mullan and Tomlyn O'Mullan together 500 acres; and others one ballyboe (60 acres) each—thirteen separate freeholds in all, calculated to total 5,980 acres. The Church, the deserving Irish grantees and Sir Thomas Phillips, as a servitor, alone were legally permitted to have natives as tenants on an area covering a little more than a third of what was to become Co. Londonderry.[11]

In November 1612 Rowley was summoned to London by the Irish Society, and there he was given detailed instructions: in Coleraine tenancy agreements were to be made for the new houses there, the gates were to be finished and the drawbridge put in place, and a prison was to be constructed at one of the gate-houses. Rowley was to see to it that the cutting of stone at the 'Leap of Castlerow' was to go ahead, ensuring that there was 'no hurt to the salmon fishings', in order to facilitate the carrying of goods up and down the River Bann.[12]

The tone of the 'Instructions Given to Mr. John Rowley, Agent, Receavour, and Treasurer for the Affairs of the City of London's Plantation in Ireland' clearly indicated much disquiet in the capital. The city fathers were aware that the forests were being plundered and timber exported 'contrary to our order and contrary to the articles' between the Crown and the City. 'Great disorder' in the woods had to be brought to an end. Much 'disorder' had resulted from workmen spending their 'time and substance' in the 'great number of taverns and alehouses'. Rowley was ordered to send 'idle and disordered' workmen back to England; smiths were not to be entrusted with iron and steel worth more than ten pounds; all except one of the ship carpenters were to be dismissed; all 'needless' officers were to be sacked; and the surveyor, Thomas Raven, 'who hath a great stipend', was to have his pay reduced to twenty marks a year. Beresford had written frequently about the 'great want of money to pay workmen and for other occasions', which had caused the Society to 'much marvel considering the sums' already disbursed. And yet the City gave Rowley gold and bills of exchange amounting to £2,017 10s to pay 'arrearages'.

The City was particularly anxious that the work planned for Derry should be speeded up. Rowley was instructed to build 'a town house at the

Derry and under the same to make a place for the court de guard and a prison' to be 'set in the market-place so as it may scour as many streets as may be' and be fitted with a bell hung 'in the top'. Rowley was to consult servitors in the area, including Captain Henry Hart and Captain John Vaughan, about the 'building of the walls of the Derry and making the ditch', who reminded him 'to beware of error committed at Coleraine in making the circuit of the town too great'.[13] The very extensive estates granted to the city had not yet been apportioned to the participating livery companies. Rowley was ordered to 'settle a course for the division of the City's lands'. He was to provide details of the lands in the four baronies divided first into four parts, then every fourth part divided into three

for the better satisfying of the Companies in London to assign every one their proportion, for thereby they will be willing to disburse the several payments and to perform their buildings, etc., which we are enjoined by the articles to perform, having a respect to the goodness or barrenness of the soil, to the nearness of the town and the largeness of the ballyboes.[14]

The Society had heard that pipe-staves had been made in the woods of Loughinsholin and exported overseas 'contrary to our order and our Articles of Agreement, which is very displeasing to us'. Since the worst offender was one of his tenants, Rowley was warned that if this destruction of the forests continued he would be held personally responsible.

The wasting of the woods led directly to a bitter quarrel between the City and Sir Thomas Phillips. Davy Mulhall, one of Phillips's men, had received a peremptory letter from Beresford ordering him to stop interfering with workmen in the woods who were cutting timber and fashioning pipe-staves. This was followed up by a curt letter to Phillips from the Society remarking on his 'intention to domineer over their jurisdiction' and requiring him to stop his meddling.[15] Phillips felt obliged to go back to London in April 1612. He did not get clear possession until 30 December, and he complained, with reason, that he should be compensated for being without land and rent for a year and a half. Bad feeling between the City and the servitor remained.

Other interests which conflicted with the City's grant had to be sorted out. The City had set aside five thousand pounds for this purpose. The old inhabitants of Derry had to wait until March 1612 to get the thousand marks agreed for surrendering their property. Other 'compositions', or compensation payments, had to be made to Sir Randal MacDonnell for the nine townlands adjacent to Coleraine, to the Bishop of Connor for Coleraine rectory, to Sir James Hamilton and Sir Arthur Chichester for fishing rights on the Bann and the Foyle, to Chichester for the castle of Culmore and to Captain Edward Doddington for the castle of Dungiven. Brian Crossagh O'Neill, a freeholder of a small proportion in Dungannon precinct, had his claim to sixteen townlands in Loughinsholin flatly rejected. By the beginning of 1613, apart from the City of London, only native freeholders and Sir Thomas Phillips continued to be proprietors in the county.[16]

Tensions arose also between the City and the Crown. In March 1612 the City presented a list of grievances to the commissioners for Ireland, including the refusal of the old inhabitants of Derry to surrender their interests there. Chichester, instructed to obtain satisfaction for the City on most of its complaints, responded that the Londoners had not yet sent over a single colonist apart from workmen. Its agents had persuaded many natives to stay who he thought would gladly settle elsewhere. Worse still, they had actually invited the Irish from all parts of Tyrone to work for them in Loughinsholin, where they were now more numerous than the Lord Deputy had ever known. Beresford had approached him to ask that natives be allowed to stay for a time. When the Londoners were faced with the Lord Deputy's accusations they responded to the commissioners that they had done more than all the other undertakers. They had spent £25,000, though their articles bound them only to lay out £15,000. They had not invited in natives from Tyrone but had asked only for their retention for two or three years.

The King himself now intervened. On 21 December he informed Chichester that he wanted a thorough survey of the whole plantation without delay. He continued:

And because the Londoners here pretend the expense of great sums of money in that service, and yet (as we are informed) the outward appearance of it in their works are very small, we require you to give us a true account of what they have done and make as near as you can a true Valuation of it, that they may discover their ignorance or abuse of their ministers to whom they have committed that employment.[17]

Outright conflict was averted by an agreement to appoint a commission to sort out the boundaries of the four thousand acres to be annexed to Derry and the three thousand to Coleraine. An indication, later confirmed, was given that the natives could stay until Mayday 1615. The passing of the City's patent would not have to await the conclusions of the boundary commissioners.

MARKING OUT THE SOCIETY'S TWELVE PROPORTIONS IN CO. LONDONDERRY

In June 1613 the Common Council of the City of London decided to send two special commissioners to Londonderry. After so much outlay the City was anxious to know what had been done so far and to take steps to improve progress, especially in building in Derry. In particular it was increasingly unhappy with the conduct of its chief agent, John Rowley. Dr Christopher Hampton informed the Privy Council that Rowley had induced his predecessor, the late Dr Babington, to demise to Rowley eighty-one townlands for an annual rent of £65. Rowley also had got a grant of all timber on diocesan lands, leading to the felling of three thousand trees and the export of hundreds of thousands of pipe-staves to Spain. After receiving detailed instructions, two assistants of the Irish Society, George Smithes and Matthias Springham, accompanied by the City's solicitor, set off and arrived in Dublin early in August.

The Lord Deputy was more than helpful. He secured the release of a barque carrying goods to the City's plantation, which had been seized by pirates, for an outlay of fifteen pounds. The two commissioners arrived in the north, and it did not take them long to find both Rowley and Beresford guilty of negligence and of lining their own pockets at the City's expense. Both were found guilty of setting up rival markets, breweries and water mills, and of despoiling the woods of Loughinsholin. Beresford alone had made forty thousand pipe-staves. The workmen at Derry and Coleraine, numbering about four hundred, were between seven and twelve weeks in arrears of pay. The commissioners paid all their arrears and set a thousand pounds aside so that in future they would be paid at least once a month. The City had been defrauded in carting expenses, and two barques, the *Dove* and the *Lark*, plying between Derry and Coleraine, had been put to unauthorised use. The commissioners sold the *Dove,* sent the *Lark* back to London and issued a contract to carry materials between Derry and Coleraine for 6s 6d a ton, saving the City about half of previous costs. In the store at Coleraine nails had been allowed to become rusty and butter and cheese rotted. Loaves in the town were found to be three ounces under weight. Ferries across the Foyle and the Bann were overcharging.

In Coleraine, at a cost of £10,550, 116 houses had been put up, but many were badly built, and repairs cost too much. A good many had not been let because the rents were too high, as no land was attached to them. Land was allotted by the commissioners. The town had a handsome wall surrounding it, but it should have been built of stone and with a smaller circumference. £1,400 had been spent on fortifications. The streets were filthy, and the commissioners ordered that they be paved before they left. The 'Cutts'—a passage hewn into the Salmon Leap to help boats down the river to reach the sea—should never have been begun, the commissioners thought; but they set money aside to ensure that it would be completed.

In Derry the commissioners set out land for the bishop and dean. The fishery, the principal source of profit, was re-let for three years at a higher annual rate of £866 13s 4d, raised from £600 a year. The commissioners 'trod out' the ground for the city's fortifications with the advice and assistance of a Captain Panton and then of other 'Captaynes of speciall note and good experyence'. Work should not begin until enough stone and lime had been made available. The castle of Culmore, a fort downstream vital for the city's defence, was in a ruinous condition and its keeper unfit for the job. Captain John Baker, an alderman of the city, was put in charge. The commissioners presented the church in each town with a communion cup of gilt plate.[18]

Smithes and Springham, assisted by Captain Doddington, then had to carry out their instruction to divide the county lands of twelve proportions of approximately equal value. To the surprise of their mapmaker, Thomas Raven, these proportions were not of equal area; as the City's journal explained, the division was made 'according to the goodness or illness of each severall ballyboe . . . due considerac'on being had of the neareness or remoteness to the townes and Rivers and of the meanes for materials to build and plant them'.[19] This task completed, Springham remained in Ireland, and Smithes returned to make his report to the Common Council on 8 November. The commissioners were praised for their actions, and, not surprisingly, it was decided to dismiss Rowley from the City's service. He was ordered to hand over any money still in his hands to Springham and return to London to face charges. It was time now to allot the proportions to the livery companies.

THE LUCK OF THE DRAW

Meanwhile the fifty-five London Companies, regularly levied for contributions to the enterprise, were busily arranging themselves into twelve associations to obtain by lot the proportions divided up by Smithes and Springham. The companies had to put forty thousand pounds up front, and the larger companies combined with smaller ones, each to form a consortium to gather together enough cash to entitle them to one of the twelve proportions. For example, the Goldsmiths, with a share of £2,999, were joined with the Cordwainers, Paint-Stainers and Armourers, whose shares were £250, £44 and £40, respectively. The Drapers had one associate only, the Tallow-chandlers, while the Vintners had nine: Curriers, Plumbers, Poulters, Blacksmiths, Weavers, Woodmongers, Fruiterers, Tylers and Bricklayers. The Coopers and Brownbakers surrendered their interests to the City, and the Haberdashers to two of their own members. The Bowyers and Fletchers, contributing £2 10s and £10, respectively, joined the Clothworkers. Others were to sell their interests later. The Fishmongers, associated with the Glaziers and Basketmakers, bought out the Leathersellers (who had already bought out the Plasterers' share) in 1611.

On 17 December 1613, at a court of the Common Council, the City sword-bearer, with great pomp and ceremony, drew the lots for the twelve proportions of the Londonderry Plantation. Some of the proportions were split to avoid taking in church lands and lands assigned to the natives. The result of this lottery was as follows: New Buildings (Goldsmiths), Muff (Grocers), Ballykelly (Fishmongers), Artikelly/Ballycastle (Haberdashers), Killowen/Articlave (Clothworkers), Macosquin (Merchant Taylors), Agivey (Ironmongers), Movanagher (Mercers), Vintnerstown (Vintners), Magherafelt/Salterstown (Salters), Moneymore (Drapers) and Dungiven/Crosalt (Skinners). Vintnerstown soon became known as Bellaghy, and Muff was later renamed Eglinton to avoid confusion with Muff in Co. Donegal. By the luck of the draw, the Grocers, Fishmongers and Goldsmiths got what eventually turned out to be the most fertile and accessible proportions. The Ironmongers found that their proportion was split into no fewer than seven estates not joined to each other. The Drapers and Skinners were left with the most inaccessible proportions, with much infertile land. To the dismay of representatives of all the companies, Alderman Cockayne (soon to be succeeded by Alderman George Smithes) announced that all the forty thousand pounds already raised had been spent, and the court felt that it had no choice but to levy another five thousand to be paid to the chamberlain by 1 February 1614.

The actual total area of lands in the new county of Londonderry was 508,700 acres, or 794.9 square miles. The livery companies had 57.3 per cent, the Church 22.8 per cent, the native freeholders 10.2 per cent, the

Hugh O'Neill, Earl of Tyrone, described by Henry IV of France as the third-greatest general in Europe, came close to breaking English royal power in Ireland, but his ultimate defeat and exile paved the way for the Plantation of Ulster. No contemporary portrait survives: this is a nineteenth-century painting, possibly a copy of one in the Vatican. (© *Getty Images / Hulton Archive*)

Charlemont Fort, built by Mountjoy in 1602, by the River Blackwater on the borders of Armagh and Tyrone. The construction of strategically placed forts, none more than four hours' gallop from another, completed the subjugation of Gaelic Ulster. (© *Topfoto / National Archives*)

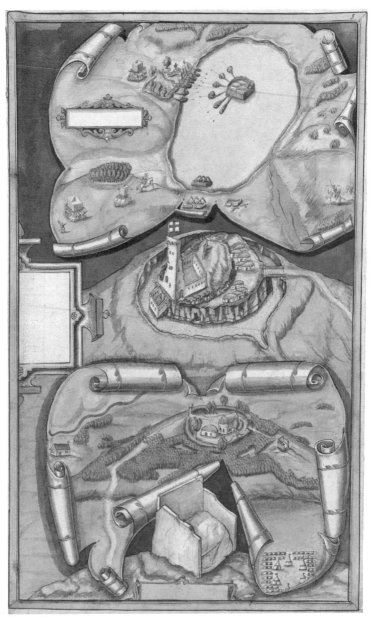

Richard Bartlett's depiction of Mountjoy's final victory in Tyrone in 1602–3. At the top, Crown forces make a successful assault on a crannóg used for storing munitions; in the centre, the flag of St George flies over the Earl of Tyrone's castle of Dungannon; and below is the O'Hagan rath of Tullaghoge and the O'Neill inauguration stone chair, subsequently smashed by the Lord Deputy. (© *National Library of Ireland*)

A portrait of James 1, painted by Daniel Mytens in 1621, four years before the King's death. The first ruler of England, Scotland, Wales and Ireland, James regarded the Plantation of Ulster as the most important project of his reign. (© *Alamy / World History Archive*)

Monument in St Nicholas's Parish Church in Carrickfergus to Sir Arthur Chichester, Lord Deputy of Ireland, 1605–16, his wife, Lady Letitia, and between them their son, who died in infancy. Chichester had charge of affairs during the most critical phase of the British colonisation of Ulster. (© *Crown copyright. Reproduced with the permission of the Controller of Her Majesty's Stationery Office.*)

The fifteenth-century O'Donnell castle of Donegal, taken over by Sir Basil Brooke in 1603. Given a grant of £250, Brooke renovated the castle, added an extension in the English style (to the left of O'Donnell's keep in this picture) and erected a bawn to surround it. Later his heirs acquired a great estate in Fermanagh, confiscated from the Maguires. (© *Photolibrary*)

Contrary to the popular view, Dunluce is a planter's castle. Sir Randal MacDonnell built this fortress on the site of the ruined MacQuillan Castle. Though a fervent Catholic, Sir Randal (who became the 1st Earl of Antrim) successfully enticed many Scots Presbyterians to settle on his lands. His son, the 2nd Earl, spent large sums erecting a magnificent hall attached to it for the benefit of his wife, the dowager Duchess of Buckingham. (© *Getty Images*)

Sir Josias Bodley
headed a survey
of confiscated
lands in 1609.
Accompanied by
eight
cartographers, he
produced maps
for naming and
marking the
'mears and
bounds' of every
townland to
assist King James
in his allocation
of estates. This
one shows the
barony of
Strabane (east is
at the top of the
map), with the
Mourne and its
tributaries, the
Derg and the
Finn, flowing
into Lough Foyle.
(© Topfoto /
National Archives
/ HIP)

The map of the barony of Loughtee in Co. Cavan, showing 'polls' and other land divisions, produced by the Bodley Survey of 1609 and coloured in in England. This land was granted to English undertakers. Here John Taylor of Cambridgeshire (probably the only undertaker to arrive anywhere in Ulster) got the proportion of Aghateeduff. The Attorney-General, Sir John Davies, received most land in this barony. (© *Topfoto / National Archives / Heritages*)

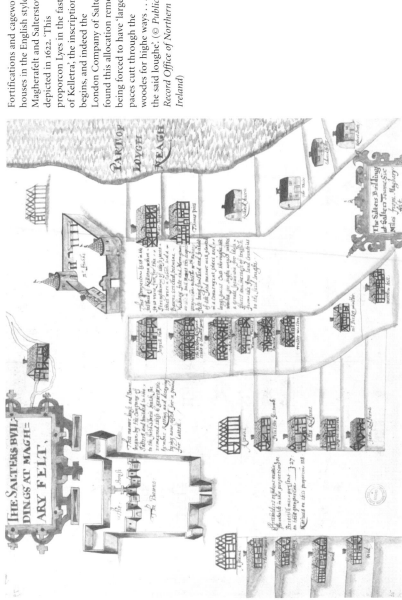

Fortifications and cagework houses in the English style at Magherafelt and Salterstown, depicted in 1622. 'This proporcon Lyes in the fastnes of Kelletra', the inscription begins, and indeed the London Company of Salters found this allocation remote, being forced to have 'large paces cutt through the woodes for highe ways . . . to the said loughe'. (© *Public Record Office of Northern Ireland*)

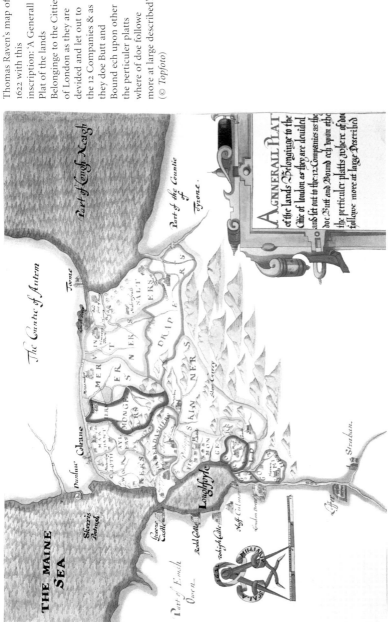

Thomas Raven's map of 1622 with this inscription: 'A Generall Plat of the lands Belonginge to the Cittie of London as they are devided and let out to the 12 Companies & as they doe Butt and Bound ech upon other the perticuler platts where of doe followe more at large described'. (© Topfoto)

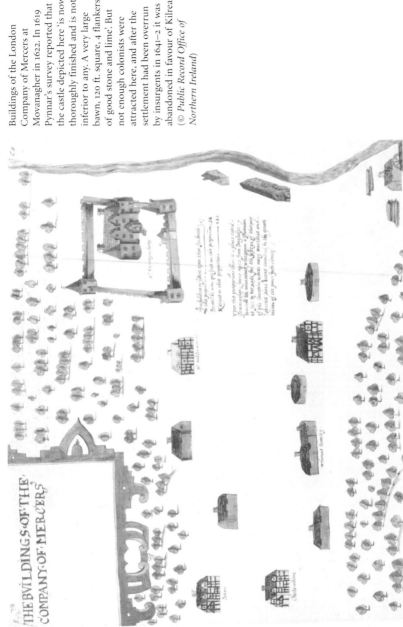

Buildings of the London Company of Mercers at Movanagher in 1622. In 1619 Pynnar's survey reported that the castle depicted here 'is now thoroughly finished and is not inferior to any. A very large bawn, 120 ft. square, 4 flankers, of good stone and lime'. But not enough colonists were attracted here, and after the settlement had been overrun by insurgents in 1641–2 it was abandoned in favour of Kilrea. (© *Public Record Office of Northern Ireland*)

'The Platt of the Cittie of London: Derrie as it Stand built and Fortyfyed', a picture-map by Thomas Raven completed for the Phillips Survey in 1622. In that year there were 109 families living in slated houses with long back gardens. The Bishop's Palace dominates the centre. In the right-hand corner, just beyond the walls, kilns are burning lime for making mortar. (© *Public Record Office of Northern Ireland*)

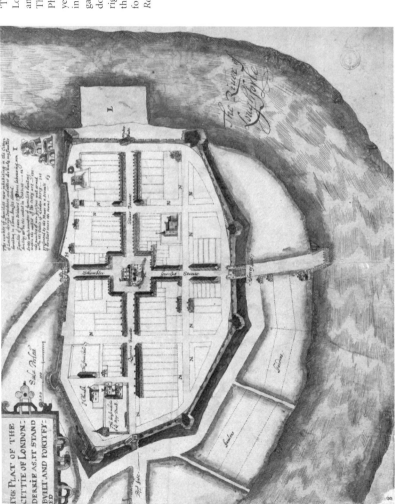

Monea Castle, built for Archbishop Malcolm Hamilton six miles north-west of Enniskillen. An imposing structure in the distinctive Scots baronial style, it bears a striking resemblance to Claypotts Castle at Broughty Ferry in Angus. The strong bawn surrounding it had two flanker towers, one of which housed pigeons to provide fresh meat in winter. (© *Getty Images*)

St Columb's Cathedral in the city of Londonderry. The foundation-stone was laid in 1628, and the building, constructed by William Parrott for £3,400 and supervised by Sir John Vaughan, was completed in 1633. Though much altered since, it has a claim to be the finest building put up during the plantation. (© *Ordnance Survey of the County of Londonderry, 1837*)

The walls of Derry, with St Columb's Cathedral behind (*above*). Londonderry was the last city or town in Ireland to be enclosed by stone walls, and it was probably the last walled city to be constructed anywhere in Europe. Though they were exposed to cannon fire from higher ground, the walls—24 feet high and 6 feet thick—proved impregnable in the siege of 1688–9. (© Photolibrary)

The Watergate, Enniskillen (*right*). Next to the wall of Hugh Maguire's 'broken castle', Captain William Cole erected this imposing fortification in front of the keep, with its own well, upper walkway and brick chimney. The flankers—two attractive corbelled turrets—were projected in such a way as to protect the wall on both sides. (© Alamy / EcoJoe)

Thomas Raven's map of Coleraine, begun by Sir Thomas Phillips and taken over by the London Companies. The commissioners of 1622 found the earthen rampart walls too weak for effective defence; the stone flankers and wall by the river (between A and D) are depicted as a suggested improvement, as is the bridge (C). The Clothworkers' castle and settlement at Killowen can be seen on the left bank of the Lower Bann. (© *Public Record Office of Northern Ireland*)

A nineteenth-century copy of a ground plan of Belfast in 1685. The plan looks south: Belfast Castle (accidentally burned down in 1708) dominates the town; the Farset is dammed to power mills and flows down what is now High Street, with the market house (at Cornmarket) and the parish church (rebuilt as St George's) on the right bank; ships anchor where the Farset joins the Lagan (now the site of the Albert Memorial Clock). (© Public Record Office of Northern Ireland)

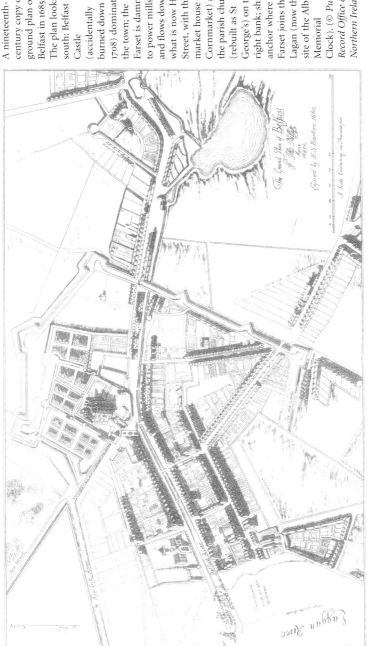

The Grand Plan of Belfast
Ano 1685

Copyed by H.S. Barton 1860.

A Scale Containing one Thousand feet

Laggan River

Bellaghy Bawn, erected by the London Company of Vintners. The original fort had two circular towers at opposite corners and a square tower at another corner. Built of brick on stone footings, with a gun platform inside one wall, the bawn (though much altered and modernised) is still in use, and the original tower, seen here, is a museum to the poet Seamus Heaney, born and raised nearby. (© *Alamy / JoeFox CountyDerry*)

A contemporary English propaganda sheet publicising the 1641 massacres. The most notorious atrocity was at Portadown in the middle of November. According to Elizabeth Price, the insurgents drove the British colonists 'off the bridge into the water and then and there instantly and most barbarously drowned the most of them . . . or else shot them to death in the water'. (© *Topfoto / Topham / Fotomas*)

Irish Society 5.9 per cent (the city of Londonderry and Coleraine with attached lands) and Sir Thomas Phillips 3.8 per cent.[20] Like the other Ulster undertakers, the companies were bound by the Articles of Plantation (which included removing all natives from their proportions); but unlike them they had to submit to the permanent supervision of the Honourable the Irish Society and contribute to the upkeep of Coleraine and the city of Londonderry.

SIR JOSIAS BODLEY'S SURVEY OF 1614: STIRRING UP THE 'COMPANIES TO BE PLANTING & BUILDING'

During an early stage in planning the plantation, Sir Francis Bacon had urged King James to monitor the progress of colonisation by regular surveys. The King certainly took this advice. Beginning with the Carew Survey of 1611, he ordered another in December 1612 (which has not survived). Then, in June 1614, Lord Deputy Chichester was ordered to have a new survey to make a valuation of the work done by the City of London on its lands. The experienced royal servant Sir Josias Bodley, the Director-General and Overseer of Fortifications in Ireland, was appointed to carry out this task.

The King was deeply perturbed by Bodley's report, which opened with this disquieting paragraph:

> Haveing taken an exacte survey of the works and plantacon performed by the Cittie of London, I cannot find that either in the one or the other they ever intended his Majesties satisfacc'on and regarded the true end and drifte of his favourable graunte soe that whatsoever they talke of great masses of wealth by them expended, naming what somes they please, yet of anie reall plantacon for fortificacon to the purpose (the onlie meanes of settinge and secureing these partes which they have undertaken) they have little or nothing to say.

Apart from workmen and labourers and a few voluntary colonists, the City had not sent over any colonists to either Coleraine or the city of Londonderry. The walls around Coleraine, though completed, were weak and needed larger ramparts, the surrounding ditch needed to be deepened, and the gates were constructed only of timber cagework. Few houses there were capable of withstanding the weather. In the city three hundred pounds had been spent in preparing stone and moving earth, but no work had begun on erecting the walls. In fact he could not understand the engineer's design and doubted whether the defences when finished would be any use. Had it not been for the Lord Deputy's conscientious activity in colonising his Inishowen grant and seeing to fortifications there, the whole district would be in constant danger. Not enough adjacent land had been made available to the citizens in both towns, and so they were likely to be impoverished and alienated. Bodley was scornful of the City's expenditure:

I dare confidentlie affirme that if their collec'ons from the Cittie to this end amount as they saye to above fifteen thousand pounds, then hath above twentie thousand of those poundes gone some other waies then directlie towards their buildings and plantings in this Country.

In the county lands almost nothing had been done apart from sending over agents—men Bodley thought were poorly qualified—and from something of a start made by the Salters. Some of the companies, contrary to the King's wishes, had made over their proportions. In short, Bodley concluded, the Londoners

have neither builte the number of houses required nor fortified their townes as they ought, nor planted the country as the verye name of plantation itself enioyneth them, nor given anie testimonie by their course of proceeding hitherto that they have anie purpose by their endeavour to deserve his Majesties soe Royal and bountiful graunte unto them, as if nothing els hade beene intended by it but to make them gainers.[21]

Some of Bodley's charges were incorrect: the proportions he named had not been alienated, and a larger number of British settlers were arriving than he stated. Nevertheless, there is no doubting that a slow start had been made.

The City was only too well aware that it was obliged to remove all the native Irish from their proportions by 1 May 1615. This was an impossible deadline, and so, early in the year, the City petitioned the City Council, asking that those Irish who were prepared to take the Oath of Supremacy, conform to the established church and adopt English customs might be allowed to stay as tenants. The Privy Council commended this proposal, but before anything could be done the King received Bodley's report. He was furious and fired off an indignant letter to Chichester on 25 March. He acknowledged Bodley's 'care and industry' in preparing the report, and continued:

> We have examined, viewed, and reviewed with our own eye every part hereof and find, greatly to our discontentment, the slow progression of that plantation, some few only of the British undertakers, servitors, and natives having as yet proceeded effectually to the accomplishing of such things in all points as are required of them by the Articles of the Plantation.

Most seemed only concerned with 'present profit'. The King could have

> converted those large territories of our escheated lands to the great improvement of the revenues of our Crown here. But we chose rather, for the safety of that country and the civilising of that people, to depart with the inheritance of them at extreme undervalues and to make a plantation of them.

For that reason James had decided to give them further time, to 31 August 1616, to carry out their obligations. Another survey would be carried out then to assess progress:

> And we are resolved shall be final and peremptory unto them; and at which time we are determined to seize into our hands the lands of any man whatsoever, without respect of persons, whether be a British undertaker, servitor, or native, that shall be found idle in performing any of the Articles of the Plantation to which he was enjoined.

The difficulty the London Companies had in finding suitable men to carry out their obligations is illustrated by the fact that some of them engaged the disgraced Beresford and Rowley as their agents. Rowley, indeed, had been elected member of Parliament for the county of Londonderry. Now he indicated that the King's letter was having some effect. Acting as their agent, he wrote to the Drapers in May 1615 warning them that 'the king's last l're hath not onlie stirred upp the most that are for the other companies to be planting & building, but also all the Servitors & undertakers, soe as manie of those workmen whom I intended to have imploied . . . are now unwillinglie settled with others'. He added: 'There is now noe expectation of favour to any and the least to London, much being looked for at your hands'.[22]

BUILDING THE CITY WALLS

With the King's deadline of 31 August 1616 very much in mind, the Irish Society set about finding colonists, beginning with Coleraine and the city of Londonderry. In March 1616 each of the twelve companies was instructed to provide one or two craftsmen and their families, with tools and other necessary equipment, ready for sailing from London by the end of May. These were not to be disreputable or drunkards but men 'that fear God'. The most suitable craftsmen would be weavers of common cloth, fustians and new stuffs, trimmers of hats and hatband-makers, locksmiths, farriers, tanners and fellmongers, feltmakers, ironmakers, glassmakers, pewterers, turners, tallow-chandlers, dyers and curriers, basketmakers and coast-fishermen. The Society would be sending over twelve boys from Christ's Hospital and other poor children to serve as servants and apprentices—native Irish were not to be taken on as apprentices. The companies had to repair the churches on their proportions and furnish each one with a bible, prayer book and communion cup.

At the same time Alderman Peter Proby and Matthias Springham, accompanied despite his protests by the City's solicitor, Clement Moss, were sent to see what progress was being made and how the money was being spent. In Dublin they were entertained by the Lords Justices, who praised the work being done in the city of Londonderry and gave advice on how to remove the natives. Arriving in Coleraine, they found that constant labour was needed to keep the earthen walls in repair but that the ditch surrounding them was fitted with pens and sluices to hold in the spring water, and that next the River Bann palisades had been built. The commissioners themselves supervised the completion of two large drawbridges. By now there were 116 houses in the town, but because the timber walls were being damaged by the weather the commissioners ordered that the dormers be slated. All future houses were to be constructed of stone. A subsidy of twenty pounds and a long lease of sixty years were offered to anyone who would build a new house of four or five rooms.

Proby and Springham called a town meeting to inquire into complaints made by the recently dismissed town recorder, John Wilkinson. By a show of hands the citizens agreed that Wilkinson's allegations had been untrue, malicious and frivolous. The cutting at the Salmon Leap was considered of little value, considering how much had been spent on it. A harbour had been proposed for Portrush, but after visiting it the commissioners decided that it was too rocky and exposed. If the town decided to build a harbour there it would be at the citizens' own expense, though the City would contribute two hundred pounds towards its construction.

In the city of Londonderry, Proby and Springham found the walls half built. The supervision by Captain Baker of Culmore attracted praise. The walls would be strong when finished, but the commissioners ordered that their height be raised from sixteen to nineteen feet. Two drawbridges had been finished, and a gate was being erected. As the church being planned would not be able to accommodate half the citizens, the commissioners advised the City to authorise a larger one on a new plan. All but five or six of the city's 215 houses were finished, and some others had been privately built both inside and outside the walls. The commissioners appointed William Castle as water-bailiff and searcher, with instructions to supply and maintain sufficient beacons and buoys. As a philanthropic gesture Matthias Springham financed the building of a Free School, and three hundred acres were then allocated for its maintenance. Swords of office were presented to the mayors of the two towns. The sum of £95 was allocated to cover the expenses of the four burgesses—two each from Coleraine and the city—and of the two knights of the shire of Londonderry, John Baker and John Rowley, for their attendance at the Irish Parliament of 1613–15. The value of the salmon fishery is indicated by the fact that the two lessees offered a thousand pounds to have their lease renewed.

The commissioners left on 12 August and gave their report to the Common Council on 1 October. In spite of continuing anxieties about Coleraine's defences, it was clear that great progress was being made in the city of Londonderry and that blatant asset-stripping and corruption had been rooted out. The Council authorised another levy of £2,500; this raised the total raised since the allotment of the lands to £60,000.[23]

The native Irish of the new county of Londonderry received only 10.2 per cent of the land. Their principal lord, Donal Ballagh O'Cahan, was languishing in the Tower of London, his fate still undecided. Their most cherished lands and fisheries had been seized; their forests were being plundered; new fortifications rising up gave visible proof of their subjugation; their beliefs were now castigated as being Romish and barbarous; and they lived in daily expectation of expulsion from their native territories to make room for newcomers speaking an alien tongue, abiding by laws they hardly understood and abiding by a religion they found heretical.

Chapter 10 ～

'NOT A MORE DISCONTENTED PEOPLE IN CHRISTENDOM': THE NATIVE IRISH AND THE PLANTATION

'THE GREATEST CRUELTY THAT WAS EVER INFLICTED UPON ANY PEOPLE'

In the spring of 1613, during elections for the forthcoming meeting of the Irish Parliament in Dublin, Sir Turlough MacHenry O'Neill of the Fews made his way to the shirehouse in Armagh. There, as a candidate for one of the two county seats, he arrived with a large party of his freeholders to cast his vote. The sentry refused him entry. Turned away, Sir Turlough and his followers held their own election, returning Sir Turlough and Henry McShane O'Neill as the county members. Of course this was not approved, and Sir Toby Caulfield and Sir John Bourchier were duly elected to represent Co. Armagh.

Sir Turlough was the most prominent of the 'deserving Irish' in the Plantation of Ulster. He had been granted 9,900 acres, the largest single allocation of lands to a Gaelic Irishman. A half-brother of the Earl of Tyrone, now languishing in exile in Rome, Sir Turlough was the most senior O'Neill remaining in Ulster. The immediate reason for the government authorities blocking Sir Turlough at the poll was that they were determined to prevent a Catholic majority in Parliament. Armagh had not yet enough British Protestant settlers to prevent freeholders there electing Catholic natives. Thirty-eight additional seats had been assigned to Ulster. This was achieved by the creation of new corporations, so hastily carried out that several did not receive their charters until after the election. Some, such as the city of Londonderry and Coleraine, deserved incorporation, but many were no more than villages—sites upon which plantation towns were still to be built. The creation of new boroughs ensured that the former Old English recusant majority disappeared; the aggregate result was a Protestant majority of thirty-two members of Parliament. Old English lords of the Pale protested to the King against the packing of Parliament through the elevation of 'beggarly cottages' to the status of corporations, 'that by the votes of a few elected for that purpose, under the name of burgesses, extreme penal laws should be imposed upon your subjects'.[1]

Sir Turlough's treatment was an open admission that the term 'deserving' was fast becoming meaningless when applied to the Gaelic Irish of Ulster. Lord Deputy Chichester, who, with the help of Attorney-General Davies, had engineered this packing of Parliament, nevertheless had for some time been anxious about the way the indigenous population had been treated. Commenting on how the Gaelic Irish 'repine greatly at their fortunes and the small quantity of land left to them', he observed in 1610 how the natives of Ulster

> especially those of the counties of Tyrone, Ardmagh and Colerayne, who, having reformed themselves in their habit and course of life beyond others and the common expectation held of them, (for all that were able had put on English apparel, and promised to live in townreeds, and to leave their creaghting) had assured themselves to better conditions from the King than those they lived in under their former landlords: but now they say they have not land given them . . . which is very grievous unto them.[2]

Sir Toby Caulfield, before he became a member of Parliament, remarked that as a result of the plantation 'it will shortly be many of their cases to be woodkerne of necessity, no other means being left for them to keep a being in this world than to live as long as they can by scrambling'. He wrote again to the Lord Deputy late in 1610 warning him that the Irish were seething with discontent, daily anticipating the return of the Earl of Tyrone with a Spanish army and hoping

> that the summer being spent, before the Commissioners come down, so great a cruelty will not be offered as to remove them from their houses upon the edge of winter, and in the very season when they are to supply themselves in making their harvest, and they think, that by

the next spring, if ever Tyrone can or will come, he will wait for no longer time, since delays and further deferring cannot be less prejudice to him than the utter ruin and extirpation of his dearest friends.

They hold discourse among themselves, that if this course had been taken with them in war time, it had had some colour of justice; but having been pardoned and their lands given them, and having lived under law ever since, and being ready to submit themselves to mercy for any offence they can be charged with since their pardoning, they conclude it to be the greatest cruelty that was ever inflicted upon any people.

In his view there was 'not a more discontented people in Christendom'.[3] Now, as the Irish Parliament met in 1613, the King expressed his concern that the Gaelic Irish were engaging in the 'preparation of arms', mentioning that he had heard that weapons were being concealed in 'woods and other secret places' in the vicinity of Belturbet, Co. Cavan.[4]

'HER CHIEFTAINS HOLD NOT THEIR ANCESTORS' SOIL'
Immediately after the Flight of the Earls a proclamation was issued from Dublin Castle promising the Gaelic inhabitants of the north that they would 'not be disturbed in the peaceable possession of their lands so long as they demean themselves as dutiful subjects'. Ten days later Lord Deputy Chichester made a promise 'to every man of note or good desert so much as he can conveniently stock and manure by himself and his tenants and followers, and so much more as by conjecture he shall be able so to stock and manure for five years to come.'[5]

The Commissioners on Irish affairs in London, however, had decided against this generous approach. In 1610 the Lord Deputy had been instructed to allocate land to the Irish amounting to only 58,000 acres or thereabouts. This land was for large grants intended for the greater Irish lords. Another 37,000 acres were to be assigned in smaller lots to lesser lords. Altogether 280 native Irish obtained plantation land grants in the six escheated counties, but of these only 26 were given estates of a thousand acres or more.[6] The list of the names of the main Irish beneficiaries was effectively a roll-call of the rivals of the O'Neill, O'Donnell and Maguire lords who had sailed out of Lough Swilly in September 1607. They included Sir Turlough MacHenry O'Neill, who had been pardoned in 1603, and other O'Neills who had often been allies of the Crown; and Mulmory MacSweeney, who had testified against the earl. O'Hanlons, who had fought against the Earl of Tyrone, got 1,340 acres—indeed, Sir Oghy (Eochaidh) O'Hanlon also received an annuity of eighty pounds in spite of the bad behaviour of his son Oghy Óg in joining O'Doherty's revolt.

Conor Roe Maguire had surrendered his three baronies in Co. Fermanagh in full expectation that, as a reward for his loyalty, they would be returned to him. Instead he received back 5,980 acres, less than a third of his lands, and his ancestral seat of Lisnaskea was assigned to a Scottish undertaker. It was particularly galling to him that the Enniskillen branch, headed by Brian Maguire, was allotted 2,380 acres, though these men had fought for Hugh O'Neill until near the end of the war. In addition, Brian's brother Turlough received the 500-acre estate of Inseyloughgease (shortly afterwards renamed Tempo).[7] In Co. Cavan, Mulmory MacHugh O'Reilly got 2,000 acres in the barony of Clanmahon, Hugh O'Reilly and Mulmory MacPhilip O'Reilly 1,000 acres each in the barony of Tullygarvey, and Phelim McGauran 1,000 acres in the barony of Tullyhaw.

The descendants of Shane O'Neill, pushed aside by the Earl of Tyrone, received considerable grants in Armagh and Fermanagh, but their hopes of greater reinstatement were dashed. Davies disliked Gaelic chroniclers and 'rhymers' but appreciated their help during the land surveys, and several received modest grants. About a fifth of the confiscated lands in the six counties were allocated to the 'deserving' Irish, but extensive grants were only for the lifetime of the recipients. The Earl of Tyrone's half-brother Art MacBaron O'Neill got two thousand acres, but this grant was to revert to the Crown after the death of himself and his wife. He too was obliged to move from Oneilland—the most sought-after area in Co. Armagh—to the less fertile barony of Orior, in the south of the county.[8] In the new county of Londonderry the native Irish were assigned only 10.2 per cent of the land.

In Co. Donegal, Lady Ineen Dubh O'Donnell, who had outlived her sons Red Hugh and the Earl of Tyrconnell and had given information against Niall Garbh O'Donnell (for long her sons' rival), got 596 acres. The earl's grand uncle Hugh MacHugh Dubh O'Donnell received 1,000 acres; but both he and Lady Ineen got these estates only for the term of their lives. When they died their lands were to go the servitors Sir Richard Hansard and Sir Ralph Bingley. In this county the MacSweeneys and the O'Boyles, former tributary lords of the O'Donnells, were the most fortunate native Irish grantees. The four remaining sub-chieftains—Donal MacSweeney Fanad, Sir Mulmurry MacSweeney Doe, Donagh MacSweeney Banagh and Turlough O'Boyle (the Lord of Boylagh)—each received a grant of 2,000 acres. Another MacSweeney from Fanad, Walter MacSweeney, was given 896 acres. These were smaller than their previous lordships but larger than the lands they had had formerly in demesne; while they had to pay rent and other dues to the Crown, these were probably less burdensome than paying tribute to the O'Donnells, supplying fighting men to them and having troops billeted on their lands. However, many had to uproot themselves to the new barony of Kilmacrenan, west of the River Swilly, and all lost their castles, including Doe, considered the strongest in Ulster.

Amongst the large number of native Irish who received small grants—many of them a 'quarter', thought to contain 128 acres—were Caffar O'Donnell, the eldest son of Hugh MacHugh Dubh, the O'Donnells of Portlough, and Lughaidh Ó Cléirigh, who was to write a life of Red Hugh O'Donnell. Others got nothing, including the O'Gallagher chieftain, Brian MacTurlough O'Gallagher, foster-father to the Earl of Tyrconnell—no doubt this was for fear that he would remain loyal to surviving O'Donnells in exile in Flanders. The O'Donnells of Glenfinn had possessed forty-three quarters of land, thought to be 12,900 acres. Their chief, Niall Garbh, who had long striven to be nominated the Earl of Tyrconnell, now languished in the Tower of London on suspicion that he had been embroiled in O'Doherty's rebellion, dying there in 1626. His family received no grants. A poem written to commemorate his death summed up the plight of all the conquered natives:

His descendants are without a patch of ground to stand on,
They who of old were beams of strength,
Conn of the Hundred Battles' race,
Long the disgrace, they for whom
Fiontain's soil was once fittingly bespread with colours . . .

Her hunting woods are streets,
Her people are but vassals,
Her chieftains hold not their ancestors' soil,
The hero's wounds are the reason of it.[9]

The Gaelic Irish in the six escheated counties had been granted only about 20 per cent of the land. In addition, the native grantees had to pay higher rents than the British planters (£10 13s 4d for every thousand acres), carry out substantial building obligations, give up transhumance ('creaghting'), farm by methods prevailing in the Pale, abide by English law and adapt to English practice in estate management. Many had to move and begin again away from their home territories. Some historians regard the treatment they received as reasonably generous. Most, however, would now agree with the opinion expressed by Aidan Clarke in 1976:

> Few of the favoured Irish received grants of the land which they actually occupied; none received as much as they believed themselves entitled to. They had every reason to remain resentful and unreconciled, and their discontent merged with that of the majority, who had received nothing, to generate a hostility that endangered the success of the project.[10]

The great majority of the 'deserving Irish' were to find it difficult to adapt to the new regime, particularly in managing their estates and financial affairs. All over Ulster in the years that followed, native proprietors were to be found mortgaging much of their land, selling off townland after townland, and many became hopelessly indebted. The aftermath of the Elizabethan-Jacobean conquest was felt most acutely by the Gaelic elite. The Antrim poet Fear Flatha Ó Gnímh regretted that he had not been taught a practical trade:

> Alas that the fosterer in lore did not teach the breaking of steeds
>   or the steering of ships, or the yoking of ploughs behind oxen,
>   to the men who compose lays.
> Woe to the scholar who knows not some craft that would be no cause
>   to censure, that he might join timbers, or shape a vat, ere he attained
>   the service of learning.
> The honour of poesy is departed;
> The credit of guardianship is gone,
> So that the school of Ireland's land were better
> As husbandmen of the ploughland.[11]

Those who actually farmed the land had in most cases simply changed their landlords, but that does not mean they were content. On the undertakers' estates they lived in constant fear of being forcibly removed. With no security of tenure, with their burdensome rents set by informal arrangements from year to year, and with their status severely reduced, the natives yearned for a return to the old order. All societies at various stages in their history have had to adjust to the dislocation resulting from invasion, subjugation and confiscation. In time, often the resulting wounds have healed, and the trauma of conquest has become but a distant memory. In Ulster not only were the wounds given insufficient time to heal before being reopened but also the tension between the Gaelic Irish and the British newcomers was fatally aggravated by conflicting religious beliefs. In short, the natives were confronted by alien colonists speaking an alien language, adhering to a variety of Protestantism far distant from their own Catholicism.

THE CATHOLIC CHURCH: STRUGGLING FOR SURVIVAL

In 1599 about three hundred people took refuge in the Church of Aghenlurcher in Co. Fermanagh. By 1602 there were only thirty survivors. One of those who had travelled north from Munster after the Battle of Kinsale came upon this group, 'fearful to behold, emaciated by hunger and want'. They implored the visitors for food 'in honour of Christ Jesus, His Virgin Mary, and all the saints'. They had been subsisting on roots, and when one person died 'the survivors feasted by lot on his remains'.[12] Along with much else besides, the Church in Ulster was in ruins in the wake of English conquest and subjugation.

Hardly a church building remained intact. Native chiefs had been responsible for some of the destruction. Back in 1566 Shane O'Neill had set fire to Armagh Cathedral to prevent the English recapturing it for military use. Leading MacMahons burned all the churches in Farney lest any garrison be laid in them. Most of the destruction, however, was the work of English troops as the Ulster Irish were going down to defeat. The Franciscans had thirteen foundations in Ulster by 1583. By 1602 they had no choice but to hold their provincial chapter in the open, near Creevelea, Co. Leitrim.

All the friaries were either severely damaged or completely destroyed. No church was left in Derry when Sir Henry Docwra landed there in 1600. Hardly a single church in the whole province still had its roof intact. The destruction of parish churches was so great that Lord Deputy Sir Arthur Chichester observed in 1608 that it was 'as if it were in a wilderness, where neither Christianity nor religion was ever heard of'.

Some commanders had gone out of their way to desecrate venerable shrines. Captain Edward Cromwell in 1599 had set fire to the Church of Down in 1599, and what were believed to be the relics of Patrick, Brigid and Columba were destroyed in the blaze. Provost-Marshals, Sir Moses Hill in particular, hunted down those clergy who refused to conform. In Derry the Dominican prior John Ó Luinnín and his brother were executed. Another Dominican, John O'Mannin, was left crippled as a result of torture. Archbishop Magauran had been killed in 1593 and Bishop Redmond Gallagher in 1601. Only three elderly Catholic bishops remained in the north. Desultory persecution continued. The Bishop of Down and Connor, Conor O'Devanny, was brought captive to the camp of Sir John Davies in 1611 and executed, along with the priest Patrick O'Loughran, by the King's order the following year.[13]

Traditional church lands were assigned to the state church as soon as King James had begun to reign. Crown officers had therefore to familiarise themselves with the way in which the Church had been manned and maintained in Gaelic Ulster. Church lands in each parish were in the hereditary occupation of usually one family, whose head was called an 'erenagh'; as Sir Oliver St John reported in 1609, 'there is no parish church in Ulster, but is built upon the erenagh lands, and has an erenagh belonging to it.'[14] Some hereditary heads were each known as a 'coarb', and the English used the terms coarb and erenagh interchangeably. These parochial lands were inherited by families who simply paid rent to the bishops. The erenagh shared the cost of maintaining the church building with the parson and the vicar, and provided hospitality to visiting clergy when required. Other church lands of a similar nature were known as 'termon' lands, where sanctuary could be sought.

Oxford had been the principal seminary for the training of Irish priests until the Reformation. For some time after that, novices had travelled to the University of Glasgow to complete their training, until the triumph of Presbyterianism in Scotland closed off that route also. The great majority of clergy in Ulster were trained locally by being apprenticed to priests. The priests Davies met in Co. Cavan were 'poor, ragged, ignorant creatures', but all had some knowledge of Latin, which proved to be of great service to surveyors and plantation commissioners who knew no Irish. In this remote part of the Catholic world, priests had usually married, and their children bore surnames such as MacEntaggart (son of the priest), MacAnespie (son of the bishop), Mac an Abbot, McVicar and MacParson. At the behest of the Jesuits the Earl of Tyrone had made some attempt to promote celibacy and to separate clergy from their concubines. Those with ambitions, no longer able to train to take holy orders in Oxford or Glasgow, now had to raise funds to travel further afield to study at Salamanca and other seminaries on the Continent. They returned fired with the spirit of the Counter-Reformation to rebuild the Catholic Church in Ulster.

Here the Catholic Church was to make a strong recovery, in highly adverse circumstances, as the plantation got under way. The Franciscans took the lead in this reconstruction. No longer able to live in their former convents, they sought safe houses amongst the native population and then began to build new convents, generally in dense forests, constructed of wood and wattles and thatched with straw or reeds. They subsisted entirely by questing, that is, by begging, and attempted to feed people in turn when required. St Anthony's was founded at Louvain in the Spanish Netherlands in 1607 and became the powerhouse of Franciscans serving Ulster. Returning to their homeland, these Franciscans were, Chichester observed during O'Doherty's rising, 'the very furies and firebrands of this rebellion'. Captured during the revolt with Shane Carragh O'Cahan, Donagh McRedie, chaplain and confessor to Sir Donal O'Cahan, attempted to argue that no secular power could condemn a priest for any offence. This was, of course, rejected, and he was hanged, drawn and quartered with Shane O'Cahan. A grisly execution, Chichester was sure, 'so taught the people better doctrine by the example of his death, than he had ever done in all his life before'. Edmund O'Mullarkey, who had served as a provincial of the Irish Franciscans, managed to evade capture. Described by the Solicitor-General, Sir Robert Jacob, as 'the first plotter and contriver of O'Doherty's treasons', O'Mullarkey remained at large during 1609 with another friar, Turlough O'Gallagher, 'like Satan compassing the earth, seducing the people, and persuading them to run into rebellion'.[15]

'A UNIFORM ORDER SET DOWN FOR THE SUPPRESSION OF PAPISTRY'

The government sought to bring 'civility' to Ulster not only by plantation and law but also by bringing the native inhabitants into the state-sponsored church—by persuasion if possible, by force if not. In 1604 the English Privy Council informed Adam Loftus, Archbishop of Dublin, that King James believed 'true religion is better planted by the word than the sword', but Loftus and Thomas Jones, the Lord Chancellor (who was to succeed Loftus in that post), responded that they were unable to see 'how, without some moderate course of coactions, they can be reclaimed from their idolatry to come to hear the glad tidings of the truth'. In short, 'coaction' (force) might be required to bring about the conversion of natives to the reformed faith. Another Crown official, Sir Parr Lane, presented this view in his verse pamphlet *News from the Holy Isle*:

Religion must be squared by the word,
And that must be maintained by the sword.[16]

King James and his Privy Council expressed the view in 1606 that the 'least civil' natives in the most remote parts would prove to be the easiest to win over to civility and true religion. Attorney-General Davies felt that this was particularly true of Ulster. Though as yet wild and unreformed, here, he wrote in 1606, conformity could be easily established once the 'work of reformation' was undertaken. He was certain that the Church in the north was so barbarous that these Irish were ready to embrace Protestantism if only there were suitable preachers to evangelise them. He looked forward to the arrival of Bishop George Montgomery and thought 'all the people of that province, at least the multitude, are apt to receive any faith if the bishop of Derry . . . would be a new St Patrick among them'.[17] Montgomery proved a bitter disappointment: he concerned himself almost exclusively with the lands and incomes of his three dioceses of Derry, Raphoe and Clogher.

Could the priests still present in the north be persuaded to become clergy of the established church? Irish-speaking ministers were the only clergy capable of presenting the reformed faith to the native population. Montgomery showed no interest in cajoling local priests. Instead he obtained licence to bring over nineteen preachers, arranging that they should continue to receive income from their Scottish and English benefices. In July 1607 Montgomery wrote to Salisbury from Dublin, 'having spent almost a whole year in the north and the most barbarous parts of Ulster not without some hope of doing good', noting that his experience there had taught him 'the great difficulty of reducing this people to civility'. In fact he had devoted little time to missionary and pastoral work.

After Montgomery had been translated to Meath in 1610, his successors—Brute Babington, who took over the Derry diocese, and Andrew Knox, the new Bishop of Raphoe—showed themselves energetic in attempting to enforce the conformity of their clergy. Knox had delighted King James by his missionary campaign in the Western Isles, and after a year in Raphoe he was reported to be 'zealously affected to correct and reform the errors and abuses of priests and people; he has done more good in a short time there than his predecessor, in all his time'.

Babington, a fellow of Corpus Christi College, Cambridge, was one of the few advocates of a persuasive missionary approach. He steered clear of coercion, being certain that there would be 'a tumultuous and general refusal' from these 'very averse and refractory' priests. 'Notwithstanding this their stubbornness I did not violently go to work with them nor urge them by authority, but endeavoured rather to persuade their consciences by arguments and reasons.' By 'dealing with them lovingly and kindly', Babington eventually got a diocesan chapter to agree to a compromise programme of change. This included an oath of allegiance to the King (but not the Oath of Supremacy), a recognition of royal supremacy over the Church, the use of the scriptures, and approved liturgy translated into Irish. But the bishop died unexpectedly in September 1611.[18]

Knox did not show anything like the same sensitivity. He enthusiastically set about destroying surviving religious artefacts. It was actually on Babington's suggestion that Bishop Knox set out to destroy a wooden statue of the Virgin at the chapel of Agivey, which, as it had a reputation for miraculous cures, drew pilgrims from as far away as the Pale. Knox's servants refused to harm the statue, so the bishop himself pulled it down and carried it to Coleraine, there to have it destroyed in a large fire laid in the centre of the town. Devout Catholics were told afterwards that only when a carpenter bored holes in the statue and filled them with sticks coated in pitch and gunpowder did the wood ignite, and that Babington's sudden death soon afterwards was proof of divine wrath.[19] Knox brought over seven Scottish clergy to his new diocese who were speakers of Gaelic, then easily understood by Ulster Irish-speakers. However, such was the resentment against the reformed religion in his diocese that they were forced to live in the bishop's residence. Knox was a firm believer in rigorous measures against priests and recusants (those failing to attend worship at the parish church): 'There must be a uniform order set down for the suppression of papistry'. This view was hardened by his sojourn in Raphoe, where he encountered hostility and 'deadly hatred'. Chichester agreed that coercion was essential; as he wrote to Salisbury in 1611, 'how mild and favourable soever they be dealt withal, I think there is little assurance of their obedience longer than they are kept down by force'.[20]

The state-sponsored church took possession of all the parish churches, delivering another shock to local people, as these buildings were usually associated with local saints. The Donegal poet Eoghan Rua Mac an Bhaird, in his lament on the death of the Earl of Tyrconnell, wrote: 'Worse than all other misfortunes the honour of her fine old mansions and the veneration of her saints and sanctuaries were desecrated—a cause of grief'. Where British colonisation was showing most success, churches were repaired or new ones were erected, and the Scots in particular brought over clergy to minister to them. In much of Ulster, however, very few colonists had yet arrived. Here Protestant clergy, where they were present, felt that they had no choice but to allow the local people to worship in the traditional way. The old rites continued in the parish churches, roofless though they were. A traveller in 1616 found that often the Protestant clergyman and the priest had come to an accommodation, 'the minister afraid of the priest's wood-kerne, and the priests as fear of the ministers apprehending or denoting them'. The clergyman 'for mere submissions sake will give way to the priest, to mumble mass in his church, where in all his life made never prayer nor sermon'.[21]

The process of seeking the conformity of resident native clergy had begun as early as 1603 in Co. Down. In Carrickfergus the majority of priests had taken the Oath of Supremacy by 1605, and—particularly after the Lord Deputy had published his proclamation against popish clergy there—more came into the town from the countryside offering to conform. The success of this campaign was short-lived. In Kilmore and Ardagh it was noticed that 'no divine service or sermon' was to be heard. The Franciscans took a lead in opposing this drift towards conformity. By the time the plantation was under way in 1611, resistance was stiffening. In any case, as more British arrived the clergy who came with them concentrated on ministering to the settlers. Those priests who had conformed were steadily sidelined, being regarded with suspicion because nearly all their wives and children remained Catholics. Soon hardly any native conforming clergy remained.

In eastern Ulster numbers of native Irish did conform, usually as the outcome of mixed marriages. More Gaelic Irish in Antrim and Down became Protestants in the years to come, but elsewhere in the province conversion was exceptional and usually transient. The clergy who had conformed were generally let alone, because they were regarded as utterly ineffective, but the imported Scottish ministers faced constant hostility. The hereditary church families stayed where they were (native Irish on church lands had no obligation to move), but as sub-tenants their status was severely reduced. They attempted to carry out some of their ancient duties, in particular caring for relics that had not been seized or smashed up. In this way some priceless treasures of ancient Ireland were preserved by erenagh families. The O'Mulhollands of Co. Tyrone kept the Bell of St Patrick and its shrine; the Book of Armagh, which included St Patrick's Confession, was looked after by the MacMoyers of the Fews; and the *cathach*, or psalter, of St Colmcille—Ireland's oldest manuscript, probably penned by Colmcille himself, and used for centuries as a talisman in battle by the O'Donnells—was guarded by the McRortys of Ballymagroarty, in the barony of Tirhugh, Co. Donegal.[22]

The University of Dublin had been established to provide education for uncivil and barbarous Irish youth. Modelled on the Puritan college of Emmanuel in Cambridge, it was expected to supply graduate clergy capable of preaching the reformed religion to the native Irish. This it signally failed to do. Even in its most productive years the college was sending out on average fewer than five graduate clergy a year. Certainly it failed to attract students from Ulster, and it did not supply the state-sponsored church in the north with a significant number of clergy. The 1622 royal visitation established that in all eight Ulster dioceses there were only thirteen graduates of the University of Dublin. The Archdeacon of Clogher admitted to the commission that many of his clergy were 'scarce endowed with a mediocrity of learning'. William Lithgow, travelling in Ireland in the early 1620s, observed that many unsuitable men, including mechanics and soldiers, were admitted to the ministry in Ireland—the example of their 'lewd lives', he thought, had been 'the greatest hindrance to that land's conversion'. James Ussher, the primate who famously dated the creation at 4004 BC, lamented in 1630 that the scandalous life of 'many unworthy ministers gives exceeding much hindrance to the progress of the gospel amongst us'.[23]

Actually the quality of Protestant clergy was much higher in Ulster than elsewhere in Ireland. In part this was because of the generous allocation of land to the Church in the plantation—in particular the proviso that glebe land was to be set aside for each pastor in every parish. This helped to ensure that in areas where British settlement was most successful the colonists were eventually well served. A good many incoming clergy seemed to have had a genuine spiritual call to evangelise the natives, but the variety of Protestantism they carried with them was unlikely to attract those who had so recently been subjugated, reduced in status and deprived of their lands.

The British colonisation of Ulster created a sudden demand for clergy. The hierarchy of the Church of Ireland was in no position to impose rigorous standards on ordinands or on ministers who crossed over from Britain to present themselves for preferment. Bishops tolerated Puritan clergy to present a united hostile front to Catholicism. Ministers in Ireland were not faced with the same necessity to accept the Book of Common

Prayer and to subscribe to the Thirty-Nine Articles, as they were in England. This liberal attitude to Puritanism was most evident in Ulster. English Puritan clergy, finding it difficult to get livings because of their beliefs, often found refuge in the north of Ireland. Above all, Scottish Presbyterian ministers were readily accepted as parish clergy in Ulster without being forced to subscribe to prescribed liturgy and articles of faith. This explains why there was no serious attempt to set up a presbytery in Ulster until 1642.

Tensions between settlers and natives militated against any prospect of mass conversions to the reformed religion amongst the Gaelic Irish. In any case an alien religion which vilified their cherished beliefs and traditions would be preached by men speaking an alien tongue, who often regarded them as pagans, savages and barbarians. Further alienation was brought about by the manner in which the established church imposed its exactions on the native population. Resistance to conversion was strengthened by the eagerness of bishops and clergy of the state church to punish and exploit them through the ecclesiastical courts.

Church levies, imposed on a native population still recovering from the ravages of war, included tithes, recusancy fines, fees arising from the rites of passage and fines imposed by church courts. Apart from Antrim and Down, in the six counties of the plantation the Church had been generously provided with 75,000 acres (actually not far short of half a million acres), and each parish had sixty acres of glebe land assigned to it. In addition, the Church was entitled to collect tithes for the upkeep of the church. In 1608 Eoghan Rua Mac an Bhaird witnessed Bishop Montgomery's new regime in Co. Donegal, castigating the 'stewards of heretic bishops' along with 'the sect of Luther, the legions of Calvin'.

Just before Christmas 1614 local people dragged a native Irish minister who had conformed out of his house in south Tyrone and stabbed him to death. Francis Blundell, a government officer, reported that this was because he had been 'so severe in demanding of his tithes', adding that 'ministers there are much to blame, for exacting their duties so strictly of such men, as never knew what it was to pay tithes, until within these few years'. Tithes were collected in kind, and the amounts demanded varied greatly from place to place. Ministers, most of them absentees, imposed a tithe on milk—a vital part of the diet of the native Irish—which had never been levied before. This was particularly burdensome during the winter of 1614/15, which was so severe that it was reckoned that up to one in five of cattle died. Lord Deputy Chichester himself felt compelled to issue an order 'for observance of a milder temper hereafter in tithing'.[24]

In the reign of Elizabeth it had proved impossible to impose fines for recusancy in most of Ulster. Now ministers regularly went to the assizes to name parishioners who were not attending, and Protestant juries had no difficulty in enforcing the levying of these fines. James Dundas, Bishop of Down, was notoriously active in this respect. The money raised proved sufficient, for example, to build and restore the Cathedral Churches of Kilmore and Dromore. Sir Oliver St John observed in December 1614 that 'to indict so many in Ulster and Connacht and the remote parts of this kingdom seems as yet unreasonable, because they have few churches and few ministers to supply them, the people rarely understanding English, and very few of the ministers that can speak Irish'. That did not stop St John a few years later from using the proceeds of recusancy fines to put up a new church on his proportion in north Armagh.[25] Not surprisingly, some native Irish tenants began to attend parish churches to avoid being fined, and these were then nominally classed as having conformed.

The native Irish were used to making payments to clergy for christenings, marriages and funerals. They had no particular difficulty in paying the usual fees even to those ministers who had conformed. The situation changed when British clergy appeared, unable to speak Irish and demanding the right to levy charges, ranging from 6s 8d to 13s 4d, for these services. When local people turned to Catholic priests they had to be paid, but the established church demanded a 'composition' for each service performed by priests. In short, local people found that they had to pay twice for rites of passage. Death duties, known as 'mortuaries', bore heavily on the poor. In 1607 they were levied at a fifth of property in Derry and a third in Raphoe. In one parish in Farney in Co. Monaghan, when a wife died the parson took a cow from the husband and all the cloth obtained to make her clothes. When Dumnagh McConill, who owned three cows, died there, in 1621, the clergyman's agents left him unburied in the church until they got one of his beasts. When his wife died, a fortnight later, they seized another cow. If a beggar died, 2s 6d was demanded of the person in whose dwelling he had breathed his last. For the parents of stillborn babies, charges were still imposed: in Farney, Patrick MacMahon had to pay 7s 8d for the christening and burial of his child in 1620.[26]

THE CONSPIRACY OF 1615

After an adjournment of almost five months the third session of the Irish Parliament opened at eight o'clock on the morning of Tuesday 18 April 1615. For James I and Lord Deputy Chichester the most urgent task was to persuade members to vote for the levying of a subsidy. The Irish government was virtually bankrupt. In 1612 income had been £24,000, but expenditure had been £33,000, and the situation had deteriorated since then. Advocates of plantation had argued that colonisation would bring substantial profits for the Crown. So far the Plantation of Ulster had signally failed to achieve this.

Then, to everyone's surprise, Chichester informed Parliament that a plot had been discovered in Ulster, that the main conspirators had been seized and that the English Privy Council had been informed. The Lord Deputy's ploy was to get Parliament prorogued (so that peers of the realm and members of Parliament from Ulster could make haste northwards to secure the province's defence) and to get the subsidy rushed through. He knew that Old English recusants intended to filibuster in an effort to secure concessions for Catholics. Now, the Lord Deputy argued, the subsidy was needed urgently to pay for the defence of Ulster. Chichester succeeded. As John Sutton, a Catholic member representing Kildare, observed during the debate on the subsidy Bill:

Little said soon amended,
Subsidy granted, the parliament ended.[27]

Chichester may have exaggerated the danger posed by the plot, but he did not doubt that the native Irish in Ulster were seething with resentment and in daily expectation of the return of the Earl of Tyrone with a great Spanish army. During the winter, he had been told of a priest in Co. Tyrone preaching that the English were heretics, that the Pope had expressed the wish that the Irish should rise up in rebellion, that the King of Spain would supply eighteen thousand men, and that, according to a prophecy in a book in Rome, English rule would end in Ireland in two years' time. Sir Robert Jacob, the Solicitor-General, rather dismissed the plot announced by the Lord Deputy, but the English Privy Council took it very seriously. Sir Dudley Carleton had written from Venice in March 1614 that Tyrone was preparing to leave Rome to go to Flanders, there to marshal Irish regiments serving with the Spanish ready for an invasion of Ireland. Then, a year later, a Catholic priest arriving at Cork brought news that Tyrone's invasion of Ulster was imminent.

The Earl of Tyrone was indeed urgently seeking permission to leave Rome and head an invasion of Ireland. Actually both the King of Spain and the Pope were discouraging the earl: they had no wish to damage relations with London at a time when Philip IV was negotiating to have his daughter betrothed to Charles, son of James I. Chichester, however, entertained the liveliest fears. In March 1615 he reported that over the previous six months there had been an alarming increase in cruel murders, as the native Irish were confident of Tyrone's return. He was convinced that 'the hearts of the natives are against the state'.[28]

The Lord Deputy got permission to use judicial torture to extract evidence of the plot. Probably for the first time in Ireland the rack was used, on Cúchonnacht Ó Cianáin, one of those arrested. He was merely 'a rhymer or chronicler belonging to Connor Roe Maguire' who had been reduced to begging; but he was also the brother of Tadhg Ó Cianáin, a poet who had been with the earls during their flight in 1607 and who was the author of the memorable account of their subsequent plight on the Continent. His evidence, and that supplied by others under duress, proved the existence of a conspiracy, but one with no prospect of success.

The conspirators had met in May 1614 in an alehouse by the banks of the Bann at Macosquin, south of Coleraine. They included Rory O'Cahan, Shane MacGilladuff Óg O'Mullan, Alexander MacDonnell and his uncle Loder MacDonnell. They planned to seize Derry, Coleraine, Lifford, Culmore and Limavady. Alexander promised to seek the aid of Collo MacGillenaspig from the Isles, and they sent out letters to Art Óg MacDonnell O'Neill and Brian Crossagh O'Neill, an illegitimate cousin of the Earl of Tyrone, asking them to organise the revolt on the south and burn Dungannon, Mountjoy and Charlemont (where Conn O'Neill, Tyrone's son, was being held prisoner). The arms they had were pitifully inadequate, and there was no coherent plan. Brian Crossagh finally agreed to play his part in August.

Brian Crossagh was a 'deserving' native who could have expected nothing in the old order and had been fortunate to be granted a thousand-acre proportion in 1611. By 1614, however, he was hopelessly in debt, and he was snubbed by the new regime. Justice Aungier, he said, 'was ready to revile me like a churl'.[29] The most determined plotter was Alexander MacDonnell, nephew of Sir Randal, who—with some justification— believed he had as much right to the vast estates in Antrim as his uncle. Shadowy leaders of the woodkerne, including Hugh MacShane O'Neill, promised support.

The plot was barely past the planning stage when the leading conspirators were arrested. The trial followed in July 1615 in the city of Londonderry before the two assize judges for the county and a jury which included two native Irishmen. Eleven men, including Alexander MacDonnell, were acquitted for lack of sufficient evidence. Six men were convicted of treason, including Brian Crossagh O'Neill, Cúchonnacht Ó Cianáin and Rory O'Cahan. They were condemned to be drawn through the streets of the city in chains, to be hanged and, while still alive, to be disembowelled and beheaded, and to have their bodies cut into quarters and then burned.[30]

The plotters must have believed that once they had risen in revolt the Earl of Tyrone would hasten to join them with a Spanish army. The earl, still in Rome, continued to fire off letter after letter to King Philip and his advisers, never giving up hope that he could lead a Spanish expeditionary force to Ireland. At the beginning of 1616, now aged sixty-five, Tyrone appeared to be in robust health. Then, in July of that year, the new Spanish ambassador in Rome, Cardinal Gaspar de Borja y Velasco, in one of his first letters sent this report to his King:

The Earl of Tiron died on the 20th of this month in the same Christian and exemplary manner in which he lived, leaving the Countess and those of his nation in great affliction and without the protection he afforded them.

The English ambassador in Brussels, Sir William Trumble, wrote that the earl had died of a fever in Rome 'and was buried with great pomp and solemnity'. His body was laid beside those of his son Hugh and the Earl of Tyrconnell at San Pietro in Montorio.[31]

Later, by the banks of the River Drowes in Co. Leitrim, the Franciscan compilers of the Annals of the Four Masters made this judgement:

Although he died far from Armagh, the burial-place of his ancestors, it was a token that God was pleased with his life that the Lord permitted him a no worse burial-place, namely Rome, the head city of the Christians. The person who died here was a powerful, mighty lord, endowed with wisdom, subtlety, and profundity of mind and intellect; a warlike, valorous, predatory, enterprising lord, in defending his religion and his patrimony against his enemies; a pious and charitable lord, mild and gentle with his friends, fierce and stern towards his enemies, until he had brought them to submission and obedience to his authority . . . A lord with the authority and praiseworthy characteristics of a prince, who had not suffered theft or robbery, abduction or rape, spite or animosity, to prevail during his reign, but had kept all under the authority of the law, as was meet for a prince.[32]

With the Earl of Tyrone's passing, there also passed any prospect of help from abroad.

Chapter 11 ∾

| PROGRESS AND PROBLEMS

DERRY'S WALLS: 'VERY WELL AND SUBSTANTIALLY DONE'

Londonderry was the last city or town in Ireland to be enclosed by stone walls. Indeed it was probably the last walled city to be constructed anywhere in Europe. In September 1614 Sir Josias Bodley, Overseer of Fortifications in Ireland, saw for himself that work there had hardly begun. He found that about three hundred pounds had been 'disbursed at the Derry in casting up of earth and breaking of quarries towards the walling thereof, which how it shall be continued either for form or strength, being that . . . no part of the stonework is yet raised, I cannot precisely deliver'. Two years later substantial progress was being made. Peter Proby and Matthias Springham, sent over by the Common Council of London, reported:

> For the fortification at Derrie we have exactly viewed the same and find it very commendable and when the same is finished will be very strong and that the walls thereof are wellnigh half done . . . Also there are two drawbridges finished and one gate was in erecting.

Their recommendation that the walls be raised from sixteen to nineteen feet was accepted. Captain Nicholas Pynnar, who had succeeded Bodley in his post, in making his survey of the plantation between December 1618 and March 1619 was duly impressed. The walls, he found, were even higher than Proby and Springham had suggested. He described the city as being

> now encompassed about with a very strong wall, excellently made and neatly wrought; being all of good lime and stone; the circuit whereof is 283 perches and $^2/_3$, at 18 feet to the perch; besides the four gates which contain 84 feet; and in every place of the wall it is 24 feet high, and six feet thick. The gates are all battlemented . . . The bulwarks are all very

large and good, being in number nine; besides two half bulwarks; and for four of them there may be four cannons, or other great pieces . . . The rampart within the city is 12 feet thick of earth; all things are very well and substantially done.

The design of the city of Londonderry was in part inspired by the Renaissance fascination with classical ideas. Many new towns and cities on the Continent took as their model the rational and geometric layout of Roman military camps. The city thought most likely to have influenced the planners was Vitry-le-François, a hundred miles east of Paris, designed by the Italian engineer Hieronimo Marino in 1545 for Francis ii, the first husband of Mary Queen of Scots (mother of James i). The design of Derry, in turn, was to be used as a model when the city of Philadelphia was being designed. The fortifications were set out and measured by the surveyor Thomas Raven, assisted by Simon Kingsland, who had prepared maps of proportions in 1613. The actual design of the walls was by Sir Edward Doddington, who had already built a castle at Dungiven on the site of the former Augustinian priory there. Peter Benson, a master-bricklayer and tiler from London, supervised the building of the walls. The circuit extended to about 1,700 yards. A large fosse, or ditch, ten feet deep and thirty feet wide, ran outside the walls for almost half their length on the south and east sides. The total cost of construction was £10,357. Though it could be exposed to cannon fire from the surrounding rising ground on both sides of the river, the Londoners had created perhaps the most impregnable fortified urban centre in Ireland.[1]

The foundation-stone of St Columb's Cathedral was laid on 21 August 1628, and the building was completed in 1633. Edmund Kinsman, Master of the Masons' Company in 1635, was probably involved in the design. The builder was William Parrott, who was contracted by the Irish Society to put it up for £3,400 and had been much involved in developing the Merchant Taylors' settlement at Macosquin. The work was supervised by Sir John Vaughan, who later became Mayor of Coleraine. He is commemorated in an inscription (VAUGHAN AED., 'Vaughan edified') in the western vestibule under the tower, which reads IN TEMPLO VERVS DEVS EST VEREQ COLENDUS ('the true God is in the temple and is truly worshipped'), ANO DO [anno domini] 1633, CAR REGIS 9 ('in the ninth year of King Charles'), and

IF STONES COVLD SPEAKE
THEN LONDONS PRAYSE
SHOVLD SOVNDE WHO
BVILT THIS CHVRCH AND
CITTIE FROM THE GROVNDE
VAUGHAN AED.

This was to be both a parish church and a cathedral, built in a con-servative 'Gothic Survival' style. According to the architectural historian James Steven Curl, 'this stylistic conservatism may have had its origins in a desire to build a reassuringly familiar type of building that would remind settlers of home' and, perhaps, in the fact that the Stuart court was then resisting classical innovations.

St Columb's Cathedral, though much altered since, deserves to be regarded as the finest building put up during the plantation. It consisted of a six-bay nave, containing a short chancel, lean-to aisles with lead-covered low-pitched roofs concealed behind crenellated parapets, a short four-stage western tower, a south porch and circular towers set at the south-east and north-east corners of both the main tower and the aisles. Rubble from ruined buildings was used in the construction and finished with sandstone dressings. The windows and lights were of a late-Elizabethan Gothic variety, defined with stone mullions and cusped heads. In 1634 the Irish Society got a royal licence to grant St Columb's in perpetuity to the Bishop of Derry, to be consecrated and dedicated as the Cathedral Church of St Columba of Derry and also as the parish church for the use of the citizens of the city and the parishioners of Templemore. King Charles provided the cathedral with bells at a cost of five hundred pounds (which he probably had to borrow from the City of London), and Lord Deputy Thomas Wentworth wrote that these were 'merrily ringing forth as well his Majesty's piety and bounty'.[2]

A DIAMOND AS BIG AS A SQUARE: WILLIAM COLE AND ENNISKILLEN

The British colonisation was taking deep root. Admittedly, many of the original grantees had pulled out of the plantation in the six escheated counties and sold their interests. The result was that some planters, with comparatively modest holdings initially, were to rise to prominence and leave an indelible stamp on the whole enterprise.

One of these was William Cole, son of a member of the Goldsmiths' Company of London, who began his military career in Holland and came to Ireland in 1600. There he was in the thick of the fighting in the Moyry Pass in 1601, fought at Kinsale and carried letters from there to the Secretary of State in London. He had charge of vessels operating on Lough Erne and custody of the Maguire castle of Enniskillen. Within a short time of getting as a servitor the estate of Cornagrade, in the barony of Coole and Tirkennedy adjoining Enniskillen, Cole bought from a Scottish grantee the undertaker estate which became known as Portora in the barony of Magheraboy. He was also patron of the new town to be established at Enniskillen. In 1610–11 he was paid £266 13s 4d for 'building and finishing of the castle and bawn of Enniskillen, utterly defaced in the late rebellion'. In 1613 he got a second payment of £133 6s 8d for 'finishing and perfecting' the works begun by him because they were 'lying open both to ruin and decay and also to the hazard of surprise or assault if it should be attempted'.[3] On condition that he maintained the fortifications, Cole was granted the lands of the island of Enniskillen in 1612.

Like other patrons of towns, Cole had his instructions for developing Enniskillen. He had to 'bring or cause to be brought' within four years 'twenty persons being English or Scotch and chiefly artificers and mechanics to make, erect and construct a town in a convenient place'. He was to set aside sites for a church and cemetery, a market house, a gaol for the county, and a public school with a court and garden adjoining. It was stipulated that he should 'build and erect edifices and buildings . . . in streets and squares, in such manner and form as shall best suit its site and situation, and for the defence and decency of the said town'. Land had to be set aside for the townspeople and their cattle.

Enniskillen was one of those towns incorporated in 1613, with the right to send two members each to the Irish Parliament as part of Lord Deputy Chichester's scheme to boost the New English (and Protestant) representation there. Cole was made the first provost, or mayor. The 'diamond' was a striking feature of Ulster Plantation towns, and Enniskillen was no exception. Essentially, diamonds were town squares with streets entering them at midpoint on each of their four sides. The diamond in Enniskillen was similar in size and shape to that in Belturbet, Co. Cavan. By 1641 there were about fifty houses in Enniskillen, most of them of one storey, with attic accommodation lit by dormer windows above a second floor (which would effectually make them one-and-a-half storeys). One house, leased to a yeoman named John Hickes for a hundred years, gave Cole a rent of ten shillings a year and two 'good fat hens' every Christmas.

Cole proved an energetic coloniser. Sir Josias Bodley found that he was building two bridges 'over the lough', had 'divers carpenters and other artificers that purpose to settle there' and had seen to the firing of 300,000 bricks and 'tile proportionable'. The Church of St Macartin's was finished in 1627 and a tower added ten years later; the 'Agnus Dei' on the date stone of 1637, with a lamb and cross symbolising the Resurrection, was probably repellent to this Puritan provost of the town, but at a time when King Charles was intent on imposing High Church orthodoxy Cole probably had no choice in the matter.

In the 1630s the names of some fifty to sixty adult British males were recorded, suggesting that there were about two hundred men, women and children in the town. The English surnames were mostly from the West Country and included Browning, Nicholls, Pearse, Ford, Hayes and Grible. There may have been as many Scots there; their surnames, notably from the Borders, included Johnston, Buchanan, Armstrong, Caldwell and Maxwell. This mixing of English and Scots was to be found by that time all over the province: the desire of James I that colonists of both nations should be together—and be proud to be considered British—was being realised at an early stage. A few native Irish managed to remain, including Cole's employee John Carmick, who had a 'chamber' in his castle.

Cole built his castle at Enniskillen using the base of Maguire's 'broken castle'. To this he added what is today the most famous feature of the town, the Watergate. The name is misleading, because it is a defensive structure linked to surviving portions of Maguire's original wall, not an entry point. This was an imposing fortification in front of the keep, with its own well, upper walkway and brick chimney. The flankers—two attractive corbelled turrets—were projected in such a way as to protect the wall on both sides. In addition to other defensive buildings (including 'other convenient houses' for 'store and munition'), Cole put up a 'good timber house after the English fashion' as his own residence, with a 'fair garden'. He also had three 'good boats . . . ready to attend all services'.

Cole started out with a grant of a thousand acres, soon augmented by the purchase of the Portora proportion. He, like other planters, was able to take advantage of the many native Irish who had received plantation grants but who—unable to run their estates efficiently on English lines, floundering in their attempts to comprehend English common law and sinking inexorably into hopeless debt—found that they had no choice but to sell off their lands piece by piece. By the 1630s Cole had acquired lands originally granted to about six of the local native Irish owners. He also took over the lands first allotted to the servitor Peter Mostin. His main tenant at Cornagrade, Clinton Ogle, was a former lieutenant from Lincolnshire. James Spottiswood, Bishop of Clogher (subsequently buried at Westminster Abbey), was for a time Cole's tenant at Portora, where evidence of impressive defences remain.

Cole was singled out, at least on his undertaker's estate, as a model planter—surveyors in 1622 stated that they could not 'learn' of any Irish tenant remaining on the land there. He had erected mills, one of them a windmill, on both his estates. He was a natural choice as one of Fermanagh's two county members in the Parliaments of 1634 and 1640 and served on several committees. Indeed, Cole (by now Sir William) was a member of the delegation sent to present the grievances of the Irish House of Commons against the conduct of the government.[4]

CATHOLIC PLANTERS: THE HAMILTONS IN THE BARONY OF STRABANE ...

To King James the Plantation of Ulster would be a civilising enterprise which would 'establish the true religion of Christ among men . . . almost lost in superstition'. In short, he intended that his grandiose scheme would bring the enlightenment of the Reformation to one of the most remote and benighted provinces in his kingdom. Yet some of the most determined planters were, in fact, Catholics. How can this be explained? James was anxious to persuade men of position and substance to give a lead in this plantation, and he was disappointed that not more of the highest nobles in England and Scotland proved willing to involve themselves. It was one of the King's strengths—and later, in the case of Lord Buckingham, a serious weakness—that he was unswervingly supportive of those who had shown him friendship and steady loyalty and who had rendered him a vital service at crucial moments during his reign. In such cases he was prepared to overlook their adherence to the Catholic faith. Already the devout Catholic Sir Randal MacDonnell was proving an assiduous coloniser in Co. Antrim.

James Hamilton, created Earl of Abercorn in 1603, had served on the Commission for Union between England and Scotland. He was 'induced' by the King to become a chief undertaker 'for a countenance and strength to the rest' and was granted the great proportion of Dunnalong—described as an estate of 2,000 'profitable' acres but in reality 10,217 acres—and the small proportion of Strabane in Co. Tyrone. Though not a Catholic, his father had been a devoted supporter of Mary Queen of Scots, and many of his relatives were Catholics. The earl saw to it that other members of his family received grants, including his brother Sir Claude Hamilton of Shawfield, who got the adjacent proportion of Killeny and the proportion of Eden in the Plumbridge area. In 1612 Sir Claude purchased the proportion of Tirenmurietagh jointly with William Stewart (who built one of the finest plantation castles at Aughentaine). In October 1614 Sir Claude was 'now at Straban taking ordour for his buildingis', but he died before the month was out. As his children were still minors, they were placed under the guardianship of their uncle Sir George Hamilton of Greenlaw, who had acquired lands in Leckpatrick and Ardstraw.

Sir George was a Catholic and saw to it that William, Sir Claude's eldest son and heir, was brought up a Catholic. The result was that over the ensuing decades many Catholic Scots—no doubt finding that the Kirk was making it increasingly difficult for them to prosper in their homeland—were persuaded to settle in this part of Tyrone. The plantation certainly prospered here. A castle in a commanding position on a steep bank overlooking the Burndennet River was described by Pynnar as 'both strong and beautiful'. The 1622 survey noted that here there was a 'good Castle of stone & Lyme, 3 stories high ... and about a Bawne 54 foot long, 42 foot broad and 6 foot high, with two open Flanckers'. Indeed in 1617 Abercorn was commended for having built 'many well fortified castles for the defence of Ulster'. William Lynn, agent to the Abercorns, listed twenty-four leaseholders, most of whom had built houses of stone, and stated that the manor had a stone water mill and a 'good quay built this year' and a ferry with 'sufficient boates for men and horses'. The 1st Earl died in 1618, to be succeeded by his eldest son, James. In 1634 the earl's fourth son, George, inherited the manor of Dunnalong. Under the guardianship of his uncle Sir George, he too became a Catholic.

On 4 January 1630 Thomas Plunkett, 'a man lately reclaimed from Popery', made a deposition before George Downham, Bishop of Derry, reporting that there was 'a great meeting of priests last November' led by the Catholic Vicar-General, Tirlagh O'Kelly, who 'lives with Scottish papists at Strabane'. He was often entertained by Claude Hamilton, who 'lodged him when the Bishop of Derry and the Provost of Strabane thought to arrest him'. Plunkett continued:

There is evidence of the holding of mass on Sunday at Sir George Hamilton's, and in other houses where it is attended by the Irish and forty Scotch from about Strabane. Sir George is praised for having made many converts during his residence in Ireland, both at Strabane and at Killybegs.

Downham added this covering letter:

> Sir George Hamilton, who is otherwise a courteous and civil gentleman, has tried to draw people to Popery.
>
> Claude Hamilton, Master of Abercorn, would be a hopeful young gentleman were he not poisoned with Popery, but maintains Papists so much that there will be a revolt in Strabane if any more of the Scotch Papists come there. The Archbishop of Glasgow has sent to me hoping that I will not harbour in my diocese Papists who have been expelled from Scotland.
>
> Sir William Hamilton, a good scholar, was a Papist, and perverted his wife, a daughter of Lord Ards, who had been a Protestant. He used the influence of Blackney, the Jesuit, who perverted Lady Hamilton's waiting maid.

Robert Algeo, Sir Claude's Catholic agent, saw to it that good relations were established with the native Irish. This part of Tyrone had been the heartland of Turlough Luineach O'Neill's lordship. Most of the old Gaelic elite had been swept away, but Algeo won the co-operation of lesser families there, most notably the O'Devins (now Devines), who had been the erenaghs of church land. Flouting the strict conditions laid out in the Articles of Plantation, the agent leased out land to the natives, most notably Patrick Groome O'Devin, who rented (by modern measurement) more than three thousand acres. In November 1613 Patrick travelled to Scotland to deliver £23 10s to Sir Claude in person. Without the collaboration of these Gaelic Irish the Hamiltons would not have prospered so well. Details of some of these leases survive. Brian Crou O'Devin's rent for the townlands of Rousky and Drain was made up of £9 in cash, thirty-two days' labour service, six barrels of barley, ten sheep, ten pigs and twenty-four hens and capons. In these O'Devin lands the only non-Irish tenant was Dr Robert Hamilton, who was given the townland of Killycurry for no rent, possibly in return for an earlier loan. (Together with Peter Lowe, Dr Hamilton had established the faculty of Physicians and Surgeons at Glasgow in 1599.) Nevertheless, many Scottish Presbyterians were attracted to these Hamilton lands. One of them was Hugh Hamilton of Lisdivin, a trader in luxury goods from Priestfield in Blantyre, who had to pay either a rent of six pounds in cash or 'one hogshead of Gascoign wine, one pound of good pepper, four pounds of loaf sugar and a box of marmalade containing at least two pounds of the preserve'. An early port book of the city of Londonderry records that he imported goods from Scotland in 1614 to the value of £34. He built a stone house at Lisdivin, owned four houses in Strabane and acquired an interest in the abbeylands of Grange. Pynnar reckoned that there were fifty settler families in Eden and Killeny, and the muster of those capable of bearing arms in the manor of Dunnalong came to 106.

In 1628 the government allowed owners of undertakers' estates to lease up to a quarter of their lands to native tenants. Sir Claude's son, by now Sir William, was fined in 1631 for exceeding this quota. He was forced to borrow five thousand marks from James Spence, a merchant from Edinburgh, and in December 1631 Spence 'took instruments' to secure the money in the presence of the Provost of Strabane. As a devoted Royalist, he lost everything in Cromwell's time and travelled to the Continent with the exiled Charles II. However, Sir William was one of the very few Catholics in Ulster to have his estates returned to him during the Restoration.[5]

... AND LORD AUDLEY IN THE BARONY OF OMAGH

In July 1609 George Tuchet, 18th Baron Audley, a member of one of the most ancient baronages in England and a Catholic, presented himself to the Privy Council in London. There he put forward by far the most ambitious plan for the Plantation of Ulster. He proposed that in return for 100,000 acres in the counties of Tyrone and Armagh he and his son Sir Mervyn Tuchet would build no fewer than thirty-three castles and thirty-three towns, setting aside 600 acres to each castle and 2,400 acres to each town. He declared that he would settle thirty families in each town, including footsoldiers, craftsmen and cottagers. He would pay the Crown £533 in rent each year, beginning after four years. He asked for manorial rights and permits to hold markets and fairs and for a licence to set up iron mills and to make iron and glass for forty-one years.

What is surprising is that the English Privy Council did not reject this grandiose scheme out of hand. No doubt the fact that the Irish Attorney-General, Sir John Davies, had married the baron's daughter Eleanor ensured that Audley received a sympathetic hearing. Davies wrote to Lord Salisbury, the King's secretary, pointing out that in earlier times the Audleys had helped to conquer north Wales, and that one of them had accompanied John de Courcy, the Norman knight who had overrun the coastlands of eastern Ulster at the end of the twelfth century, 'in testimony whereof Audley Castle is standing in Lecale, inherited at this day by one of the same surname'.[6]

When Lord Deputy Chichester read the Privy Council's letter of recommendation in Dublin he was appalled. Audley had been an indifferent planter in Munster, where he had been granted lands about Rosscarbery and Castlehaven in west Cork. In reply Chichester disparagingly referred to Audley's 'manner of life in Munster, and the small cost he has bestowed to make his house fit for him'. He did have a good service record in the Nine Years' War and had sustained severe injuries during the Battle of Kinsale, but he had been cashiered during the peace. Audley petitioned King James, asking him to help prevent 'the ruin and downfall of an old and decayed house'.

The Lord Deputy's protests were in vain. Lord Audley was made the chief undertaker in the barony of Omagh, with the right to allot proportions to others. In fact the land of the entire precinct went to him and his family: the Finagh and Rarone proportion of 3,000 acres for himself, the 2,000-acre proportion of Brad to his son Sir Mervyn Tuchet, 2,000 acres to his other son, Sir Fernando, at Fintona, the 2,000-acre proportion of Edergoole and Carnbracken to his son-in-law Edward Blunt, and the proportion of Clonaghmore and Gravetagh to his other son-in-law, Sir John Davies. By modern measurement these lands totalled not far short of the 100,000 acres Lord Audley had originally requested. In addition, he obtained 500 acres in the barony of Orior as a servitor, and in the same precinct he and his heirs would receive the 2,000-acre estate of Art MacBaron O'Neill (granted for life only) when he died.

Audley threw himself into the enterprise with energy and enthusiasm. Indeed, he seems to have taken over the management his sons' estates, Blunt's estate and Davies's proportion (probably because the Attorney-General had his hands full with state business, not to speak of coping with the growing mental instability of his wife). The extent of the land under Audley's management was vast, but much of it was infertile mountainous land. An even more serious drawback was that these estates were poorly forested, making it difficult to obtain sufficient timber for building. His family had once owned iron mines near Tunstall in Staffordshire; now, without enough wood to burn charcoal, Audley could not realise his dream of making great profits by smelting iron.

Undaunted, Lord Audley set about building with a will. By the Christmas of 1612 he was close to completing a castle three miles south of

Omagh at Ballynahatty on Blunt's estate when this 'great work', as Sir Josias Bodley reported,

> was much hindered and cast behind by a violent storm of thunder, lightning and tempest, which overthrew part of the said building, slew one of his workmen, and hurt divers others. The same he is now again re-edifying and purposeth to encompass with a bawn of good circuit.

In 1622 the commissioners described this rebuilt castle as 'a good stone house, in forme of a crosse, 54 foote everie way, being 2 stories high, and covered with slate', surrounded by a 'bawne of stone & lyme 96 foot long, 78 foot broad, and 10 foot high'.[7]

This was a modest structure compared with the two buildings he put up on Davies's proportion. At a cost of three thousand pounds he supervised the erection of Castlederg on the site of the O'Neill tower-house, commanding a ford on the north bank of the River Derg. This was still being worked on when he died, and it was completed by Davies himself 'at great chardge'. The 1622 commissioners were impressed: 'There is about Castledirge a bawne of stone and lyme, not finished being 100 foot long, 80 foot broad, and five foot high, wth 3 open flankers, of the same height with the walls'. This fortress was strong enough to withstand the assault of the rebel commander Sir Phelim O'Neill in 1641.

In 1615 the King wrote to congratulate Audley for settling English and Scottish tenants and bringing in English cattle on his estate, planting the 'most barren and rough land in all that country'. Perhaps the most elaborate and expensive building erected under Audley's direction was Castle Curlews, in the townland of Kirlish, north-west of Drumquin. Unlike Castlederg, defence was clearly not the first priority. Castle Curlews was put up on the slopes of Slieveglass and Bolaght Mountain; Davies admitted that it was a house 'being erected, noe place soe unfit for habitation'. Only at the basement level were there gun-loops for protection. A wing of two-and-a-half storeys with canted bay windows on three sides provided delightful views but no defence of any consequence.

Audley died in 1617 at the age of about sixty-six on his way from Castle Curlews to Ballynahatty. His problem, and that of his heirs, was that most of his lands had little appeal for prospective British tenants. In 1619 there were only sixty-four colonists on his Omagh lands, an estate 'so weak and uncertain, that they are all leaving the land'. Most of the land was let to twenty Irish 'gentlemen', who had about three thousand 'souls of all sorts' under them. Audley's successor, Sir Mervyn, Earl of Castlehaven, speeded up the exodus of the British by trebling rents. The earl neglected his estates and—following a conviction for homosexuality and the rape of his wife— was executed in England in 1631. He had already sold much of his property in Ulster to his mother's relatives, by whom it descended to Sir Audley Mervyn—an unflinching champion of the Protestant cause.[8]

DEFENDING THE PLANTATION

All over Ulster new castles, defensive works and mansions were rising up, providing outward and visible signs of the arrival of a new order. Some veterans were confident and secure enough to erect buildings almost devoid of defensive features. This was certainly true of Lord Deputy Chichester, who had Jacobean mansions with splendid bay windows in the latest English fashion put up in both Carrickfergus and Belfast. Joymount at least was next to a great defensive wall that Chichester caused to be put around Carrickfergus, but Belfast Castle, and the town rapidly emerging round it, was eventually protected only by a 'rampier' (rampart) of earth of dubious value. However, Sir Moses Hill erected a strong tower at Castle Chichester, further east at Whitehead.[9] Dalway's Bawn at Bellahill, near Carrickfergus, a rectangular enclosure with three round flankers built in 1609, remains the best-preserved bawn in Ulster. And, of course, the confiscated lands of the province were already encircled by forts constructed at the Crown's expense.

Sir Richard Fiennes, Lord Say and Seale, had been granted three thousand acres in order to exercise a leadership role in the barony of Oneilland in Co. Armagh. Though he took out a patent in June 1610, he was now an old man and passed it on to Sir Anthony Cope, a substantial Oxfordshire landowner at Hanwell, near Broughton. His son, also called Anthony, put up a grand cross-shaped house at Castleraw which reflected a style prevailing in the English midlands. The Savages, one of the few surviving Old English landed families in Ulster, built a tower-house at Kirkistown in the Ards in 1622—an old-fashioned structure, complete with a spiral stair and ogee-headed windows in the traditional Irish style.[10]

In Donegal, Sir Basil Brooke repaired and strengthened the fifteenth-century O'Donnell stronghold but added a Jacobean manor-house wing in the English style next to it, surrounded by a bawn. Sir Richard Wingfield completed Benburb Castle on a site of one of Shane O'Neill's strongholds; this veteran ensured that the bawn walls, circular tower and rectangular flankers were plentifully supplied with gun-loops. Sir Toby Caulfield's house, Castle Caulfield, was fitted with splendid bay windows, rendering it indefensible, but at least the strong fort of Charlemont was not far away.

By the 1620s Lough Erne had been ringed with castles, their architectural styles reflecting the origins of the grantees. On the northern shore of the lower lough they included those of the English planters, the Blennerhasset brothers. Thomas and Sir Edward Blennerhasset jointly bought the thousand-acre estate of Tollimakein from John Thurston to add to their own proportions in Lurg precinct, making them the pre-eminent landlords in north Fermanagh. Sir Edward erected Hassett's Fort (later Castle Caldwell), according to Pynnar 'a strong bawn of lime and stone . . . and a stone house 3 storeys high, all furnished himself and family dwelling in it'. Thomas's fortified house of Castlehasset (now Crevenish) in Kesh attracted similar approval. The most imposing castle on the northern shore of the lough was (and remains) Termon Magrath, erected close to Pettigo. The Magraths had been the erenaghs of church land here, and Queen Elizabeth granted the Franciscan friar Mieler Magrath these lands in gratitude for his conversion to Protestantism. He became Bishop of Clogher and was Archbishop of Cashel by the time of the plantation. A Franciscan visiting him in 1617 reported that he was 'cursed by the Protestants for wasting the revenues and manors of the ancient see of Cashel, and derided by the Catholics who are well acquainted with his drunken habits'.[11] Termon Magrath was put up by the archbishop's fifth son, James.

Unlike the English, the Scots were still putting up castles in their homeland, where security was a higher priority than comfort. Monea Castle, built for Archbishop Malcolm Hamilton six miles north-west of Enniskillen, is an imposing structure erected in the distinctive Scots baronial style. Well provided with gun-loops at the ground-floor level, the rectangular tower-house had its entrance protected by two tourelles, or circular towers, capped with crow-stepped gables joined by a high arch with a murder-hole in the medieval style. The strong bawn had two flanker towers, one of which seems to have housed pigeons so as to provide residents with fresh meat in winter. Monea bears a striking resemblance to Claypotts Castle at Broughty Ferry in Angus. Tully Castle, overlooking Lower Lough Erne on the southern shore, was built for Sir John Home in a mixture of styles, and its rubble walls and ground-floor vault indicate that Irish masons built it. It had corbelled rounds projecting over the bawn wall and in the towers at the angles of the bawn.

The Scots baronial style is also evident in Castle Balfour and Crom Castle, by Upper Lough Erne, Sir James Hamilton's castle at Killyleagh, Co. Down, and especially in Ballygalley Castle, with corbelled cylindrical tourelles capped with conical roofs, put up on the Antrim coast in 1625 for James Shaw of Greenock. The Londoners sank most of their money for defence into the walls of Derry and Coleraine, but they erected bawns on most of their twelve proportions, evidence of which can still be best viewed at Bellaghy, Ballykelly and Salterstown. The Skinners already had Captain Edward Doddington's castle at Dungiven, but they put up another bawn, Crossalt, at Brackfield. The 1st Earl of Antrim built defended houses at Kilwaughter, Glenarm and Ballycastle, but he lavished most of his attention on Dunluce Castle. Here the two-storey inner great hall with tall windows to the west was put up in the English style as a gracious manor house, with fine moulded stones at the parapet level to support the roof. The 2nd Earl, anxious to make it fit for his wife, the dowager Duchess of Buckingham, spent large sums on furnishings and extensions. However, parts of the domestic quarters and kitchens fell into the sea in a disastrous collapse in 1639, taking some of the servants with it to a watery grave.[12]

ESTATES FREQUENTLY CHANGING HANDS

A feature of the Plantation of Ulster was the rapid turnover in the ownership of proportions. How this happened can be illustrated by examining the career Sir Ralph Bingley in Co. Donegal. Shipped over from Chester, Bingley arrived in Ulster as Captain of Foot in 1598. This professional soldier from Broughton was already a veteran: he had taken part in the raiding voyage led by Sir Francis Drake and Sir John Hawkins to Panama and Puerto Rico in 1595, and had served the following year as a muster-master for trained bands in Hampshire defending Portsmouth. In 1600 he was part of Sir Henry Docwra's amphibious operation in Lough Foyle and took command of 150 men lodged in Rathmullan priory engaged against the MacSweeneys of the Fanad Peninsula. Even before the end of hostilities in May 1602 he obtained a lease of the monastic land of Rathmullan, the island of Inch and the entire fishing rights of Lough Swilly. Next year his acquisitions extended to Carrigans and the monastic lands of Kilmacrenan, and he was joined by his brother Richard, who also got access to neighbouring lands. Though Bingley was knighted in 1603, he was paid off as a colonel and became involved in shady 'doings at sea', being imprisoned briefly when he made unauthorised raids on Spanish vessels after Philip III had signed a peace with James I.

The rebellion of Sir Cahir O'Doherty in 1608 enabled Bingley to rehabilitate himself, leading the assault on Tory Island and ordering the treacherous slaughter of MacSweeney's garrison there. Bingley was allotted a thousand acres (actually 7,120 statute acres) as a servitor-grantee in the barony of Kilmacrenan, with the responsibility of establishing a settler town at Rathmullan. Richard, now constable of Doe Castle, got a proportion adjoining the fortress, but he sold up to become surveyor of the Royal Navy and to assist Chichester in transporting rounded-up woodkerne to Sweden. Within a few years Sir Ralph had become a major proprietor, somehow becoming the owner of two undertaker proportions, one which had been granted to Sir Robert Remington, who had died before the year 1610 was out, and the other to Sir Maurice Berkeley, a Somersetshire landowner and active member of Parliament knighted at Cádiz in 1596. Like Cole at Enniskillen and many other servitors, Bingley took advantage of the precarious financial condition of those Irish fortunate enough to be left some land. He appears to have bought out the patents of at least eleven native grantees. Bingley's dealings, even by the standards of the time, appear to have been corrupt and forceful, leading to complaints from local Irish that he had 'detained' their land.

Rather suddenly Bingley sold most of his land, about 26,420 acres, some to former military associates, and his Rathmullan estate to the Bishop of Raphoe, Andrew Knox, who was to prove an energetic coloniser. Bingley himself was no more than average in performance as a planter. He erected a fortified house and bawn at Farsetmore, overlooking the River Swilly, considered in 1619 'well seated for service', and houses for his tenants 'at his own charge'. He put up a strong house for himself at Drumboe and developed Ballybofey, where he was licensed in 1619 to hold fairs and markets, and which in 1622 contained twelve thatched houses and cottages 'inhabited for the most part with British'. Pynnar reckoned that there were fifty families in 1619, some of them recruited in Flintshire and Cheshire, and others were Scots.

When Charles 1 decided to go to war with France in 1627, Bingley leapt at the chance to renew his military career. He wrote to the Duke of Buckingham, the King's favourite, appointed to lead the expedition to La Rochelle, offering to command a force from Ireland, as 'it swarms with idle men that are more fit for the wars abroad than to disturb the peace . . . at home'. He did indeed join that disastrous expedition and was killed in action on the Ile de Rhé in October 1627. His widow sold his estates for £5,850, much of which had to be used to pay off creditors.[13]

In every barony of the six escheated counties estates continued to change hands, in places with bewildering frequency. The precinct of Lifford, the south-west portion of the barony of Raphoe, provides a typical example of this kind of turnover. Here nine Englishmen had been selected in London to be granted proportions. Sir Robert Remington dropped dead before he could get from Yorkshire to his proportion of Tawnaforis, and his heir sold on to Sir Ralph Bingley. Sir Henry Docwra, anxious to pursue his career in Dublin, immediately sold out to William Wilson, a lawyer from Norfolk. Sir Henry Clare, a Norfolk landowner and veteran of the Irish wars, passed on his estate of Stranorlar to Peter Benson, the contractor who had built Derry's walls. Edward Russell, a Londoner who had seen service in Newry, sold out to Captain John Kingsmill, the younger son of a Hampshire landowner. Sir Thomas Cornewall, one of a family group from Shropshire which had originally applied for the entire precinct, sold Corlackey proportion in 1613 to Robert Davies of Gwysaney in Flintshire, where he had made his money in coal-mining; but he seems to have lost his fortune in Bohemia, being amongst the Protestants overwhelmingly routed at Prague in 1620, and so Davies sold on to Paul Davis (no relation), a former clerk of the Irish Privy Council. The estate of Sir William Barnes was sold in three portions to Thomas, brother of William Wilson, to Sir Richard Hansard and Captain Kingsmill. Sir Maurice Berkeley sold his great proportion of Dromore and Larga to Bingley in order to concentrate on his interests in Virginia.

Of the original grantees in Lifford precinct, only the army veterans Sir Thomas Coach and Ralph Mansfield remained. And yet the plantation here was progressing well. The stipulated number of colonists for the nine proportions was 150 settler families or 360 adult males; in 1619 Pynnar recorded 193 settler families, which included 536 British adult males.[14]

COLONISING COUNTY ANTRIM

Despite all the government attention given to the plantation in the six confiscated counties, British colonisation was at its most successful in Antrim and Down. The only government survey which reported on the two counties was that of 1611. Even at that early stage the commissioners' 'Reporte of the Voluntary Worke Done by Servitors and Other Gentlemen of Qualitie upon Lands Given Them by His Majestie or Purchased by Themselves' indicated encouraging progress. In Belfast, Chichester's mansion and castle were close to completion, and 'there is a strong Bawne almost finished which is flankered with foure half Bulwarkes'. The report continued:

The foundacion of the wall and bulwarkes to the height of the water table is made with stoane, and the reste, being in alle 12 foote high above the ground, is made with bricke. The Bawne will be compased with a lardge and deep ditche or moate which will always stand full of water.

The Castle will defend the Passage over the Foorde at Bealfast between the Upper and Lower Clandeboye, and likewise the Bridge over the Owynvarra between Malon and Bealfast. The work is in so good forwardness that it is lyke to be finished by the mydle of the next Somer.

The 'Owynvarra' (Abhainn Bhearra) is now called the Blackstaff (a close translation). The commissioners found that Belfast had 'many famelyes of English, Scotch, and some Manksmen already inhabiting, of which some are artificers who have buylte good tymber houses with chimneys after the fashion of the English palle, and one Inn with very good Lodginge which is a great comforte to the travellers in those partes'. After the finishing of the house, the castle and the bawn, the 1.2 million bricks that Chichester had fired would provide enough 'for the buyldinge of other tenementes within the said Towne'.

Sir Arthur Chichester's heir, Viscount Edward Chichester, seems to have rebuilt much of his brother's mansion. Having seen Joymount in Carrickfergus, Sir William Brereton found Belfast Castle most pleasing:

At Belfast my Lord Chichester hath another dainty stately house (which is indeed the glory and beauty of the town also), where he is most resident, and is now building an outer brick wall before his gates. This is not so large and vast as the other, but more convenient and commodious; the very end of the lough toucheth upon his gardens and backside; here also are dainty orchards, gardens and walks planted.

The ecclesiastical commissioners of 1622 reported that the church in Belfast had been rebuilt from the ground. This was not the old parish church of Shankill but was on the site of the medieval chapel of ease where the Farset River joined the Lagan, almost certainly where St George's now stands. Measuring 150 feet along its east-west axis and 100 feet from north to south, and with a prominent tower, six bays, two transepts and a large window in the north transept, this rivalled St Columb's in Derry. Chichester saw to it that Belfast, along with other British colonial towns, was incorporated in 1613 to enable the town to send two members to the Irish Parliament. As 'Lord of the Castle', Chichester chose the 'sovereign', or mayor, and the twelve other burgesses. In 1615 the corporation ordered that fines be levied on those who did not attend church 'within the said corporation', and it repeated the order two years later.

The 1611 commissioners reported that Belfast was 'plotted out in a good forme', but it was not so grandly planned as the city of Londonderry, for example. The main street was parallel to the Farset on the north side, named Broad Street, which later became Waring Street. Only in the next century did High Street become the hub of the town, especially after the Farset had been covered over in stages in the 1770s. Plots for houses in Broad Street backed on to the Farset, and other dwellings in time were put up in Skipper Street and on the road to Carrickfergus, which became North Street. The town's market-place was probably in what is now Bridge Street. By 1639 the corporation laid down that there was to be no forestalling of grain and no trading until the ringing of the market bell at ten o'clock.[15]

Close to Belfast—probably in the area now known as the Oldpark—Chichester had fenced off 'a Parke of three myle compasse' and erected a timber house with brick chimneys. Other retired soldiers were busy between Belfast and Carrickfergus. Humphrey Norton, lieutenant of the Lord Deputy's Foot Company, had put up a large house with chimneys on land leased from Chichester which was 'well intrenched, rampiered, and fenced with a strong palisade of timber'. Near Carrickfergus, Ensign Michael Newby had built 'a pritie stone house with chimneys, two storie high', thatched, but it was to be slated the following summer. A mile inland the late Cornet Thomas Walsh had erected a large house 'enclosed with a rampier of earth, soddes and flanker'd . . . now inhabited by Lieutenant Barrye who marryed the saide Walsh his wyddowe'. All around, the commissioners found many other 'tenementes inhabited, some of them by such cyvell irish as doe speak English, and dyvers of them have byne servitors in the late queen's tyme'. On the whole,

upon dyvers other portions of the Lord Deputy's lands there are many English famelies, some Scottes, and dyvers cyvell Irish planted, and there are three myles already buylte upon several partes of the said lands; and tymber and other materials are also provided for the buydinge of another mylle neere unto Belfast.

On the other side of Belfast, Sir Moses Hill had leased from Chichester 'a good scope of lande'. Hill had 'a stronge forte buylte upon a passadge on the playnes of Moylon with a strong palisade and a drawbridge called Hilsborowe. Within it is a fayre tymber house walled with brickes, and a towre slated'. This fortification was not at Hillsborough but by the Lagan, close to Shaw's Bridge. Hill was also constructing a house and bawn down-stream, 'where the sea ebbes and flowes in a place called Strandmellis'.[16] The ruins of this structure were known in the nineteenth century as Sir Moses' Cellars. Sir William Brereton, travelling this way in 1636, found that Arthur Hill, son and heir to Sir Moses, 'hath a brave plantation' which

> doth yield him a £1000 per annum. Many Lancashire and Cheshire men are here planted; with some of them I conversed. They sit upon a rack rent [rent raised year by year], and pay 5s or 6s an acre for good ploughing land, which is now clothed with excellent corn.[17]

Chichester had chosen Carrickfergus, not Belfast, as his main place of residence. Though it would soon be by-passed in size and population by the city of Londonderry, Carrickfergus was still Ulster's largest town when the 1611 commissioners reported on it. Here they observed the defensive walls ordered by the Lord Deputy under construction:

> At Knockfargus we founde many masons and laborers at worke aboute the erection and building of the walles of that towne and sunderye quarie men and laborers at worke aboute a quarter of a myle from the Towne in breakinge of rough stones for the works.
> We also founde 4 oxe teemes 2 horse teemes and many garrons which carres drawing of stones and of other materialles for the same worke and we found 4 lyme kills on fyre employed in burning lyme stone for the same.

Sir Fulke Conway informed them that men were 'employed continually in breaking of limestone about three myles from the Towne at a place called the White heade'. Other masons were busy forty miles away—presumably at Cushendun—'in breaking and skaffoldinge of free stones for coynes for the Bullworkes and to face the wall 6 foot high all along the southe part of the Towne by the sea syde'. They heard that this operation was fraught with difficulty, 'because the boates cannot come neere the place but in very calme weather and as wee weare enformed there have byne sundrie boates brocken and spoyled there since that worke begane'. Chichester was also erecting a large mansion for himself on the east side of Carrickfergus, which he would call Joymount, 'with a good quantitie of grounde for an orchard', strongly built and predicted to be 'a good strength to the Towne on that side'.

Sir Moses Hill had erected Castle Chichester on land close to Whitehead, and the commissioners observed that neighbouring Islandmagee 'is well inhabited by English and Scotishmen and by other civill Irishmen such as for the most part can speake English and many of them doe goe in the English habbitt'. In the hinterland north of Carrickfergus and Belfast, Baptist Jones was developing an estate at Marshallstown, enclosing fields 'trenched with a deepe ditche and stronge palle . . . in many places sett with wyllowes'; John Dobbs was building 'a fayre Castle' on land leased from Ensign John Dalway; Dalway himself was busy constructing the bawn close by which still bears his name; Lieutenant Humphrey Norton was finishing a castle 'with two great flankers . . . at a place called Tymplepatricke upon the said Sir Arthur Chichester's lande by the River of Sixmylewater'; and Captain Roger Langford had built a stone house at Muckamore 'which is a good strength and countenance to that part of the countie'. Captain Hugh Clotworthy, in charge of the King's boats on Lough Neagh, next to Massereene Fort, 'in the midst of the Ryver some smale distance from the lough', had seen to the erection of 'fayre tymber houses after the English manner . . . covered over with good shingle togeather with necessarie houses to keepe his Majesties stores of victualles and munition'. Clotworthy had command of a barque of thirty tons, another of fourteen tons and others between ten and eight tons equipped to take stores across the lough 'into the centre of Tyrone and Armagh to relieve his Majesties forces and garrisons there'.[18]

The greatest proprietor in Co. Antrim was not Sir Arthur Chichester but Sir Randal MacDonnell, who had secured legal title in 1603 to 333,907 acres in the Route and the Glynns. He had surrendered nine townlands next to Coleraine to facilitate the City of London, but the King, in very generous compensation, agreed to reduce by half the rent for the remainder of his estates. Sir Randal, more wholeheartedly than any other Gaelic lord in Ulster, adopted British ways, in particular quickly comprehending how to run his vast estate in a modern, commercial way. Aware that he had many who would like to see him fall, he also kept his antennae constantly raised to discern the King's priorities and to respond promptly to seek to satisfy them.

Devout Catholic though he was, Sir Randal did not hesitate to invite Protestants from the Scottish Lowlands to lease his lands. This would not only please the King but would also augment his income, as Lowlanders were accustomed to paying economic rents rather than the traditional render given by natives to their superior lords. Though his lands were not covered by the Articles of Plantation, he erected fortifications on them as if they did apply there. As early as 1611 commissioners reported that the 'towne of Dunluce consists of many tenements after the fashion of the palle people for the most part with Scotishmen'. Here Sir Randal had his principal stronghold; he had built 'a fayre stone walle aboute the whole Work, within which he hath erected a good house of stone with many Lodgingis and other Roomes'. This would later be enhanced in an elegant English style to rival any other in the province. Other castles were repaired and modernised at Ballycastle and Red Bay, and his brother 'buylte a good neowe stone house at Glenarme', where he would put up a new castle shortly before his death. In turn, his tenants would build castles at Ballygalley, Kilwaughter and elsewhere.

By 1629 the Earl of Clanrickard was observing that Sir Randal 'hath good tenants and is very well paid his rents'.[19] Sir Randal, created the 1st Earl of Antrim in 1620, let out land to twenty-five Lowland Scots between 1609 and 1626. Admittedly the leases were long: the shortest was for 51 years, most were for 101 years, and one man obtained a 301-year tenure. Long leases kept rents at a fixed level, which created problems for Randal and his son and heir. Those who had taken out large estates were able to sub-let to other incoming British: the rent roll for May 1641 records 375 acres rented to a yeoman, John Stirling, and another 347 acres to a 'husbandman', John Skeagh.

The O'Neills of Lower Clandeboye, the part of the sixteenth-century lordship north of the River Lagan, had been the principal losers in Co. Antrim. Niall Óg O'Neill of Killileagh was left with the remnants of what had once been an extensive lordship on the northern shores of Lough Neagh. This included Edenduffcarrick Castle, the site of the later Shane's Castle. Chichester described him as very poor with many dependants. When Niall Óg died, in 1616, it was revealed that he was heavily in debt to Sir Robert McClelland of Bomby. All his lands were mortgaged to pay debts, apart from a jointure for his wife worth £250 a year, leaving his son Sir Henry O'Neill with lands worth £40 per annum.[20]

Nevertheless, Sir Henry proved an astute and level-headed survivor and was acknowledged as a man of culture and learning. He took care to cultivate the friendship of his neighbour Sir Hugh Clotworthy and his politically influential son and heir, Sir John Clotworthy. This family was to emerge from all the vicissitudes of the century remarkably unscathed, and it remains prominent today, with Lord O'Neill of Shane's Castle at its head.

Some Scots struck out on their own in Co. Antrim. Among them was William Edmonston of Duntreath, Stirlingshire, who originally crossed to Ireland with Sir Hugh Montgomery. In 1609 he moved from Down to Antrim, where he bought 2,870 acres at Broadisland in the barony of Belfast, near Carrickfergus, much of it from John Dalway. Here he began by building two slated houses. Clearly he decided that his future lay in Ireland, because he mortgaged his Duntreath estates for fifteen years. By the time of his death, in 1626, when he was succeeded by his son, he could raise 151 British men (almost all of them Lowlanders), according to the muster of about 1630. William Adair, who had settled in the barony of Toome, came from Kilnahilt in Wigtownshire. Like Edmonston, he was prepared to lose most of his lands in Scotland to make a success of his venture in Antrim. In 1620 he was forced to sell some of his Wigtownshire land to Sir Hugh Montgomery, and he was 'put to the horn'—that is, taken to court in Scotland for debt—to satisfy his creditors. He was highly successful in attracting tenants, and the muster of 1630 listed 137 British men, 90 per cent of them Scots. That muster, giving a total of 2,008 British males for Co. Antrim, demonstrates the rapid progress of colonisation there. That figure includes 956 on the earl's lands, 377 from Islandmagee and 387 English from other estates.[21]

COLONISING CO. DOWN

Sir James Hamilton and Sir Hugh Montgomery deserve to be regarded as the principal pioneers of British colonisation in Ulster. They might have been even more successful if they had not become embroiled in expensive legal disputes. Sir William Smith, a descendant of Sir Thomas Smith (who had been granted the Ards by Queen Elizabeth), tried to revive his family's title to this land. Despite the finding of an inquisition of 1612 that Sir Thomas had forfeited the lands for failure to fulfil the terms of his grant, Sir William pressed ahead with a claim on the lands now being settled by Hamilton and Montgomery. Sir William failed, but the two Scottish lairds had been obliged, at considerable cost, to defend their titles.

Much more distracting and expensive were 'several tedious and chargeable law-suits' between Hamilton and Montgomery concerning 'the marchis of their landis', mostly over townlands Montgomery had bought or otherwise obtained from Sir Conn O'Neill. The dispute—described in the Montgomery Manuscripts as 'divers debates, controversys, and suits'— became so intractable that the Earl of Abercorn was called in in 1614 to arbitrate. The award he handed down on 2 August 1615 tended to favour Hamilton. The two lairds were to share the woods and lands acquired from Sir Conn, and Hamilton was to hand back abbey lands apportioned to Montgomery in 1605. Montgomery refused to let the matter drop, arguing that the decision had been unfair because Abercorn was cousin to Sir James Hamilton. However, in December 1616 King James confirmed the earl's award. The dispute rumbled on and seems to have been finally resolved only in 1626. In the view of William Montgomery, author of the Montgomery Manuscripts, it took the horrors of the rebellion of 1641 to erase the bad feeling between the two families, all 'differences sirceasing that last named year, and so were sedated, or buried, or forgotten'.[22]

This long wrangle did reveal that Hamilton had taken land illegally from the Church. In 1611 the English Council was informed that John Todd, Bishop of Down and Connor and Dromore, had attempted to separate himself from his wife by gathering false testimony against her. The scandalised Council ordered that the bishop be removed, but Todd fled to Scotland to escape punishment. The investigation revealed that Todd had embezzled most of the church property in his diocese, some of it alienated to Hamilton. Mounting legal costs seem to have forced Hamilton to sell the proportion he had been granted in Co. Cavan in 1621. However, Hamilton did acquire, legally, the entire barony of Dufferin on the western shores of Strangford Lough, which he leased from the Old English White family. In 1616 he augmented his holdings still further by leasing eighteen townlands between Saintfield and Belfast from Sir Conn and establishing a half interest in another forty of O'Neill's townlands.

After spending time in Co. Down in 1614 mediating between the two lairds, the Earl of Abercorn observed that he found two thousand well-armed Scots there ready to serve the King. This was a very rough estimate (apparently made while out hunting), but it is an indication that the process of colonisation was forging ahead. Actually the total number was probably higher. The muster of 1630 listed 1,401 British males on Hamilton's lands and 1,317 on Montgomery's, more than three-quarters of them bearing Scottish surnames.[23] The 1611 commissioners commented favourably on 'voluntary works' in the county:

Sir James Hamyton Knight hath buylded a fayre stone house at the towne of Bangor in the upper Clandeboye within the Countie aforesaid about 60 foote longe and 22 foote boade the towne consistes of 80 new houses all inhabited with Scotyshmen and Englishmen. And hath brought out of England 20 artifficers who are making materilles of tymber bricke and stone for another house there.

Hamilton was also preparing 'to build another house at holly woode three miles from Bangor and two hundred thowsand of brickes with other materialles ready at the place where there are some 20 houses inhabited with English and Scottes'. At Newtownards 'Sir Hugh Mountgomery Knight hath repayred parte of the Abbey of Newtowne for his owne dwelling and made a good towne of a hundred houses or thereabouts all peopled with Scottes'.

Thanks to the Montgomery Manuscripts, more is known about this laird and his family than about any other in Co. Down at this time. After completing his mansion, Sir Hugh saw to it that the church in Newtownards was 'repaired, roofed, and replenished with pews (before his death), mostly by his Lady's care and oversight, himself being much abroad by his troubles aforesaid'. His son later erected another church with a steeple beside it. Differences between the Hamiltons and the Montgomerys were set aside so as to bear the cost together of reconstructing the church on the abbey lands of Comber. Montgomery also erected a large church and bell-tower in Donaghadee and one to match it on the other side of the North Channel in Portpatrick (then known as Port Montgomery). He also repaired the church at Greyabbey and another on the episcopal lands of Kilmore, and he supplied these churches with bells bearing his coat of arms and with Bibles—not the Authorised (King James) version but the 'Dutch', or Geneva, translation, published in 1603. In spite of his Presbyterian sympathies (which were not as strong as those of his son and heir), he also saw to it that these churches had copies of the Book of Common Prayer.

About 1626 the harbour at Donaghadee, 'a great and profitable work', was completed. In that year King Charles I instructed the Lord Deputy, Viscount Falkland, to grant Viscount Montgomery, who, 'having lands in our Kingdom of Scotland, may have occasion frequently to repair thither, and specially at this time being to build a church at Port Montgomery', a licence to pass into Scotland, so often as his occasions shall require, and likewise, that the Viscount have liberty to transport all such materials, victuals, and other necessaries from his own bounds in Ireland as are requisite for his own use and advancing of the work intended at the port of Scotland, with as much liberty and immunity as can be granted, in regard of the barrenness of the place of the country where the port doth lie.

Clearly the King had been urged to do this by planters all over Ulster, for the letter refers to the construction of the harbour, 'the doing whereof hath been often recommended to us by our British undertakers as a thing very necessary for our service'. Thanks to Montgomery, Donaghadee continued to be the busiest port for passengers between Scotland and the north of Ireland for at least a century to come.

Sir Hugh built a 'great school' at Newtownards for pupils of both sexes, endowing it with twenty pounds a year to pay a 'Master of Arts'

> to teach Latin, Greek and Logycks, allowing the scholars a green for recreation at goff, football, and archery, declaring, that if he lived some few years longer, he would convert his priory houses into a College for Philosophy; and further paid small stipends to a master to teach orthography and arithmetic, and to a music-master, who should be also precentor to the church (which is a curacy), so that both sexes might learn all those three arts.

The author of the above, William Montgomery, is almost certainly the first person to refer to the game of golf in Ireland. He mentions that he was a scholar at this school in 1646 and that past pupils told him that no better music, 'without a full quire and organs, could be made':

> For the precentor's method was this—three trebles, three tenors, three counter-tenors, and 3 bass voices, equally divided on each side of them (besides Gentlewomen scholars which sat scattered in their pews) which sang their several parts as he had appointed them, which overruled any of the heedless vulgar, who learned thereby (at least) to forbear disturbing the congregation with their clamorous tones.—The scholars of the great school also came in order, following the master, and seated themselves in the next form in the loft or gallery, behind the Provost, who had his Burgesses on each hand of them.

Clearly the British settlement on the parts of Down granted to the two Scottish lairds was doing very well. What is more, this colonisation was spreading into the hinterland of the county. The Upper Clandeboye O'Neills were not the only losers: Montgomery and Hamilton, veterans who had served the Bagenals in Newry, and servitors, leasing land from Chichester and moving up the Lagan Valley, were finding ways to acquire fresh estates—by fair means or foul—from the natives in Iveagh, Kinelarty, Lecale and Killultagh. This was a piecemeal process, unaccompanied by violence. In the end, however, it was dangerously dislocating, generating a profound feeling of insecurity amongst the surviving Gaelic proprietors. The Magennises, MacCartans and other natives began to feel they could take no more.

UNEVEN COLONISATION

Government officials may have been disappointed by the number of British colonists in Ulster, as revealed in repeated surveys, but the migration was impressive enough. Bodley had come up with the figure of 2,000 adult British males in 1613. The surveys of 1619 and 1622 raised that number to 6,000 or more, and the 1630 muster lists drawn up to record those available for local military service listed about 6,500 adult British males in the six escheated counties, and a further 5,600 in Antrim and Down. By 1630 the rough total is reached of 16,000 adult British males in Ulster. Harvest failures in Scotland from 1633 tempted more Scots to come over, and by 1641 the settler population of Ulster stood at between 40,000 and 45,000 adults, two-thirds of them Scots.[24]

Within three years, undertakers, including the London Companies, were all required to plant their lands with a minimum of twenty-four adult English or Lowland Scots males, representing at least ten families, for every thousand acres granted. The proportions for English and Scottish undertakers were stated to contain 162,500 acres, and the London Companies were granted another 38,520. In all, the undertakers, including the London Companies, were to settle a minimum of 4,825 adult males. In addition, the bishops were expected to settle eight adult British males for every thousand acres. Corporate towns were supposed to be exclusively British, and, while they had no obligation to colonise, servitors and even some of the 'deserving Irish' were expected to bring in colonists as tenants.

The time-frame set down was far too tight. The Carew Survey of 1611 and the Bodley Survey of 1613 revealed that a great many undertakers had yet to meet their obligations, and so King James, becoming ever more frustrated, extended the time limit to the end of August 1616. Another survey by Bodley in 1616—apart from a few fragmentary reports on the Londoners' lands—has not survived, but it is clear that the report revealed a disappointing situation. The King issued a proclamation in 1618 setting a new deadline of 1 May 1619, by which date all the Irish were to have been removed from the undertakers' estates. Pynnar's survey of 1619 demonstrated that very little progress had been made in forcing the natives to move, and so the King felt he had no choice but to agree in 1621 that the undertakers should set aside a quarter of each proportion for the Irish. A final survey—sometimes known as the Phillips Survey, as Sir Thomas played a leading role in conducting it—reported in 1622.

What emerges from these reports is that most of the undertakers did indeed colonise their lands with the requisite number of British settlers. Some far exceeded their quotas (compensating for those who neglected to meet them), and, considering that the colonisation of much of the counties of Antrim and Down was more impressive than anywhere else in the province, Ulster was in the process of being transformed. The negative conclusions and often caustic language of the survey reports tend to hide the success of the whole colonising enterprise. Much of the frustration at court was brought about by evidence that many of the plans laid down in London were going awry. In part this was the fault of the planners who had made it too easy for the original grantees to sell up, with the result that some of the more determined colonisers were able to augment their holdings, creating estates which, from the experience of the Munster Plantation, were considered in London to be too large. The colonists were expected to live in towns, but most of them found that this was far too inconvenient, necessitating daily travel to their farms. The outcome was quite the reverse of that recommended by theorists such as Spenser, Smith and Bacon. Also, British settlers brought over by undertakers were mobile and, in time, were able to move to lands which were more fertile and accessible to markets, and—above all—which were not isolated and in danger of being attacked or plundered by woodkerne and other native Irish. In short, the settlers clustered in fertile valleys and near the coasts and navigable rivers, finding safety in numbers.

British colonisation was therefore uneven. By 1622 it was becoming clear that preferred areas of settlement were emerging: mid-Ulster, to the south and west of Lough Neagh, especially east Tyrone, north Armagh and the Clogher Valley; the Foyle Basin, particularly in the vicinity of Londonderry and Strabane; the Lower Bann Valley and the north coast;

around Upper and Lower Lough Erne; and the middle of Co. Cavan. In the counties of Down and Antrim the most densely colonised areas were in the Lagan Valley, north and east Down, the Lecale and Ards Peninsulas, south Antrim and Ballymena, and in the Bush Valley. For the most part these were the very areas which had been inhabited most densely by the native Irish before their conquest.[25]

During the sixteenth-century phase of migration from Spain to the New World the total annual human flow averaged 2,583 a year. The British migration to Ulster in the early seventeenth century can be considered comparable, particularly when it is remembered that the population of Britain was less than half that of Spain and Portugal together. The proportion of women amongst those going to the New World did not exceed a third of the total in any year and was usually considerably less. The proportion of women coming over from Britain to Ulster was notably higher.[26]

Of course the distances British colonists had to travel were much shorter than for those setting out from Spain. However, for most of the time the passage from Spain to America was relatively secure and well charted. For Scots making their way from Galloway to Ulster the passage was short and generally safe. For those who decided to migrate from East Anglia to become tenants on the Blennerhasset estates in Co. Fermanagh, for example, the journey to western Ulster was altogether more daunting. George Canning, agent for the Ironmongers' Company in Co. Londonderry, was one of the few to keep a record of his travel times. In 1614 he had been involved in the Londonderry Plantation for four years, so the route was familiar to him. He left London on 30 September and arrived in Chester on 2 October; finding no ship available, he waited for a passage from the little port of Hilbree between 14 and 21 October. Boarding the *Bride of Derry*, he got to the Foyle three days later, and he finally got to his destination at Coleraine on 26 October. Surviving the hazards of crossing the Irish Sea and navigating the treacherous headlands of the north coast must have been almost as taxing for British immigrants to Ulster as it was to be for the 21,000 who emigrated from the south of England to New England in the 1630s.[27]

SETTLING IN

The first settlers had to bring enough provisions with them to survive the first winter before planting their corn in the spring. They usually had to provide their own shelter before beginning the task of erecting permanent homes. This generally involved enlisting natives not only to guide them to their properties but also to build houses—which explains why many made do with coupled houses put up in the traditional Irish style. Another man who served as agent for the Ironmongers, Thomas Perkins, remarked that his progress was hindered because of the 'rain which made great rivers . . . full of difficulty and danger in this country for want of boats and bridges'. Thomas Blennerhasset, while urging fellow-Englishmen to join him in this great colonial enterprise, nevertheless warned that new arrivals should have their weapons at the ready for 'the cruel wood-kerne, the devouring wolf, and other suspicious Irish', who might well 'put on the smiling countenance' but did 'threaten every hour'.[28]

Everywhere, the native Irish were waiting to be moved or dispossessed, and in the forests lurked the woodkerne, landless men and former soldiers of O'Neill, who threatened the settlements. At Charlemont, Co. Armagh, Sir Toby Caulfield was forced 'every night to lay up all his cattle as it were in warde, and doe hee and his what they can, the woolfe and the wood-kerne (within caliver shot of his forte) have often times a share'. John Rowley, the mayor of the city Londonderry, informed the Drapers' Company in 1615 that his men were building Moneymore 'as it were with the Sworde in one hande and the Axe in thother'. The following year Canning reported to London that his labourers were 'fearful to work in the woodes except they be 10 or 12 in a companie'. Again and again woodkerne emerged from their forest and mountain retreats to plunder the settlers, despite Lord Deputy Chichester's drive to 'take up the lewd Kerns or such as have bin Rebells or are idle Livers' and ship them for military service to Sweden.[29] Some, of course, were in constant expectation that Hugh O'Neill would return to Ulster with a Spanish army, a hope which did not dissolve until the earl's death in 1616.

The papers of the Ironmongers' Company provide some insight into the manner in which colonisation got under way. The Ironmongers' lands lay upstream of Coleraine on the west bank of the Lower Bann. Here the initial problem was the complete lack of suitable stone for building. Their first agent, Lieutenant Thomas Perkins, found clay on site suitable for making bricks and suggested oak instead of freestone for the surrounds of doors and windows. The price he proposed was too high, and he was dismissed and replaced by George Canning. Canning decided to do what he could with the stone available and gathered together slate and timber.

As building began, in 1615, he had grave misgivings, fearing that it might be 'necessary to frame your buildings round because the stone is so bad it will not make Quynes for the corner'. With some difficulty he recruited men from Coleraine and, not waiting for London's permission, engaged two carpenters based in the town, Abraham Wott and Edward Elice, to build a village close to the castle due to be erected at Athgeave. Six two-storey houses with brick chimneys were put up, constructed of 'half timber', that is, 'timber sawed to 5 or 6 inches square, and five inches square between each piece, and between those nogged, as we call it, with short pieces of cleft oak driven hard between and plastered, so it is very strong and equal to stone building'. But that winter of 1615 storms stripped off slates, and thatched houses put up by the English workmen were 'torn almost naked'. He ruefully observed that, though the dwellings of the natives were not suitable for civilised colonists, the 'Irish build low that a man may reach to the top with his hand and covered with turf and straw together bound on with ropes of straw and wattles so the winds little trouble them'.

Here, in addition to imported carpenters, masons and slaters, other workmen (presumably Irish) were needed to square timber in the woods, cart stone from quarries and bricks and lime from kilns from further afield, and float logs down the Bann. All this involved the Ironmongers in considerable expense. While it cost only a pound to bring iron from London to Coleraine, another five shillings were needed for 'boatage' from the town upstream, with a further cost of five shillings a day to bring material a short way overland from the riverside to Athgeave. Canning got £615 from his company between September 1615 and August 1616; £593 had been spent even before the castle was ready for occupation.[30] Those not close to navigable rivers incurred greater costs.

The servitor John Leigh had replaced his brother Edmund as custodian of Omagh Fort, with abbey lands adjacent, in 1608. He then bought out Sir Francis Willoughby's interest in the 2,000-acre proportion of Fintona in the barony of Clogher in Co. Tyrone. It was not long before he found it difficult to meet his obligations to build and to attract the requisite number of British colonists who were prepared to take the Oath of Supremacy. In August 1622 he wrote to Lord Caulfield, a member of a commission inquiring into the Irish government, including into plantations. Aware that the commissioners would find him falling behind in implementing the Articles of Plantation, he was keen to provide explanation.

Leigh began by stating that the soil of half the proportion 'is generally so bad, being only heath and boggy mountain land, and the measure of the little arable land that it is so small, that no British tenant will be drawn to inhabit upon it upon any terms or conditions, be they never so reasonable'. On the remaining thousand acres, 'whereas I have made estates of divers kinds unto British tenants . . . I do raise of clear yearly rent from them from their lands that they hold from me, being six hundred and four score acres, but only £18 15s', and 'my yearly rent of all my 2,000 acres doth not rise to £120 *per annum*'. Above all, 'I have been driven to build with much more charge than any other undertaker that I know in all the county of Tyrone', because of

> the want of most of the chiefest materials belonging to building, at first being forced to fetch all my timber about 12 or 14 miles at the nearest over bogs and mountains, and some above 22 miles, and to draw all the same at garrons' tails, the barbarousness of the country and the badness of the ways not admitting any other kind of carriage for that purpose.

Actually, the quality of the soil about Fintona was far higher, for example, than in the thin, acid and leached lands washed by the Atlantic in Boylagh precinct in Co. Donegal. Leigh's principal difficulty, in short, was inaccessibility:

> In like sort am I driven to fetch all my lime, every barrel whereof stands me at the least in 18d a barrel, and all my hewing stones in like sort I fetch 10 or 12 miles and to draw all at garrons' tails over filthy boggy mountains, all which inconveniences and defects notwithstanding what my expense and charge hath been in so barren a part of the country in building and enclosing and reducing of the soil to a better condition and what my intent and endeavours are yet further to perform.[31]

The Haberdashers, with land in Loughinsholin, south-west of Coleraine, were far less conscientious than the Ironmongers in attempting to meet their building and colonising obligations. They did not even have their own agent but employed Tristram Beresford, who was representing the interest of all the companies in Coleraine. Nevertheless, the Haberdashers had spent £1,124 by 1623 to cover the costs of surveying, map-making and fees for Beresford and his assistants; and those of iron, lead, nails, glass and iron shipped from London and—their biggest outlay—the erection of a water mill and their castle. Even then, money had to be found to build a church.[32]

The Fishmongers were allotted lands amounting to some 24,000 statute acres in two blocks: an area around Greysteel on the southern shore of Lough Foyle; and a long, narrow tongue of land from Lough Foyle around Ballykelly south to include Loughermore Mountain, and down to Foreglen and Feeny. This they named the manor of Walworth after Sir William Walworth, a former mayor of London and a fishmonger, who had helped to suppress Wat Tyler's Rebellion in 1381. On receiving their proportion, in December 1613, they chose as their agent Alexander Fookes, a buyer of fish at Rye, who, at a fee of 3s 4d a day, travelled to Ulster with the cartographer Thomas Raven. Though there was to be 'much suspicion' of 'untrue dealing', Fookes appears to have been energetic; he chose Ballykelly as the core of the Fishmongers' settlement, and by 1616 he had seen to it that there was a 'great house newly built . . . fifty feet square', with sixteen rooms, enclosed with a bawn with four flankers 125 feet square. The company sent Robert Whitney out to check on Fookes, giving him sixty pounds, which he thought not enough, because of 'the danger that he was in by his journey, escaping very hardly with his life'.

By about 1617 the Fishmongers had spent about three thousand pounds on their proportion and were wondering whether they would ever get a sufficient return on their investment. Like other companies, they were approached frequently by a range of individuals seeking to lease their lands. Among them was Raven, who offered to pay 4½ pence an acre each year and to discharge all the company's plantation obligations. He was told that, as the company had as yet 'no intelligence or information of the value of those things', it could not 'conclude with any man for anything'.

In the end they picked James Higgons, a London merchant who lived on London Bridge, close to the Fishmongers' Hall. Two townlands, Carrickhugh and Tullamaine, were leased to Lawrence Rathbone, an associate of Sir Thomas Phillips based in Coleraine. The fertile and accessible lands north of Loughermore Mountain and by Lough Foyle attracted at least the required number of British tenants. By about 1630 there were close to a hundred British males there, including the tradesmen 'Penticost the smith' and 'Peter the cooper'. Most of them were English, but, as in almost every English estate, Scots were present in numbers also.

Upstream of the bawn and 'great house' at Ballykelly, Higgons and his associate George Downing erected a mill and a large stone-built mill-house; the present Milltown House incorporates much of the original building, making it one of the oldest dateable structures in the area. The construction of a long and deep water course to power the mill must have been a substantial and labour-intensive feat of engineering. Higgons was to 'cause the land to be measured over, butted, bounded, doled or staked out'. Fields were enclosed by 'railing'—clearly a major task, as Downing had to bring fifty thousand lath nails from London to complete it. The collection of rents was increasingly by bills of exchange to ease the safe transmission of large sums to the City.

As on other Londoners' proportions, the native Irish were not expelled, even though the government persisted with threats to the companies if they were not. The attention of the Fishmongers was brought to a warrant from the Lord Deputy demanding removal. They responded that if this were to happen 'the tenants cannot pay their rents', which would 'redound to all the companies' general hurt and loss'. Therefore they paid the fines imposed. Two tenants, questioned about arrears, referred in extenuation to 'the great yearly imposition laid upon them for continuance of the Irish'. And so O'Mullans, O'Cahans, O' Harrans and other Gaelic Irish, tolerating the insertion of a layer of British above them, stayed on to farm the land.

Even in the densely colonised lands about Ballykelly there were still thirty Irish present in 1659, compared with forty-five English and Scots. In the more remote lands of the proportion, in Foreglen and Feeny, the 1622 commissioners found hardly any British; they concluded that it 'were fit there were another plantation into the land . . . for the better defence of the inhabitants thereof who are daily spoiled'.

Londoners defied the government by taking on priests to rent the land, finding them good farmers and prompt payers. This incensed Sir Thomas Phillips, who drafted a list of priests in the Derry diocese. He found that the sheriff of the county, Richard Kirby, had allowed suits involving priests to be heard in his sheriff's court. On Phillips's list for the Fishmongers' estates were Father Dermot O'Lynn (described earlier as 'speaking Irish, Latin and English' and as 'guileless and able'), Father Eugene McCloskey, Father Neice O'Devanny of Banagher and Father Donnogh O'Cahan of Cumber. Phillips stated that nine 'mass houses' had been erected on the Londoners' lands, one of them on the Fishmongers' proportion and another on the Grocers', 'near to one another'.[33]

Meeting building obligations proved easier than finding Protestant British tenants who would generate income. Canning, the Ironmongers' agent, started out by entering into short-term arrangements with the natives who were already there, urging his company to plead with the government that he could retain them, provided they went to church and took the Oath of Supremacy. The response was that this could not be done and that the company was likely to incur financial penalties if natives were kept on. He was urged to bring over artisans from London, who, once they had completed the erection of the castle and other buildings, 'after or rather presently may be set down upon our land as tenants'. Canning had found it impossible to cajole English and Scots already in the province to become tenants: money in Ireland was 'verious pretious', making it almost impossible for them to make the usual down-payments for leases, known as entry fines. Likely 'takers of land' had been able to get leases very advantageously for seven years' purchase and were therefore 'very unwilling . . . for the most part unable, to disburse money for fines or purchase of land.'

Canning did have some success in persuading artisans, mostly recruited in Coleraine, to become tenants. For example, Roger Holden, a sawyer, got a lease of two townlands at a rent of seven pounds per annum for a term of thirty-one years. Holden had to sublet only to British 'according to His Majesty's book of plantation'. To make room for these approved subtenants he was 'to expel and put out of the said lands all the Irish tenants upon lawful warning'. By 1 August 1616 he was to erect two houses of 'brick, stone or timber after the English manner' and 'enclose a garden, orchard, and homestall with ditching and quickset about each house'. In short, as the 'Printed Book' specified, farming had to be done as in England or the Pale. Transhumance, or creaghting—taking cattle on to the hills in summer and temporarily fencing off land for the cultivation of corn—was forbidden, and fields had to be permanently enclosed. Field boundaries were henceforth to be surrounded by fences or by walls of drystone or clay (confusingly still referred to in rural Ulster today as 'ditches') and planted with 'quicks', that is, fast-growing hawthorn capable of keeping out domestic stock. (Hawthorn saplings are labelled to this day in the Donegore Garden Centre as 'thornquicks'.)

The most usual lease all over Ulster was for thirty-one years or for 'three lives'—an arrangement whereby the lessee named three living persons. The lease, with a fixed rent and specified obligations, only fell in when the last of the three died—a risky arrangement which nevertheless, with luck, could be very advantageous, especially for those in the eighteenth century who named the long-reigning George III as one of the lives.

Canning drew up leases with nine Englishmen and four Scots (though one of them soon after had given him 'the slip'). By Michaelmas 1616 he expected to see the castle finished, with an adjoining village of six houses together, 'which is a great town in this country', along with another fifteen houses for tenants. The outcome would be 'a good plantation' for the Ironmongers' Company, and he himself intended to settle here permanently and 'to have my wife and family out of Warwickshire, for me thinks it is uncomfortable living as I do'.[34]

The London Companies came to the conclusion that leasing or 'farming' out most of their proportions in large blocks was the most convenient way of managing lands so remote from the capital. The only exception was the Mercers' Company, which retained direct control, unsuccessfully as it happened, on their Movanagher estate. The fact that the 'farmers' had to pay substantial entry fines at least helped to ease, however temporarily, the companies' cash flow. These leaseholders included Sir Robert McClelland, who leased the Haberdashers' 'Manor of Freemore' at Ballycashlan and Artikelly and the Clothworkers' estate at Killowen; Sir John Clotworthy, who took over the Drapers' proportion, centred on Moneymore, from Peter Barker in 1633; John Freeman, the 'Manor of Goldsmiths' Hall' at New Buildings; the 'Manor of Pellipar', centred on Dungiven, apportioned to the Skinners, to Sir Edward Doddington and then to Tristram Beresford and George Carey from 1627; the Merchant Taylors' 'Manor of St John the Baptist' at Macosquin, to Valentine Hartopp and then to Ralph Wall; the Salters' 'Manor of Sal', to William Finch and then to Ralph Whistler; the Vintners' manor at Bellaghy, to John Rowley and Baptist Jones, and from 1625 to Henry Conway; and the Ironmongers' 'Manor of Lizard' at Agivey, to George Canning. The descendants of some of these men—notably Canning and Beresford—would play notable roles in the later history of Ireland and Britain.

This passing on of major tracts of the Londoners' grants to 'farmers' on long leases, however, was particularly displeasing to King James.[35]

THE KING FINDS, 'GREATLY TO OUR DISCONTENTMENT, THE SLOW PROGRESSION OF THAT PLANTATION'

On 25 March 1615 King James expressed his frustration in a long letter to his Lord Deputy, Sir Arthur Chichester:

Right trusty and well-beloved, we greet you well.

We received lately from you a relation of the present state of the plantation of Ulster, set down with so much clearness and order by the pen of Sir Josias Bodley, according to the exactness of the survey hereof taken lately by himself by our commandment, that we do acknowledge his care and industry in performance of that service and do require you to give him thanks in our name for it. We have examined, viewed, and reviewed with our own eye every part hereof and find, greatly to our discontentment, the slow progression of that plantation, some few only of the British undertakers, servitors, and natives having as yet proceeded effectually to the accomplishing of such things in all points as are required of them by the Articles of the Plantation. The rest, and by much the greater part, having either done nothing at all, or so little or, by reason of the slightness hereof, to so little purpose that the work seems rather to us to be forgotten by them or to perish under their hand than any whit to be advanced by them: some having begun to build and not planted, others begun to plant and not build, and all of them in general retaining the Irish still upon their lands, the avoiding of which was the fundamental reason of that plantation. We have made a collection of their names as we find their endeavours or negligences noted in this service, which we will retain as a memorial with us, and they shall be sure to feel accordingly the effects of our favour and disfavour as there shall be occasion.

The King said he could simply 'have converted those large territories of our escheated lands to the great improvement of the revenues of our Crown'. But he chose rather, 'for the safety of that country and the civilising of that people, to depart with the inheritance of them at extreme undervalues and to make a plantation of them'. Much as he would be justified in taking back the lands of those 'who have failed to perform according to the original intention the Articles of the Plantation', he was pleased 'to assign them a further time'. James fixed a new deadline of 31 August 1616, 'which we are resolved shall be final and peremptory unto them'. He was 'determined to seize into our hands the lands of any man whatsoever, without respect of persons, whether he be a British undertaker, servitor, or native, that shall be found idle in performing any of the Articles of the Plantation to which he was enjoined'. He would ask Bodley to carry out another survey then, and 'whosoever he shall certify to be deficient in any point touching the plantation' Chichester was to 'seize into our hands the proportion or proportions of those his lands wherein he hath made his omission'. Having signed and sealed this letter, the King wrote underneath in his own hand:

My lord, in this service I expect that zeal and uprightness from you that ye will spare no flesh, English nor Scottish, for no private man's worth is able to counterbalance the perpetual safety of a kingdom which this plantation being well accomplished will procure.[36]

James gave his Lord Deputy little time to carry out his wishes. In November 1615 he decided to terminate Chichester's viceroyalty. Chichester had presided over the government of Ireland for a decade—an unusually long tenure. He was frequently unwell and had suffered a serious fall from his horse on the way to London in the spring of 1614. Sir Oliver St John, Master of the Ordnance in Ireland, reported that the Lord Deputy 'had long used to lace up his legs to avoid a swelling in them, and so made a stopp of tumours in his body'. Chichester spent much of his convalescence at Carrickfergus with his ailing wife, Letitia, and saw the completion there of his mansion of Joymount in 1618. In 1620, as the Thirty Years' War got under way in central Europe, Chichester's last service to his King was to be sent abroad as England's ambassador to the Habsburg Empire. Chichester retained his Protestant zeal to the end. Not long before he died, in 1625, he fired off an indignant letter to Sir Edward Conway, the English Secretary of State, complaining that troops were being sent into action without being accompanied by 'ministers of the word of God':

> How can we expect that God will bless our endeavours when we neglect to serve Him and how can soldiers serve Him without teachers to instruct and call upon them to humble themselves before Him? I pray think upon this as a matter of greatest moment and spare not to put the King in mind of it.[37]

His brother Edward inherited his extensive properties, and, as the largest estate extended over almost all of the peninsula of Inishowen, it was appropriate that when he was ennobled after the Restoration it was as the 1st Earl of Donegall.

Sir Oliver St John, raised to the peerage as Viscount Grandison, succeeded Chichester as Lord Deputy. Bodley's survey, presented in 1616 (which has not survived), once again made it apparent that the undertakers were failing to meet their obligations in full. The King would expect a determined response. In August 1617 Grandison gave warning that all natives were at once to transfer themselves to the lands of servitors and natives and those of the Church. This removal was to be effected by 1 May 1618, after which time any natives who had failed to obey this order would be liable to such penalties as the Lord Deputy should think fit to impose. This failed to produce the result intended, and so on 1 October 1618 the Council issued a proclamation requiring all the Irish to clear out of the British undertakers' lands before 1 May 1619. If they did not do so they were to pay a fine of ten shillings each and thereafter submit to be fined at the Lord Deputy's pleasure. This was the first open admission that the King's grand plan to segregate the natives and colonists could not be enforced.

King James demanded retribution. As the Privy Council informed the Lord Deputy in March 1618, the slackness of the undertakers had so provoked the King that, after a full investigation, he was resolved to 'take that advantage of those that have soe grossly failed, as eyther in lawe or policy of state hee may justly doe'.[38] James ordered another survey, more searching and systematic than previous ones, to discover exactly how far the undertakers had performed their obligations. It was led by Pynnar. He began on 1 December 1618 and completed an extremely comprehensive report on 28 March 1619.

Pynnar found that in the six escheated counties there were 6,215 adult British men: 1,106 in Donegal, 642 in Londonderry, 2,469 in Tyrone, 642 in Armagh, 645 in Fermanagh and 711 in Cavan. However, 'partly by observing the habitations of these lands, and partly by conferring with some of knowledge among them', he conjectured that there were to be found on the plantation at least 8,000 men of British birth and descent able to do the King's service. He reckoned that in the six counties there had been built 107 castles with bawns, 19 castles without bawns, 42 bawns without castles or houses and (besides many other houses he had been unable to see) 1,897 dwelling-houses of stone and timber in villages after the English manner.[39] His report concluded:

And yet there is a great want of buildings upon their lands, both for townreeds and otherwise. And I may say, that the abode and continuance of those inhabitants upon the lands is not yet made certain, although I have seen the deeds made unto them. My reason is, that many of the English tenants do not yet plough upon the lands, neither use husbandry, because I conceive they are fearful to stock themselves with cattle or servants for those labours. Neither do the Irish use tillage, for they are also uncertain of their stay upon the lands; so that, by this means, the Irish ploughing nothing . . . the English very little; and were it not for the Scottish tenants, which do plough in many places of the country, those parts may starve.

In short, the English planters in particular had become very dependent on the Irish, who were prepared to pay higher rents than the colonists, 'and if the Irish be put away with their cattle, the British must either forsake their dwellings, or endure great distress on the sudden. Yet the combination of the Irish is dangerous to them, by robbing them, and otherwise'. The Londoners had been particularly negligent:

I observe the greatest number of Irish do well upon the lands granted to the City of London; which happeneth, as I take it, two ways, First, There are five of the proportions assigned to the several companies, which are not yet estated to any man, but are in the hands of agents; who, finding the Irish more profitable than the British tenants, are unwilling to draw on the British, persuading the Company that the lands are mountainous and unprofitable, not regarding the future security of the whole: secondly, The other seven of the proportions are leased to several persons for 61 years, and the lessees do affirm that they are not bound to plant English, but may plant with what people they please; neither is the City of London bound to do it by their patents from his Majesty, as they say; and by these two actions, the British that are now there, who have many of them built houses at their own charges, have no estates made unto them, which is such a discouragement unto them, as they are minded to depart the land; and without better settlement will seek elsewhere.[40]

To enforce his proclamation of 1 October 1618 King James appointed Edward Wray, one of the grooms of his bedchamber, to be the collector of all fines and forfeitures payable by the natives inhabiting the British undertakers' lands within the succeeding seven years, in return for an annual rental of a hundred pounds. This was a further indication that the government was beginning to shrink from its plan to eject the Irish there.

'YOUR MAJESTY'S GREAT BOUNTY AND GODLY INTENTION IS GENERALLY FRUSTRATED': THE 1622 SURVEY

Meanwhile the government in London was becoming increasingly concerned at the cost of governing Ireland. Confiscations and plantations were supposed to yield a substantial revenue to the Crown, but the subsidy required by the administration in Ireland amounted to an annual average drain of £47,170 upon the English exchequer between 1604 and 1619. Indeed, that exchequer in London itself was close to insolvency. The

English Lord Treasurer, Lionel Cranfield, Earl of Middlesex, was anxious to find explanations for this state of affairs in Ireland. He was the main driving force behind the establishment of a commission in 1622 to make a thorough inquiry into how the government of Ireland could be made self-financing. This would include yet another survey of the state of the plantation in Ulster.

The work of the commission was seriously hampered by the interference of the King's favourite, George Villiers, Duke of Buckingham. Robert Cecil, Earl of Salisbury, had died in 1612. King James attempted to take over the direction of government himself, but he was unable to prevent the accumulation of debt. Just before his death, Salisbury had in desperation created a new order of knighthood, the baronetcy, which, at £1,095 for each title, raised about £90,000. This was not enough: the government debt was in the region of £500,000, and the King's annual deficit was some £50,000. Villiers first appeared at court in 1614 and immediately captivated James. The King's beloved heir presumptive, Prince Henry, had died suddenly in 1612 at the age of eighteen, and James does not seem to have been much taken with his second son, Charles, a reserved boy of twelve. Despite his dalliances with other men, the King was bereft by the death in 1619 of his queen, Anne. Addressing her at times as 'my little wiffe-waffe', he had assured her: 'God is my witness I ever preferred you to all my bairns, much more than to any subject'.[41] Now, frequently ailing and prematurely aged, James lavished honours on Villiers, raising him to the peerage. Buckingham exploited his monarch ruthlessly and acquired extensive properties and revenues in Ireland for himself and his family.

Buckingham had to acknowledge that the government of Ireland needed looking into, but he feared that the commissioners would discover too much about the questionable activities there of his agents, relatives and hangers-on. His claim to be upholding the interest of the King might well be challenged. The commissioners began their work in April 1622. An inquiry into the state of the plantation in Ulster was only one part of their remit. For much of the time they were in Dublin, looking into the condition of the established church on Mondays, examining the revenue on Tuesdays and investigating the courts of justice on Wednesdays. Fridays were devoted to plantations, and Thursdays and Saturdays were kept free for other matters which might arise. Despite attempts by Buckingham's favourites and allies to disrupt their work, the commissioners had achieved a great deal by the autumn.

The parlous condition of the royal finances in both England and Ireland was aggravated by a downturn in trade and a succession of bad harvests. Viscount Grandison had been forced to resign as Lord Deputy early in 1622, and his replacement, Henry Cary, Viscount Falkland, felt he had no choice but to bring over from England his own supply of grain and cheese. In desperation the government issued a proclamation on 23 November forbidding the export of corn from Ireland. Ulster was particularly hard-hit, and the commissioners took care to carry enough food with them to keep them fed while they were in the province.

Sir Thomas Phillips, engaged in a bitter and protracted vendetta against the London Companies, had lobbied successfully to assist the commissioners, and now, unpaid, he joined them. His jaundiced findings certainly must have coloured the commissioners' findings. The final report, made up of 125 closely written large folios, which included a great sheaf of 'certificates' (lists of tenants on each proportion submitted by undertakers, subsequently checked by the commissioners), was extremely thorough.[42]

Students of migration and settlement are likely to conclude that the mass of evidence provided by the 1622 commission demonstrates that British colonisation was progressing rather well in Ulster. The planters, however, were not adhering strictly to the terms of their patents, as the report made plain. The commissioners did not mince their words:

It appeareth sufficiently by the forementioned certificates how ill the above written conditions have been observed, and albeit some have performed much better than others, yet your majesty's great bounty and godly intention is generally frustrated. For notwithstanding the many surveys made at your majesty's great charge and your majesty's pleasure often signified by letter and published by proclamations for the performance of the conditions of plantation, yet now in so long a space after the time limited for building and planting, there is a general defect in a greater or lesser measure as appeareth in the former certificates, which is like to increase if some speedy course be not taken for reformation thereof.

The commissioners listed and explained 'these many defects'. Many of the undertakers were 'not resident but live in England or Scotland or remote from their proportions'. Most of them 'retain great store of Irish families upon their lands, which is the cause the British can get no reasonable bargain'. They were reluctant to give British tenants formal leases, preferring 'verbal promise or by writing imperfect without form of law', giving them power to rack-rent or 'to put poor men out of their holdings'. Few undertakers had 'performed their building within the time limited', and many of the defensive works were next to useless: 'Divers of the bawns are made of stone and clay and some of sods, which are to little purpose but ruinous and decaying already. And many of them have no houses within them nor gates to keep them shut, and therefore of no use when nobody dwells within them'. Few undertakers had placed their tenants in villages or towns 'as they ought to do' but 'do let them live scattering and dispersed in woods and coverts, subject to the malice of any kern to rob, kill and burn them in their houses'. Many colonists 'have not ready in their houses convenient store of arms . . . as by the conditions of plantation they ought to have'. The commissioners were particularly concerned that undertakers were selling on their grants without permission, leading to the creation of over-large, unmanageable estates:

> Proportions are sold from man to man without licence, by which means divers proportions are come into one man's hands, which is a principal cause that the conditions are not performed and chief freeholders extinguished.

Servitors did not have the obligation to plant, but the commissioners found much to criticise. Some of the bawns had 'no houses, people or gates . . . to little purpose but left waste', some people were never resident, some 'are recusants and will not take the oath of supremacy', and most of the servitors' tenants 'are not planted in villages and town reeds, as by the articles of plantation they ought to be, but do live dispersed so as a few kerns may easily take victual from them by force, if they give it not willingly'. The 'defects of the natives' included putting up 'bawns of sods to no purpose', allowing their tenants to 'live dispersed and not in town reeds' and continuing to 'take Irish exactions, as heretofore'. Their tenants 'do generally plough after the Irish barbarous manner by the tails of their garrons and not after the manner of the English Pale, as they ought to do by the articles of plantation'.[43]

Why were the undertakers, servitors and—indeed—the 'deserving' native Irish failing so blatantly to abide by the Articles of Plantation?

'HOW ILL THE ABOVE WRITTEN CONDITIONS HAVE BEEN OBSERVED': SOME EXPLANATIONS

In the autumn of 1824 the Ordnance Survey staff, directed by Thomas Colby, arrived at the Phoenix Park in Dublin to begin mapping the whole of Ireland on a scale of six inches to one statute mile. It was a great undertaking carried out with dedication. At the height of the project some two thousand men were employed, and for a time Dublin was at the cutting edge of cartographic innovation. For a brief moment in history it could be said that Ireland had been mapped more meticulously and accurately than any other country in the world.[44] The survey's maps and statistics were available to the Rev. George Hill when he came to write his monumental work on the Plantation of Ulster. In his footnotes—far more voluminous than the main text—Hill was able to compare the stated number of acres in each barony or precinct with those provided by the Ordnance Survey.

By then it was well known that the actual area of each barony and proportion was far greater than that stated in patents. What Hill did was to demonstrate the scale of the mismatch: even if it is taken into account that 'plantation' acres were larger than statute acres, and that 'waste' was not included, it was obvious that those who had surveyed the escheated counties had grossly underestimated the area of land to be apportioned. Examples taken from Hill (which he punctuated with exclamation marks) include the barony of the Fews, Co. Armagh, reported as 6,000 acres, os 77,000 acres; Boylagh, Co. Donegal, 10,000 acres, os 158,480 acres; Knockninny, Co. Fermanagh, 9,000 acres, os 28,000 acres, 'exclusive of water surface'; Magheraboy, Co. Fermanagh, 9,000 acres, os 80,000 acres, 'exclusive of water'; Tullyhunco, Co. Cavan, 6,000 acres, os 39,000 acres; Clankee, Co. Cavan, 5,000 acres, os 64,377 acres; Orior, Co. Armagh, 11,000 acres, os 75,000 acres; Clanawley, Co. Fermanagh, 8,500 acres, os 75,000 acres; and Clanmahon, Co. Cavan, 8,000 acres os 50,000 acres, 'exclusive of water and a few scraps of Church land'.[45]

The failure to attempt a measured survey of the confiscated lands resulted in proportions vastly greater in acreage than that stated in the grants. In time, undertakers were to settle at least the minimum number of British families specified in their patents, but they could not possibly find the cash to obtain enough English and Scots tenants to farm lands far more extensive than had been expected. Finding the necessary capital to build castles and bawns to ensure the security of such large sweeps of territory was clearly beyond the means of most undertakers, servitors and native Irish receiving grants.

King James and those who guided and represented him did not blame themselves for poor planning or accept that surveying 'by inquisition' had its shortcomings. Neither the Pynnar report nor that of the 1622 commissioners mention such failings, but these investigators did otherwise identify many of the reasons for the grand scheme as laid out in the 'Printed Book' not taking shape as envisaged. The expulsion of the Gaelic gentry was achieved with comparative ease, but the insistence that all the native Irish be expelled from undertakers' proportions was completely impractical. Not only did the planters lack the military might to drive them out but the reduced King's army in Ireland, even if concentrated exclusively in Ulster, rightly shied unhesitatingly away from such a task. Certainly Lord Deputy Chichester did not think it at all possible. Quite apart from humanitarian considerations, the extermination of the natives was not contemplated—no doubt royal officials would have agreed with the observation by Sir Henry Sidney in Queen Elizabeth's time that such mass slaughter would involve 'a marvellous sumptuous charge'.

Newly arrived colonists found the ordinary native Irish—desperate not to be driven out and wishing as a consequence to ingratiate themselves with the newcomers—useful to them from the outset. Local people acted as guides and helped to erect dwellings to enable English and Scots to survive the first winter. Even if they did plough by the tail, the Irish played a critical role in working the land and preparing for harvest at a time when British tenants had either not yet arrived or were still thin on the ground. Only a few colonists had brought enough domestic stock across the sea to meet all their needs. Cattle to stock their proportions were mostly bought locally, and even though Irish-made butter matured in wooden raskins and sunk in bogs was not much to their taste, settlers were grateful for the opportunity to buy it. The new proprietors were only too willing to pay the natives to fell timber, quarry stone and dig the earth to create bawns and assist in raising up fortifications. Close to the southern shore of Lower Lough Erne in Co. Fermanagh, for example, Monea Castle is clearly the work almost exclusively of Scots settlers; but Tully Castle, a few miles further west, gives every indication not only of being built by local Irish but also of being partly designed by them.

And yet the commissioners of 1619 and 1622 were right to point out that retaining the native Irish on undertakers' proportions did impede rapid and thorough-going plantation. Undertakers, with the exception of those in the most favoured locations, could only attract British incomers, prepared to take the Oath of Supremacy, to become tenants on their estates if they offered them very favourable terms. Actually, they often made matters worse by refusing to make out binding leases, preferring to make informal arrangements in the hope of being able to get higher rents in the future by rack-renting.

Certainly undertakers could not make written and binding contracts with natives they were retaining illegally. The local Irish were glad to offer rents far higher than the freshly arrived British were willing to pay, or to render labour services in lieu. Contrary to the popular view in England, but attested by the correspondence of military commanders as they suppressed rebellion in Ulster in Elizabeth's final years, the northern Irish did cultivate corn on a considerable scale. Now, constantly expecting to be moved on, the natives often could not risk ploughing the lands they could lose access to at any time. For them it was far better to cherish their herds, that is, to look to the care of their wealth, such as it was, in a mobile form. The outcome, at least in the short term, was that the plantation in many places actually brought about a decline in arable farming. This was in sharp contrast with the more secure settlements in Down and Antrim, where the Scots had assiduously set about ploughing.

The archives for this period contain ample evidence of the disappointments of many of those British who crossed the sea with expectations which were too high. Surviving members of the Gaelic learned classes wrote principally of the sufferings of their high-born fellow-countrymen. Records revealing how the Irish who actually farmed the land responded to the new regime in Ulster are all but non-existent. They were a conquered people, and their illegal presence on lands assigned to undertakers and, to a lesser extent, to the Church depended on the whim of landlords. Rack-rented and forced either to accept paltry wages or to give their labour unpaid in return for uncertain tenures, these Gaelic Irish could not but have resented the appearance of newcomers speaking a foreign tongue and despising their cherished beliefs.

Prospective planters had been assured that the lands they had applied for were 'utterly depopulated'. Soon they found that this was not so. On the lonely settlements by the Sperrins or Glenveagh the baying of the wolf at the moon must have sent a chill down the spine of many a colonist who had never heard the sound before. The fear of woodkerne lurking in the thickets was better founded. The greatest threat, however, was the smouldering resentment of the native Irish who worked and farmed with the settlers. In 1628 Sir Thomas Phillips warned the government that 'it is fered that they will Rise upon a Sudden and Cutt the Throts of the poore dispersed Brittish'. In the parish of Donegore in Antrim a Protestant minister had a vision on his deathbed: "'The dead bodies of many thousands, who this day despise the glorious gospel, shall lie upon the earth as dung unburied." And whilst one said "Is there no remedy?" he cried thrice, "No remedy, no remedy, no remedy!"'[46] That was in 1634; the blundering policies of Charles I seemed almost to be willing the prophecy to come true.

Chapter 12 ∿

| REBELLION

CHARLES I AND THOMAS WENTWORTH

James I died on 27 March 1625. The last years of his reign had been ignominious. The ailing King had become ever more dependent on George Villiers, elevated to the peerage as Duke of Buckingham. James had been seeking the hand of the Infanta of Spain for his son and heir. In a ludicrous outing, Buckingham had set out for Madrid in March 1623 with Prince Charles, both of them incognito, to secure the hand of the princess. Philip IV put forward impossible terms for the match: complete toleration for Catholics ratified by Parliament, and any child of the marriage to be raised a Catholic. War with Spain followed.

By the time the English were fitting out an expedition bound for Cádiz, Charles was King. He appeared to be everything his father was not: clean, sober, personable, handsome and chaste. He gave every indication of becoming a fine ruler, but he would quickly squander the reserves of good will with which he had come to the throne. Above all, he put every bit as much faith in Buckingham as his father had. Then, as the war went from bad to worse, and as Buckingham was attempting to quell a mariners' mutiny in Portsmouth, on the evening of 22 August 1627 an assassin took the hated duke's life with a ten-penny butcher's knife. Henceforth Charles I would attempt to rule alone.

Charles did not share his father's enthusiasm for the Plantation of Ulster, and no further surveys were authorised. Instead the King sought to increase his personal power, and for this he needed money which did not have to be sanctioned by Parliament. James I's grandiose scheme for Ulster was fast unravelling. In 1619 James had doubled Crown rents and imposed fines on those who had failed to abide by the Articles of Plantation. In 1621 it had been conceded that undertakers could retain natives on a quarter of their proportions. Then the 1622 commission made it plain that the Irish were still outnumbering the colonists on every proportion. This was confirmed by a census of natives on undertakers' estates, completed by Easter 1624. When Charles came to the throne, and as the expedition to Cádiz was in preparation, the most urgent need was for money. In return for cash fines, the Privy Council on 31 August 1625 dropped its insistence that natives remaining on estates attend church and that the old patents be surrendered to be replaced with new ones. From now on failure to adhere to the conditions laid down in the 'Printed Book' was simply used to raise more revenue for the Crown.

The ambition of Charles I was to become a monarch whose power was absolute, just like the King of Spain or the Holy Roman Emperor. To do this he had to rule without the consent of Parliament, and therefore Charles had to find alternative sources of income. Ireland was one of those alternative sources. In 1626 the King presented the gentlemen of Ireland with what he called 'matters of grace and bounty'. These 'graces' were particularly appealing to the Old English Catholics because they offered religious toleration, the right to hold government posts and—above all— the right to secure legal titles to their landed estates and halt current schemes for further plantations. In return, the King sought substantial and regular 'subsidies', to be approved by the Irish Parliament. After some hesitation, planters in Ulster came to the conclusion that in such an uncertain climate it might be politic to back the graces and pay the new taxes to sweep away the danger of forfeiture, which James had threatened more than once.

After protracted negotiations a delegation of leading landlords— including Andrew Stewart, representing Ulster—travelled to London in January 1628 to finalise the deal. In return for three successive annual subsidies of forty thousand pounds, English money, to be used principally to support the army, the graces would be conceded. Crucially, the King in effect terminated the careful policy of segregated settlement in Ulster: undertakers' titles were to be confirmed without reference to their observation of the plantation conditions. Implementing the deal proved more difficult than expected: the war with Spain and then with France prompted a fresh drive for religious conformity, antagonising the Catholic Old English lords forced to pay heavy recusancy fines.

Then, in January 1632, King Charles announced his decision to appoint as his Lord Deputy his trusted servant Thomas Wentworth. Taking up his post the following year, Wentworth proved to be arrogant, overbearing and insensitive. He called his policy 'thorough'. It had only one purpose: to make certain that his master, Charles I, had supreme power in both

Church and state. The Lord Deputy called an Irish Parliament to meet in July 1634. The first session was to raise money for the King, Wentworth warning that he would enforce fines rigorously for failing to attend services of the established church if the subsidies 'be not freely and thankfully given'. Fully expecting the implementation of the graces, the Irish Parliament voted more generous payments to the King for the next four years.

Having got his money, Wentworth then showed his true colours. He had no intention of granting toleration to Catholics or, indeed, to Presbyterians. He reneged on the promise to give landlords secure legal title to their estates, even if these lands had been in their possession for centuries. A Commission for Defective Titles (similar to that launched in Ulster in 1605) began a series of rather disturbing inquiries.[1] At the same time as Charles was getting himself into deeper and hotter water on the other side of the Irish Sea, his Lord Deputy was alienating just about every interest in Ireland. Wentworth even managed to turn many of his natural allies, the 'New English', against him.

Wentworth owed his eventual fall not to the New English, not to the Old English, not to the Gaelic Irish but to the planters in Ulster and their friends at Westminster.

TRIAL IN THE STAR CHAMBER: THE CONFISCATION OF THE LONDONERS' LANDS

During the autumn of 1625 the Privy Council threatened to sequester all the revenues of the London Companies in Ulster and to use them towards implementing the Articles of Plantation. The Irish Society moved swiftly to collect the revenues before they could be seized. It was instructed not to interfere with the next sequestration, scheduled for May 1626. The Crown argued that it had borne the cost of the defence of the county of Londonderry for the past sixteen years and that this would not have been necessary if the Londoners had 'planted with British, as they were bound by their contract'. The Society responded that the royal troops had been of no benefit; they had been a burden, because they had to be fed and housed, and the companies had received no payment for these services.

When Charles declared war on France in 1627 his need for money became ever more urgent. An expedition to support the Huguenots at La Rochelle during the summer and autumn turned out to be a humiliating failure. That year commissioners drawn from the Irish government, led by the Lord Deputy and assisted by Sir Thomas Phillips, began an inquiry into the City of London's plantation. By the spring of 1629 a mass of evidence had been collected. This included a report that there were 1,412 able British men and 2,293 Irish on the City's lands.

The evidence, with recommendations, was presented to the King along with a detailed account by Phillips of the plantation for the years 1610–29. Phillips calculated that the City's income had been £98,665 and its expenses £68,730. This was an unfair calculation: it included £10,000 made from the spoliation of the woods, but there was no evidence that the City (apart from unscrupulous individuals) had made money from this source, and it did not include the great cost of the Cutts at the Salmon Leap at Coleraine. In fact the annual income to 1641 had never exceeded £2,000. Phillips urged King Charles to 'cast . . . his princely eye upon the important and material things contained' in his report, to 'revoke the Londoners' Patent' and to reassume the plantation 'into his royal hands'.

Charles took this advice. In 1630 the Attorney-General, having looked through the work of the commissioners, and regularly consulting the Privy Council, recommended that a trial be prepared. The City was swamped with inquisitions, and Phillips obsessively supplied yet more material to the prosecution. The Londoners were charged with having obtained a grant of exorbitant rights and privileges and of violating the Articles of Agreement—they had betrayed the trust of King James, imperilling the kingdom of Ireland, leading to the decay of 'true religion' and threatening the Plantation of Ulster with 'utter ruin'. An offer of twenty thousand pounds and Admiralty rights was rejected. Wentworth intervened and pressed for the confiscation of the Co. Londonderry proportions.

The trial in the Star Chamber—a room in the Palace of Westminster—could not be expected to produce justice. Membership of the court—a tribunal without a jury—was confined to privy councillors. After four years the trial ended; the City and the Irish Society were found guilty on all counts. A huge fine of seventy thousand pounds (reduced in 1637 to twelve thousand) was imposed, and the patent was to be surrendered. Wentworth's ally, John Bramhall, Bishop of Derry, was appointed to collect rents from the confiscated estates. Rents obtained from the city of Londonderry and Coleraine were doubled, and those from the twelve proportions were tripled. Various friends of the King lobbied to take over the plantation on the his behalf, including Wentworth himself.[2]

The alienation of the City of London was complete.

OPPRESSING PRESBYTERIANS: THE BLACK OATH

Thomas Wentworth, the Lord Deputy, continued ruthlessly to enforce the King's will in Ireland. Charles aspired to supreme dominance in religious as well as in temporal affairs of state. Wentworth, after denying Catholics the right to public office, now turned on Protestants who did not toe the line. Until now the Church of Ireland had tolerated a wide range of Protestant beliefs and practices. This suited Scots very well: most of those settling in Ulster were Presbyterians, who, since they did not yet have their own church here, were content to join the Church of Ireland. And all over Ireland, Protestants in this, the established church, tended to be Puritans, favouring plain forms of worship and plain dress.

Wentworth was determined to change all that. Bishops using the High Church pomp, ceremony, chanting and liturgy favoured by the King replaced the ones that the Irish Protestants preferred. Bramhall, who had accompanied Wentworth to Ireland as his chaplain, was appointed Bishop of Derry in 1634, and from 1636 he led a court of high commission to supervise diocesan courts and enforce state policy, with the power to confiscate and imprison. He was joined by Henry Leslie, appointed Bishop of Down and Connor in 1635, and together they set about enforcing conformity in Ulster. Leslie carried out a special visitation of his diocese in 1636. On 10 August he summoned his clergy to a meeting in Belfast. Leslie chose as his text Matthew 18:17: 'But if he neglect to hear the church, let him be unto thee as an heathen man and a publican'. Then the bishop castigated those clergymen who had succumbed to Presbyterianism:

Hee that will take upon him the office of a minister, not being called by the Church, is an intruder and a thief that cometh not in by the doore, but climbeth up another way ... They think by the puff of preaching to blowe downe the goodly orders of our church, as the walls of Jericho were beaten downe with sheepes hornes. Good God! Is this not the sinne of Uzziah, who intruded himself into the office of priesthood? ... They have cryed downe the most wholesome orders of the church as popish superstitions.

Some of the clergy present had the cheek to answer back. They did indeed regard the forms of worship prescribed in the Book of Common Prayer as popish. These clergy who refused to change their tune were then deprived of their office and financial support.

Forced to leave Ireland, they decided to join other Presbyterians determined to go to New England to preserve their religious liberty. In the autumn of 1636 the *Eagle Wing*, a ship of 150 tons built at Groomsport, was ready to sail to the New World. Setting out from Belfast Lough with 140 passengers on 9 September, the ship was driven across the North Channel to Loch Ryan by contrary winds. After repairing a leak, they sailed out into the Atlantic and got almost as far as the Newfoundland Banks. One passenger, the excommunicated Minister of Killinchy, John Livingston, wrote an account of what happened next:

> But if ever the Lord spake by his winds and other dispensations, it was made evident to us, that it was not His will that we should go to New England. For we met with a mighty heavy rain out of the north-west, which did break our rudder, which we got mended . . . Seas came in over the round-house . . . and wet them all that were between the decks . . . We sprung a leak that gave us seven hundred strokes in two pumps in the half-hour glass. Yet we lay at hull a long time to beat out the storm, till . . . it was impossible to hold out any longer.

After prayer they decided to return, reaching Belfast Lough on 3 November.

Meanwhile, King Charles was attempting to impose the prayer book on Scotland. There opposition was led by Robert Blair, former Minister of Bangor, excommunicated by Bishop Leslie, and by Livingston, who had made his way across the North Channel almost immediately after stepping ashore from the *Eagle Wing*. Both rallied support for the Covenant, a bond of union among the King's Scottish opponents. Scottish planters in Ulster needed no encouragement to sign the Covenant. Wentworth, Bramhall and Leslie lost no time in taking action against them. Leslie told the Lord Deputy: 'They do threaten me for my life, but, by the grace of God, all their brags shall never make me faint in doing service to God and the King'. Wentworth drafted a command that all Scots in Ulster over the age of sixteen, male and female, must take an 'oath of abjuration of their abominable covenant'.

The Lord Deputy was raising an army in Ireland with the principal aim of adding muscle to the King's attempt to recover royal authority in Scotland. He sent most of these recruits northwards to Carrickfergus to 'amuse' the Scots while the King advanced on Berwick. As it happened, the King's forces were too weak to bring the Scots to heel; he was forced to agree to a pacification in June 1639, leaving the Scots in control in their own country. Meanwhile the troops billeted in Ulster not only bore heavily on the planters but also gave the government the force required to impose religious conformity. Wentworth's intention was to frighten Scots in Ulster back to Scotland, thus weakening the British colony there still further.

The oath—soon known as the Black Oath—had to be taken kneeling, and if it was refused Bishop Leslie had the power to fine, imprison and excommunicate. For Sir John Clotworthy, an Englishman with estates in Antrim, this was the last straw. He resolved to go to London, there to rally his friends in Parliament to bring about the downfall of Wentworth. Clotworthy had rented the Drapers' proportion in Londonderry, and this estate he had lost when the Star Chamber sequestered the City's estates in 1635. He was in a strong position to present a challenge: he had a seat in the House of Commons at Westminster; he was related by marriage to John Pym, the leader of the opposition to Charles I; and he could count on the support of powerful individuals alienated by Wentworth in Ireland.

The King had summoned Wentworth back to England, creating him Earl of Strafford, to be his principal officer charged with enforcing his will. Charles, forced by his lack of money to call Parliament, now had to face the pent-up wrath of those who had endured his 'eleven years' tyranny'.

Clotworthy led the charge. On 7 November 1640 he presented a long petition to the Commons on behalf of the Presbyterians and Puritans of Ireland. These people, he began, had 'translated themselves out of several parts of his Majesties kingdoms of England and Scotland, to promote the infant plantation of Ireland', only to be oppressed by the King's ministers and High Church bishops. Very many, he continued, were

> reviled, threatnd, imprisoned, fettered together by threes and foures in iron yoakes, some in chaines carried up to Dublin, in Starre chamber fined in thousands beyond abilitie, and condemned to perpetuall imprisonment; Divers poore women but two dayes before delivery of children were apprehended, threatnd, and terrified . . . They therefore most humbly pray that this unlawful hierarchicall government with all their appendices may bee utterly extirpate.[3]

He declared to fellow-members of Parliament that Strafford had claimed the previous year that, with an Irish army behind him, the King could 'have what he pleased in England'. Pym then stood up to demand that Strafford be impeached as 'the greatest enemy to this country and the greatest promoter of tyranny that any age has produced'.[4] Clotworthy seconded the motion.

On 11 November the House of Commons voted to impeach Strafford. Sixteen of the twenty-eight accusations against him related to his tyrannical rule in Ireland. In April 1641 the House of Lords found him guilty of treason, and, on 12 May, Thomas Wentworth, Earl of Strafford, was beheaded—'as he well deserved', the Earl of Cork noted in his diary.[5]

Everything now was going wrong for Charles I: his most faithful minister had been executed; his attempts to overawe the Scots had failed; his Parliament was defying his will; and he was almost bankrupt. Perhaps the large Irish army, mainly made up of Catholics, recently raised by Wentworth, could help? No, it was too late: that army melted slowly away simply because there was no money to pay the men.

NATIVES LOSING LAND

Only in precincts assigned to undertakers were the native Irish forbidden to buy land, but all over Ulster they were literally losing ground. The experience of the Magennises in Co. Down was typical. The Lordship of Iveagh comprised almost all of western and central Down and included some territory spilling into south Co. Antrim. In 1605 the Commission for the Division and Bounding of the Lords' and Gentlemen's Livings had been appointed to apply widely the arrangement made in Co. Monaghan in the 1590s, known as the 'native plantation', to reduce the power of 'overmighty lords'. Before this had been abandoned in favour of planting British colonists on confiscated lands, it led to a new arrangement for the Magennis lands. Art Roe Magennis applied to the commission to be appointed Lord Iveagh. He was to regret doing this. In February 1607 the commission promulgated its decision. It decided to divide the Lordship of Iveagh into freeholds in accordance with a scheme drawn up by the Solicitor-General, Sir Robert Jacob. A locally based commission and assizes held at Newry duly divided up the lordship between 1607 and 1610. King James approved the recommendations in June 1610.

The lordship was divided into fifteen freeholds, thirteen of them to leading members of the Magennis family. Altogether the native Irish got 85 per cent of the townlands in the lordship. Land was set aside for the established church, in particular for the see of Dromore, where John Todd had been appointed bishop in 1608. Officers in the Crown forces made sure that they got a share also. This was inevitable, given that the superintendents in this process of creating freeholds included Sir Toby Caulfield, Sir Fulke Conway, Sir Francis Roe, Sir Edward Blaney and Captain Edward Trevor, all of whom had served under Sir Samuel Bagenal of Newry in the closing years of the Nine Years' War. These officers were to use every means open to them to extend their new possessions, and this could only be at the expense of the natives of Iveagh.

Here the Gaelic Irish had to adapt to a much-altered regime. Many proved unable to cope. Letting out lands by leases, which, after entry fines had been paid, yielded fixed rents for many years, was a new departure for the natives. Above all, there was a constant need for ready cash to pay for estate management, capital improvement, legal fees (which were often rapacious), marriage portions for female children, and the education of male heirs seeking careers in the army or in the legal profession by attending the Inns of Court in London.

Art Roe Magennis of Rathfriland, granted the largest Magennis freehold, did succeed in being elevated to the peerage as Lord Iveagh in 1623, but his financial position soon became precarious: sending his son Hugh to Oxford involved heavy expenditure with a poor return, for it was reported that the three years Hugh spent there 'has in no way bettered him in those things which we specially desired'. As freeholders they now had to pay regular rents to the King's sheriff and find money to pay for feudal incidents such as suing out of livery by heirs, wardship and marriage, and to pay for pardons and fines, including recusancy fines for failing to attend Protestant church services. This was a big change from a dependence on tribute paid in kind. The result was that most of the native Irish borrowed heavily, mortgaging land for ready money. They added to their problems by continuing to adhere to previous practice, in particular subdividing their property to give all sons a share in the land. This determination to make provision for every child could prove ruinous: Glassney McAholly Magennis of Clanconnell, for example, married four times and had at least seven children, and all were provided for. The newcomers ruthlessly exploited the frequent inability to understand the newly introduced legal system and the management of estates in the English way. Phelim McCartan sold swathes of his ancestral lands in Kinelarty and Lecale to the retired soldier Sir Edward Cromwell.

Captain Edward Trevor worked assiduously to augment his holdings. Owning a modest estate in Brynkinalt, near Chirk, in the marcher country of north Wales and Shropshire, Trevor had established his base near Warrenpoint at a spot that became known as *Ros Treabhair* (Trevor's wood). His wife, Agnes, had died in childbirth at Narrow Water in 1610, and then he had married Rose, daughter of Henry Ussher, Archbishop of Armagh. Trevor had served as sheriff and was one of the commissioners during the division of Iveagh into freeholds. He imposed fines for the making of freeholds and was able to keep a third of these from 'those of ability and less from the poorer sort'. The freeholders, without cash to pay for legal services, often had no choice but to alienate lands instead to Trevor and his associates. His pension of £96 14s a year meant that he had some ready money to hand to lend to the Irish.

Native proprietors borrowed money using their lands as collateral. When they could not pay their debts in time, they lost their land. The mortgaging of land was being eased in these years not by actually physically occupying the lands but by granting the rents to the mortgagee. However, if repayments of the principal had not been completed within twenty-one years the land was lost for ever. By 1641 Trevor and his son Mark between them had more than sixteen thousand plantation acres throughout Upper and Lower Iveagh, including the entire Magennis estate of Milltown. It is reckoned that by 1641 lands held by native Irish proprietors in Iveagh were reduced from 85 to 48 per cent and that much of the territory remaining to them was encumbered with debt.

Sir Marmaduke Whitchurch, lieutenant of Bagenal's horse company at the Battle of the Yellow Ford in 1598, secured almost the entire estate of Loughbrickland because its owner, Art Óg McBrien Óg McEdmond Boy Magennis, failed to pay a debt incurred in 1611. The Crown escheator, George Sexton, acquired a large though scattered estate made up of bits of land which had been granted to Magennises in Rathfriland, Milltown, Kilwarlin, Clanconnell and Loughbrickland. Many of Sexton's acquisitions were of dubious legality: he used his position to ignore normal procedures and buy land at knock-down prices. When he died, in 1632, it was revealed that he had evaded paying 'fines' (in these cases a form of purchase tax) on at least eight occasions.

The most spectacular failure was that of Brian Óg MacRory Magennis, who alienated about 28,000 acres in Kilwarlin—forty-five townlands in the modern parishes of Blaris, Hillsborough and Annahilt, and eight more in Dromore and Dromara. The problem was that he had let out his lands on long leases with low fixed rents but with high entry fines, which were quickly spent. Beneficiaries amongst the newcomers included the Hill family, Edward Trevor, Trogmorton Stotisbury, George Sexton and a lawyer, John Jennings. By 1641 Arthur Hill possessed a third of the whole barony of Upper Iveagh.

Meanwhile, from their first holdings in the Lagan Valley and in the vicinity of Carrickfergus and Belfast, captains who had served Sir Arthur

Chichester began to look out for opportunities offered by Magennis freeholds. Sir Moses Hill, starting out in the Lagan Valley, had accumulated his initial capital in a fraud over whiskey supplies to the army. He and Arthur, his son and heir, engulfed the greater part of the Magennis lands in Kilwarlin, the remainder going to Sir William Reeves, and Sir Faithful Fortescue absorbed lands in Magherally and Seapatrick. Sir Fulke Conway augmented his estate about Lisnagarvey (now Lisburn) to the extent that when he died, in 1624, his land—inherited by his nephew Edward, later Viscount, Conway—was valued at two thousand pounds a year, about the same income as the City of London collected from all its lands in Ulster. Lands held by the O'Lawry family in Moira and Magheralin were lost in a series of alienations to Edward Trevor, Francis Kinnaston, Edward Brugh and David Boyd. All of these carpetbaggers, with the exception of Boyd, were English or Welsh. But, in time, they would bring in very considerable numbers of Scots to rent and farm their new acquisitions.[6]

Sir Hugh Montgomery and Sir James Hamilton, the Scottish lairds now firmly embedded in north and east Down, looked around them for fresh opportunities. They, like most of the newcomers, could muster the cash required far more easily than the natives could. Conn MacNéill O'Neill of Castlereagh sold off his townlands one by one until he was left with nothing. His sole memorials are a fetid stream and a shopping centre in east Belfast bearing his name, Connswater, and his stone inauguration chair in the Ulster Museum at Stranmillis. Conn's son Daniel managed to live on his wits at court in London. Montgomery was able to find the money to buy many of O'Neill's townlands by borrowing it in Edinburgh and mortgaging his Braidstane lands. As well as purchasing much of Conn's land, Montgomery claimed that he had given him two thousand pounds, and, 'beside this, Conn has received continual and daily benefits from me in money, horses, clothes and other provisions of good value and also has been chargeable unto me in divers other disbursements'.

Sir Arthur Chichester raised £1,700 in bonds from London to purchase more estates in Lower Clandeboye. Sir Fulke Conway bought property in south-east Antrim by selling his English lands as well as his wife's jointure, ensuring that his descendants would be major proprietors here for generations to come. Army officers who had retired or had been cashiered found that their pensions were only payable in Ireland; nevertheless, they were able to use them to extend their Ulster lands.

Sir Hugh Clotworthy had £91 5s as captain of the King's boats on Lough Neagh, which helped him not only to consolidate his estate in

Templepatrick but also to 'farm' or rent land from the Londoners. The Crown's casual manner of issuing patents, compounded by chaotic record-keeping, was systematically exploited by newcomers *in situ*: lands were often grossly undervalued by juries of native Irish, which made decisions on the annual value of estates not by ideas of economic rent but by the much less onerous traditional renders which had been paid in the past to superior lords.

Even the Anglican clergy became involved in shady deals. John Bramhall, Bishop of Derry, and Wentworth's ally, complained that many landlords in Co. Down were manipulating royal grants to get access to church land; they 'first found offices to entitle the King to this land and tithes' and then 'passed them by patent from the Crown, the bishops sometimes conniving'. These included two speculators from Dublin, John King and Thomas Hibbotts. Bishop Todd of Dromore was certainly conniving. He made fee farm grants of his diocesan lands: fourteen townlands to Edward Trevor; forty-three to his brother-in-law, William Worsely of Nottingham; and seven to Arthur Bagenal of Newry. Chichester was so furious when he heard of this that he had the bishop arrested. Worsely had to give most of his ill-gotten land back, but Trevor and Bagenal held on to theirs by agreeing to change their outright grants to sixty-year freeholds.[7]

There were some rare examples of native Irish families improving their position. The O'Haras of Crebilly, Co. Antrim, became close allies of the Earl of Antrim and were rewarded by being given a favourable lease of four townlands, including Loughguile, which had been MacQuillan territory. The 2nd Earl granted them these lands outright in 1629. O'Hara also bought the church lands of Kells from Sir Arthur Chichester, and by 1630 he had become one of the most prominent native landowners in eastern Ulster.

Downward social mobility, however, was the fate of most of the Gaelic Irish. This was the experience of the O'Hara neighbours, the family of Ó Gnímh, obliged to become tenants on their lands when it was granted to Sir Patrick Agnew, and thereafter to subtenants when the estates were let out to Captain Alexander Dundas. (Confusingly, many Ó Gnímhs later anglicised their surname to Agnew.) The MacQuillans of the Route had already lost Dunluce to the MacDonnells and were left with nothing when all the lands of north Antrim were granted to Sir Randal in 1603. In sympathy, the government gave them the 'tough' (estate) of Clangartity in mid-Antrim; but their chief, Rory Óg, was forced by debt to sell it in 1619 to Sir Faithful Fortescue, who in turn sold it to William Adair. Rory Óg lived the rest of his life on a modest royal pension and loans from Adair. The contraction of estates held by the Gaelic Irish was to be found throughout Ulster. In Co. Cavan the decrease was from 20 per cent in 1610 to 16 per cent in 1641, and in Co. Armagh from 25 per cent to about 19 per cent over the same period.[8] These estimates do not take into account the fact that some estates were so heavily mortgaged by Irishmen hopelessly in debt that they were certain to be lost entirely.

THE HIGH-SPENDING EARL

By 1641 the most indebted Ulsterman of all was the 2nd Earl of Antrim. Named Randal after his father, Sir Randal, the 1st Earl, he was brought up as a Gaelic-speaker and had 'neither hat, cap, nor shoe, nor stocking' until he was seven or eight years old. At the tender age of four Randal was engaged to Lucy, the daughter of James Hamilton, the 1st Earl of Abercorn—this was to make certain that he would be regarded as the legitimate heir, as Sir Randal had already fathered at least one illegitimate son. The 1st Earl, despite his unwavering support for King James, and the enthusiasm with which he promoted the colonisation of his lands by Protestant Lowlanders, remained a devout Catholic. He built a chapel in honour of St Brigid near Athlone, put up a religious house at St Patrick's Purgatory at Lough Derg and funded and supported the Franciscan friary at Bonamargy, near Ballycastle. It was primarily to expose his son to continental Catholicism that the young Randal, by now Viscount Dunluce, was sent to France in 1627. When Dunluce returned in the spring of 1627 he was presented at court to King Charles I and his French queen, Henrietta Maria. There Dunluce, 'a tall, clean-limbed, handsome man with red hair', made a very favourable impression. At the King's insistence he remained at court thereafter.

Lady Lucy was thrown over, and the MacDonnell heir began to look elsewhere for a suitable wife. The English nobility regarded him with some suspicion—after all, he was the grandson of the Earl of Tyrone, a deceased traitor. Katherine Villiers did not share such prejudices. Her husband, the Duke of Buckingham—the loathed favourite of Charles I—had been knifed to death at Portsmouth in 1627. Immensely wealthy, she was by far the most eligible widow in the land.[9] Dunluce did not hesitate when she indicated her interest, and, though she was nine years older than Randal, they were married in April 1635. Before he died, the following year, the 1st Earl had the satisfaction of learning that his daughter-in-law had become a Catholic.

On the eve of his marriage Dunluce had debts of more than £3,000. By 1639 the 2nd Earl, according to Lord Deputy Thomas Wentworth, had debts of £50,000. His biographer, Jane Ohlmeyer, reckons that 'Antrim's debts hovered between £40,000 and £42,000 during the late 1630s'. His extravagance was extraordinary: he spent £22,000 just to furnish his houses at Dunluce in north Antrim and Bramshill in Hampshire. According to one report, in one night's play he lost 'at the Wells at Tunbridge almost £2,000 at ninepins'. Great numbers of creditors waited in vain to be paid, including three goldsmiths, five jewellers, two physicians, one shoemaker (owed more than £3,500), one stocking-seller, two upholsterers and the court painter, Anthony van Dyck. In desperation the earl leased out any land in Antrim not yet tied up at extremely low rents in return for high entry fines. In November 1637 he mortgaged the entire barony of Cary, the lordship of Ballycastle and Rathlin Island for ninety-nine years in trust for the payment of selected debts.[10]

The Earl of Antrim's debts were so immense that he became like some large financial institutions early in the twenty-first century: too big to be allowed to fail. He retained the unswerving support of King Charles. Unlike other Gaelic Ulstermen facing financial ruin, he was not contemplating rebellion.

ECONOMIC DISLOCATION: 'GREAT NUMBERS ... LEAVE THEIR CORN STANDING IN THE GROUND'

The financial plight of surviving Gaelic lords had become acute following the disastrous harvests of 1638 and 1639. Indeed, the last years of Wentworth's viceroyalty brought severe dislocation to all in Ulster, planters and natives alike. This was a sudden reversal: until now Ulster's economy had been doing rather well.

The annual supplement to the Irish government from the English treasury had been reduced from £48,000 in 1613 to slightly more than £3,000 in 1623, and in 1638 Wentworth had been able to send over £10,441 to England from the Irish treasury. In part this was a reflection of an expanding economy. Bad harvests between 1621 and 1623, together with the Spanish war of 1626–9, had resulted in temporary downturns, but on the whole the island's output and exports grew steadily, especially during the 1630s.

British colonisation had not yet transformed agriculture in Ulster, which continued to depend heavily on the grazing of cattle; but the influx of settlers certainly did much to raise output. Though their farming techniques were probably not yet much more advanced than those of the native Irish, the Scots settlers appear to have cultivated their lands in eastern Ulster more intensively than they had been before. Sir George Rawdon, agent on the Conway estates in south Antrim, assiduously promoted the introduction of the most up-to-date agricultural practices. Exports of linen yarn, mostly produced in the north, rose from 627 packs in 1621–2 to 1,257 by 1640. Exports of cows and oxen, which had been 4,000 in 1621–2, were 46,000 by 1640–41. In 1621–2, 590 horses had been exported from the Ards Peninsula alone, and for 1637 the number had risen to 2,484. In 1632–3 exports from the city of Londonderry by-passed those of Galway for the first time. George Monck, undertaking a survey of customs in Ulster in 1637, observed that he was 'very glad to see such store of shipping in the Derry and the good increase of boats and barques in all the ports by the way'.[11]

Then, from 1638, the economy of Ulster was thrown into crisis. Disastrous harvests were primarily to blame, but the situation was made all the more desperate by Wentworth's actions. He attempted to improve the quality of linen. The traditional method, which involved knotting the threads, was to be replaced by numbering them and dividing them 'into hundreds'. In the long term this was the right direction for the domestic linen industry to go in, particularly to meet the demands of the English market; but the new regulations were brought in too rapidly and were unfeelingly enforced. Serious problems arose because the yarn was 'made and winded by thousands of old women . . . that can hardly be taught to number their fingers'. However well the yarn was made, if it was knotted it was seized by officials and 'converted . . . into wine or ale' in front of those who had made it. As a result, many women 'are now starving that were able to live'.[12]

Even more dislocating was the confrontation between Charles I and his Scottish subjects. Wentworth himself admitted that these 'troubles have already a great operation upon the trade of this kingdom', and Christopher Lowther, an importer of iron ore, remarked that conducting business was difficult, because 'these Scotch wars hindereth us in all things'. Wentworth's drive to enforce religious conformity on Presbyterians and Puritans in Ulster had a profoundly damaging effect. Many settlers fled across the North Channel. In January 1639 the Earl of Antrim wrote that those sympathising with the Covenanters flock over daily to them, 'fearing the high commission court here'. Lord Conway's agent in Antrim warned his employer that summer that rents would be late, because his Scots tenants were leaving. Viscount Chichester informed Wentworth that 'great numbers' were fleeing to Scotland, taking with them 'their horses, cows, sheep and what else they have, and leave their corn standing in the ground'. By December 1639 the value of land in Co. Antrim had fallen by half.

Wentworth added to these woes by billeting in Ulster the army of nine thousand men he had raised to assist the King in his attempt to face down Scotland. The presence of five hundred soldiers in the city of Londonderry, then with an adult population of only a thousand, pushed food prices up to ruinous levels. Writing from Co. Tyrone in April 1640, Bishop Bramhall warned that 'all places and all sorts of men' were 'full of discontents and complaints'. Troops were quartered on tenants' lands so that, Chichester wrote, the 'poor people . . . are so much impoverished that they can no longer subsist, and the plantation which was here begun and brought to some perfection is now so much ruined as there is little hope to recover it'.[13]

PLOTTING REBELLION

During the final months of 1640 and the spring and summer of 1641, no fewer than three plots against the state were maturing in Ireland. One was being hatched by colonels, *émigré* Irish veterans recruited by Wentworth from overseas to train his army. When the cost of maintaining this force, thought to be about a thousand pounds a day, was proving ruinous, the men were put on half pay and billeted in winter quarters in Belfast, Derry, Moneymore and Armagh. Then the decision was made to disband the army in May 1641: the colonels were now out of work. Catholics, like the men they had been training, these officers now plotted to take advantage of the King's woes to advance the cause of the Counter-Reformation by organising rebellion in Ireland.

Meanwhile, in the Spanish Netherlands, Eoghan Roe O'Neill, nephew of the Earl of Tyrone, had emerged as the acknowledged leader of the exiled Irish. A veteran commander of one of Philip IV's regiments, Eoghan Roe had distinguished himself during the Siege of Arras in 1640. Now, as he observed Charles's bungled attempts to force the Scots to submit to his will, and the British Parliament's mounting hostility to the King, Eoghan Roe concluded that the time had come to lead an expeditionary force to Ulster.

Nothing much came of the colonels' plot, and Eoghan Roe needed time to find backers for his invasion plan. In the end it was a group of Gaelic gentlemen in Ulster, members of the Irish Parliament, who set the rebellion in motion, plunging the whole island into a state of perpetual warfare for more than twelve years.

Sir Phelim O'Neill appeared to be one of those 'deserving Irish' who had done well for himself under the rule of the Stuarts. He gave every indication of blending in successfully with the new ruling class. Well educated in the English manner, attending Lincoln's Inn for three years as a young man, a convert to the state-sponsored Reformed Church (but, as it turned out, only for a time), he possessed a substantial estate of 4,500 acres in the counties of Armagh and Tyrone centred at Kinard (now Caledon). Indeed, he had gone out of his way to attract Protestant British settlers on to his lands. He had been able to purchase a knighthood for himself in 1627 and had been elected to the Irish Parliament, where he had been active on several of its committees. But Sir Phelim was one of those many Gaelic Irishmen who had been quite unable to manage estates in the modern, commercial way. By 1641 he had mortgaged his lands for at least £13,066. He was not alone. Conor Maguire, Lord Enniskillen, declared that he was 'overwhelmed in debt and the smallness of my nowe estate'.[14] His brother Rory Maguire and Philip McHugh O'Reilly of Cavan, both of them members of Parliament, were also in grave financial difficulties. Rory Maguire had married Deborah, widow of Sir Leonard Blennerhasset of Ederny and sister of Lieutenant-Colonel Audley Mervyn of Trillick, who bore him three children in addition to the six she had borne her previous husband.

These men had hoped for some time that the graces, the concessions offered by Charles I, would provide religious toleration, security and respect from the ruling elite. Despite protracted debates in the Irish Parliament, nothing tangible had resulted. Much as these men loathed Wentworth, they found that his fall had led to the appointment in his place of Lords Justices (appointed to deputise for the viceroy), known for their hard-line anti-Catholic views. In the 'Bishops' Wars' the Scots were demonstrating the effectiveness of direct, extra-parliamentary action. At the same time, however, the victories of the Scots and their 'godly' allies in Westminster posed an ominous threat: a ferocious Puritan crackdown on the Catholic majority in Ireland.

The man who galvanised these Gaelic gentlemen into organising rebellion was Rory O'More, an army officer from Longford with lands in Kildare and Armagh. He was able to convince the Ulstermen that the Catholic Old English of the Pale could take no more—given a lead, they would join the Gaelic Irish of the north. In February 1641 O'More approached Lord Maguire while he was attending Parliament in Dublin;

he referred to his lordship's great debts, the sufferings of the Irish on planted lands and the opportunity the King's conflict with Scotland offered to recover lost estates. Philip O'Reilly, Turlough O'Neill (Sir Phelim's brother) and the head of the MacMahons, Colonel Brian MacMahon, met in Monaghan soon after. There the opportunity to bring over to their cause men of Wentworth's new army, 'all Irishmen, and well armed', before they were disbanded and dispersed was discussed. More meetings followed. Meanwhile Sir Phelim O'Neill had been conducting an elaborate coded correspondence with his cousin Eoghan Roe O'Neill in Flanders. Sir Phelim O'Neill's wife died unexpectedly, and her funeral took place on 5 September 1641; O'More and the Maguires were amongst the mourners. Only then, at the wake in Kinard, was Sir Phelim approached, brought into the plot and, indeed, appointed leader.

In their earlier plotting the colonels had come up with the idea of making a carefully planned surprise attack on Dublin Castle. This strategy the Ulstermen adopted, arranging for it to be accompanied by an uprising of the native Irish in the north. It was also agreed that the Scots settlers in Ulster should be left alone unless they proved hostile. Final arrangements were made on 5 October in the house of Turlough O'Neill at Lough Ross in Co. Monaghan: Dublin Castle would be seized on 23 October, and Sir Phelim would lead a simultaneous insurrection in Ulster with the object of taking the walled city of Derry.

'THE SUDDENNESSE OF OUR SURPRISALL': THE 1641 REBELLION ERUPTS

In Dublin, on 22 October, Lord Maguire disclosed the plot to Owen O'Connolly of Moneymore, foster-brother to Colonel Hugh Maguire and employed by Sir John Clotworthy on his lands in Co. Londonderry. Maguire concluded: 'And whereas you have of long time been a slave to that Puritan Sir John Clotworthy, I hope you shall have as good a man to wait upon you'. What Lord Maguire did not know was that O'Connolly had become a Protestant convert. O'Connolly joined conspirators at the *Lion* in Winetavern Street in Dublin to pick up as many details as he could. Then he leaped over a wall and two fences to bring the news to Lord Justice Parsons in Merchants' Quay. Parsons only half believed the story but, just to be sure, put Dublin Castle in a high state of defence. Soon afterwards Lord Maguire and other leading conspirators were seized and imprisoned in the fortress they had planned to capture. The plot had been foiled, but that same night the rebellion in Ulster began.

Just before eight o'clock on the evening of Friday 22 October, Sir Phelim O'Neill called on his neighbour Lord Caulfield at Charlemont and invited himself to dinner. There was nothing unusual in this: both men were members of Parliament and justices of the peace, and knew each other well. Once inside, Sir Phelim and his men seized the fort and imprisoned the garrison and its commander; then they galloped to Dungannon, which had fallen by a similar ruse, reaching it by midnight. Just before dawn next day O'Neill surprised Mountjoy with the help of the O'Quinns, and at the same time the O'Donnellys took Castlecaulfield. Before nightfall that Saturday, Sir Conn Magennis, uncle of the 2nd Viscount Iveagh, had led a successful assault on Newry, and Lurgan was in flames, Sir William Brownlow surrendering the castle there next day. On Sunday, Sir Phelim issued a proclamation from Dungannon, declaring that the rising

is noe ways intended against our Soveraine Lord the King, nor the hurt of any of his subiets, eyther of the Inglish or Schotish nation, but onely for the defence and liberty of our selves and the Irish natives of this kingdome.

So far the rebellion had limited objectives, and no appeal had been made to foreign powers. And so far, under the direction of the native Irish gentry, the insurgents had shed comparatively little blood. 'I protest that no Scottsman should be touched', Sir Phelim's brother declared, while Philip O'Reilly in capturing Cavan ordered his men 'not to meddle with anie of the Scotishe natioun, except they give cause'. Within days the insurgents were striking south to Dundalk, north to Moneymore, which had been seized by the O'Hagans, and west towards Fermanagh, where the Maguires had risen.

Arthur Champion, a wealthy Dublin merchant, had established himself as a country gentleman in Co. Fermanagh by buying land from Thomas Flowerdew, an original grantee, and his son Edward. Then, in 1640, he had purchased the manor of Coole from the ageing and childless servitor Roger Atkinson, and in the same year he was simultaneously a justice of the peace, sheriff of the county and a member of Parliament for Enniskillen. After a meeting of his manor court on 22 October, Champion invited his friends to dinner at his castle of Shannock and to stay the night. Just after dawn next day a party of his tenants, led by Donn Carrough Maguire and Edmund Carrough Maguire, appeared at the gates saying they had a prisoner accused of stealing cattle. As soon as he opened the gates the tenants threw off their long mantles, stabbed Champion and three of his companions to death and took possession of the castle.[15]

Rory Maguire had signalled the start of the rising in Fermanagh by burning the village of Lisnarick. Then, joined by his brother-in-law Richard Nugent and the McCaffreys, he took Archdalestown. After seizing Irvinestown, Rory forced the capitulation of Lisnaskea on 25 October. Maguire also took prisoner his relative by marriage Francis Blennerhasset and his wife and children, keeping them locked up in Castlehasset (now Crevenish) for seven weeks. Francis was shot dead by the rebels on Christmas Eve, and his son-in-law Thomas Redman was hung up on tenter-hooks and left to die.[16] The McMurrays and McLaughlins seized Garrison on the shores of Lough Melvin.

At nine o'clock on the evening of Saturday 23 October, Bishop Leslie wrote in haste from Lisburn to Sir Hugh Montgomery, 2nd Viscount Ards, warning him that Sir Phelim was in revolt 'with a huge multitude of Irish souldiers, and that this day they are advanced as far as Tonregee'. This was followed by another message that

> the newes which I sent unto your Lordship about 4 houres agoe are too true, and a great dale worse than I then understood. For the Newry is taken and we expect them here this night . . .

Robert Lawson, a merchant and sheriff of Londonderry, returned from doing business with Sir James Hamilton, Viscount Clandeboye, at Killyleagh to call on his wife at the New Forge ironworks, near Belfast. He found most of the townspeople 'fled and flying, and carrying their goods to Carrickfergus', the elderly Viscount Chichester already on board ship. He beat a drum through the streets, raised about 160 men and reached Lisburn at four o'clock on Monday afternoon, 25 October. Sir Conn Magennis, having burned Dromore, approached Lisburn that night, but, 'making show of six or seven lighted matches for every piece, to astonish the enemy', Lawson's men forced him back. It was to no avail that the Irish drove a hundred head of cattle at the gates next day and, on Wednesday, Lord Montgomery and Lord Hamilton brought up reinforcements. Lisburn continued to hold out. Belfast and Carrickfergus were thus saved, and Colonel James Clotworthy had time to secure Antrim, the Agnews to defend Larne, James Shaw to fortify Ballygalley, and Archibald Stewart, Lord Antrim's agent, to place garrisons in north Antrim.

Elsewhere in the province the insurgents seemed to sweep all before them. Portadown fell, all Cavan was overwhelmed, and on 28 October, after holding out for some days, Armagh capitulated. All the planter castles in Co. Fermanagh came under siege. Sir William Cole had time to make the island town of Enniskillen impregnable. Colonel Audley Mervyn, who rallied settlers in west Tyrone in their defence, in a long address he made to the House of Commons at Westminster the following summer, gave an account of what had happened in his part of Ulster:

> Though the poison of this rebellion was diffused through the veines of the whole kingdome, yet it broke the skin with its plague-tokens in the county of Tyrone, and Fermanagh first.
>
> The suddennesse of our surprisall, and the nature of it, was so unexpected, that the inhabitants could scarcely believe themselves prisoners, though in their chaines, and the Irish servant which over-night was undressing his master in duty, the next morning was stripping master and mistres with a too-officious tyranny.
>
> Here in the twinckling of an eye, the corporations, townes and villages proclaimed their situation a farre off by their fire and smoake; here you might see hundreds of men, women, children, of all con-ditions and estates, that had lived in most plentifull and secure habitations, exposed to the rocke for shelter, to the heavens for cloathing, so that hundreds in a few dayes starved upon the mountains.[17]

ATROCITY: THE GENTRY LOSE CONTROL

On 4 November, Sir Phelim O'Neill and Rory Maguire issued a joint declaration stating that the King had given them a commission under the Great Seal of Scotland, addressed to 'all Catholics of the Romish party both English and Irish', giving them power to 'seize the goods, estates and persons of all the English Protestants'. This was a forgery, but, adorned with a royal seal detached from a land patent, it was widely believed and undoubtedly encouraged many hesitating native Irish to take up arms.[18]

Everywhere, the Catholic gentry depended on an uprising of the Gaelic peasantry, and after the first fortnight they lost control. All attempts to distinguish Scots from English were abandoned. Hungered by harvest failures, and listening to wild prophecies and rumours of a Puritan plot to massacre them, the Gaelic Irish threw themselves with merciless ferocity on the settlers. The Irish victories were so rapid in the first few days that the leaders did not know what to do with those who had surrendered.

After they had robbed and stripped the settlers in Cavan, the O'Reillys simply released them, 'turned naked, without respect of age or sex, upon the wild, barren mountains, in the cold air, exposed to all the severity of the winter; from whence in such posture and state they wandered towards Dublin'. Perhaps two-thirds of those who perished before the end of the year died of exposure and hunger. Others, like Viscount Caulfield and Francis Blennerhasset, were simply shot dead.

The massacre at Portadown in the middle of November is well authenticated. William Clark told how Manus Roe O'Cahan drove

> with such other English as they could find to the number of threescore persons which belonged to the said Parish of Loughgall and put them all in the Church there . . . imprisoned for the space of nine days with at least 100 men, women and children during which time manie of them were sore tortured by strangling and halfe hanging . . . after which time of imprisonment hee with an 100 men, women and children or thereabouts were driven like hogs about six miles to Porte of Doune to a river called the Band and there they forced them to goe upon the Bridge . . . and the stripped the said people naked and with theire pikes and swords and other weapons thrust them down headlong in to the said river and immediately they perished and those of them that assayed to swim to the shore the rebels stood to shoot at.

Elizabeth Price confirmed that the prisoners were driven

> off the bridge into the water and then and there instantly and most barbarously drowned the most of them. And those that could not swim and came to the shore they knocked on the head, and so after drowned them, or else shot them to death in the water.

Like William Clark, Mrs Price was kept alive because she was thought to be hiding money; in an effort to find it, her tormentors 'had the soles of her feet fried and burnt at the fire, and was often scourged or whipped'.

After the massacre at Portadown, other Protestant settlers were herded into a house at Shewie, nearby, and burned to death. Ann Smith and Margaret Clark escaped through a hole in the wall; they were knocked on the head and left for dead but survived to give evidence of the atrocity. Ellen Matchett gave one of several accounts of settlers burned to death in houses where they had taken refuge; she herself was 'miraculously preserved by a mastiff dog that set upon these slaughtering and bloody rebels' and survived with others in hiding, emerging 'sometimes to get the brains of a cow, dead of disease, boiled with nettles, which they accounted good fare'.

Tully Castle, on the southern shore of Lower Lough Erne, held out for weeks against Rory Maguire's forces. Behind the walls were about fifteen men and some sixty women and children. On Christmas Eve, Lady Hume decided to surrender, assuming that the lives of at least the women and children would be spared. But, as the survivor Captain Patrick Hume stated later in sworn evidence, 'the rebels having stripped the Protestants of all their clothes (except the said Lady Hume), they imprisoned them in the vaults or cellars of the said castle, where they kept them with a strong guard all that night'. Next morning, Christmas Day, they incarcerated Lady Hume and her family in a barn 'within a stone's cast from the castle', planning to transfer them to Monea Castle. Then all the other prisoners were led out into the bawn, and

> the rebels did most cruelly and barbarously murder the said Protestants to the number of men and 60 women and children or thereabouts . . . After the said rebels did pillage and plunder the said castle, they did burn it on the day and year aforesaid.

Captain Hume's evidence can be found in more than thirty manuscript volumes filled with the sworn statements of survivors of 1641, gathered largely to justify a massive confiscation of land held by Catholics. Certainly much of the evidence in these depositions is fantastic, grossly exaggerated and based almost exclusively on hearsay; but much is also supported by other evidence. Atrocities followed the collapse of all authority in a climate of fear and want, perpetrated by people inflamed by rumour, religious passion and a lust for revenge. They were not the outcome, however, of a concerted drive for massacre. A great many of the incidents of cruelty could be classed as acts of war, incidents which would have been considered run-of-the-mill in the Thirty Years' War, then still raging in Germany.

Just how many British settlers in Ulster were massacred or murdered in the final months of 1641 is extremely difficult to determine. Pamphlet literature in England soon laid claim to anything up to 150,000 Protestants massacred, a figure far in excess of the total British population in the province. In a detailed study of the violence in Armagh, Hilary Simms has calculated a maximum of 1,259 and a minimum of 527 killed in the county, that is, at least 17½ per cent and at most 43 per cent of Armagh's British population. Even multiplying the highest total for Armagh by nine in order to get an estimate for the nine counties of Ulster would still bring the total for the province to less than 12,000.[19]

The bloodshed was not all one-sided. Sir William Cole and his men made a sally from Enniskillen and, having rounded up about two hundred Irish, butchered them all. In any case, the killing had only begun.

Chapter 13 ～

RECONQUEST AND RECOVERY

'FORCE AND FEAR UNITED THE TWO PARTIES': THE OLD ENGLISH AND THE ULSTER IRISH JOIN FORCES

On 23 October 1641 the Ulster Irish had risen in revolt. In the weeks that followed, thousands of British colonists had been driven out; thousands more had been murdered; and about two-thirds of the nine-county province had fallen to the rebels.

The victorious insurgents took Dundalk and began to lay siege to Drogheda. The Lords Justices in Dublin Castle announced the existence of 'a most disloyal and detestable conspiracy by some evil-affected papists'. The Catholic Old English gentlemen had responded to the Dublin government's call to arms. As they marched north to Drogheda, however, they wondered whether they too were being branded as 'disloyal and detestable'. For years they had been persecuted on account of their religion, and, despite their long record of loyalty to the Crown, they had been threatened with the confiscation of their lands. As they approached the walled town, they turned aside. In December 1641 they had meetings with the Gaelic Irish commanders at Tara and Knockcrofty. The momentous decision they arrived at was to join the native Irish rebels of Ulster. For centuries these Old English lords, descendants of the Norman colonists, had fought loyally for the English government. Now they had been pushed too far. Richard Bellings, who had been at the meetings, knew how significant this decision was:

> And thus, distrust, aversion, force, and fear united the two parties which since the conquest had at all times been most opposite, and . . . publicly declared that they would repute all such enemies as did not assist them in their ways.[1]

ULSTER 'NOT ONLY LOOKS LIKE A DESERT, BUT LIKE HELL': NEW ARMIES IN ULSTER

During the first weeks of the uprising it looked as if the whole British colony in Ulster would be overwhelmed. But the garrison of Lisburn held the rebel advance at bay. Lord Hamilton and Lord Montgomery reinforced the defenders, now under the command of Sir Arthur Tyringham, with men from north Down and the Ards. In response, the insurgent commander-in-chief, Sir Phelim O'Neill, brought up a large force from mid-Ulster. About nine thousand rebels massed in an attempt to break through the defences of Lisburn. Three times they attacked, on 8, 22 and 28 November 1641, and three times they were repulsed, on the last occasion with great loss.

Sir Phelim's original objective had been to take Derry, but the element of surprise was lost, and, under the command of Sir William Stewart and Sir Audley Mervyn, the settlers held the insurgents back along a line stretching from Augher to Newtownstewart and north to Strabane. Support for the rebel cause in Co. Donegal was weaker than Sir Phelim expected. There the insurgents, led principally by Manus O'Donnell of Glenfinn (the son of Niall Garbh, who had died a prisoner in the Tower), expended much of their energy in seeking plunder. The settlers, organised by Captain John Stewart and Captains James and John Cunningham, formed four large regiments, which became known as the Laggan Army, named after the densely colonised area in the barony of Raphoe. In their ferocious counter-attacks the settlers kept the western approaches to the city of Londonderry secure. Further south Sir Ralph Gore, though mortally wounded in an engagement in the Barnesmore Gap, saw to it that Donegal Castle, Ballyshannon and Castle Murray were held securely against the insurgents.[2]

Everywhere, the native Irish nevertheless outnumbered the colonists. The plantation clearly remained in peril. Strabane fell to the rebels in December, and refugees crowded into Derry; and in Coleraine, where some were killed when the parish church was struck by lightning, a hundred died each day from disease. Atrocities continued to be perpetrated by both sides. Insurgents ignored the pleas of their commander, Miles O'Reilly, when they murdered unarmed settlers in Kilmacrenan, including the Rev. Robert Atkins, 'because he would not confess more money than he had', and—according to a deposition later made by Mulrony Carroll—rebels killed three women, 'one of whose bellies they ripped up, she being great with child, so as the child sprang out of her belly'. In north Antrim some

Catholic Scots joined the rebellion. Alasdair MacDonnell, a kinsman of the Earl of Antrim, leading men to bring protection to a Protestant settler at Portna, suddenly got the Catholics in his party to murder the Protestants in the force. Sixty of them were killed. In revenge, colonists killed Catholic tenants of Henry Upton in Templepatrick and more than thirty Catholics in Islandmagee. Hearing of this, Sir Conn Magennis had seventeen captives being transferred to Newcastle for an exchange of prisoners, including Lieutenant Hugh Trevor and his wife, taken to a wood and hanged. Sir James Montgomery, commanding a force in south Down, wrote that he could not contain his men—who had learned of this atrocity—for they

> had seen . . . their houses burned, their wives and children murdered. So they were like robbed bears and tygers, and could not be satisfied with all the revenge they took . . . being full of revenge . . . most partys killing many, and giving no quarter.

This place of slaughter, at the foot of the Mourne Mountains, is known as Bloody Bridge to this day.

At Movanagher settlers took shelter in 'little Hutts, pestered and packed with poore people'. More than five hundred Ulster colonists took refuge on the Isle of Bute alone, and in the presbyteries of Ayr and Irvine some four thousand others were in danger of starving. The Scottish Privy Council ordered a special collection, explaining that 'by famine they will miserablie perish if they are not tymouslie supplied'.[3] At the same time the Scots were cautiously approving an urgent plea from London to send a relief army to Ulster.

Major-General Robert Monro, after landing at Carrickfergus on 3 April 1642, set out southwards with his Scots army in pursuit of the insurgent Irish. A hardened veteran of the Thirty Years' War, he simply slaughtered his captives, first at Kilwarlin Wood, then at Loughbrickland and finally at Newry, where, after shooting and hanging sixty men, he stopped his soldiers throwing women in the river and using them as targets, though only after several had been killed. The rebels hid in the woods, so in marching north again he seized their cattle and slaughtered any Irish men, women and children he found. Along the Lower Bann thirty or forty Irish making for the river were 'cutt downe, with sume wyves and chydrene for I promis,' reported Adjutant-General Peter Leslie, 'such gallants gotis but small mercie if they come in your comone sogeris handis'. Mountjoy and

Dungannon were recovered, and in desperation the Ulster Irish prepared to capitulate.

Just then, at the end of July 1642, Eoghan Roe O'Neill disembarked at Doe Castle in Donegal. He had sailed from Dunkirk up the North Sea and around Scotland. Only after strong pressure had been applied by Pope Urban VIII had O'Neill been permitted to retire from the Spanish army and allowed to slip away. Nephew of Hugh O'Neill, the Earl of Tyrone, who had died in Rome in 1616, Eoghan Roe had been brooding in Spanish service in Flanders and now used his prestige and military experience to stiffen the ranks of the Ulster Irish. The task was not easy, for Ulster, the province he had left forty years before, 'not only looks like a desert, but like Hell . . .'[4]

THE WAR OF THE THREE KINGDOMS BEGINS

It was on 22 August 1642 that the English Civil War broke out. All the Stuart realms would be engulfed in this conflict, which for many in Ireland would be remembered as the War of the Three Kingdoms. Now that the forces raised by the British Parliament were marching against Charles I's Cavaliers, English government in all parts of Ireland was threatened with collapse. Certainly there were as many as 37,000 Protestant men in arms in the island. But their loyalties now were dangerously divided between King and Parliament.

Members of the Catholic hierarchy, meeting in Kilkenny, had declared that all Catholics who did not take part in this just war would be excommunicated. Elected representatives of the Old English and the native Irish came together to form the Confederation of Kilkenny in October 1642. The Confederation's Supreme Council acted as the government of Ireland, appointed generals, issued writs and minted a new coinage. There is little doubt that at this moment the Confederate Irish, working together, could have seized control of the whole island. Fatal hesitation, conflicting aims and wasting disputes, however, prevented them from achieving that objective.

Few periods of Irish history are as confusing as the 1640s. During most of this time the English Civil War raged. In Ireland these were years of massacres, innumerable sieges, dozens of battles, hundreds of skirmishes; this was a time of religious hatred, burnt crops, smoking ruins—a time when the defeated and the innocent were cut down without mercy again and again. Generals and their men changed sides, sometimes with bewildering frequency. In command in Cork, the Protestant Lord Inchiquin, known as Murrough of the Burnings, fought for Charles I, then for Parliament, then again for Charles I and finally became a Catholic. Major-General Robert Monro, his Scots troops in Ulster and the Co. Down lairds, Viscount Hamilton and Viscount Montgomery, were Royalists, then Parliamentarians and then Royalists again.

The Confederates, instead of driving their opponents into the sea, opened negotiations with Charles I. Their view was that King Charles was more likely to give them religious freedom than Parliament's Puritans and Roundheads. The Confederates' faith in Charles—like almost everyone else's—was completely misplaced. Pointless negotiations dragged on for years. On behalf of the King, the Earl of Ormond finalised a 'cessation', that is, a truce, with the Confederates on 15 September 1643. This did not mean an end to the fighting, however. Many Protestants on both sides of the Irish Sea were horrified that the King had done a deal with 'malignants' and 'idolatrous butchers' of this 'popish party'.

Divisions began to weaken the Confederate cause. The Old English, despite everything, remained loyal to Charles I. Eoghan Roe O'Neill, along with many other Gaelic Irish, sought complete Irish independence. The arrival in October 1645 of Archbishop Giovanni Battista Rinuccini, representing the newly elected Pope Innocent X, swung the pendulum in O'Neill's favour. Rinuccini brought with him arms, 20,000 pounds of gunpowder, 200,000 silver dollars and a determination to stop the Confederation of Kilkenny continuing its deal with Charles I. Against his better judgement, Eoghan Roe had been persuaded to engage the Ulster settlers in battle at Clones, Co. Monaghan, on 13 June 1643. Outnumbered two to one, his raw recruits were comprehensively routed by the Laggan Army, commanded by Robert Stewart. O'Neill was not to lose another battle. He pulled back to Connacht, there assiduously to train his Ulster army in modern fighting methods.[5]

'THE LORD OF HOSTS HAD A CONTROVERSIE WITH US': THE BATTLE OF BENBURB, JUNE 1646

Eoghan Roe was ready when Monro moved out of Antrim to march south in June 1646. With fresh Scottish reinforcements, Monro advanced with six thousand men and six field pieces drawn by oxen. On the River Blackwater at Benburb, O'Neill attacked from the rear. As his men were pounded by Monro's cannon, Eoghan Roe harangued his men:

> Let your manhood be seen by your push of pike! Your word is *Sancta Maria*, and so in the name of the Father, Son, and Holy Ghost advance!—and give not fire till you are within pike-length!

With no field guns but with an equal number of men, the Irish steadily pressed the Scots back to the river, slaughtering them. Monro escaped only after he had cast away his coat, hat and wig. Between a third and a half of the Scots were killed, the Irish sustaining only trifling losses.

When the news reached Rome, Pope Innocent himself attended a *Te Deum* in Santa Maria Maggiore to thank God for the triumph. In 1598, not far from this battleground, Eoghan Roe's uncle the Earl of Tyrone had won the greatest victory the Irish ever won over the English. Now, in 1646, this Battle of Benburb was the most annihilating triumph in arms the Irish ever won over the British. Monro ruefully observed: 'For ought I can understand, the Lord of Hosts had a controversie with us to rub shame in our faces'.[6]

Yet this great victory at Benburb was thrown away. Though all the north was now at his mercy, Eoghan Roe instead turned south to help Rinuccini take control of the Confederation in Kilkenny. Fatally divided, the Confederates would soon be in no condition to face the victors in the English Civil War—the Roundheads—and their leader, Oliver Cromwell.

CROMWELL: 'A RIGHTEOUS JUDGEMENT OF GOD'

During the summer of 1647 the fields of Ireland were once more drenched in blood. At least three thousand Irishmen were cut down at Dungan's Hill, Co. Meath, and another four thousand died at Knocknanuss Hill, Co. Cork. And these were only two battles in an endless series of armed engagements.

By the end of 1648 the Confederates had joined with Presbyterian Scots and Royalists, both English and Irish. These men, bitter enemies until recently, now united behind their captured King. But in England the cause of Charles I was lost. Soon he was on trial for his life, and on 30 January 1649 the King was executed. In common with the Scots, the Presbyterians of the Laggan army were horrified at the news. When Sir Charles Coote, in command of the Derry garrison, declared his support for the parliamentary regicides, they laid siege to the city in April. Parliament made sure that the garrison was well supplied by sea, as one of the besieged recorded in his diary on 13 June:

> After three month's siege there is not one sick or feeble body among us, and now in a better condition than the first day of the siege: our greatest want is and will be firing, there being no other firing than old houses, and trees got out of orchards; for we suppose provisions will be plentifully sent us by the parliament.

Lord Montgomery joined the Royalist besiegers with substantial reinforcements, but to no avail. Meanwhile Eoghan Roe O'Neill—bizarrely seeking a temporary alliance with the republican Parliamentarians—was marching on the city and on 8 August drove off the Royalist besiegers and entered the city. There he was entertained by Coote, whose father had been killed in action against the Irish in 1642.[7]

A week later Oliver Cromwell, appointed Lord Lieutenant of Ireland by Parliament, set out from Milford Haven with 130 vessels. He had at his disposal a war chest of £100,000, a great train of artillery and twelve thousand 'Ironsides'—seasoned veterans of many victories. Cromwell faced no opposition when he stepped ashore from his frigate on 15 August 1649. From the outset he made it clear that he intended to avenge the 1641 massacres in Ulster. 'You, unprovoked', he declared, 'put the English to the most unheard of and most barbarous massacre without respect of sex or age, that ever the sun beheld, and at a time when Ireland was in perfect peace'. After taking Drogheda, Cromwell forbade his men 'to spare any that were in arms in the town'. Some two thousand were put 'to the sword. This, he reported to Parliament, 'is a righteous judgement of God upon these barbarous wretches, who have imbrued their hands in so much innocent blood'. Then the Lord Lieutenant forged his way southwards, down the coast to the port of Wexford. There, after another successful siege, a further two thousand were massacred.[8]

The firm hand of the Commonwealth also began to come down on Ulster. While Cromwell continued his campaign in the south, Colonel Robert Venables marched north. This veteran of Naseby took Newry and Belfast without difficulty, laying siege thereafter to Carrickfergus. As the Lords Hamilton and Montgomery summoned their men to Newtownards and Comber, Coote sped southwards from Derry and made camp at Lisburn. Early in December 1649 Venables and Coote, acting in concert, cut the settlers' army to pieces near Lisburn, killing a thousand men, with many hacked down in a relentless cavalry pursuit. General Tam Dalyell, the Scots Royalist commander, then surrendered Carrickfergus.

Eoghan Roe O'Neill died in November, and Bishop Heber MacMahon of Clogher was elected to lead Catholic resistance. Next spring, when MacMahon took Dungiven and put all the men there to the sword, the colonists realised that their best interests were served by supporting Venables. The Parliamentarians routed the Irish at Scarrifhollis, overlooking Lough Swilly, on 21 June 1650. The victor, Sir Charles Coote, put his prisoners, senior officers included, to the sword. Soon afterwards

Bishop MacMahon was captured in Enniskillen and hanged; his head was then fixed on one of the gates of Derry. Charlemont Fort, the last Confederate stronghold in the north with Sir Phelim O'Neill in command, surrendered on 14 August. O'Neill escaped, but, after taking refuge on an island hideout in Tyrone, he was betrayed in February 1653. At his trial, much to the annoyance of the judges eager to blacken the name of the executed King Charles, he admitted the forgery of the royal commission of 1641, thereby forfeiting any chance of escaping a traitor's death. Sporadic guerrilla fighting in Ulster lasted until Philip MacHugh O'Reilly formally capitulated in April 1653 after a successful assault on Lough Oughter. Rory O'More, O'Reilly's fellow-plotter in 1641, was last seen swimming away in the vicinity of Inishbofin, off the Galway coast.[9]

THE LAND SETTLEMENT

Cromwell had returned to England in May 1650, leaving his son-in-law Henry Ireton in charge. The destruction of war was evident everywhere. Dr William Petty, the army's Physician-General, estimated that 504,000 native Irish and 112,000 colonists and English troops had perished between 1641 and 1652. Petty reckoned that another 100,000 Irish men, women and children had been forcibly transported to the colonies in the West Indies and North America. Colonel Richard Lawrence wrote:

> About the years 1652 and 1653 the plague and famine had swept away whole countries that a man might travel twenty or thirty miles and not see a living creature, either man, beast, or bird, they being either all dead or had quit those desolate places.

The Gaelic poet Seán O'Connell described Cromwell's subjugation of the island as 'the war that finished Ireland'. This was close to the truth. Feeding on corpses of cattle, horses and—no doubt—people, packs of wolves became numerous and audacious, even invading the streets of Dublin. The government made an appeal for charitable donations for 'the great multitudes of poore, swarming in all partes', including 'poore children, who lost their parents . . . some of them fed upon by ravening wolves and other beasts of prey'. Military commanders received orders to organise wolf hunts in their area. By March 1655, £243 5s 4d had been paid out in rewards for killing wolves.

Retribution did not end with the fighting. Cromwell's intentions for Ireland were revealed in the Act of Settlement (1652). The first clause laid out five categories of individuals who would be exempted from pardon for life or estate; under this, no fewer than eighty thousand adult males were liable for execution. After two years more than two hundred men had been tried and executed by authority of a special high court of justice; but by then the thirst for judicial blood-letting had largely been slaked. For the great majority throughout the island, the clauses in the act which mattered were those concerning land.

Cromwell, the Lord Protector of the Commonwealth, was not only concerned to punish. He had to find the cost of his conquest—a sum reaching £3,500,000. His soldiers were owed £1,750,000 in back pay. Back in 1642 Parliament needed to raise money urgently to suppress rebellion in Ireland; it passed the Adventurers' Act to invite men to 'adventure' money to the government and receive Irish land in return for their investment when the war was over. In short, the only way to meet the English government's debts was to confiscate vast tracts of land in Ireland, most of it held by Catholics.

Cromwell had once declared that the Catholics of Ireland could go 'to Hell or Connacht'. The Act of Settlement spelled out what he meant by this. Only those who could prove 'constant good affection' to the cause of Parliament could keep their estates intact. Very few could prove such constant support. Protestant proprietors failing the test were to relinquish a fifth of their estates. Catholic landowners were to have their estates confiscated entirely and to receive alternative ones, two-thirds the size, wherever Parliament might decide. It was soon revealed that these alternative lands would, indeed, be in Connacht.

THE PLANTATION STRENGTHENED

Cromwell's military victories and the Commonwealth's draconian legislation which followed them ultimately ensured the recovery and reinvigoration of the British colonisation of Ulster. By the end of the seventeenth century much of what had been laid out in the grandiose scheme adopted by James I in 1610 had been realised. To many settlers in Ulster, however, it was not immediately apparent that their future was secure.

Those Presbyterians who had rallied to the Royalist cause were uncertain about how the regime would treat them. The omens were not good. The Anabaptists in power in Dublin despised Presbyterian doctrine and intolerance of other Protestant sects. Colonel Robert Venables, having routed the Presbyterian Royalists in Ulster, now demanded that

Presbyterian ministers swear allegiance to the Commonwealth. Patrick Adair, a Scot who answered a call to be minister to the congregation at Cairncastle, near Larne, was one of the majority who refused to do so. Many fled to Scotland. Those who stayed, according to Adair,

> though their stipends were sequestered, yet changing their apparel to the habit of countrymen . . . taking what opportunities they could to preach in the fields or in barns and glens and were seldom in their own houses.

These ministers were hunted down, and those who were caught were imprisoned in Carrickfergus and transported to Scotland. By the end of 1651 only six ministers were left in Ulster.[10]

The Scottish colonists in Antrim and Down were due to forfeit a fifth of their estates. Leading members of the government met Colonel Venables in Carrickfergus in April 1653 to discuss how this could be implemented. It did not take them long to conclude that forcing such determined colonists to give up land might be well-nigh impossible. Instead they proposed 'the transportation of popular men . . . of whose dutiful and peaceful demeanours' they 'had not assurance'. Some of these were incarcerated in Carrickfergus. There too were Presbyterian ministers who had refused to sign an oath to support the regime and suspects accused of taking part in the massacre of inhabitants of Islandmagee in January 1642.

On 24 April, Venables wrote to Charles Fleetwood to tell him of his plan of 'transporting some of the Scotch inhabitants into some of the towns of the south, if we can fit grounds to hold out for this removal'. In May the recalcitrant Presbyterian ministers were informed that they were to be transplanted with their congregations to Co. Tipperary, 'where they promised to give them estates here, a proportional value of land there'. The list of 260 transplantees was headed by Sir Robert Adair of Ballymena and James Shaw of Ballygalley, and included Lord Montgomery of the Ards. Charles Fleetwood, Edmund Ludlow, Miles Corbet and John Jones sent Venables a letter to the effect that

> the time for the persons named in the list for to be moved out of Ulster into the places before mentioned shall be at or before the First of November next. And that the respective families of those persons so removed as aforesaid shall also remove out of Ulster to the places chosen by them—Munster as aforesaid at or before the 16th of April next ensuing.[11]

Oliver Cromwell himself intervened in March 1654 to secure the exemption of Sir Robert Adair. By then, however, the government was fast abandoning the idea of detaching a fifth of each estate from every Protestant landowner who had failed to show constant good affection to the cause of Parliament. The scheme to transplant Scots dissidents to Munster was dropped. In September 1654 Cromwell allowed Protestant colonists whose lands had been confiscated for their royalism to compound for their delinquency by the payment of a composition fine of twice the annual value of the estates. In short, Protestants failing to show 'constant good affection' were let off with fines, most of which were never paid. The regime was now concentrating on the transplantation of Catholics to the province of Connacht.

Since 1641 many Ulster Catholics had been killed in action fighting for the rebel cause. Others had been tried and executed. Their lands had been forfeited. Others joined the thousands transported by the Commonwealth to the West Indies and other colonies. More thousands—including many MacSweeneys of Co. Donegal—made their way to the Continent to enlist in the armies of France, Spain and the Holy Roman Empire. A great many had fled the province, in particular from the Earl of Antrim's estates, as Monro's Scots army began its campaigning in 1642. Lord Antrim himself had refused to join the rebellion, but he was an ardent Royalist throughout. As he was overseas in the service of Charles ii, his estates were confiscated by the Commonwealth.

Confiscations earlier in the century ensured that, apart from Co. Antrim, there was less land to be forfeited by Catholics in Ulster than in most other counties in the rest of Ireland. Nevertheless, Ulster Catholics were amongst the miserable groups gathering at Loughrea, Co. Galway, carrying passports and certificates issued by revenue officers. There five commissioners considered their claims to land west of the River Shannon. Among them was Turlough O'Neill of Dungannon precinct, who obtained 400 acres in the barony of Costello in Co. Mayo. Richard O'Cahan of Co. Londonderry got 600 acres in the barony of Gallen in Co. Mayo but quickly sold his land to a local merchant. The family of Niall Garbh O'Donnell, now led by his grandson Rory, left Glenfinn to settle on lands allocated to them at Ballycroy, close to Blacksod Bay. The family of his brother Hugh Boy got land close to Castlebar—indeed, virtually all the O'Donnells of Glenfinn ended up in different parts of Co. Mayo. Sir Turlough MacHenry O'Neill of the Fews had been granted the largest single estate in the Plantation of Ulster. When he died, in 1639, this estate was inherited by his son Sir Henry. Sir Henry did not join the rebellion, but his sons and kin were involved, and the estate was confiscated. The lands he received in compensation in Co. Mayo were supposed to be the equivalent of two-thirds of what he had lost, but, like many others transported to Connacht, it was no more than a third.

In Co. Down the seizure of forfeited lands was carried out by a commission of the revenue under Colonel Arthur Hill of Hillsborough and including Major George Rawdon, Lord Conway's agent. All the Magennises of Iveagh, with the exception of those of Tollymore, had their estates confiscated. Four leading Magennises were transplanted to Connacht. The 'adventurers' William Hawkins, Joseph Deane and William Barker got some 27,000 plantation acres between them, carved out of the Rathfriland and Castlewellan estates. Other land went to ex-soldiers, three thousand acres to Hill's younger son Moses, and Rawdon made sure of a generous portion for himself. The poll-tax returns of 1659 revealed 1,352 English and Scots adults and 1,381 Irish in the barony of Lower Iveagh—there was not a single Magennis surname on the lists. The Magennis family was disappearing from its ancestral territory.[12]

In Co. Donegal all Catholics who owned land in 1641 had their estates confiscated by the Commonwealth. Some, leading their men out against the settlers in 1641—including Mulmurry MacSweeney and Turlough McCaffar O'Donnell—were to be sentenced to death if captured. Turlough O'Boyle, the largest landowner to forfeit an estate in Donegal, had not joined the rebellion, but he had been elected as a representative to the Confederation in Kilkenny and supported the policies of Rinuccini and Eoghan Roe O'Neill. About twenty Gaelic Catholic noblemen forfeited their estates in Co. Donegal, with the exception of three MacSweeneys with small estates, who retained their holdings by becoming Protestants.[13]

A poem written in Ulster in about 1650, 'An Síogaí Rómhánach', bemoaned the divisions within the Confederation of Kilkenny, which the poet argued had led to so much loss. As the author is lying on the tombs of O'Neill and O'Donnell in Rome he has a vision of a beautiful maiden. She asks why the Gaels, alone of the race of Adam, who had preserved the faith since Patrick's time, should be punished by God while the 'Saxon brood', the 'heretics' who had 'scoffed at the Mother of the only son', were exalted. She blamed the Old English, the 'treacherous foreign Gaels', for refusing to support Rinuccini and Eoghan Roe O'Neill. The vision ends with the hope that, next time, the Irish will unite 'to drive out the strangers and set Ireland free':

Then none shall league with the Saxon,
Nor with the bald Scot,
Then shall Erin be freed from settlers,
Then shall perish the Saxon tongue.
The Gaels in arms shall triumph
Over the crafty, thieving, false sect of Calvin.[14]

During Cromwell's rule there was not the slightest prospect of this vision becoming a reality.

'THIS POOR CHURCH HAD A NEW SUNSHINE OF LIBERTY': TOLERATION RESTORED TO PRESBYTERIANS

On 9 July 1655 Henry Cromwell, the Lord Protector's son, arrived as Major-General of the army in Ireland. In effect he had come as the supreme governor of Ireland, easing to one side his brother-in-law Charles Fleetwood. Irish Protestants had found Fleetwood, a rigid Anabaptist, imperious and deaf to the advice they proffered. Henry Cromwell they found much more accommodating. In lieu of their back pay, 33,419 soldiers got what were called 'debentures'—pieces of paper entitling them to Irish land. As one official observed, another Ireland would have to be found to accommodate them. It was fortunate, then, that only about twelve thousand of them stayed to become Irish farmers. Quite contrary to Cromwell's plans, these men went native very quickly. They were thinly scattered across the countryside and defied an ordinance forbidding them to marry Irish women. Many, in time, became Catholics. Forty years later a visiting Englishman commented on the survival of Irish culture: 'We cannot wonder at this when we consider how many there are of the children of Oliver's soldiers in Ireland who cannot speak one word of English'.[15]

The rest of these cashiered soldiers sold their debentures, usually at great loss, to land speculators. Well to the fore amongst the purchasers were British men who had successfully colonised Ulster before the rebellion had begun. They now had the opportunity to augment and consolidate their estates, and they now had available to them a fresh influx of British eager to become tenants on their lands. For the most part these were Scots. Even Fleetwood lost his enthusiasm for suppressing Presbyterianism before his departure. Scots who had fled across the North Channel during the rebellion steadily returned to Ulster to bring the land back into full production. Sir John Clotworthy, a Devon Puritan, had always done what he could to protect the interests of Presbyterians. Lady Clotworthy began by persuading Colonel Venables to allow her minister, Mr Ferguson, to return to Antrim. The Rev. Patrick Adair recalled that the condition of his fellow-ministers, 'the brethren', improved:

> After this, the rest of the brethren returned from Scotland with passes from the English government there . . . For Cromwell did labour to ingratiate all sorts of persons and parties . . . Upon this favourable reception by those in power for the time, the brethren thought it their duty of meeting together presbyterially, as they had formerly done . . . They met at Templepatrick, Cairncastle, Comber, Bangor, &c., for a while, till at last they settled their meetings as before. This was in the year 1654, when this poor Church had a new sunshine of liberty.[16]

Henry Cromwell was even more accommodating and saw to it that the incomes of Presbyterian clergy, in the form of glebes and tithes, were fully restored. Between 1653 and 1660 the number of Presbyterian ministers grew from about half a dozen to seventy. This reflected the very considerable growth in their congregations. By 1660 the population of Ulster was somewhere between 217,000 and 260,000, a substantial recovery from the setbacks experienced during the 1640s. Immigration in the 1650s was estimated by contemporaries to be about 80,000 persons, Scots for the most part. Even though this estimate is almost certainly too high, it indicates that the plans made by James I and his courtiers were at last being realised. Hearth Money Returns in the 1660s for the counties of Tyrone, Londonderry and Antrim show that new surnames of British householders increased by between 50 and 80 per cent in most districts. A census of 1659 (taken to levy a poll tax), together with the Hearth Money Returns of 1660, show that the ratio of British settlers to native Irish was becoming more equal than that revealed by the census of 1624. For Co. Londonderry the number of adults recorded in 1659 was 4,428 English and Scots and 5,306 Irish; and, in the returns for the 1660s, 1,770 British households and 1,000 Irish. The corresponding figures for Co. Donegal are 3,412 English and Scots, and 8,589 Irish adults in 1659; and 1,645 British and 1,779 Irish households in the 1660s.[17]

The same figures demonstrate that the tendency for colonists to concentrate in favoured areas, with fertile land and good access, which had been apparent before the rebellion, was becoming more marked. As more British immigrants arrived to seek tenancies, the native Irish found that they were being forced onto poorer or more inaccessible land. The English appear to have been more prepared than the Scots to keep the Irish on their lands. During the early 1660s immigration from Scotland slowed down. To a very considerable extent, this was due to a new drive to impose conformity on Presbyterians.

THE RESTORATION

On 14 May 1660 Charles Stuart was formally proclaimed King Charles II in Dublin. A similar proclamation had been made in England a few days before. This restoration was greeted with great enthusiasm by the majority of Irish Catholics, who had high hopes that the Cromwellian land settlement would be overturned. King Charles, as he said himself, had no wish to go on his travels again, however. He would do what he could for prominent men, Catholic as well as Protestant, who had stood by him during his years of exile, but he could not remove all those who had received grants in his absence. He began by issuing an elaborate declaration in November 1660: soldiers and 'adventurers', other than those to whom pardon had been refused, were to keep what they already held on 7 May 1659. However, provision was also to be made for 'innocent papists' and named individuals who had served the King with special fidelity, and who were to be given preferential treatment. An Act of Settlement followed in the summer of 1662, which led to the establishment of a court of claims. Attempts to resolve the land question continued for the rest of the decade. This included an Act of Explanation in 1665, which provided for the surrender by soldiers and adventurers of a third of their holdings to satisfy Catholic claims. But most Catholics were to be disappointed.

The most spectacular reversal in Ulster was the restoration of Lord Antrim (the 2nd Earl had become the 1st Marquis in 1645). It could be said that no party had enjoyed his 'constant good affection', and he had survived by doing deals with agents of the Commonwealth. His wife, Katherine, had died in 1649, and soon after he married Rose, the daughter of Henry O'Neill of Killeleagh, Lord of Lower Clandeboye. It helped that Rose was a Protestant and had inherited, on her father's death in 1638, his estates in the barony of Toome. Antrim's creditors in London worked hard to ensure his survival. Then, when he heard that Charles II had been restored, he made his way to London. When he arrived he was arrested by the King's special order and committed to the Tower. There he languished between July 1660 and May 1661. Antrim's long-term rival, the Earl of Argyll, had also hurried to London, only to be found guilty of treason and then executed in Edinburgh. The marquis survived only by lying: he denied planning to raise an army at the behest of Charles I for use in England in 1641. Then, on 10 July 1663, Charles II declared the marquis 'innocent of any malice or rebellious purpose towards the crown'. This was followed by a public hearing in August, attracting an enormous amount of publicity. The King's letter was decisive, Pepys noting in his diary that the 'king hath done himself all imaginable wrong in that business of my Lord Antrim in Ireland'. However, the marquis was not formally restored to his estates until 1665.[18]

Few other Catholics in Ulster were successful. Father Patrick Maginn, chaplain to Charles II's queen, Catherine of Braganza, lobbied without success to have his lands acquired by the Hills in Co. Down returned to him. In Co. Donegal, Colonel Mulmurry MacSweeney returned from exile to take a lead in pressing the case of family members and neighbours who had fought loyally in the Royalist cause. The King examined his petition in person at Whitehall in December 1660. Only Colonel MacSweeney got anything, a small estate confiscated from his mother given back to him because, as royal officials stated, he was 'signally merited of your Majesty's most Royal Father, and your Majesty for his faithfulness and fidelity'. Henry O'Neill of Killeleagh, Co. Antrim, and Phelimy Magennis and his son Ever were restored to their Castlewellan estates, probably because they had become Protestants. King Charles personally lobbied to have Arthur Magennis, 3rd Viscount Iveagh, restored, but Rawdon and other local landowners rallied enough opposition to prevent it. Iveagh was fobbed off with a pension, which, irregularly paid, was in arrears of £1,600 at the time of his death in 1684.[19]

The London Companies, fervent backers of the cause of Parliament, began to resume possession of their proportions in Co. Londonderry as soon as conditions permitted. Cromwell provided them with a fresh charter in 1657. This was then replaced by Charles II with his own charter in April 1662, which granted all the rights that had been forfeited in 1635. By the end of the reign, outside of Co. Antrim less than 4 per cent of the land in Ulster remained in Catholic ownership. The confiscations of the 1650s and 60s virtually wiped out Catholic ownership in Co. Fermanagh, for example. Here the principal beneficiary was the Donegal landowner Henry Brooke, who had distinguished himself in the wars. He was granted the Maguire lands of Magherastephana, reckoned then to be 10,000 acres. In 1707 his son, also called Henry, was granted a patent creating of these lands the manor of Brookeborough. Sir John Cole received more than

4,000 statute acres in the barony of Clanawley, which became the kernel of the family's Florencecourt estate. James Caldwell, an Enniskillen merchant who was made a baronet, was granted extensive lands to add to the estate around Belleek, which he had bought from the Blennerhassets. Others receiving grants ranging from 100 to 300 acres included Lieutenant Walter Johnston, Arthur Foster, Gabriel Montgomery and James King. Jason Hassard, of a family which had travelled over from Lyme Regis with Sir William Cole, was granted 450 acres by patent in 1668 and acquired further lands by lease or purchase. John Corry, a Scot who had established a successful business as a merchant in Belfast, completed his purchase of the manor of Castle Coole in 1656, and his heirs became the Earls of Belmore.[20]

The restoration of the King was followed by the restoration of the established Church of Ireland. John Bramhall, who, as Bishop of Derry, had assisted Wentworth in enforcing conformity, now returned as Archbishop of Armagh and Primate of All Ireland. For the first time in Ireland, Bramhall insisted on adherence to the Thirty-Nine Articles, as in the Church of England. In January 1661 the Lords Justices forbade all meetings of 'Papists, Presbyterians, Independents and Anabaptists and other fanatical persons' as unlawful assemblies. These included Presbyterian congregational kirk sessions, which not only enforced church discipline, excommunicating if necessary, but also had functions similar to those of a court of petty sessions. Lord Charlemont warned Bramhall that he faced many difficulties in Ulster, 'abounding with all sorts of licentious persons but those we esteem most dangerous are the Presbyterian factions'.[21] Jeremy Taylor, appointed Bishop of Down and Connor, lost no time in dealing with those ministers who refused to acknowledge the rule of episcopacy and the prescribed liturgy of the state-sponsored church. Before the year 1661 was out, sixty-one ministers were turned out of their churches, thirty-six of them in one day by Taylor. Only about seven or eight ministers conformed, and the rest, deprived of their livings, had to flee or continue their ministry by preaching in barns, houses and even open fields.

The situation improved after the death of Bramhall in 1663, and by the end of the decade the ministers had returned. These ministers were not restored to their livings, but in 1672 they were given a regular stipend, known as the *regium donum*. Presbyterians, however, like Catholics, were excluded from public office, and this became official in the Test Act (1673)—the test being proof of the receipt of communion in a Church of Ireland church.

FROM DEARTH TO PROSPERITY

Economic conditions were difficult for much of the 1660s, and then a severe contraction of trade set in during the Dutch wars of 1672–4. Dr Robert Mossom, Bishop of Derry, in a representation to the London Companies in 1670, stated that his churches were in a state of bad repair because of the extreme poverty of the inhabitants; 'the country is generally so impoverished through want of trade that the tenants cannot pay their rents'. Widespread famine followed in 1674–5. In Co. Fermanagh it was remembered that the lands of most 'proprietors in the country were waste and continued so for some years after'. On the Conway estate in south Antrim it was reported that 'a great part of their cattle are dead' and that many 'tenants have not so much as will sow their land, nor bread to eat'. William Waring of Clanconnell, Co. Down, said in March 1675 that 'our country is in a very poor condition and many poor people like to famish and many tenants leave their farms when they have ploughed the land for want of seed and whole families going a begging'.

This dearth was followed by a sustained recovery over the next ten years. Once again Scots arrived in numbers, particularly after the suppression of the Bothwell Bridge uprising in 1679. In 1678 the Scottish Privy Council expressed concern that 'sundry tenants and other persons of mean quality' were either leaving or planning to leave for Ireland, 'to the great prejudice of heretours and others . . . who are lyke to be left destitute'.[22] This time, however, large numbers of English came in, particularly from the north-west, moving up the Lagan Valley and into Armagh. Here Quakers had been arriving since the 1650s. A detailed examination of baptism, marriage and burial data for the parish of Blaris, with a Church of Ireland community numbering between 3,500 and 5,500, indicates that names appear and vanish with great rapidity. Clearly these were people on the move, settling in south Antrim briefly before moving on to Oneilland in north Armagh and spreading out from there.[23]

In 1682 Dr William Molyneux in Dublin was commissioned to collect statistical accounts of Irish districts for inclusion in Moses Pitt's *Grand Atlas*. The publication fell through before it got to Ireland, but a few manuscript descriptions survive. They paint a picture of a province which was settled and growing in prosperity. In his account of the barony of Oneilland, William Brooke observed:

The soile of this Barony of O'Nealand is very deep and fertile, being productive of all Sorts of grain, as wheat, Rye, Barly, Oats, &c. The vast quantity of wheat that is yearly carried hence into the County of Antrim, besides the maintenance of above two thousand Familys with bread, which Number I find to Inhabit this Small Barony, most whereof being English, do plainly demonstrate it to be the granary of Ulster, and one of Ceres's chiefest barns for Corn; and as it Excells all the rest for Corn, so it challenges the preference for fruit trees, good sider being sold here for 30 shillings the hogshead.

As, under the terms of their leases, tenants were made to plant apple trees, Brooke predicted that 'this County twenty or thirty years hence will be little inferior to the best sider county in England'. In and about Lurgan 'is managed the greatest Linnen manufacture in Ireland', and he concludes that 'the fertility of the Soile, the curious inclosures, the shady Groves and delicate seats, that are everywhere dispersed over this Barony doe all concur to make it a Paradise of pleasure'.

William Montgomery described the Ards Peninsula, giving an impression of a peaceful and flourishing settlement, where from

the Northeast coast of the whole barroney let us note that All along: from hence to the barr of Strongford river the Inhabitants doe Manure & Dung the land with sea oar by them called Tangle which being spread on it and plowed down makes winter grain & summer Barly grow in aboundance & clean without weeds cocle or tares; the roads are pleasant & smooth in depth of winter.

He shows himself very knowledgeable about the abundant wildfowl and fish in Strangford Lough, and he observes the shortage of timber. The gentry had to send to Scotland for coal, while their tenants found 'aboundance of fewel cut by the Spade (and dryed in the sunn)'. This turf from the bog would have been described by Scots settlers as 'peats from the moss'. Oysters could be got in the lough, then as now, and a salt marsh near Newtownards was so valued for its medicinal herbs that 'the Netherland Duch' offered to lease it for two thousand pounds but were refused by Lord Montgomery.

Richard Dobbs of Carrickfergus, in his eccentric and chaotic description of Co. Antrim submitted to Dr Molyneux, remarks that the timber bridge over the Lower Bann at Portglenone is one of the best 'in the three kingdoms; there are seats upon it to rest and view the Pleasures of the Band water', while another at Coleraine was 'able to vie with Port

Glenoyne Bridge'. He estimated Islandmagee to be 5,500 acres, 'whereof 5000 I am sure is fit for fork and scythe, nor did I ever see better ground for so much together, whether for grain or cattle', and at Brown's Bay the land was 'sandy, dry, and fit for rabbits; but the people here think that no profit can be made but by ploughing, in which the men spend their whole time, except the summer quarter in providing and bringing home fireing; and the women theirs, in spinning and making linen cloth, and some ordinary woollen for their family's use.' He discusses the excellent fox-hunting there, the value of the Gobbins Caves for hiding stolen horses before they were smuggled to Scotland, and the collection of seabirds and their eggs from the cliffs, where he could not 'look down from the top to the bottom, without some horror, and yet I have been shown a boy of about 16, that would take the Leather of a horse, drying the leather, stake it into the Ground, would for eggs, or a sea Gull go down as far as the leather reached'.

These are descriptions of colonial Ulster: Brooke observes that 'the few Irish we have amongst us are very much reclaimed of their barbarous customs, the most of them speaking English'; and Dobbs writes that there were no Irish in Ballycarry, while in his home parish of Kilroot—apart from his own Church of Ireland family and servants—the people were 'all presbiterians and Scotch, not one natural Irish in the Parish, nor papist'.[24] In short, despite the growing attractions of English colonies in America, Ulster was continuing to draw in a steady flow of English and Scots.

'IF IRELAND BE LOST, ENGLAND WILL FOLLOW': KING WILLIAM'S WAR AND PEACE

Political instability in Britain, as well as in Ireland, had done much to precipitate rebellion in 1641. Renewed instability across the Irish Sea following the accession in 1685 of a Catholic king, James II, was to plunge the island once more into turmoil and blood-letting. It was not long before King James was sending tremors of alarm not only through the length and breadth of England but also through the Protestant settlement in Ireland. His actions correspondingly raised the hopes of Catholic gentry, who had lost so much in Cromwell's land settlement. With the country again thrown into conflict, the fate of Britain and much of Europe, for a time, seemed to hinge on the outcome of the contest in Ulster.

Created Earl of Tyrconnell in 1685, Richard Talbot arrived in Dublin as Lord Deputy in February 1687. One of the few Catholic officers to survive Cromwell's massacre at Drogheda, Talbot had risen from being the sixteenth child of an impoverished Kildare gentleman to become James II's principal agent in promoting the revival of Catholic fortunes in Ireland. Soon he was busy clearing Protestants out of the Irish army and the country's administration. Following the birth of a male heir to the throne in June 1688, thereby ensuring the Catholic succession, the Protestant gentlemen of England became convinced that King James would have to go. Fearing that Tyrconnell was about to send a Catholic army across the Irish Sea, they turned to William of Orange, ruler of the Dutch Republic, for aid. William accepted their invitation and landed with an imposing army at Torbay on 5 November 1688. After fatal vacillation, James fled to France just before Christmas. The following February, William and his wife, Mary, James's eldest daughter, were declared joint sovereigns of England, Scotland and Ireland.

This bloodless revolution gave the English Parliament new constitutional powers, but members were not stirred to action until news came in March 1689 that James had landed at Kinsale with a formidable French army. 'If Ireland be lost', one member of Parliament observed, 'England will follow', and another declared: ''Tis more than an Irish war, I think 'tis a French war.' For a brief moment in history the fate of much of Europe turned on events in Ireland.

Very suddenly the British colony in Ulster appeared to be in peril. Alarm became acute when a letter found lying in the street in Comber on 3 December 1688 warned Lord Mount-Alexander that 'all our Irishmen through Ireland is sworn that on the ninth day of this month they are to fall on to kill and murder man wife and child'. Whether genuine or bogus, the letter raised the spectre of 1641 and galvanised the Protestant gentry to action. The Comber letter was being read out to citizens in Derry when a messenger arrived warning that Alexander MacDonnell, Lord Antrim, was approaching with 1,200 Redshanks. Tyrconnell had ordered Antrim's regiment to replace the largely Protestant garrison he had unwisely left in the city.

When the Redshanks entered the Waterside and began to cross the Foyle, thirteen apprentice boys famously closed the gates. The epic siege had begun. Early in 1689 Protestant gentry met at Loughbrickland to organise resistance to Tyrconnell, but in March their forces shattered their men at the 'break of Dromore'. An assault on the Catholic garrison of Carrickfergus failed completely. King James was rapturously greeted in Dublin, and, strengthened by professional French troops, the supporters of King James—the Jacobites—were soon in control of all of Ulster, save for the island town of Enniskillen and the walled city of Derry.

In addition to a garrison of more than seven thousand men, perhaps thirty thousand Protestants sought sanctuary in Derry. In a very real sense, therefore, the fate of the Protestant settlement in Ulster depended on the city's ability to hold out. If Derry fell, James would be ready to use Ireland as a·base from which he could make an assault on England to recover his throne, and Louis xiv would be one step nearer to neutralising England and overrunning Holland. For 105 days the city resisted all attempts to take it, until on 28 July 1689 Major-General Percy Kirke's vessels broke the boom that French engineers had stretched across the Foyle and brought relief to the city. The price colonists had paid was high: Captain George Holmes reckoned that fifteen thousand men, women and children died, many of them from fever, during the siege.

Derry's defiance gave King William time to send an expeditionary force, under the Duke of Schomberg, to Ireland. Coming ashore at Ballyholme Bay on 13 August 1689, this force recovered Carrickfergus, but the next ten months were expended in inconclusive campaigning. With a heavy heart William realised that he had no choice but to go to Ireland himself. Sir Cloudesley Shovell's squadron of warships escorted William's fleet of about three hundred vessels across the Irish Sea into Belfast Lough on 14 June 1690. An army of continental size disembarked and advanced southwards. The international composition of this force of thirty-six thousand, which took up position on the left bank of the River Boyne on 30 June, underlined the fact that it represented the Grand Alliance against France, the world's greatest power: here were regiments of English, Dutch, Danes, French Huguenots and Germans. The planters acted principally as skirmishers, most notably the men of Enniskillen, who had crushed the Jacobites at Newtownbutler on the same day as the *Mountjoy* had broken through the boom at Derry. These 'Inniskillingers' were described by an army chaplain as being 'half-naked with sabre and pistols hanging from their belts . . . like a Horde of Tartars'.

The Battle of the Boyne, fought on 1 July, was not a rout. The Irish and French retired in good order to fight doggedly behind the Shannon for another year. Yet the battle was decisive: it was a severe blow to Louis xiv's pretensions to European hegemony and was celebrated by the singing of the *Te Deum* in Vienna; James, who made a precipitate flight to France, could no longer think of Ireland as a springboard for recovering his throne. For the English the 'Glorious Revolution' and parliamentary rule were made secure; for the Old English in Ireland the defeat dashed hopes of recovering their estates; and for Ulster Protestants the battle ensured the survival of their plantation and a victory for their liberty, to be celebrated from year to year:

> Let man with man, let kin with kin
>> Contend through fields of slaughter—
> Whoever fights, may freedom win,
>> As then, at the Boyne Water.

ULSTER AND THE 'SEVEN ILL YEARS'

The province of Ulster recovered rapidly as soon as the war between the Jacobites and Williamites was transferred to the south and west. Certainly, there had been severe loss of life and much destruction, but no comparison could be made with the blood-letting and devastation experienced in the 1640s. Now it was in Limerick and Athlone that lives were expended promiscuously, and at Aughrim, on the plains of east Galway, seven thousand Irishmen lost their lives in one afternoon. When news of that victory on 12 July 1691, the bloodiest battle in Irish history, spread north, the Protestants of Ulster set bonfires ablazing, as they would do every year thereafter. Aughrim effectually ended the war: although Limerick, like Derry, had resisted all attempts to storm its walls, peace was agreed on 3 October.

The defeat of the Jacobites was so complete that it was followed by the longest peace Ireland had ever known. From being the poorest of the four provinces at the beginning of the seventeenth century, Ulster became the most prosperous by the end of it.

King William did what he could to limit the scope of land confiscation, but if the Glorious Revolution meant anything it meant that the monarch had to bow to the wishes of Parliament. In Ulster the Catholics did not have much more to lose—except, that is, for the Marquis of Antrim. 'I feare hee will be restoured,' observed an agent of Londonderry Corporation, 'for wee have no evidence against him'.[25] The luck of the MacDonnells held out, and the marquis was duly restored. The last Catholic O'Neill proprietor, Sir Neill O'Neill of Killeleagh, Co. Antrim, had died soon after fighting on King James's side at the Boyne, and his estates in the counties of Londonderry and Monaghan were confiscated. Cúchonnacht Maguire, grandson of Brian Maguire of Tempo, was killed at the Battle of Aughrim, but his widow and son successfully contested the confiscation of his lands. A swathe of Co. Down Magennises fell at Athlone, Aughrim and Limerick, and Lord Iveagh was amongst those who chose exile abroad. Virtually all the Magennises had fought for King James. Only the Protestant ones got back their lands, but by the 1740s they were so encumbered with debt that they had to be sold by auction, the Corgary Magennises to Joseph Innes, a Belfast merchant, and the Castlewellan Maginneses to William Annesley of Dublin. The largest forfeiture in Ulster was the estate of Claude Hamilton, the Catholic Earl of Abercorn, though it was later repurchased by his Protestant nephew.[26]

Catholics had retained 22 per cent of the country in 1688, but the Williamite confiscations reduced the proportion to 14 per cent. When the King's grants to his favourites had been firmly revoked at Westminster, and all Jacobite claims had been met or denied, nearly half a million acres (mostly forfeited by the Old English) were available for sale. By then the bottom had dropped out of the market for land which had been won with so much blood, especially as only Protestants could buy. Half the land was bought at a knock-down price by a consortium of London merchants calling itself the Company for Making Hollow Sword-Blades in England. The merchants sold out six years later, and, indeed, many estates changed hands. William Conolly was one of those with ready cash and a good business head who made a fortune from land-jobbing; his forebears were reputedly native Irish innkeepers in Ballyshannon who had become Protestants. Ultimately Conolly became Speaker of the Irish House of Commons and the richest man in Ireland.

Presbyterian Scots poured into Ulster even before the Williamite War was at an end. It was observed that 'vast numbers of them followed the Army as Victuallers . . . and purchased most of the vast preys which were taken by the Army in the Campaign and drove incredible numbers of cattel into Ulster'. Then, in 1693, the volcano of Hekla in Iceland erupted with terrible force, spewing huge quantities of volcanic dust into the sky. At the same time, on the other side of the world, the volcanoes Serua and Aboina erupted in the Dutch East Indies, adding to the atmospheric haze filtering out the sun. The result was what climatologists call the Little Ice Age. Ruined harvests resulted in a terrible famine in Scandinavia, and Finland lost a third of its population. In Scotland the harvest failed in 1693 and in every following year to the end of the century. The Scots called these the Seven Ill Years. Some parts of Scotland suffered more than during the Black Death in the fourteenth century. The starving tried to survive by eating nettles and grass and then, fever-ridden, pouring into the towns, dying there in thousands. Andrew Fletcher of Saltoun, in an address to the Estates, the Scottish parliament, said:

There are at this day in Scotland two hundred thousand people begging from door to door. These are not only no way advantageous, but a very grievous burden on so poor a country . . . It were better for the nation they were sold to the galleys or West Indies, than that they should continue any longer to be a burden and curse upon us.

Fletcher reckoned that one in five died from hunger, and others reported that a third of the people starved to death. It seems likely that the Seven Ill Years killed about a tenth of Scotland's population as a whole. Patrick Walker, an itinerant pedlar, wrote:

Meal became so scarce, that it was at two shillings a peck, and many could not get it . . . I have seen, when meal was all sold in the markets, women clapping their hands, and tearing the clothes off their heads, crying, 'How shall we go home and see our children die in hunger?' Through the long continuance of these manifold judgements, deaths and burials were so many and common, that the living were wearied in the burying of the dead.

The Scottish Privy Council again and again debated the 'present scarcity and dearth'. Proclamations were issued and extended, lifting restrictions on the importation of meal from Ireland, particularly to the western shires between the mouth of the Annan and Kintyre. A Lowlander in the Highlands reported:

Some die by the wayside, some drop down in the streets, the poor sucking babs are starving from want of milk, which the empty breasts of their mothers cannot furnish them, everyone may see death in the face of the poor that abound everywhere.

The Kirk attributed the famine years to the sins of the nation, and ministers recommended fast days for the starving.[27] Ireland escaped the worst effects of this climatic downturn. Many survivors of the Scottish famine headed for the narrow sea to begin a new life in Ulster.

SCOTTISH EMIGRANTS SWITCH FROM POLAND AND SCANDINAVIA TO ULSTER

Not until the second half of the seventeenth century did Ulster become the principal destination for emigrants from Scotland. Until then most Scots leaving their country had been crossing the North Sea to serve in the armies of the kings of Sweden and Denmark, and to settle in Poland. This migration eastwards had begun about 1570 and reached a peak between 1610 and 1619. One English commentator, writing in 1606, expressed the fear that his country would be swamped with Scots as a result of the union of Crowns three years before:

> We shall be over-run with them, as cattle pent up by a slight hedge will over it into a better soyl, and a tree taken from a barren place will thrive to excessive and exuberant branches in a better, witness the multiplicities of the Scots in Polonia.

The Polish ambassador in London in 1621 thought that there were about thirty thousand Scots in Poland. William Lithgow, visiting Poland in 1616, found there 'abundance of gallant rich Merchants, my Countrey-men' and described that country as

> Mother and Nurse, for the youth and younglings of Scotland, who are yearely sent hither in great numbers . . . cloathing, feeding and inriching them with the fatnesse of her best things; besides thirty thousand Scots families, that live incorporate in her bowels. And certainly Poland may be termed in this kind to be the Mother of our Commons, and the first commencement of all the best Merchant's wealth.

The bad harvests of 1621–3, which affected Scotland as severely as Ulster, sustained this migration. Ulster attracted colonists principally from the Lowlands and the south-western shires of Scotland, whereas emigrants to Poland and Scandinavia were principally from the east and north-east, especially Fife and Aberdeenshire.

The rulers of Sweden and Denmark had an almost insatiable appetite for Scottish fighting men to swell their armies, particularly after the beginning of the Thirty Years' War in 1618. In the first half of the seventeenth century it was reckoned that 10 per cent of the population of Bergen had been born in Scotland. About 20 per cent of the young men of Scotland left during this period. For example, Robert Hamilton of Stanehous had been granted the middle proportion of Dirrynefogher in Magheraboy precinct in Co. Fermanagh. In 1612 it passed to his son Malcolm, rector of Devenish, created Archbishop of Cashel in 1623. Three of his brothers—Hugh, Alexander and Lewis—were serving in the Swedish army. Lewis, created Baron Hamilton de Deserf by King Gustavus Adolphus, married Anna Catharina, daughter of the Lord of Ry Nabben, and inherited the Fermanagh estate in 1662. He died on the way from Sweden to Ireland, but Anna took up residence in Monea Castle. Her son Gustavus Hamilton, half Swedish by blood, inherited the estate and won fame as the successful defender of Enniskillen in 1688–9. (Anna, incidentally, married three more times, outliving her husbands, Richard Dunbar of Derrygonnelly, Captain William Shore and James Somerville of Tullykelter Castle. She died in 1705.)[28]

For the years 1600–1650 the best estimates are that between 20,000 and 30,000 Scots left for Ireland, between 30,000 and 40,000 left for Poland, between 25,000 and 30,000 left for Scandinavia, and between 10,000 and 15,000 went elsewhere, that is, between 85,000 and 115,000 in total—a remarkable number, considering that the population of Scotland was no more than 1.2 million in the middle of the century.

After 1650 the emigration across the North Sea dropped to a trickle, and most emigrating Scots headed for Ulster.[29]

'CALVINISTS ARE COMING OVER HERE DAILY IN LARGE GROUPS OF FAMILIES'

The last decade of the seventeenth century and the first years of the next witnessed an unprecedented surge of British, the great majority of them Scots, coming in to Ulster. The Bishop of Tuam, Edward Synge, estimated that fifty thousand Scots families came to Ulster between 1689 and 1715. This was certainly an exaggeration, but the true figure was high. The Catholic Bishop of Clogher, Hugh MacMahon—who, by law, should not have been in the country—wrote in 1714:

Although all Ireland is suffering, this province is worse off than the others, because of the fact that from the neighbouring country of Scotland, Calvinists are coming over here daily in large groups of families, occupying the towns and villages, seizing the farms in the richer parts of the country and expelling the natives.

As Catholics were forbidden by law to buy, land in Ireland was available for Protestants to purchase at exceptionally low prices. Landlords, many of them with rentals heavily in arrears, were anxious to have these new immigrants as tenants. According to one pamphleteer, the church proprietors, who for some small advance in the rent of their lands, preferred numbers of those Presbyterians, who had swarmed from Scotland after the late revolution. These new adventurers were in many respects able to out-bid the old tenants, who had been in a great measure ruined in the late troubles.

The Scottish Privy Council felt moved to issue proclamations against 'those who run away from their landlord' and attempted to prohibit 'vessels to transport any of the yeoman that cannot show a pass . . . because many procure boats from Ireland to transport them and their goods thither without passes and are received to dwell and take land there'. Estimates of the numbers involved in this immigration during the 1690s range from 50,000 to 80,000. Over a wider period, 1650–1700, between 60,000 and 100,000 people probably left Scotland for Ireland, that is, between three and four times as many as had migrated in the first half of the century. The anonymous Jacobite author of *The Light to the Blind*, written about 1711, observed of Ulster landlords that 'their tenants for the most part were Roman Catholics until after the battle of the Boyne in the year 1690 when the Scottish men came over into the north with their families and effects and settled there so that they are now at this present the greatest proportion of the inhabitants of Ulster'.[30]

The Hearth Money Returns of the 1660s, used to establish the number of British households in a barony, can be compared with the Protestant Householders' Returns for 1740. Of course natural increase has to be taken into account, but the rapid rise in Ireland's population did not really begin until after the later year. An analysis of the figures shows a startling increase, particularly for the west of the province, which can only be accounted for by immigration and internal migration. The counties of Antrim and Down, and the Laggan district of north-east Donegal, had benefited most from the migrations of the 1650s and 60s. After the Williamite War the fresh influx sought out parts of the province which, so far, had been lightly settled by the British. The most striking increase in the number of British households was in the barony of Loughinsholin (the territory detached from Co. Tyrone to help create Co. Londonderry): from 308 households in the 1660s to 2,572 in the 1740s—an increase of 735 per cent. Other large increases occurred in the barony of Inishowen, Co. Donegal (376 per cent), and in the Co. Londonderry baronies of Tirkeeran, (232 per cent), Keenaght, (318 per cent) and Coleraine (242 per cent).[31]

Though there was no census to provide proof, it does seem clear that by the end of the seventeenth century there was a Protestant majority in the population of the nine counties of Ulster. By 1732 the balance had altered still further, with an estimated 313,120 Protestants and 192,295 Catholics. The proportion of Catholics in each county was Antrim, 19 per cent; Down, 27 per cent; Londonderry, 24 per cent; Armagh, 35 per cent; Fermanagh, 42 per cent; Donegal, 43 per cent; Tyrone, 52 per cent; Monaghan, 64 per cent; and Cavan, 76 per cent.[32]

Clergy of the Church of Ireland were particularly alarmed by the influx of Scots immigrants. In several parts of Ulster, Presbyterians formed overwhelming majorities—Jonathan Swift was unhappy at Kilroot not only because he was thwarted in love but also because he had almost no Anglicans living in his parish. Ulster Presbyterians threatened the privileges of the established church and made inroads on Anglican congregations too often neglected by worldly or absentee clergy.

Presbyterianism was particularly well organised and disciplined. Congregations grouped into presbyteries which supervised their affairs through regular visitations. There were five presbyteries in 1689 and seven by 1691. From 1691 ministers and selected elders began to meet annually at the Synod of Ulster. Discipline was strict: ministers and elders could punish offences such as adultery, fornication, drunkenness, slander, failure to pay debts and Sabbath-breaking. Dr Edward Walkington, Bishop of Down and Connor, indignantly complained that 'they openly hold their sessions and provincial synods for regulating of all matters of ecclesiastical concern'. William King, Archbishop of Dublin, distrusted Ulster Presbyterians: 'They are a people embodied under their lay leaders, presbyteries and synods . . . and will be just so far the King's subjects as their lay elders and presbyteries will allow them'. Archbishop King was determined that what for him were the arrogant pretensions of the Presbyterians must be curbed. In 1704 he made sure that appropriate clauses were included in the 'act to prevent the further growth of popery'.[33]

BELFAST: 'NEVER LESS THAN FORTY OR FIFTY SAIL OF SHIPS BEFORE IT'

Lord Edward Chichester, Viscount of Carrickfergus, died in England and was succeeded by his son Arthur, who was created the 1st Earl of Donegall. As the family property had been confiscated by the Commonwealth in 1644 and was not restored to him until 1656, Lord Donegall had accumulated great debts. He returned to Belfast from England in August 1660 to recover his lands, duly confirmed by charter in 1668. In his absence, Belfast had been growing fast.

By the end of the 1630s English and Scots had settled in roughly equal numbers in a town which was barely larger than Bangor or Newtownards. Belfast had no walls, though an earthen 'rampier' had been hastily thrown up by its citizens in 1642. Its defences were never really put to the test, and Belfast escaped the destruction suffered by so many other towns and villages since 1641. During the Commonwealth, when a great many Scots poured into Ulster, many made Belfast their home. Before the rebellion most Scots had come from the south-west, Irvine and Ayr in particular; now they were drawn from a wider area which included Glasgow, Wigtown and Kirkudbright. These immigrants began making Belfast the most dynamic centre of trade in Ulster and, possibly, the fastest-growing town in Ireland.

Even before he returned, Lord Donegall did all he could to encourage British newcomers to settle in Belfast. These included George Macartney of Auchinleck, who obtained a lease of ninety-nine years of a 'half burgage' share of High Street, and his kinsman 'Black' George Macartney of Blacket, who built a large house on the same street close to the quay. It was important for any merchant or artisan who was in business on his own account to be a 'freeman' in order to be excused, or pay at a lower rate, a series of customs, tolls, fines and court fees. Since in Belfast—unlike in the city of Londonderry and Coleraine—freemen had no political rights, no attempt was made to restrict their numbers. In 1666 the town corporation ruled that artisans had to apply for their freedom within three months of completing their apprenticeship. It took thirteen years for an artisan to become a freeman in Glasgow. Until 1691 freemen were legally obliged to take the Oath of Supremacy; Lord Donegall, with strong Puritan sympathies, made no attempt to force Presbyterians to take it. In short, Lord Donegall was making Belfast an exceptionally attractive place for incomers to do business.[34]

By the early 1660s about 3 per cent of Irish customs was being raised in Belfast, by which time it ranked as the ninth-largest port in Ireland. It had bypassed the city of Londonderry, and in 1666 the French traveller Jorevin de Rocheford noted:

I arrived at Belfast, situated on a river at the bottom of a gulf, where barks and vessels anchor on account of the security and goodness of the port; whereof several merchants live here who trade to Scotland and

England, whither they transport the superfluities of this country. Here is a very fine castle, and two or three large and straight streets as in a new built town. One may often procure a passage here for Scotland.[35]

Certainly Belfast Castle dominated the town. It was nearly a square, each side being 120 feet long, with a central courtyard and chimneys placed all around the edge; this suggests that the centre of the building, although roofed with a cupola on top, may have been left open as a grand entrance space. It had no fewer than forty hearths in 1666. Belfast Castle had elaborate formal gardens (similar to those at Newtownards, Lisburn and Tully Castle, but absent at Joymount), which included an apple orchard, a cherry orchard, a garden for strawberries, gooseberries and currants, cinder paths and a bowling-green. Lord Donegall may have lacked the capital to develop the town himself, but simply by residing there he made a significant contribution to the town's status. In consequence, several country gentlemen, including Sir Hercules Langford, built houses in Belfast. Lord Donegall found enough money to fund a mathematics fellowship in Trinity College, Dublin, and to set up a well-regarded school in Belfast—a surviving exercise book indicates that it provided a good grounding in mathematics, trigonometry, astronomy, navigation and surveying.[36]

The Englishman Thomas Waring settled in Belfast in the early 1640s, setting up business there as a tanner, bringing in oak bark and hides from his property in Killultagh in north-west Down. In the Restoration period he had become one of the most prosperous merchants in the town and a ship-owner, leasing a substantial holding made up of six 'half burgage' shares. Edward and Thomas Pottinger had come from Orkney to set up business principally on the Co. Down side of the Lagan, facing the town. Macartney of Auchinleck became the tenant of four water-powered corn mills, a tuck mill and a 50 per cent share of the sugar refinery.

In 1673 Black George Macartney, sovereign (or mayor) in that year, led a consort of merchants to petition successfully that the custom house be removed from Carrickfergus to Belfast. A warehouse was converted into a custom house on the north side of Waring Street, and by 1682 it was equipped with a beam and scales, tables and an iron chest for money. Quays were built on each side of the Farset at the bottom of High Street— indeed, quarrymen were admitted to the freedom of the town in 1681 on condition that they provided stone for their completion. Water was brought to the Great Bridge (the site of the present Boyne Bridge) from the tuck-mill dam at the east side of Barrack Street through wooden pipes, the sockets being strengthened by bands of iron over joints smeared with white lead. Black George Macartney also petitioned for the construction of a bridge to span the Lagan; he pointed out to Lord Conway that 'if our town prosper, your town of Lisburn certainly must, for one depends on the welfare of the other'. The grand juries of Antrim and Down put up £500, but the remaining £1,100 had to be raised by subscription from the gentry of Antrim and Down. With twenty-one arches spanning the Lagan at 2,562 feet, it was almost complete when it was damaged by Schomberg's artillery in 1689, and it was for many years after the longest bridge in the British Isles. Known as the Long Bridge (replaced by the Queen's Bridge in 1843), it brought directly into the town traffic which had previously crossed several miles upstream at Shaw's Bridge.

By 1670 three-storey houses were being put up, and in that year the military surveyor, Thomas Phillips, described Belfast as 'the third place of trade in this kingdom . . . having never less than forty or fifty sail of ships always before it, the place very rich and numerous'. Belfast was not yet as important as that, but by 1706 it had emerged as the fourth port of Ireland. With a population of about 5,000, it was still small in comparison with Dublin (with 62,000) and Cork (with 17,500), but its growth had been remarkable since 1660, when the citizens were numbered at 1,914.[37] Belfast was almost exclusively a town of British colonists. In 1707, during a Jacobite scare, the sovereign, George Macartney (son of George of Auchinleck), was instructed to arrest any Catholic priests within his jurisdiction; after making a return of all the inhabitants of the town, he reported: 'Thank God we are not under any great fears here . . . We have not amongst us within the town above seven Papists'.[38]

Belfast had become the principal port from which Ulster's agricultural produce was being exported. William Sacheverell, visiting the town at the end of the century, observed: 'The quantities of Butter and Beef which it sends into Foreign Parts are almost incredible; I have seen the barrels pil'd up in the very Streets'. Indeed, Belfast together with Youghal exported 43 per cent of Ireland's butter. Cattle driven into the town were killed close to the water, and the meat was then pickled and packed into barrels—the salt beef must have demanded long stewing, for recent archaeological investigations show that most of the beasts were ten years old when slaughtered. Detailed figures are available for 1683. In that year 2,663 barrels of beef were exported to France and Flanders, 613 to Spain and the Mediterranean, 873 to the Colonies, 368 to Holland and only 88 to England

and Scotland. France and Flanders were the main destinations for butter: 25,889 hundredweight in 1683. Other leading exports included 12,436 hides, 3,769 hundredweight of tallow, 7,017 barrels of corn, 323 pieces of linen and 181 hundredweight of linen yarn. The export lists also contain 323 fox and otter skins, 3,300 rabbit skins, 5,800 ox horns, ten barrels of 'ox guts' and 391 barrels of salted herrings.

Wood was still being exported but in rapidly diminishing quantities. In 1695 the Irish Parliament was informed that over the previous ten years 136 tons of timber, 823,605,000 barrel-staves and 4,525½ dozen clapboards had been shipped from the port of Belfast:

> To prevent this, an Act to hinder exporting any sort of timber to Scotland is proposed. The woods in Ulster in a few years will not supply casks to export our own commodities of beef, butter, salmon, herrings, or for shipping and building. Witness the great woods in the County of Down and Antrim almost destroyed.

In short, the growth of Belfast, just like that of Dublin, would not have been possible without the regular supply of coal from across the Irish Sea. Most of it was shipped from Scotland and the rest from Whitehaven. Merchants in the export trade were constantly on the look-out for produce to fill their ships on their return. For example, in March 1679 Black George Macartney wrote to his agent Andrew Marjoribank in Danzig:

> Pray let me know what goods of our country would sell with you and what goods are, if any good be got I would gladly drive some trade with you if it would turn to account.[39]

Colonial produce imported included 1,206 hundredweight of sugar, 382,640 pounds of tobacco, 317 pieces of calico, 242 pounds of indigo and 22 hundredweight of ginger. In addition to walnuts, silks, prunes, liquorice and ten dozen playing-cards, France and Spain sent to Belfast 124 butts and 213 tuns of wine and 4,419 gallons of brandy. Much of this was then taken into the hinterland on pack horses by 'chapmen' or pedlars. Ships returning from Spain carried 6,950 bushels of salt, which, added to the 12,889 bushels imported from England and Scotland, were required for the pickling of barrelled beef—the great underground deposits of salt at Carrickfergus had not yet been discovered.[40]

Carrickfergus found itself eclipsed by Belfast. It had been greatly damaged not only by the loss of customs but also by Schomberg's bombardment in 1689. In 1683 Richard Dobbs wrote that there the 'people for the most part are little given to industry or labour, many of them having little estates since the dividing of the Town Lands'. He added that Larne consisted of only one street of buildings, 'all thatched houses . . . as is generally the case where the people are Scotch'. The city of Londonderry took a long time to recover from the siege of 1688–9. Westminster voted ten thousand pounds in aid to the ruined city, but the money was never paid out. Several merchants had been made bankrupt and ended up in debtors' prisons. In 1721 their cause was championed by William Hamill in his pamphlet *A View of the Danger and Folly of Being Public Spirited and Sincerely Loving One's Country*. Despite extraordinary sacrifices, they had

> nothing for it these thirty years but royal promises, commissions without pay, recommendations from the throne to Parliaments and reports and addresses back to the throne again.

The Irish Society did abate rents and levy a hundred pounds from each of the twelve companies. A report made in May 1691 recorded that sixty tons from the Society's forests were made available 'towards rebuilding the market-house, repairing the gates, and other public buildings in Derry', and in December 'one hundred and twenty tons of timber, and forty thousand laths, were allowed for building the town-house of Derry'. In 1706 the city's population was 2,848. When the scientific writer Dr Thomas Molyneux visited the city two years later he remarked on the many new and restored buildings, but he thought that trade and commerce there had not recovered since the siege. Nevertheless, Bishop George Berkeley wrote in 1724 that the 'city of Londonderry is the most compact, regular, well built town, that I have seen in the King's Dominions'.[41]

Some plantation towns failed to survive. Movanagher was abandoned after being destroyed in the 1641 Rebellion, and the Mercers' Company chose Kilrea instead as its principal town. Only aerial photography and archaeological investigation revealed that a substantial village had been deserted close to Dunluce Castle. Tully Castle was not reoccupied after the siege of 1641, and the town beside it was abandoned. Some towns laid out by the London Companies were slow in growing, and some, such as Salterstown, failed almost completely. Towns such as Augher, Dungannon and Strabane had been burned in the 1641 Rebellion and were to suffer further, though the damage was less destructive, during 1688–9.

A report of 1704 stated that a good many houses in the town of Armagh were still 'ruined in wars'; but, visiting in 1708, Molyneux thought it a 'very pretty town and borough situated on a hill'. He found Richhill and Portadown 'pretty villages', Ballymoney 'a pretty, clean, English-like town' and Lifford a 'very nasty, ugly town'. He did not visit Ballymena, a growing town being developed by the Adairs, or Lurgan, developed by the Brownlows.

In 1689, as Schomberg was marching south towards Dundalk, the Duke of Berwick, James II's natural son, had burned Newry to the ground. Looking over the charred remains, the Williamite chaplain George Storey observed that the 'town itself had been a pretty place and well built'. With the return of peace the main proprietor, Nicholas Bagenal, threw himself into the task of reconstruction. When he died, in 1712, Bagenal's estate in Co. Down was inherited by the Jamaican planter Robert Nedham, who granted leases in perpetuity, which did much to encourage men of capital to settle in the town.

An accidental fire in 1707 completely destroyed Lisburn, but only a year later Molyneux was able to make this report:

> If the story of the Phoenix be ever true, sure 'tis in this town. For here you see one of the beautifullest towns perhaps in the three kingdoms— all brick houses, slated, of one bigness, all new and almost finished, rising from the most terrible rubbish that can be imagined.

Lord Hillsborough set about rebuilding Banbridge on a cruciform plan, and an English brickmaker was contracted to make the town of Hillsborough one of the most elegant in the north.[42]

ROYAL SCHOOLS

Captain John Leigh, High Sheriff of Tyrone, observed in a report to James I in 1608 that 'the best gentlemen' wanted to have schools established for the benefit of their sons and those of their tenants. Before the year was out the King ordered that there 'shall be one Free School at least appointed in Every County, for the education of Youth in learning and religion'. Lord Deputy Chichester made arrangements for the upkeep of the lands whereby they would be 'distinguished by mears and bounds'. Little was done thereafter until, on 21 April 1614, James issued an order that the lands be transferred forthwith for the maintenance of what became known as the Royal Schools.

The Free School for Tyrone, set up by letters patent on 13 May 1615, was the first to be established. The first master, John Bullingbroke, waiting for rent from the school lands to accumulate, began by renting premises at Belville House, about half a mile from Mountjoy Castle. The Free School for Co. Armagh was the one most generously endowed, being granted seven hundred acres near Mountnorris, where the school was first established. A warrant from Chichester, dated 5 October 1611, informed the Sheriff of Cavan that John Robinson had been appointed schoolmaster 'during his good behaviour' and ordered the sheriff to 'have collected & receaved the rents due out of the said Lands, allotted to the said free schoole since Allhalowtide last'.

In Fermanagh, Sir James Balfour got permission to build the Free School near his castle at Lisnaskea and to appoint his chaplain, Geoffrey Middleton, as the first master in 1618. In that year Pynnar's survey reported:

> There is also a school which is now sixty four feet long and twenty four feet broad and two storeys high. This is all good stone and lime, strongly built, the roof is already framed and shall be presently set up.

In Co. Donegal the first master appointed was described in the 1622 visitation survey as 'Brian Moryson Mr of Artes an Irish native who is conformable in Religion and is a very good humanist'. The school, some way outside the town Donegal, by Lough Eske, the report continued,

> is a very inconvenient place it being at the furthest part almost of the Dioces And the most convenient place for his residence is Raphoe w'ch is the Bps seate and better inhabited with British people than the other place and in the midst of the Dioceses and nearer to the Schoole lands.

Mountjoy was taken and burned by the forces of Sir Phelim O'Neill in 1641. In her deposition Anne Bullingbroke stated that 'upon the Saturday the 23rd day of October 1641, she and her said husband were robbed and stript of goods, chattels, and other personal estate etc. by Sir Phelim Roe O'Neill and other ungodly and rebellious followers'. Then the Bullingbroke family 'did for ten weeks together shelter and hide themselves in the wild woods, where they lived most miserably and poorly until the headmaster and one of his children died through hunger and cold'. Only in 1662 was the school re-established, in Union Lane in Dungannon. John Starkey, headmaster at Mountnorris, was drowned with his family by the rebels in the River Blackwater, and as peace returned the school began again in the town of Armagh on the site of the monastery of St Columba in Abbey Street. The Fermanagh Royal School transferred to Enniskillen to a site close to St Macartin's Cathedral. As had been recommended in 1622, the Royal School in Donegal was transferred to Raphoe during the Restoration.

William King was the son of a Scottish merchant who had settled in the town of Antrim. In 1703 he became Archbishop of Dublin. He recalled his time as a pupil in Dungannon, where he was expected to learn Despauterius's Latin Grammar, the Psalms of David in Latin and the Epistles of Ovid by heart, without understanding the meaning of the words. Education consisted almost wholly of the Classics. These were schools for the sons of colonists, but some natives were admitted, who presumably had to accept instruction in the doctrine of the established church.[43]

On the Irish Society's lands Coleraine did not get a Free School until 1705, though it was soon in difficulties 'from the mismanagement and incapacity of the master, and the gross negligence of the Corporation'. It fell into disuse in 1739 and was not revived until the following year. Matthias Springham, during his tour of 1616 as a representative of the City of London, had endowed a Free School in Londonderry as a philanthropic gesture and seen to it that sufficient lands were set aside for its maintenance. For the remainder of the seventeenth century this was where colonists of the county sent their sons to be educated.[44]

THE SPOLIATION OF THE WOODS

The great majority of the inhabitants of Ulster did not live in towns. The face of the province was being transformed by the rapid disappearance of the woods. Stands of timber were felled for building, charcoal-burning and export. Intent on quick profits and on opening up more land for grazing and cultivation, the colonists—unlike the native Irish and their relatives across the Irish Sea—made little attempt to preserve woodland by coppicing.

For a time, ironworks and tanneries had flourished. Sir Charles Coote once employed 2,500 men in his ironfounding concern in Co. Cavan. Along with other similar enterprises, it had been the most prodigal consumer of wood: it took 2½ tons of charcoal to make one 1 of bar iron. Thomas Waring, five times sovereign of Belfast between 1652 and 1666, had a large tannery between North Street and Waring Street, and he and his family had other tanneries at Toome, Derriaghy and Lurgan. Tanners preferred to strip bark from living oak, and eventually their deprivations deprived them of their raw material, though small pits survived at Cootehill, Killeshandra, Ballycastle, Enniskillen and Belfast. In the eighteenth century the scarcity of local wood had become acute: as early as 1718 it was noted that wood was 'extraordinary dear' in Ballyclare, and in 1735 it was noted that in Carrickfergus 'timber is so dear . . . that it is better to sell the ground than to build'.[45]

The destruction of the woodlands nevertheless increased the area being farmed. The growing season begins about three weeks later in Ulster than in Munster, but more intensive cultivation increased yields. Above all, farmers in the north were finding a fresh source of income: the growing of flax. The development of a flourishing domestic linen industry was to have a profound effect on the fortunes of Ulster as the eighteenth century progressed.

Chapter 14 ∽

| LEGACY

ULSTER AND COLONIAL AMERICA

Fynes Moryson, Lord Deputy Mountjoy's former secretary, described Ireland in 1617 as 'this famous island in the Virginian Sea', indicating that it was no longer a rugged outpost on the north-western edge of the known world and that it had become the eastern fringe of Britain's expanding Atlantic empire. For much of the seventeenth century the colonisation of Ulster and of the eastern seaboard of North America shared many characteristics. After all, Virginia in America and Virginia in Co. Cavan were founded at the same time and in the same spirit.

For some time Ulster and North America were equal in attraction, and the outflow from Britain to them was equal in volume. As late as 1680 the physician and cartographer Sir William Petty could not make up his mind whether America or Ireland offered the better prospect. By 1622 between 25,000 and 35,000 Scots and English had settled in Ulster. In that year there were only a few thousand settlers in British North America, but by 1650 the number had risen to between 40,000 and 50,000. Between 1586 and 1700 Ireland as a whole took in at least 150,000 British immigrants and possibly as many as 250,000. This figure is far higher than that of those who had migrated from Spain and Portugal to Latin America from 1500 to 1650. This population movement across the Irish Sea and the North Channel constituted one of the earliest and largest European migrations of the period—the beginning of a far greater European exodus across the Atlantic in the eighteenth and nineteenth century. Ulster had become a colonial land of opportunity, just like tidewater Virginia.

Attempts to find parallels, however, can go too far. The short journey over the Irish Sea—despite the frustrations of waiting for a favourable wind—cannot be compared to the long, hazardous voyage across the Atlantic. Even Ulster possessed some long-established ports, which the American seaboard initially entirely lacked. Ireland's northern province was underpopulated by English standards, but the density was at least thirty times that of pre-colonial America. Despite much familiar vegetation, North America had a climate subject to continental extremes. The native Irish could provide cheap and much-valued labour, so much so that undertakers in Ulster almost universally defied James I's orders to expel them from their proportions. Native Americans, in contrast, either contracted European diseases, with fatal results, or withdrew into the back country. In addition, the extent of land which became available to the British in Colonial America was vastly greater than in Ulster.[1]

Nevertheless there are many indications that in Britain for some time Ulster and America were viewed in the same light. As many as 35 per cent of all merchants putting capital into Irish plantations between 1586 and 1620 also had investments in overseas companies, most notably the Virginia Company. Though some planters, such as Lord Audley, were to find that the estates they had been granted were almost devoid of wood, much of Ulster, like America, was wreathed in dense, mature forests, which not only yielded ample building materials but also provided the opportunity for colonists to make quick profits by smelting iron and exporting barrel-staves, laths and ship timber in great quantities. To British newcomers much of Ulster was as wild and barbarous as the American coastlands. After campaigning in Co. Donegal in 1608, Lord Deputy Chichester found the country as inaccessible as 'the kingdom of China', being 'one of the most barren, uncouth, and desolate countries that could be seen, fit only to confine rebels and ill spirits into'.

Neither in Colonial America nor in Ulster did the settlers represent a cross-section of British society. English and Scottish nobles did provide financial support for colonial enterprises in Ireland and America, but only very few of them could be persuaded to participate in person—no doubt they remembered the disastrous outcome of the Earl of Essex's colonial scheme in Ulster in the 1570s. It was unfair of the Rev. Andrew Stewart of Donaghadee to describe the English and Scots coming over as 'generally the scum of both nations', and of Fynes Moryson to conclude that

all the English in general that voluntarily left England to plant themselves in Ireland . . . were generally observed to have beene eyther papists, men of disordered life, bankrots, or very poore . . . by which course Ireland as the heele of the body was made the sincke of England, the stench whereof had almost annoyed very Cheapside the hart of the body.[2]

Nonetheless, most of those who took the lead in the plantation were younger sons inheriting little or nothing at home, and few of those British they took in as tenants were substantial yeomen, a class to be described later in Ireland as 'strong farmers'. Many who became settlers were discharged soldiers or the unemployed and underemployed, who knew little about up-to-date agricultural techniques. For some decades after the plantation had been launched, farming in Ulster, with the exception of the Montgomery and Hamilton estates in Co. Down, continued as it had been since the Gaelic lords held sway. More intensive agriculture arrived only with the great influx of Scots in the second half of the seventeenth century.

Similarly in America it proved difficult to entice men over 'brought up to husbandry'. Proprietors in Virginia complained in 1620 of 'a great scarcity, or none at all' of 'husbandmen truly bred'. A great many British immigrants in Colonial America were vagrants who had come to London to escape the rigours of the Poor Law. Numerous descriptions of the work force in Virginia mentioned that they were 'full of mutenie and treasonable intendments' and that 'the common sort . . . were active in nothing but adhearing to factions and parts, even to their own ruine'. Some arrived as convicted criminals or stowaways, deserting soon after to become pirates 'with dreams of mountains of gold and happie robberies'.[3]

THE COLONIAL VIEW OF INDIGENOUS POPULATIONS

The cultural gulf between native Americans and European settlers was far wider than that between the Gaelic Irish and British newcomers in Ulster. However, settlers tended to regard natives in both places as uncouth barbarians to whom normal standards of decent behaviour towards their fellow-humans did not always apply. In Leinster and Munster the New English encountered the bilingual and partly gaelicised descendants of medieval Norman conquerors and those they had brought over with them, proud now to be described as the Old English. These Old English could provide a cultural buffer, helping to promote greater mutual understanding. Apart from some Nugents, Savages and others clinging on in Lecale and at the tip of the Ards, Ulster did not have an Old English population. Here the Reformation turned a cultural gap into a great chasm. The stubborn refusal of the Irish to accept the reformed faith enabled Protestant newcomers to dismiss them as uncivilised people, to be treated as such. In 1610 Barnaby Rich, who had gone out of his way to convince the City of London to take part in the Plantation of Ulster, expressed a view widely held by his fellow-countrymen:

It is popery that hath drawn the people from that confidence and trust that they should have in God, to believe in saints, to worship idols, and to fly from God's mercy to other mens merits, and to set up a pope-holy righteousness of their own works. It is popery that hath alienated the hearts of that people from their faith, fidelity, obedience, love and loyalty that is required in subjects towards their sovereigns. It is popery that hath cost the lives of multitudes, that hath ruined that whole realm and made it subject to the oppression of thieves, robbers, spoilers, murderers, rebels and traitors.[4]

That the souls of Gaelic natives of Ulster were thought to be beyond saving is demonstrated by the lackadaisical efforts to convert them. In the same way, colonists in Virginia made little attempt to preach their faith to the native Americans, unlike the Spanish and Portuguese, who were remarkably successful at bringing the indigenous peoples of Latin America into the bosom of the Church.

Patterns of behaviour regarded as unacceptable at home were widely adopted by those who co-ordinated and spearheaded the subjection of natives on both sides of the Atlantic. At the close of the Nine Years' War, English army commanders had felt justified in routinely inflicting atrocity and in starving the Gaelic Irish into submission by a relentless destruction of their food supplies. Distant from central control, these officers, after the Treaty of Mellifont, felt free to administer arbitrary rule at the local level; indeed Dublin Castle gave them martial powers to do so. Those in authority in Colonial America (some of whom had previous military experience in Ireland) appear to have acted with even greater impunity. Both in Ulster and America the perceived backwardness of the natives—in their dwellings, dress, farming methods, customs, beliefs and the like—was used to justify harsh and arbitrary means to bring about subjugation. Propaganda tracts printed to encourage the British to settle in freshly conquered lands on both sides of the Atlantic were remarkably similar. Prospective immigrants were likened to Israelites following Moses to a promised land flowing with milk and honey. Lord Mountjoy had established control in Ulster by ordering woods to be felled to create routeways for his armies and by ringing the province with garrisoned star-shaped forts. This was a strategy closely followed in British Colonial America.

COLONIAL DIRECTIONS ADOPTED AND IGNORED

Planning the colonisation of Ulster, in particular the settling of the six confiscated counties, was much more meticulous than it had been for earlier plantations in the island. Planning for the new territories across the Atlantic was very similar: settlement was preceded by surveys, however rudimentary by later standards; development corporations, such as the Virginia Company, closely paralleled the Honourable the Irish Society; the Irish county was replicated in the colonies as a key administrative unit; and frontier outposts, designed to fasten control in hostile countryside, became planned towns (twenty-three of them in the Plantation of Ulster). Classical styles favoured by Renaissance Europe can be seen in the grid-iron street plans and diamonds enclosed by the town halls, gaols and market-houses of many Ulster Plantation towns, most notably Coleraine, Belturbet, Enniskillen and the city of Londonderry. Charleston in South Carolina, Frederica in Georgia and Philadelphia in Pennsylvania appear to have been laid out following Ulster models.[5]

The carefully laid plans of those directing colonial schemes in London were often frustrated by immigrants soon after their arrival: organisers quickly lost control over those to whom they had entrusted the task of settling newly conquered lands. Colonial theorists such as Sir Thomas Smith and Sir Francis Bacon had argued in favour of placing settlers in towns to ensure the emergence of a 'civil' society. Both in Ulster and America colonists found it too inconvenient to travel each day from urban centres to their farms, and this resulted in dispersed settlement; it was in vain that migrants to North America and the West Indies were instructed in 1672 to 'plant in towns and not build their houses stragglingly—such solitary dwellings being incapable of that benefit of trade, the comfort of society and mutual assistance which men dwelling together in towns are capable of one to another'.[6] British families brought over by undertakers to become tenants on estates which they found too infertile or isolated could not be stopped from moving to more accessible and attractive parts of Ulster, just as many in America moved on, sometimes even to Spanish colonies.

By the 1630s the outflow of English emigrants to Colonial America was beginning to exceed that to Ireland. By the late seventeenth century the migration of English to Ulster had almost ceased, just when Scots were arriving there in unprecedented numbers. Then, about the time of Queen Anne's death, in 1714, the influx of Scots rather suddenly came to a halt. After a string of bad harvests in the 1690s, yields of corn in Scotland were so good that there was a surplus sufficient even to supply the burgeoning gin trade in London. Standards of living in Scotland soon were as high as, or higher than, in Ulster—the need to migrate across the North Channel had disappeared. Meanwhile British settlers and their descendants in the north of Ireland began to cast their eyes across the Atlantic and consider the benefits a fresh start in the New World might offer. The consequences for the future history of Ulster and North America were to be profound.

LINEN, FLAX SEED AND SCOWBANKERS: 'IT PUTS OUR PEOPLE TO SOWING A GREAT DEAL'

Huguenots—French Protestants—seeking refuge in Ireland have frequently been given credit for bringing the linen industry to Ulster. Of course, from very early times the native Irish had grown their own flax and made their own linen. This type of cloth, known as 'bandle linen', was still being made for local sale in the eighteenth century; however, its width was too narrow to succeed in the export market. It was really the Scots, and families from the north of England (Quakers in particular), settling in Ulster, who established the manufacture of linen suitable for sale abroad. In 1700 half of all Scotland's exports to England by value were made up of linen. Scots and many English making a new home in Ulster in the seventeenth century brought their skills with them, and the majority set parts of their farms aside for the growing of flax.

Some of the leading Ulster planters, such as the Clotworthys of south Antrim, encouraged their tenants to grow and spin flax to tide them over hard times. Not only could flax be easily sold for ready cash in the market but it could also be kept at home and processed, spun and woven into linen for sale to drapers. These merchants then took the linen webs in solid-wheeled carts to the Linen Hall in Dublin, and from there the cloth was exported to London. Huguenots—many enticed over by an act for encouraging 'Protestant Strangers' to settle in Ireland—certainly introduced more sophisticated techniques, particularly in Lisburn, until they were dispersed by a disastrous fire in the town in 1708.

During the early decades of the eighteenth century the domestic weaving of linen became the main economic activity of eastern Ulster: Antrim, Armagh, Down, Monaghan and the eastern parts of Londonderry, Tyrone and Cavan. By the end of the 1720s linen, nearly all of it produced in Ulster, accounted for a quarter of the total value of exports from Ireland. It is almost perverse to state that the very success of this industry in turn greatly stimulated emigration from the north of Ireland to the

American Colonies. The emergence of a flourishing trade in flax seed does much to explain this development. Just as its blue flowers were fading, the flax was pulled up, roots and all, so that no part of the stem was lost and the fibres in the stem were as long as possible. This had to be done before the plant went to seed. It was therefore more economic for a family of flax-growers and weavers to buy the seed from elsewhere. Early in the century seed was nearly all from the Baltic, shipped to Ulster by Dutch merchants. Then, in 1731, Westminster permitted the shipment of flax seed directly to Ireland from the Colonies. In 1733 it further stimulated the trade with a bounty, and America became the exclusive supplier of flax seed to Ulster.[7]

European settlers in North America had found that flax grew readily there and raised crops every year, letting the plants mature well into the autumn. There labour was too expensive to be engaged in the time-consuming and often physically exhausting process by which flax was retted, broken, scutched, hackled, spun, wound, woven, bucked, boiled, beetled and bleached before it was ready for sale in the form of good-quality linen cloth. The Governor of New York observed in 1698 that 'hemp and flax are better for the production in the soil of Ireland and to be manufactured there where labour is cheaper by three-fourths than here in New York or New Hampshire'.[8]

Most settlers in America growing flax confined themselves to one procedure: in a process known as 'rippling' they drew the sheaves of flax through large fixed combs to detach the seeds. At this stage their flax made a durable thatch, but it was no longer good for making fine linen; the seed, however, commanded a ready price. Hogsheads of flax seed were bought by travelling dealers, known as 'scowbankers', and taken downriver to New York, Philadelphia, Boston and other ports. In 1743 the Philadelphia merchant Samuel Powel wrote that 'the call for flaxseed to Ireland continues & increases ... It puts our people to sowing a great deal'.[9] By 1751 Philadelphia alone was shipping out more than 69,000 bushels of seed a year, all of it destined for Ireland. In turn, settlers in America were eager to buy finished Irish linen with the money they had raised in selling flax seed, tobacco and cotton. By 1760 Ulster was exporting 17 million yards of linen a year, most of it bound for the Colonies.

Costly fine linen did not take up nearly so much room as seed in the hold on the return voyage from Ulster to America. Ship-owners landing flax seed at Belfast, Derry, Coleraine and Newry did not want to return across the Atlantic in half-empty vessels. The most lucrative additional cargo proved to be people anxious for a fresh start in the New World.

Ship-owners therefore competed with each other to fill the vacant space with passengers. The flax-seed trade and the emigrant trade were thus two sides of the same coin in this transatlantic commerce.

'THE HUMOUR HAS SPREAD LIKE A CONTAGIOUS DISTEMPER'

So that the Bible could be consulted every day for guidance, Presbyterian elders laid great emphasis on teaching their congregations to read. Incoming Scots did much, therefore, to make Ulster the most literate corner of Ireland. Presbyterians there could also read handbills advertising the opportunities awaiting them across the Atlantic. In 1726 the Justices of Assize for the north-west circuit of Ulster remarked on the lure of the New World for Protestants aggrieved at increases in rent. They noted the success of agents sent around the province by ships' masters who

> assure them that in America they may get good land to them and their posterity for little or no rent, without either paying tithes or taxes, and amuse them with such accounts of those countries as they know will be most agreeable to them.[10]

Political stability and a rapidly growing population enabled proprietors, in particular middlemen and 'farmers' who leased the Irish Society's lands, to increase rents, though these were still low by English standards. In addition, cattle disease and harvest failure caused great distress during the early decades of the eighteenth century. Arriving in his diocese as Bishop of Derry in 1718, William Nicholson found 'dismal marks of hunger and want' on the faces of the people. 'We seem to be brought to the brink of a famine', he wrote later. 'God defend us from the pestilence'. In February 1727 Hugh Boulter, Archbishop of Armagh, informed the Archbishop of Canterbury that 'we met all the roads full of whole families that had left their homes to beg abroad . . . so that this summer must be more fatal to us than the last; when I fear many hundreds perished by famine'.

This scarcity of 1726–7 was followed by a severe famine in 1728–9. Huge numbers of cattle and sheep were killed in 1740, 'the Year of the Great Frost', and this in turn was followed by a year of storms and a prolonged drought, causing the worst famine of the century. The Irish called this year of 1741 *Bliain an Áir*, 'the Year of the Slaughter'. The Rev. Philip Skelton, curate of Monaghan parish, reported that there were

> whole parishes in some places . . . almost desolate; the dead have been eaten in the fields by dogs for want of people to bury them. Whole

thousands in a barony have perished, some of hunger and others of disorders occasioned by unnatural, unwholesome, and putrid diet.

Out of a population of 2.4 million, between 310,000 and 480,000 died as a direct result of famine and fever that year throughout the whole island.[11] A greater proportion of the population died in this one year than during the six years of the Great Famine of the 1840s, when the population was more than three times what it had been in 1741. All Europe suffered famine in 1741, but no country except for Norway suffered as much as Ireland. The people in Ulster who died first and suffered most were the poorest of the Catholic Irish; but the Scottish and English settlers had come to the north of Ireland to find a better life, and when the expectations of many had not been fulfilled, and rents were rising, they and their descendants moved on across the Atlantic to the New World.

Small numbers of Ulster Presbyterians had emigrated to America in the late seventeenth century, mainly from the Laggan in north-east Donegal, but it was not until 1718 that the exodus began in earnest. In the summer of that year five ships left Derry Quay for Boston. James McGregor, minister of the Aghadowey congregation and the leader of this expedition, got a grant of land on the frontier north of the Merrimac River in what is now New Hampshire, which he named Londonderry in honour, he said, of Ulster Protestants' 'finest hour'. The authorities in Dublin were beginning to be alarmed at this draining away of a Protestant population which had been so painstakingly settled in Ulster during the previous century. Archbishop William King informed Dublin Castle in 1718 that 'no papists stir . . . The papists being already five or six to one, and being a breeding people, you may imagine what condition we are like to be in'. The momentum of emigration gathered pace, reaching a peak in 1728–9. In November 1728 Primate Hugh Boulter, deputising for the viceroy as a Lord Justice, informed the Duke of Newcastle:

The humour has spread like a contagious distemper, and the people will hardly hear any body that tries to cure them of their madness. The worst is that it affects only protestants, and reigns chiefly in the north, which is the seat of our linen manufacture.

Ezekiel Stewart of Portstewart observed in 1729:

The Presbiteirin ministers have taken their shear of pains to seduce their poor Ignorant heerers, by Bellowing from their pulpits against the

Landlords and the Clargey, calling them Rackers of Rents and Scruers of Tythes . . . There are two of these Preachers caryed this affair to such a length that they went themselves to New England and caryed numbers with them . . .'[12]

The great majority of these migrants were Presbyterians, though considerable numbers of members of the Church of Ireland left also. Up to this time, few Catholics were attracted to make a voluntary journey across the Atlantic. Writing in the 1760s, the English agricultural improver Arthur Young, after touring Ulster, commented: 'The Catholicks never went; they seem not only tied to the county but almost to the parish in which their ancestors lived'.[13] In any case, most of Colonial America was a comparatively bleak environment for Catholics. Protestants were more likely to be able to raise the money for the fare—about six pounds per person in 1718, with reductions for children, and down to four pounds by the 1760s—by selling the interest in their leased farms to incoming tenants (the origin of the 'Ulster Custom'). There might even be some cash left over to buy some land across the Atlantic. American merchants put up money to pay fares for passengers who, in return, signed indentures before the mayor of the port of embarkation to work for no pay for about four years. The services of these 'indentured servants' were then sold, usually to farmers, for about twelve pounds each, Pennsylvania currency.

Most of the emigrants setting out from Derry, Coleraine, Belfast, Larne, Newry and Portrush disembarked at Delaware, Philadelphia, New York or Boston. The first wave of migrants went to New England. Arthur Dobbs of Castle Dobbs, near Carrickfergus, had become Governor of North Carolina, and he made energetic attempts to attract fellow-Ulstermen to settle in his colony. In 1761 the South Carolina Assembly voted to pay four pounds sterling for the passage of each 'poor Protestant' brought to the colony. In the Low Country here enslaved Africans were in a majority, and the plantation-owners feared slave insurrections if Europeans were too few in number. The Charleston merchants John Torrans and John Poaug engaged John Greg of Belfast to rustle up Ulster emigrants. Greg's ship *Falls,* of Belfast, and the *Prince of Wales,* owned by Mussenden, Bateson and Company of Belfast, soon filled with passengers. They also hired the *Success,* a brigantine of eighty-five tons built in Philadelphia and part-owned by William Caldwell of Derry.[14]

These Ulster immigrants, the great majority of them Protestants, were known in America as the Scotch-Irish. The South Carolina Assembly correctly concluded that these immigrants would be particularly adept at colonising the hinterland, the 'back country'. Skills they and their forebears had acquired in Ulster in clearing the land, constructing homesteads and defending themselves against hostile natives proved invaluable as they pushed the frontier ever westward. Just as there was almost a tribal movement of Scots into Ulster at the close of the seventeenth century, so a great flood of Scotch-Irish, journeying in family groups, opened up the back country.

Passing through settled areas to the frontier, the Ulster immigrants settled on the Octararo Creek, between the present-day counties of Chester and Lancaster. From here pioneers pressed on in a north-westerly direction along the east bank of the Susquehanna River, founding the townships of Pequea, Donegal, Paxtang and Hanover. Crossing the river at Harris's Ferry, they came to the fertile Cumberland Valley. By the 1740s the Cumberland Valley and the neighbouring York and Adams counties were densely settled. The Scotch-Irish pressed on westwards, up the Juniata Valley, founding townships with names such as Fermanagh, Derry, Tyrone and Armagh among the ridges of the Allegheny mountain range. Others struck southward through the Great Valley, across the Potomac and into the valley of Virginia. From this valley and the Carolina Piedmont, settlers moved into the mountain valleys of Appalachia, and from there they crossed the Appalachians, through the Cumberland Gap, into Kentucky and Tennessee.

In Ulster, British settlers and their descendants were long accustomed to being on the move and defending their land: woodkerne, tories and raparees at home had prepared them for frontier skirmishing with Ottawas, Shawnee and other native Americans. Writing from the Cumberland Valley in 1733, James Magraw sent this urgent message to his brother in Paxtang: 'Get some guns for us—there's a good wheen of ingens about here'.

'The good Bargins of yar lands in that country doe greatly encourage me to pluck up my spirits and make redie for the journey, for we are now oppressed with our lands at 8s. an acre', David Lindsay explained to his Pennsylvanian cousins in 1758. When economic crisis swept across the western world in 1770, emigration to America from Ulster reached a new peak of about ten thousand a year. Some forty thousand tons of emigrant shipping left Ulster ports between 1771 and 1774, and the estimate made by a Linen Board inspector—that each ton represented one emigrant—is supported by other contemporary evidence. In April 1773 the *Londonderry*

Journal reported 'that one ship, last year, had no less than £4000 in specie on board'. It continued:

> Their removal is sensibly felt in this country—This prevalent humour of industrious Protestants withdrawing from this once flourishing corner of the kingdom seems to be increasing . . . The North of Ireland has in the last five or six years been drained of one fourth of its trading cash, and the like proportion of the manufacturing people—Where the evil will end, remains only in the womb of time to determine.[15]

The American Revolution brought about a sudden halt to this flood of emigrants, but it seems likely that by 1775 at least 100,000 and perhaps as many as 200,000 people from Ulster—the great majority of them Protestants—had left for Colonial America.[16] The flow resumed when peace was agreed in 1783.

THE PENAL LAWS AND ULSTER

Between the Treaty of Limerick in 1691 and the outbreak of rebellion in 1798 Ireland enjoyed the longest peace in its history. The result was unprecedented economic growth: Ireland's exports quadrupled between 1700 and 1765 and doubled again by 1810. The island's population rose from about 1.2 million in 1650 to more than 5 million in 1800—this was a race between population growth and an increase in living standards; on the whole, living standards won the race.[17]

What did change in Ulster was the balance between Protestants and Catholics. Early in the eighteenth century there was a distinct majority of Protestants there; by the end of the century there was almost certainly a Catholic majority. The actual number of Protestants increased, but there is little doubt that the outflow across the Atlantic tipped the balance against them, just as Archbishops King and Boulter had feared. For the time being a fragile peace prevailed between those adhering to the reformed faith and those who remained loyal to Rome, but relations between two such evenly balanced groups remained dangerously volatile.

The passing of a bill in the Irish Parliament in 1697 to expel monks, friars, Jesuits and the Catholic hierarchy from Ireland marked the beginning of anti-Catholic legislation known as the Penal Laws—the last of which was placed on the statute book in 1720. The most effective of these laws prevented Catholics from buying land, becoming members of the legal profession, voting in elections, becoming members of Parliament, setting up schools or holding public office. When a Catholic proprietor died his estate would be equally divided among all his sons; if one son conformed, he could inherit the entire estate. Legislation to forbid pilgrimages, force priests to register and expel the Catholic hierarchy was largely ineffective: the Lough Derg pilgrimage continued (with the connivance of the proprietor, the Protestant Leslie family, which charged six pence for each pilgrim); later, in the eighteenth century, Catholic bishops were actually writing to the newspapers. Though they were forced to pay tithes to an alien church, Catholics were able to worship freely as they had not been able to do in Cromwell's day.

The direct impact of the Penal Laws on Ulster was not as great as in the other three provinces. This was because there the Catholic Gaelic elite had been almost completely swept away. There were some high-profile conversions by Catholic gentry eager to avoid subdivision of their estates and to find careers for younger sons in the legal profession. Virtually no Catholic estate of any significance was left in the entire province of Ulster when Alexander MacDonnell, 5th Earl of Antrim, 'turned' at the age of twenty-one, in 1734. With the exception of Newry, very few Catholic inhabitants of the north could be described as being in the middle classes and therefore affected by laws excluding them from holding public office or commissions in the militia.

A long-held myth is that the native Irish received only inferior land in the Plantation of Ulster. Confiscations during the Commonwealth and in William III's reign may have largely swept away the Gaelic gentry, but Catholics continued to farm the land throughout the province as leaseholders, tenants-at-will or subletting cottiers. As the population rose, however, Catholic tenants (the great majority of them descendants of the conquered native Irish) found that they were being steadily eased off the more fertile lowland soils. From the outset, newcomers had tended to cluster in the very parts of Ulster which previously had been most favoured by the indigenous Irish: the valleys of the Lagan, Bann, Foyle, Blackwater, Erne, Maine, Bush, Moyola, Ballinderry, Roe, Faughan, Swilly and Deele in particular. From the late seventeenth century, landlords and their agents tended to favour co-religionists in these core areas of settlement. Increasing numbers of Catholics could only obtain access to uplands and dried-out fens and bogs previously used for summer grazing. To bring such land into full cultivation involved the unremitting labour of removing or burning off whin and heather and the prising out of rocks or stumps. In 1744 the author Walter Harris described farming above Dromara on the slopes of Slieve Croob:

The face of the Country hereabouts is rough, bleak and unimproved; yet produces the Necessaries of Life sufficient to support a large Number of Inhabitants, who have little other Bread Corn but Oats ... They are an industrious hardy People, and may be properly said to *eat their Bread in the Sweat of their Face,* the Courseness of the land obliging them to great Labour.[18]

As in previous centuries, this newly cleared land was cultivated with the loy (from *láighe,* a spade with a long shaft, a foot-rest and a narrow iron blade) in ridges known—to those who never had to do the job themselves—as 'lazy beds'. In west Donegal the population rose as the thin acid soil was painstakingly enriched by seaweed and sweetened with shell sand. The exotic vegetable, the potato, tolerating a wide range of soils, increasingly formed a crucial part of the diet; by providing vitamin C it did much to eliminate scurvy, which had previously plagued the people of Ireland.

It is likely that this growing awareness by Catholics that they were losing access to the best land in the core areas of British settlement was doing as much as, or more than, the Penal Laws to foster resentment against their Protestant neighbours. Nowhere in Ulster was tension between the sects more acute than in the flourishing heart of the domestic linen industry.

PEEP O' DAY BOYS AND DEFENDERS

Drunken affrays in the vicinity of Markethill between gangs calling themselves the Nappach Fleet, the Bawn Fleet and the Bunkerhill Defenders had become openly sectarian by 1786. The combatants regrouped, Protestants becoming the Peep o' Day Boys and Catholics the Defenders, and for the next decade and more sectarian warfare raged in Co. Armagh. Better armed, the Peep o' Day Boys at first swept all before them—a 'low set of fellows', Lord Gosford observed, 'who with Guns and Bayonets, and Other Weapons Break Open the Houses of the Roman Catholicks, and as I am informed treat many of them with Cruelty'. According to John Byrne, a Catholic dyer from Armagh, some Protestant gentlemen lent arms to Catholics

to protect them from depredations of these fanatic madmen; and many poor creatures were obliged to abandon their houses at night, and sleep in turf-bogs, in little huts made of sods; so great was the zeal of our holy crusados this year.[19]

By this time Co. Armagh had become perhaps the most densely populated rural area in either Great Britain or Ireland. Here the manufacture of linen was the main economic activity. This was a domestic industry, carried on in the home by people who divided their time between farming and the production of yarn and cloth. Weavers could not allow their hands to become rough from heavy farm work—in case they would catch in the fine warp and weft—and so food had to be imported from other parts of Ireland to areas concentrating on the production of linen cloth. Often they were satisfied with holdings just large enough for a cottage which could house a loom and spinning wheels, with just enough land to grow flax and sufficient grass for a cow to supply the family with fresh milk. Co. Armagh was the core of the 'linen triangle', extending from Dungannon east to Lisburn and south to Armagh; then, as output increased, Newry was drawn in. By now drapers were buying the cloth unbleached, thus giving weavers a quicker return for their work. In effect these linen merchants became Ulster's first rural capitalists, investing their profits in bleach-greens, where, with the aid of water power, they finished the cloth to the high standard required by the English and overseas markets.

Competition to rent land became fierce in the vicinity of market towns, bleach-greens and the water-powered wash mills, dye-works and beetling mills. Few Catholics were drapers, but many were handloom weavers, competing with their Protestant neighbours. Trade rivalry easily became sectarian rivalry. Rents for the tiny farms in the linen triangle were the highest in Ireland, and Protestants, living on oatmeal, perhaps supplemented with bacon once a week, often felt that Catholics, surviving on potatoes and buttermilk, could unfairly outbid them by paying higher rents. Here, in mid-Ulster, where Protestants and Catholics lived in roughly equal numbers, the ideas of the Enlightenment had made little headway. Memories of seventeenth-century dispossession and massacre remained stubbornly alive.

'For heaven's sake don't forget the Powder & Ball with all Expedition', the Drumbanagher magistrate John Moore wrote to Lord Charlemont in July 1789. He had no hesitation in giving out arms to 'the Protestant Boys that have none', because Defenders 'are now beginning their Night Depredations and Lye in Wait behind Ditches, to murder and Destroy Every protestant that appears'. The sectarian violence fanned out to the uplands of south Armagh. Here the Catholics—still speaking Irish and wearing mantles—had the advantage of numbers and turned on the Protestants with a ferocity not seen for more than a century. A horrific climax was reached when Defenders attacked a schoolmaster and his family in Forkill on 28 January 1791, an event graphically described by the Rev. Edward Hudson, Presbyterian minister of Jonesborough:

> In rushed a Body of Hellhounds—not content with cutting & stabbing him in several places, they drew a cord round his neck until his Tongue was forced out—It they cut off and three fingers of his right hand— Then they cut out his wife's tongue and . . . with a case knife cut off her Thumb and four of her fingers one after another . . . She I fear cannot recover—there was in the house a Brother of hers about fourteen years old . . . His Tongue those merciless Villains cut out and cut the calf of his leg with a sword.

In September 1795 Defenders assembled near Loughgall at a crossroads known as the Diamond to face the Peep o' Day Boys in battle. The Peep o' Day Boys, reinforced by a Co. Down contingent called the Bleary Boys, took position on the brow of a hill overlooking the crossroads. William Blacker, a Trinity College student at home on vacation, spent his time melting lead from the roof of Castle Blacker, making bullets for the Peep o' Day Boys. Then, he wrote later, the Protestants opened fire

> with cool and steady aim at the swarms of Defenders, who were in a manner cooped up in the valley and presented an excellent mark for their shots. The affair was of brief duration . . . From the bodies found afterwards by the reapers in the cornfields, I am inclined to think that not less than thirty lost their lives.[20]

The victorious Protestants then marched into Loughgall, and there, in the house of James Sloan, the Orange Order was founded. This was a defensive association of lodges; like the Defenders, it was oath-bound, it used passwords and signs, it was confined to one sect, and its membership was made up mainly of farmer-weavers. Blacker was one of the very few of the landed gentry who joined the order at the outset. He did not approve, however, of the immediate outcome of the Battle of the Diamond:

> Unhappily . . . a determination was expressed of driving from this quarter of the county the entire of its Roman Catholic population . . . A written notice was thrown into or posted upon the door of a house warning the inmates, in the words of Cromwell, to betake themselves 'to Hell or Connaught'.

A sample of what was called 'placarding' was sent by General William Dalrymple to Dublin Castle. It warned a woman of Keady and her brother that they must not be informers,

> Otherwise be all the Secruts of hell your house Shall Be Burned to the Ground. Both his Soul & your Shall be Blwed To the Blue flames of hell. Now Teak this for Warnig, For if you Bee in this Contry Wednesday Night I will Blow your Soul to the Low hils of hell And Burn the House you are in.[21]

The 'wreckers' smashed looms, tore up linen webs and destroyed great numbers of homes. In just two months some seven thousand Catholics were driven out of Co. Armagh. Many did flee to Connacht. Lord Altamont reckoned that four thousand had taken refuge in Co. Mayo, and his brother noted: 'The Emigration from the North continues; every day families arrive here with the wreck of their properties'. Meanwhile the United Irishmen, once no more than a radical pressure group, had become a secret, oath-bound revolutionary body pledged to fight for an Irish republic with the aid of the French Directory. Now thousands of Defenders clamoured to be part of the coming revolution.

REBELLION AND UNION

Protestants were in such an overwhelming majority in the counties of Antrim and Down that they had little fear of their Catholic neighbours. Here Presbyterians had a long tradition of defending their rights against tithe-collectors, clergy and landlords of the Church of Ireland. The Enlightenment had taken deep root in Belfast, still barely a tenth the size of Dublin but growing fast. Here an energetic and confident middle class passionately debated new political ideas, coming in with their cargoes from Scotland, America and France. They had taken a lead in the successful drive for legislative independence in 1782 and in the unsuccessful campaign to make the Irish Parliament more representative in the following two years. For example, in May 1784 they attended Mass at St Mary's Chapel, which the Protestants of Belfast had largely paid for, as the several hundred Catholics in the town were too poor to meet the cost.

Then news of the outbreak of the French Revolution in the summer of 1789 electrified the citizens of Belfast. The example of France spurred them to campaign anew for the reform of Parliament. In October 1791 the Society of United Irishmen was formed in a Belfast tavern to campaign for radical change. The society spread across Antrim and north Down and south to Dublin and beyond. By then most of the Penal Laws had been repealed; the United Irishmen succeeded in persuading the Irish Parliament to give Catholics the vote in 1793 but failed to win Catholic Emancipation, that is, the removal of the oath which barred them from Parliament. In frustration the United Irishmen became revolutionaries, and by 1796 they had tens of thousands of Defenders swelling their ranks and the promise of French aid. This resulted in an extraordinary division of Protestant allegiance in Ulster. West of the River Bann, Orangemen and other Protestants eagerly joined the Yeomanry, a locally recruited defence force formed by the government. While the Yeomanry got some recruits east of the river, far more Protestants in Antrim and Down, in spite of ruthless sweeps to disarm them, got blacksmiths to forge them pikeheads for the approaching uprising.

The rebellion when it came, at the end of May 1798, was predominantly confined to Leinster. But in June, Presbyterians in Antrim and then in north Down rose up also, only to be routed in the town of Antrim and at Ballynahinch. Ballymena was the last rebel stronghold to capitulate. They had been fighting in support of the rebels further south, but it is significant that the Defenders, gathering by the graves of the MacCartan lords at Loughinisland, refused to march the few miles north to join the United Irish army at Ballynahinch.

As soon as he heard of the outbreak of the insurrection, the Prime Minister, William Pitt the Younger, resolved to press forward with a bill to unite the kingdoms of Great Britain and Ireland under one legislature at Westminster. His concern was Britain's safety during a deadly war with Revolutionary France. A majority in the Irish Parliament—a body which represented only the 'Protestant Ascendancy', the charmed circle of Anglican gentry, clergy, lawyers and their relatives—opposed the Union Bill. It would be necessary, the Under-Secretary Edward Cooke warned Pitt, to have the Union 'written-up, spoken-up, intrigued-up, drunk-up, sung-up and bribed-up'.[22] So indeed it proved.

At its headquarters in Dublin the Orange Order attempted to remain neutral on the issue. But most Orangemen in Ulster, fearing that it would be swiftly followed by Catholic Emancipation, vigorously opposed the Union: thirty-six lodges in Armagh and Monaghan alone petitioned against it. 'My occupation is now of the most unpleasant nature, negotiating and jobbing with the most corrupt people under Heaven', the Viceroy, Lord Cornwallis, wrote, but it worked—the Union Bill passed through the Irish Parliament and Westminster and became law in the summer of 1800.[23]

MIGRATION TO BELFAST

On 1 January 1801 the new Union flag, incorporating St Patrick's Cross, was run up flagpoles in all the principal towns. For the great majority of the people of Ulster it was an event of no consequence—of far more immediate concern were the hardships brought about by wartime inflation and harvest failures. Forty years later, however, the province's inhabitants would hold passionate opinions on the Union—both for and against—and, right into the twenty-first century, this would not change.

Apart from Antrim and Down, in most of Ulster sectarian bitterness had not been eased during the long peace between the Treaty of Limerick and the outbreak of insurrection in 1798. Interrupted only by a trio of pathetically ineffective and short-lived uprisings (none of them in Ulster), the nineteenth century was also largely a century of peace in Ireland. Yet the absence of widespread violence did not extinguish 'party' feeling and intercommunal antagonism. Indeed, corrosive sectarianism was to return east of the River Bann.

The slaughter of 1798 had a chastening effect on those United Irishmen in Belfast who had avoided death on the field of battle, execution and transportation. It would be quite wrong to assume, however, that they and their progeny all cast aside the tolerance they had imbibed during the Enlightenment. Why, then, did Belfast become notorious for its vicious sectarian rioting later in the nineteenth century? The answer is that Belfast was becoming the fastest-growing urban centre in Ireland, indeed in the United Kingdom. Quite simply the original citizens of the town and their descendants were soon swamped by immigrants from the overcrowded and impoverished countryside seeking work in the mills, engineering works and shipyards.

Belfast was the first place in Ireland where the Industrial Revolution had taken deep root. Streams had been dammed and steam engines installed to power cotton-spinning machines, and then, in the late 1820s, as Belfast found it increasingly difficult to compete with Manchester, the technical problems of spinning flax by power machinery had been overcome. Ulster was fast becoming the greatest centre of linen production in the world. The capital, business skills and technical expertise earlier acquired by drapers and cotton-manufacturers were now redeployed to make eastern Ulster the one part of Ireland where the

Industrial Revolution made spectacular progress in the nineteenth century.

West of the River Bann the Ulster countryside became ever more impoverished: agricultural prices sank after the British victory at Waterloo, and at the same time the domestic linen industry was being slowly but inexorably driven to the wall by unequal competition with steam-powered factories in Belfast, Leeds and Manchester. As people poured into Belfast to seek employment in the mills, in the flax-machinery works and at the docks, the religious balance of the town changed: in 1784 there had been only 1,092 Catholics, but by 1834 there were 19,712, forming 32 per cent of Belfast's population. As the traveller John Barrow observed: 'Within a few years some four or five thousand raw, uneducated Catholic labourers from the South and West had poured into the city'.[24]

The migration from mid-Ulster became a flood during the Great Famine. Contrary to the popular view, Ulster was harder hit than the province of Leinster: the number of Ulster's inhabitants fell by 374,000 between 1841 and 1851, a drop of 15.7 per cent, compared with 19.9 per cent for the whole of Ireland. Ulster suffered about 224,000, or 8.6 per cent, 'excess deaths', that is, the number over and above those who would have died from the usual causes. Fleeing from hunger and pestilence to the ports, a great many travelled on to Liverpool and from there to the United States. Scotland, which for so long had sent migrants to Ulster, now acquired a great Irish population, and those lacking the resources to go further settled in Belfast.

The population of Belfast increased by almost 47 per cent between 1801, when it was 19,000, and 1811, when it was 27,832. By 1851 it was 87,062, and by 1871 it was 174,412. The Belfast Harbour Commissioners saw to the dredging of the Lagan estuary to enable the largest ships to come up to the quays at any tide. The mud drawn out to create this channel, opened in 1849 and named the Victoria Channel, formed an artificial island in east Belfast, and here the construction of iron ships began. The official recognition in 1888 that Belfast was a city seemed somewhat overdue—it had become Ireland's largest port and biggest city. By 1901 Belfast was, after London and Liverpool, the port of third importance in the United Kingdom, then the greatest trading state on earth; and it had the world's biggest linen mill, ropeworks, tobacco factory, spiral-guided gasometer, tea machinery and fan-making works, aerated waters factory, dry dock, handkerchief factory and shipyard (launching the largest man-made moving objects on earth).

'THE DRAGONS' TEETH, SO PLENTIFULLY ... SOWN IN THIS ULSTER PLANTATION'

The majority arriving in Belfast had come from mid-Ulster, and with them they brought antagonisms etched into their folk memory. Incomers chose where they settled with care. Invisible lines marked off Protestant and Catholic districts, frontiers kept unstable by the constant influx of newcomers. Here, where the low-paid majority eked out a wretched existence, religious hatreds had ample opportunity to fester in brutalising conditions. Ancient quarrels, which had been fought out previously in the countryside, were now transferred to the narrow streets of Belfast. Readers of the *Times* in London could be forgiven for concluding that Connacht was the most disorderly and violent part of Ireland. In fact violence was more frequent and fatal in its consequences in the sectarian battles which so often raged in Belfast—more were killed in these street conflicts during the century than all those who met with violent deaths in the Emmet, Young Ireland and Fenian risings and the Land War put together.

Sectarian rioting reached a new peak of intensity during the summer of 1857. Not only was there a 'warm interchange of opinion on a basis of basalt', as the journalist Frank Frankfort Moore remembered, but gun battles raged almost every night for weeks. Head-Constable Henderson saw a ditch near Quadrant Street 'closely lined with men, having guns levelled, firing without intermission'.[25]

In many respects Belfast resembled other city ports in the United Kingdom, such as Newcastle-on-Tyne. It was the ferocity of sectarian warfare which set it apart. On 11 August 1857 the *Daily News* of London marvelled at this upsurge of ancient hatreds:

Geologists are much divided upon the question whether a volcano, whose eruptive powers have been fully developed, has ever been known to die out. Observers of social phenomena are equally at fault as to whether the destructive agency of religious fanaticism, having once been long established, can ever be safely regarded as extinct. Long lulls occur in the mischievous action of both ... But ever and anon men are startled by unlooked-for and unaccountable tremblings of the earth beneath their feet; and the premonitory signs of mad commotion fill the air, and before they have time to inquire or reason about the cause of the long-latent and almost forgotten evil it has burst over their heads and filled the tranquil home with sorrow and dismay.[26]

The Belfast riots of 1864 and 1872 were even more protracted and violent. Following the publication of a 4,500-page report by a parliamentary select committee in 1835, the Grand Lodge of Ireland was dissolved in April 1836; but the Orange Order survived in Ulster, and its members frequently defied the Party Processions (Ireland) Act (1850). 'Party' confrontations frequently besmirched the normally peaceful Ulster countryside. About fifty Catholic 'Ribbonmen' (successors to the Defenders of the eighteenth century) died in a conflict with an Orange procession at Dolly's Brae, near Castlewellan, on 12 July 1849.

These Belfast riots were even more protracted and violent than those of 1857. The Rev. George Hill, in the final paragraph of 590 pages of densely printed text on the Plantation of Ulster published in 1877, had no doubt that this violence had its roots in the early seventeenth century. His observations probably made uncomfortable reading for most of those who had purchased his book. Though Pynnar's survey of 1619 recorded 'sadly halting progress', Hill concluded:

> It would have been more than remarkable, however, had not the newcomers prospered sooner or later, seeing that they enjoyed all the encouragement and protection they could have desired, or that mere earthly power could afford—they got hold of the very best land in the province, teeming, as it did, with natural fertility, and so rested as to yield but little harvests with but little toil ... But the paradise of plenty, if not of peace, to which these strangers at times attained, was only secured by a very heavy and dreadful sacrifice of the general interests of Ireland as a nation; for to this settlement in Ulster ... may be traced the awful scenes and events of the ten years' civil war commencing in 1641, the horrors of the revolutionary struggle in 1690, and the re-awakening of those horrors in 1798 ... The dragons' teeth, so plentifully, and if so deliberately sown in this Ulster plantation, have, indeed, sprung up at times with more than usually abundant growth, yielding their ghastly harvests of blood and death on almost every plain, and by almost every river side, and in almost every glen of our northern province.[27]

A RELIGIOUS CONFLICT?

During the nineteenth century, movements within the Christian churches did much to keep alive ancient intercommunal antagonisms. In Britain the deism and scepticism fashionable amongst the upper classes were being swept aside by a fresh wave of religious enthusiasm sweeping over much of Europe. Largely funded by English evangelicals, the first major drive in more than a century was launched to convert Irish Catholics to Protestantism. By 1816 there were twenty-one Methodist missionaries operating from fourteen stations throughout Ireland. Anglicans, Baptists and Presbyterians had their own missionary organisations. Over a period of ten years the Religious Tract and Book Society alone distributed 4.4 million tracts. Between 1806 and 1823 the Hibernian Bible Society issued 218,000 copies of the New Testament and 104,000 Bibles.

This missionary campaign caused deep resentment. Many of the Catholic poor believed the prophecies of Pastorini, the pseudonym of an eighteenth-century English Catholic bishop, which foretold the violent destruction of Protestant churches in 1825. It was widely believed that 'locusts from the bottomless pit'—the Protestants—were about to meet their end. Admittedly, Catholic clergy and Catholic gentlemen were deeply embarrassed by this millenarianism and even more by attacks on Protestant churches.

Meanwhile many Presbyterians in Ulster who had been 'out' in 1798, horrified by the realities of violence and disillusioned by failure, were finding solace in the certainties of evangelical religion. In 1830, as he strove to unite all Presbyterians into one church, the Rev. Dr Henry Cooke succeeded in purging liberal clergy, who had argued that a range of beliefs could be tolerated within Presbyterianism. Public debating duels between Protestant and Catholic clergy—especially a three-day contest at Ballymena in July 1827—did nothing to improve community relations. Lord Farnham, founder of the Association for Promoting the Second Reformation, was an example of how tactless and provocative proselytising could be: week by week the earl proclaimed the numbers of souls freshly won over from Popery on wall posters or on placards hung from the backs of people walking the town of Cavan. Farnham was responsible for major evictions of Catholics on his estate south-east of Lough Ramor that were carried out in order to bring in more politically compatible Protestant tenants. Other clearances of this kind in Co. Cavan followed on the property of Sir George Hodson, on the Headfort estates and on the lands of the Rev. Marcus Beresford.

A great campaign for Christian spiritual renewal launched in America in 1858 surged across the Atlantic and reached the shores of Ulster the following year. With tireless zeal, the Rev. S. J. Jones got the revival under way in mid-Antrim, holding as many as a hundred prayer meetings a week in Connor and Ballymena. From there the movement spread rapidly to neighbouring counties and as far south as Cavan and Monaghan. The Rev. David Adams of Ahoghill remembered:

> In the end of April and the beginning of May the wind of the Spirit calmed, but about the middle of May it blew a heavenly hurricane, and the mighty wave of mercy swelled gloriously mountain high, sweeping across the dead sea of our rural population, and washing the rocky hearts of formal worshippers.

According to the *Ballymena Observer*, the revival 'is advancing wave after wave, like some resistless tide upon the strand; each surging swell marking its onward progress to a predestined limit, but no human eye can see the boundary'. On Sunday 29 June 1859 nearly forty thousand people crowded into the Botanic Gardens in Belfast, where twenty separate meetings were held. Not all approved: the Rev. Isaac Nelson, a Presbyterian minister in Belfast, described 1859 as 'the Year of Delusion . . . having really no more to do with Christianity than the phenomena of electro-biology'.[28]

When an Austrian Redemptorist held a mission in Enniskillen in 1852 he found that Catholics in the town 'had never even witnessed benediction of the Blessed Sacrament, never seen incense rise from a thurible'. Within a few years such a discovery became more and more unlikely. Regular attendance at Mass had previously been limited to a pious minority of educated and prosperous Catholics; now, probably for the first time in Irish history, it became universal. Archbishop Paul Cullen, made Ireland's first cardinal in 1866, set out energetically to regularise devotional practice, root out religious customs of doubtful Christian origin, campaign for denominational education at every level and launch a counter-attack on Second Reformation missionary activity.

Belfast presented the Catholic Church with a special challenge. Cornelius Denvir, Bishop of Down and Connor since 1835, had been quite unequal to the task of providing adequate pastoral care for his rapidly expanding urban flock, who in any case were often too poor to pay for the upkeep of their church. In May 1865 he was replaced by Patrick Dorrian, who proved a more dynamic standard-bearer of Catholic renewal than Cullen had dared to hope. Soon after his consecration Dorrian launched a general mission in Belfast. Twelve additional priests were brought in to help the eight parish clergy of the town hear Confessions for ten hours a day over a month. The delighted bishop reported to the Vatican that 'persons who have not been at Confession for years are coming in crowds'—his final estimate was that thirty thousand had been to Confession and Holy Communion. Adults who had missed Confirmation as children were now confirmed in great numbers, parochial societies and confraternities sprang up, and by 1877 the Society of St Vincent de Paul alone recorded more than two thousand boys attending its Sunday schools. Great numbers of new church buildings could be seen rising from the ground. In Co. Monaghan alone twenty-five chapels were put up between 1783 and 1842; St Peter's church—soon to be Belfast's pro-cathedral—was dedicated by Cullen in 1866; and it took from 1840 to 1904 to complete St Patrick's Cathedral in Armagh.

A visitor from the Ottoman Empire would have had difficulty distinguishing between the Protestant Evangelical Revival and the Catholic Renewal. Both displayed intense religious fervour and a triumphalist assertiveness; both made faith the cornerstone of their beliefs and laid new emphasis on regular prayer, private devotions, participation in church services and Sunday instruction for children; both embraced a fervent Puritanism and were opposed to sexual permissiveness, strong drink and 'pernicious' literature; both accepted infallibility, one of the Pope and the other of the literal truth of the Bible as God's word; and both adopted 'Victorian morality' with a greater enthusiasm than the English themselves.

And yet most Catholics and Protestants were acutely aware of what divided them, particularly in the sectarian enclaves of Belfast, Portadown and the city of Londonderry.[29]

ETHNIC CONFLICT?

As railways and other modern communications steadily eroded parochial sentiment, people throughout Europe were discovering their national identity. Poets and other writers, historians, musicians and artists—who routinely used the word 'race' when referring to their own people—fed a multiplicity of national passions. Every nationality emphasised its individuality and distinctiveness, generally using language as the badge of identity. Language was once the principal means of distinguishing between the native Gaelic Irish and incoming British settlers in Ulster. The census of 1901 showed how much this had changed: while Irish was still spoken in every county in the province, only 6 per cent of Ulster's population could speak it. In short, religion, rather than language, had now become the mark of distinction.

More clearly than ever, the inhabitants of Ulster seemed divided sharply into two ethnic groups with profoundly divergent aspirations.

During the second half of the nineteenth century Ulster had joined in in the developing European debates on racial typifications. In the 1850s readers of the *Ulster Journal of Archaeology* were informed that Protestants in Antrim and Down were Anglo-Saxon in race, possessing the inherited virtues of thrift, capacity for hard work and respect for law and order. Using such words as 'staunch' and 'stalwart' to describe themselves, northern Protestants had no difficulty in accepting this theory. Nationalists—though they might add adjectives such as 'dour' and 'mean'—largely accepted Protestants' assumption of their racial separateness, for they at the same time were emphasising their Gaelic origins and laying claim to inherent characteristics such as hospitality, passion and love of poetry.

It is not unreasonable to assume that in Ulster the great majority of Catholics are descended from the native Gaelic Irish and that the great majority of Protestants are descended from seventeenth-century British colonists. However, there is much evidence that planters and their descendants did not separate themselves from the native Irish population as much as was formerly assumed. Settlers in western Ulster, particularly those of low status, sometimes married local women, and within a generation their descendants could well be Catholics speaking Irish. On the other side of the province the incoming flood of British colonists encouraged many native Irish to embrace Protestantism, speak English and drop the O or Mac from their surnames. Before the seventeenth century was out, considerable numbers of Magennises of Iveagh and Clandeboye O'Neills had become converts to the reformed faith. Later, rather more Catholics converted to Protestantism than the Church was willing to admit—particularly those finding it convenient to attend Protestant schools or who had been swept up in successive evangelical revivals.

The nineteenth century saw a dramatic fall in the number of those who could speak Irish, and as surnames were anglicised, translated or given pseudo-translations the memory of ancestral connection was often lost. The surname Gallogley, prevalent in Donegal, derives from *Gallóglaigh*, 'foreign warriors' (Hebridean mercenaries of the late Middle Ages), but many bearing that name—assuming that *Gall* meant an English foreigner—adopted the surname English. Some Laverys on the eastern shore of Lough Neagh—aware that *lámh* means a hand or forearm—changed their surname to Armstrong. Most of the Ulster sept of Ó Dreáin anglicised to Adrian, but some, in a pseudo-translation, converted to Hawthorne, *draighean* in Irish, meaning 'blackthorn' or 'hawthorn'. Many

Donnellys in the Coleraine district became Donaldsons; some of the McBrin family of Co. Down changed their name to Burns, an Argyll surname; many names were confused and amalgamated, such as the Border surname Kerr and the Irish surname Carr; and the O'Carrolls of Dromore almost all changed their surname to Cardwell.

In short, the descendants of natives and newcomers in Ulster became almost inextricably intermingled. A cursory glance at registers in segregated schools past and present shows many British surnames in Catholic rollbooks and Irish surnames in Protestant ones. Genealogists have uncovered a far greater degree of religious conversion and native-planter, Catholic-Protestant intermarriage than might be expected.[30] However, detailed investigation would surely reveal a similar lack of clarity in the ethnic distinctions being so passionately espoused as the nineteenth century drew to a close in the Austro-Hungarian, Turkish and Russian Empires. What mattered was that Serbs, Croats, Slovenes, Poles, Czechs and others *felt* themselves to be separate nations.

POLITICAL CONFLICT

The vast majority of Ulster Catholics thought of themselves as part of an Irish nation, worthy of self-government. Ulster Protestants, always with notable exceptions drawn largely from the intelligentsia (such as the Fenian and Nationalist MP for Cavan, Joseph Biggar; Captain John White of Ballymena, who helped to found the Irish Citizen Army in 1913; and a Home Ruler from Ballymoney, the Rev. James Armour), saw themselves as Britons who should not be cut loose from the United Kingdom. These clashing aspirations continued to generate eddies of turbulence, sometimes becoming dangerous cyclones, for many years to come. Politicians at Westminster, however, often displayed a striking inability to recognise the portents of storm.

Intercommunal tensions in Ulster were now heightened by the growing debate on Ireland's political future. Sectarian conflict began in Belfast as the first Home Rule Bill was being debated at Westminster in June 1886. Though the bill was defeated, the conflict intensified to become the worst violence experienced anywhere in Ireland in the nineteenth century. Men of the Royal Irish Constabulary (most of them Catholic southerners seen as agents of the Liberal government) were attacked repeatedly, even though they retaliated with volleys from their carbines. Despite intervention by the Highland Light Infantry and repeated cavalry charges, police and military fought an unequal battle against mobs in the streets hurling salvos of paving stones. Battles raged each night across the frontier between the Falls Road and Shankill Road. Frankfort Moore was in York Street on the night of 31 July, witnessing 'dense crowds surging in every direction, and shot after shot I heard above the shouts that suggested something very like Pandemonium . . . I felt I had learned something of the impotence of every arm except artillery in the case of street fighting'.[31] When at last the riots subsided, in mid-September, the official death toll was thirty-one, though the actual number killed was probably about fifty.

It was 1912 before there was a real possibility again that Ireland would get Home Rule. This time Unionist leaders put up a meticulously organised resistance designed to avoid widespread sectarian conflict. But when it seemed certain that the third Home Rule Bill would become law, in 1913, they formed a paramilitary army, the Ulster Volunteer Force, soon to be armed with rifles brought in from Germany. Nationalists formed the Irish Volunteers before the year was out, and about half its members were in Ulster. As the two paramilitary forces paraded within yards of each other on the Falls Road and Shankill Road, civil war seemed certain. 'I see no hopes of peace', the Ulster Unionist leader Sir Edward Carson gloomily observed towards the end of July 1914. 'I see nothing at present but darkness and shadows . . . We shall have once more to assert the manhood of our race'.[32] But on 4 August the United Kingdom was at war. It was not to be in Ulster but in France that the manhood of Carson's race would be asserted.

DEVOLUTION

Civil war in Ulster was only postponed. The general election of 1918 demonstrated that Irish nationalists would no longer be satisfied with devolution. Since this was refused by Westminster, republicans launched a deadly guerrilla campaign, and as the Anglo-Irish War edged into Ulster it triggered off a sectarian conflict there more vicious and lethal than all the northern riots of the nineteenth century put together. The killing and destruction intensified as Westminster applied its elaborate constitutional solutions. The Government of Ireland Act, passed in December 1920, provided for two devolved Irish parliaments, one for the six north-eastern counties, to be called Northern Ireland, and another for the other twenty-six counties, to be known as Southern Ireland. Unionists themselves decided that the counties of Donegal, Cavan and Monaghan should not be included in Northern Ireland, as the nationalist electorate there was too large. As expected, southern republicans rejected this solution and fought on until the Anglo-Irish Treaty of December 1921 created the Irish Free State, with an independent status equivalent to that of the Dominion of Canada.

The Government of Ireland Act was really designed to create Northern Ireland. The United Kingdom's first devolved region came to be born in a welter of blood. Fighting began after taunting by both sides at the corner of Long Tower Street, Derry, in April 1920, and it spread eastwards, where virtually all Catholic residents of Lisburn, Banbridge and Dromore were driven out. Responding to the news of murders committed by the IRA further south, Catholics were expelled from the shipyards in Belfast, triggering a ferocious sectarian warfare along the frontier zones between working-class enclaves. Isolated Catholic and Protestant families were particularly vulnerable, and intimidation, house-burning, rioting and assassination drew the lines between the two communities in the city more tautly than ever. Atrocity followed atrocity, counter-assassination followed almost every death, and large areas of Belfast were virtually at war.

Special powers adopted by the Northern Ireland Government, the formation of a new police force and the great expansion of the numbers of special constables deployed did much to restore order. But it was the outbreak of civil war in the Irish Free State in June 1922 which—by drawing IRA activists south of the new political border—made it possible to bring about a solid peace. But the price in blood had been heavy: between July 1920 and July 1922 the death toll in the six counties was 557—303 Catholics, 172 Protestants and 82 members of the military and police. In Belfast 236 people had been killed in the first months of 1922, more than in the widespread troubles in Germany in the same period.

By contrast, the years following were remarkably peaceful: there was not a single sectarian murder between 1923 and 1933. Thirteen people died violently in the riots of 1935 in Belfast, but the fighting had been concentrated in a small district just north of the city centre.

Though Northern Ireland enjoyed a remarkable calm after 1922, intercommunal tensions had not been significantly reduced. While the Northern Ireland Government had not created these divisions, it did little to assuage them. Of course, the devolved administration in Belfast faced the problem that a third of the inhabitants of the region did not want Northern Ireland to survive. With a secure majority in its Parliament, however, the Unionist Governments did not make serious efforts to cajole the Catholic minority into accepting, however reluctantly, the new state of affairs. London, distracted by economic problems, the rise of dictatorships on the European mainland and imperial troubles, took its eye off the ball in Northern Ireland. Discussion of Northern Ireland affairs at Westminster was ruled out of order. Both Britain and the United States were grateful for Northern Ireland's contribution to victory in the Second World War. Criticism of how the region was run was considered inappropriate.

Because they concentrated on attempting to achieve the unobtainable objective of ending partition, nationalist politicians in Northern Ireland only belatedly turned their attention to producing a detailed analysis of unfair treatment in the manipulation of electoral boundaries to Unionist advantage, the appointment to posts in the public services and the allocation of council houses. That was to change after the Second World War as the benefits of the welfare state were extended to the region. This greatly increased expenditure at a local level, magnifying the scale of malpractice, and educated a new Catholic middle class capable of co-ordinating a sophisticated campaign to bring about internal change. This was a period of rapidly rising expectations and vastly improved international communication.

In the 1960s the Prime Minister, Captain Terence O'Neill, belatedly attempted to convince his party to bring about change. Despite his mould-breaking gestures of conciliation, however, he eventually created intense frustration within the minority by his inability to deliver thoroughgoing reform, while at the same time more and more loyalists were convinced that he was conceding too much and turned against him.

The tragedy was that the legacy of the past refused to go away. The arrival of 'New English' administrators and planters from across the Irish Sea in the sixteenth and seventeenth centuries had coincided with the deadly struggle for supremacy between the supporters of the Reformation and the Counter-Reformation. But for this religious division, a much more harmonious blending of these newcomers and indigenous inhabitants almost certainly would have occurred. Now, in 1968–9, a vibrant civil rights movement, inspired by direct action on the streets overseas, dissolved into intercommunal conflict, plunging the region into near-chaos. The unchained sectarian dragon leaped from its cage as fear, suspicion, atavistic hatred and memory of ancient wrongs gushed to the surface, inaugurating thirty years of destruction, conflict, forced population movement, mutilation and slaughter.

NOTES

Where the title of a book, article or pamphlet is not given, the complete reference will be found in the bibliography.

Chapter 1 (p. 1–24)

1. Quinn, 1966, p. 108.
2. Bagwell, 1885, vol. 2, p. 258.
3. Annals of the Four Masters, AD 1574.
4. Bagwell, 1885, vol. 2, pp 302, 324.
5. Lennon, 1994, p. 280.
6. Canny, 1976, pp 90–91.
7. Art Cosgrove in Art Cosgrove (ed.), *A New History of Ireland, II: Medieval Ireland, 1169–1534*, Oxford, 1987, p. 531.
8. Maxwell, 1923, p. 126.
9. Maxwell, 1923, p. 145; G. A. Hayes-McCoy in Moody, Martin and Byrne (eds), pp 75, 78–9.
10. Katharine Simms in James Lydon (ed.), *England and Ireland in the Middle Ages*, Dublin, 1981, pp 230–31.
11. Canavan, 1989, pp 33–5.
12. Hill, 1873, p. 37.
13. Simms, 1987, pp 28–36; Nicholls, 1972, pp 22–30.
14. Nicholls, 1972, p. 10.
15. Ibid., p. 11.
16. Ibid., pp 44–54, 80–83.
17. Ibid., p. 60.
18. Ibid., pp 84–90.
19. Gailey, 1984, p. 21.
20. Nicholls, 1972, pp 114–20.
21. Connolly, 2007, pp 404–5.
22. Nicholls, 1972, p. 68.
23. Gailey, 1984, pp 23–4.
24. Allingham, 1897, p. 62; Maxwell, 1923, pp 314–18; Dunlevy, 1989, pp 41–51; Quinn, 1966, pp 69–71.
25. Bagwell, 1885, vol. 2, p. 244.
26. Hill, 1873, p. 158.
27. Falls, 1950, pp 143–5; Maxwell, 1923, pp 170–71.

28. Lennon, 1994, pp 225–7.
29. Lennon, 1994, pp 237–49; Bagwell, 1890, vol. 3, pp 186, 224, 244.
30. Bagwell, 1890, vol. 3, p. 224.
31. Hayes-McCoy, 1969, pp 100, 103.
32. Falls, 1950, pp 239, 241.
33. Bagwell, 1890, vol. 3, p. 343.

Chapter 2 (pp 25–37)

1. Falls, 1959, p.195.
2. Silke, 1970, p. 79.
3. Docwra, 1849, p. 247.
4. Moryson, 1617, book 2, pp 223–4.
5. Falls, 1950, p. 277.
6. Silke, 1970, pp 86–91.
7. Óscar Recio Morales, 'Spanish army attitudes to the Irish at Kinsale' in Morgan (ed.), 2004, p. 92; Silke, 1970, pp 36–50.
8. Silke, 1970, p. 93.
9. Hiram Morgan, 'Disaster at Kinsale' in Morgan (ed.), 2004, pp 102, 108.
10. Ibid., p. 118.
11. Ibid., p. 118.
12. Silke, 1970, p. 112.
13. Morgan in Morgan (ed.), 2004, p. 121.
14. John McGurk, 'English naval operations at Kinsale' in Morgan (ed.), 2004, pp 151–3; Morgan in Morgan (ed.), 2004, pp 120–21.
15. *Calendar of the Carew Manuscripts,* vol. 4 (1601–3), p. 195.
16. Morgan in Morgan (ed.), 2004, p. 128.
17. Ibid., p. 129.
18. Ibid., p. 130–32.
19. Annals of the Four Masters, AD 1601.

Chapter 3 (pp 38–48)

1. Hiram Morgan, 'Disaster at Kinsale' in Morgan (ed.), 2004, p. 139.
2. Hiram Morgan, 'England's joy' in Morgan (ed.), 2004, pp 408–13.
3. Moryson, 1617, book 3, p. 197.
4. John McGurk, 'The pacification of Ulster, 1600–3' in Edwards, Lenihan and Tait (eds), 2007, p. 122.
5. Vincent Carey, '"What pen can paint or tears atone?": Mountjoy's scorched earth campaign' in Morgan (ed.), 2004, p. 208.
6. Docwra, 1849, pp 258, 260.
7. Falls, 1950, p. 328.
8. Carey in Morgan (ed.), 2004, p. 210.
9. Moryson, 1617, book 3, p. 197.

10. Carey in Morgan (ed.), 2004, p. 212.
11. Moryson, 1617, book 3, p. 199.
12. Carey in Morgan (ed.), 2004, p. 209.
13. Silke, 1970, p. 163, footnote.
14. Ibid., p. 209.
15. Ibid., p. 211.
16. Ibid., p. 211.
17. Ibid., p. 211.
18. Moryson, 1617, book 3, pp 283, 285.
19. Ibid., p. 225; Carey in Morgan (ed.), 2004, p. 213; Canny, 2001, p. 166.
20. Joseph McLaughlin, 'What base coin wrought: The effects of the Elizabethan debasement in Ireland' in Morgan (ed.), 2004, p. 195.
21. McGurk in Edwards, Lenihan and Tait (eds), 2007, p. 125.
22. Canny, 2001, pp 166–7.
23. Connolly, 2007, p. 270.
24. Falls, 1950, pp 332–4.
25. Kelly, 2003, p. 76.
26. McGurk, 2006, pp 209–11.
27. Falls, 1950, p. 337; McGurk, 2006, p. 211.
28. Bardon, 2008, p. 155.
29. McGurk, 2006, p. 213.
30. Kelly, 2003, p. 77.
31. Ibid., p. 80.
32. McGurk, 2006, p. 218; Kelly, 2003, p. 79.

Chapter 4 (pp 49–69)

1. Fraser, 1996, pp xxv–xxvii.
2. Ibid., pp xxxii, xxxiii, 37.
3. McCavitt, 1998, p. 13.
4. Ibid., pp 5–7.
5. Joseph McLaughlin, 'What base coin wrought: The effects of the Elizabethan debasement in Ireland' in Morgan (ed.), 2004, p. 197.
6. David Edwards, 'Legacy of defeat: The reduction of Gaelic Ireland after Kinsale' in Morgan (ed.), 2004, p. 285.
7. McLaughlin in Morgan (ed.), 2004, pp 200–201.
8. Edwards in Morgan (ed.), 2004, pp 285–6.
9. Ibid., pp 289–93.
10. Kearney Walsh, 1986, p. 37.
11. Edwards in Morgan (ed.), 2004, p. 282.
12. Robert J. Hunter, 'The end of O'Donnell power' in Nolan, Ronayne and Dunlevy (eds), 1995, p. 231.
13. McCavitt, 1998, p. 95.

14. Robert J. Hunter in Nolan, Ronayne and Dunlevy (eds), 1995, pp 238–9.
15. Ibid., pp 240–41.
16. Kelly, 2003, pp 79–80.
17. McGurk, 2006, pp 231–3.
18. Lacy, 1990, p. 77; Kelly, 2003, p. 30; McGurk, 2006, p. 234.
19. McGurk, 2006, pp 226, 235–6.
20. T. W. Moody, 'Sir Thomas Phillips, servitor' in *Irish Historical Studies*, vol. 1, no. 3 (March 1939), pp 251–5.
21. Benn, 1877, pp 72, 78–9.
22. Gillespie, 2007, p. 54.
23. Benn, 1877, pp 86–7.
24. Gillespie, 1985, pp 174–5.
25. Robert Hunter, 'Sir William Cole, the town of Enniskillen and plantation County Fermanagh' in Murphy and Roulston (eds), 2004, p. 118.
26. Canny, 2001, pp 79–80.
27. Gillespie, 1985, p. 34.
28. Ibid., p. 98.
29. Canavan, 1989, pp 33–7, 46.
30. Harold O'Sullivan, 'The Magennis Lordship of Iveagh in the Early Modern Period, 1534 to 1691' in Proudfoot (ed.), 1997, pp 161–9.
31. McCavitt, 1998, p. 116.
32. McCavitt, 2002, p. 80.
33. McCavitt, 1998, p. 119.
34. Ibid., p. 121.

Chapter 5 (pp 70–85)

1. Hill, 1869, p. 16.
2. Ibid., p. 17.
3. Ibid., p. 18.
4. Ibid., pp 19–20.
5. Ibid., pp 21–3.
6. Ibid., pp 26–7.
7. Perceval-Maxwell, 1973, pp 49–50.
8. Hill, 1869, p. 27.
9. Ibid., p. 29.
10. Ibid., p. 30.
11. Perceval-Maxwell, 1973, p. 1.
12. Hill, 1869, p. 31.
13. Perceval-Maxwell, 1973, p. 51.
14. Lowry, 1867, appendix 1, pp i–ii.
15. Perceval-Maxwell, 1973, p. 52; Hill, 1869, pp 32–3.
16. Hill, 1869, p. 35.

17. Ibid., pp 37–9.
18. Ibid., pp 44–7.
19. Perceval-Maxwell, 1973, pp 52–4.
20. Ibid., p. 56.
21. Hill, 1869, p. 56, footnote.
22. Perceval-Maxwell, 1973, p. 57.
23. Ibid., p. 66.
24. Ibid., pp. 85–6; Hill, 1873, p. 207.
25. Hill, 1873, p. 194.
26. Hector McDonnell, 'Surviving Kinsale Scottish-style: The MacDonnells of Antrim' in Morgan (ed.), 2004, pp 272–3.
27. Ohlmeyer, 1993, pp 18–21; Perceval-Maxwell, 1973, pp 47–8.
28. Perceval-Maxwell, 1973, p. 48.
29. McDonnell in Morgan (ed.), 2004, p. 273.
30. Perceval-Maxwell, 1973, pp 48–9.
31. Ibid., p. 62.
32. Ibid., p. 47.
33. Ibid., p. 64; McDonnell in Morgan (ed.), 2004, p. 275.
34. Hill, 1973, p. 206.
35. McDonnell in Morgan (ed.), 2004, p. 275.
36. Brian S. Turner, 'Distributional aspects of family name study illustrated in the Glens of Antrim' unpublished PhD thesis, Queen's University, Belfast, 1974, pp 64–158.
37. Hill, 1873, p. 203.
38. Perceval-Maxwell, 1973, pp 61–3; Hill, 1873, pp 203–4.
39. Hill, 1873, p. 225.
40. Perceval-Maxwell, 1973, p. 65.

Chapter 6 (pp 86–110)

1. *Calendar of State Papers, Ireland, 1606–8*, p. 270.
2. Robert J. Hunter, 'The end of O'Donnell power' in Nolan, Ronanyne and Dunlevy (eds), 1995, p. 241.
3. Ibid., p. 229.
4. Ibid., p. 234.
5. Kearney Walsh, 1996, pp 48–9.
6. Ibid., p. 49.
7. McCavitt, 2002, p. 72.
8. Ibid., p. 70.
9. Ibid., pp 67–8.
10. Ibid., p. 71.
11. Valerie McGowan-Doyle, '"Spent blood": Christopher St Lawrence and Pale loyalism' in Morgan (ed.), 2004, p. 179.

12. Ibid., p. 189.
13. McCavitt, 2002, p. 88.
14. Ibid., pp 88–9.
15. McCavitt, 2002, p. 85.
16. Kearney Walsh, 1996, p. 55.
17. Kearney Walsh, 1986, p. 46.
18. Ibid., pp 52–3.
19. Kearney Walsh, 1996, p. 59.
20. McCavitt, 2002, p. 95.
21. Ibid., p. 60.
22. Annals of the Four Masters, AD 1608.
23. Ibid.
24. Kearney Walsh, 1996, p. 64.
25. Ibid., pp 66–7.
26. Ibid., p. 67.
27. Ibid., p. 69.
28. Ibid., p. 73.
29. Ibid., p. 75.
30. Ibid., p. 76.
31. Ibid., p. 78.
32. Ibid., p. 79.
33. Ibid., p. 72.
34. *Calendar of State Papers, Ireland, 1606–8*, p. 270.
35. Ibid., p. 273.
36. McCavitt, 2002, p. 124.
37. Ibid., pp 116–17.
38. Ibid., p. 114.
39. Ibid., p. 115.
40. Ibid., p. 113.
41. Ibid., p. 123.
42. Ibid., p. 125.
43. Ibid., pp 118–19.
44. Ibid., pp 115–16.
45. Ibid., p. 117.
46. Ibid., pp 117–18.
47. Annals of the Four Masters, AD 1608.
48. McCavitt, 2002, p. 138.
49. *Calendar of State Papers, Ireland, 1606–8*, pp 504–6; McCavitt, 2002, pp 139–41.
50. McCavitt, 2002, p. 141.
51. Ibid., p. 139.
52. Ibid., p. 143.
53. Ibid., p. 144.

54. Ibid., pp 144–5.
55. *Calendar of State Papers, Ireland, 1608–10*, p. 7.
56. Ibid., pp 15, 17.
57. *Calendar of State Papers, Ireland, 1606–8*, p. 275.
58. McCavitt, 2002, pp 147–8.
59. Kearney Walsh, 1996, pp 83–4.
60. Ibid., pp 90–91.
61. Ibid., pp 90–81.
62. Ibid., p. 93.
63. Ibid., p. 86.
64. Ibid., p. 86.
65. Ibid., p. 87.
66. Ibid., p. 95.
67. Ibid., p. 107.

Chapter 7 (pp 111–41)

1. Canny, 2001, pp 195, 197.
2. Fraser, 1996, pp 85–6.
3. *Calendar of State Papers, Ireland, 1608–10*, p. 17.
4. Hill, 1877, p. 70.
5. Smyth, 2006, p. 21.
6. Ibid., pp 25–8.
7. Ibid., pp 31, 35, 49–53.
8. Robinson, 1984, p. 68.
9. Smyth, 2006, p. 352.
10. Ibid., pp 66–74.
11. McCavitt, 1998, p. 151.
12. Ibid., p. 151.
13. Ibid., p. 152.
14. Canny, 2001, p. 190.
15. Ibid., p. 191.
16. Ibid., p. 61.
17. McCavitt, 1998, p. 153.
18. Hill, 1877, p. 70.
19. Ibid., p. 71.
20. Ibid., p. 74.
21. Ibid., p. 74.
22. Ibid., p. 75.
23. McCavitt, 1998, pp 152–3.
24. Hill, 1877, p. 77.
25. Ibid., p. 78.
26. Ibid., pp 79–80.

27. Ibid., pp 78–88.
28. Moody, 1939, pp 33–4.
29. Hill, 1877, pp 93–6.
30. Ibid., pp 93–116.
31. Ibid., pp 122–5.
32. McCavitt, 1998, p. 68.
33. Ibid., pp 72–3.
34. Ibid., p. 62.
35. Ibid., p. 156.
36. Canny, 2001, p. 193.
37. Ibid., p. 195.
38. Ibid., p. 196.
39. Canny, 2001, p. 198.
40. 'In Our Time', BBC Radio 4 discussion on Foxe's *Book of Martyrs*, chaired by Melvyn Bragg, 18 November 2010.
41. Rolf Loeber, '"Certeyn notes": Biblical and foreign signposts to the Ulster Plantation' in Lyttleton and Rynne (eds), 2009, pp 24–6.
42. Connolly, 2007, pp 257–8.
43. Canny, 2001, pp 43–8.
44. Connolly, 2007, p. 259.
45. Canny, 2001, pp 51–5.
46. For the full text of 'Certeyn Notes', Rolf Loeber in Lyttleton and Rynne, 2009, pp 34–42.
47. Ibid., pp 40–42.
48. Ioan-Aurel Pop, *Transylvania between the 11th and the 14th Centuries: A Historical Sketch*, pp 157–82.
49. Moody, 1939, pp 31–2.
50. Hill, 1877, pp 133–4.
51. Ibid., p. 134; Canny, 2001, pp 204–5.
52. Moody, 1939, p. 33.
53. Ibid., p. 37.
54. Robinson, 1984, pp 85–6.
55. McCavitt, 2002, p. 155.
56. Moody, 1939, p. 36.
57. McCavitt, 2002, pp 156–7; McCavitt, 1998, pp 147–8.
58. Ibid., pp 156–60.
59. McCavitt, 2002, p. 160.
60. Kearney Walsh, 1996, p. 94.

Chapter 8 (pp 142–66)

1. Bardon, 2008, p. 173
2. Gilbert, 1879, vol. 1, pp 318–26.

3. Gillespie, 1985, p. 34.
4. Perceval-Maxwell, 1973, p. 29.
5. Ibid., pp 27, 326.
6. Fraser, 1971, pp 361–2.
7. Ibid., pp 366–73.
8. Perceval-Maxwell, 1973, p. 26.
9. Fraser, 1971, frontispiece map; see also Bell, 1988.
10. Perceval-Maxwell, 1973, p. 84.
11. Robinson, 1984, pp 77, 79.
12. Ibid., pp 77–8; R. J. Hunter, 'County Armagh: A map of plantation, c. 1610' in Hughes and Nolan (eds), 2001, pp 277–9; Hill, 1877, pp 259–62.
13. R. J. Hunter, 'Plantation in Donegal' in Nolan, Ronayne and Dunlevy (eds), 1995, pp 296–8; Robinson, 1984, pp 77–8, 202–5; Hill, 1877 pp 259–82.
14. Perceval-Maxwell, 1973, pp 323–58; Robinson, pp 205–8; Hill, 1877, pp 283–309.
15. Robinson, 1984, pp 196–8; Perceval-Maxwell, 1973, pp 359–61; R. J. Hunter in Murphy and Roulston (eds), 2004, pp 105–20; R. J. Hunter in Nolan, Ronayne and Dunlevy (eds), 1995, pp 286–319; McCavitt, 1998, pp 76–7; and Hill, 1877, pp 309–48.
16. Perceval-Maxwell, 1973, p. 115.
17. Ibid., pp 115–16.
18. Hill, 1877, pp 221–2.
19. Ibid., pp 226–8.
20. Perceval-Maxwell, 1973, p. 117.
21. Hill, 1877, pp 228–30.
22. Ibid., pp 445–6.
23. Ibid., p. 120.

Chapter 9 (pp 167–89)

1. Moody, 1939, p. 62.
2. Ibid., pp 60–65.
3. Ibid., pp 66–8.
4. Ibid., p. 70; Curl, 2000, pp 36–7.
5. R. J. Hunter, 'The Fishmongers' Company of London and the Londonderry Plantation, 1609–41' in O'Brien (ed.), 1999, pp 205–7.
6. Moody, 1939, pp 71–8.
7. Ibid., pp 79–83.
8. Hill, 1877, pp 451, 477, 480, 493–4, 499–505.
9. Ibid., pp 514, 522–3, 527–8, 538, 546, 551.
10. Ibid., p. 555.
11. Moody, 1939, pp 108–11.
12. Curl, 2000, p. 77.
13. Ibid., pp 78–9.

14. Ibid., p. 79.
15. Moody, 1939, pp 113–14.
16. Ibid., pp 117–18.
17. Ibid., pp 119–20.
18. Ibid., pp 146–51.
19. Ibid., p. 152.
20. Curl, 2000, pp 86–9.
21. Moody, 1939, pp 160–62.
22. Moody, 1939, pp 164–5.
23. Ibid., pp 167–76.

Chapter 10 (pp 190–208)

1. Aidan Clarke, 'Plantation and the Catholic question, 1603–23' in Moody, Martin and Byrne (eds), *A New History of Ireland, III*, 1978, p. 213.
2. John McCavitt, 'Rebels, planters and conspirators: Armagh, 1594–1640' in A. J. Hughes and William Nolan (eds), 2001, pp 255–7.
3. Maxwell, 1923, p. 292.
4. McCavitt, 1998, pp 157–8.
5. John McCavitt, 'Rebels, planters and conspirators: Armagh, 1594–1640' in Murphy and Roulston (eds), 2004, p. 251.
6. Robinson, 1984, pp 75–6.
7. W. A. Maguire, 'The Maguires of Tempo: Vicissitudes of a County Fermanagh family' in Murphy and Roulston (eds), 2004, pp 147–8.
8. Robinson, 1984, pp 75–7, 199–200.
9. McGettigan, 2010, pp 19–21.
10. Aidan Clarke, 'Pacification, plantation and the Catholic question, 1603–23' in Moody, Martin and Byrne (eds), 1976, p. 202.
11. Bernadette Cunningham in Brady and Gillespie (eds), 1986, p. 162.
12. Mac Cuarta, 2007, p. 17.
13. Ibid., pp 17–20.
14. Ibid., p. 23.
15. Ibid., pp 23–35.
16. Ford, 1987, pp 46–7.
17. Ibid., p. 158; Mac Cuarta, 2007, p. 37.
18. Ford, 1987, pp 164–7.
19. Mac Cuarta, 2007, pp 39–40.
20. Ford, 1987, pp 46, 167.
21. Mac Cuarta, 2007, p. 42.
22. Ibid., 2007, pp 53–4.
23. Ford, 1987, pp 74–9.
24. Mac Cuarta, 2007, pp 57–8.
25. Ibid., p. 59.

26. Ibid., pp 63–8.
27. Gillespie, 1987, pp 3–7.
28. Ibid., 11–12.
29. Ibid., p. 33.
30. Ibid., 43–8.
31. Kearney Walsh, 1996, p. 132.
32. *Annals of the Four Masters* (John O'Donovan, ed.), 1848, vol. 3, pp 2373–5.

Chapter 11 (pp 209–54)

1. Lacy, 1990, pp 92–6; Curl, 2000, pp 110–13.
2. Curl, 2000, pp 142–8.
3. Robert J. Hunter, 'Sir William Cole, the town of Enniskillen and plantation County Fermanagh' in Murphy and Roulston (eds), 2004, pp 105–9, 117–18, 122.
4. Ibid., pp 123–34.
5. Roulston, 2010, pp 21–9; William Roulston, 'The Ulster Plantation in the manor of Dunnalong, 1610–70' in Jefferies and Dillon (eds), 2000, pp 267–77; *Calendar of State Papers, Ireland, 1625–32*, pp 512–13.
6. Rolf Loeber and Terence Reeves-Smith, 'Lord Audley's grandiose building schemes in the Ulster Plantation' in Mac Cuarta (ed.), 2011, pp 82–5; Robinson, 1984, pp 200, 204.
7. Loeber and Reeves-Smith in Mac Cuarta (ed.), 2011, pp 86–9.
8. Ibid., pp 90–100.
9. Mallory and McNeill, 1991, p. 307.
10. R. J. Hunter, 'County Armagh: A map of plantation, c. 1610' in Hughes and Nolan (eds), 2001, p. 277.
11. Wilsdon, 2010, pp 123–4.
12. O'Neill (ed.), 2002, pp 17–18, 39; Hamlin (ed.), pp 56–61, 77, 112, 114–15, 121–2, 144–5; Kerrigan, 1995, pp 57–9, 70–78; Wilsdon, 2010, pp 98–162.
13. Robert J. Hunter, 'Sir Ralph Bingley, c. 1570–1627: Ulster planter' in Roebuck (ed.), 1981, pp 14–28.
14. Robert J. Hunter, 'Plantation in Donegal' in Nolan, Ronayne and Dunlevy (eds), 1995, pp 296–302.
15. Gillespie, 2007, pp 56–65, 69.
16. Benn, 1877, pp 85–7.
17. Ibid., p. 93.
18. Ibid., pp 674–6.
19. Ohlmeyer, 1993, pp 24–5; Benn, 1877, p. 677.
20. Gillespie, 1985, pp 111, 140–41.
21. Perceval-Maxwell, 1973, pp 229–33.
22. Ibid., pp 235–40; Hill, 1869, pp 72, 81.
23. Perceval-Maxwell, 1973, pp 241–6.

24. Perceval-Maxwell, 1994, pp 30–31; Connolly, 2007, pp 301–2; Gillespie, 2006, p. 54; Connolly, 2008, p. 6.
25. Robinson, 1984, pp 92–5.
26. Canny, 2001, pp 211–12.
27. Ibid., p. 212.
28. Ibid., p. 213.
29. Ibid., p. 213; Moody, 1939, p. 229; Dudley Edwards, 1938, p. 40.
30. Canny, 2001, pp 218–19.
31. Treadwell (ed.), 2006, p. 591.
32. Canny, 2001, p. 216.
33. R. J. Hunter, 'The Fishmongers' Company of London and the Londonderry Plantation, 1609–41' in O'Brien (ed.), 1999, pp 205–49.
34. Ibid., pp 219–20.
35. Curl, 2000, pp 86–7.
36. Akrigg, 1984, pp 332–5.
37. McCavitt, 1998, p. 221.
38. Moody, 1939, p. 184.
39. Ibid., p. 185.
40. Hill, 1877, pp 589–90.
41. Akrigg, 1984, pp 3, 214.
42. Treadwell, 1998, pp 186–211.
43. Treadwell (ed.), 2006, pp 607–8.
44. Paul Ferguson, 'Ordnance Survey' in Connolly (ed.), 1998, pp 415–16.
45. Hill, 1877, pp 283, 296, 300, 303, 306, 308, 309, 330, 340.
46. Stevenson, 1981, p. 13.

Chapter 12 (pp 255–78)

1. Aidan Clarke in Moody, Martin and Byrne (eds), 1978, pp 265–9.
2. Curl, 2000, pp 136–42.
3. Reid, 1867, vol. 1, pp 180–82, 189, 237, 253; Gillespie, 1985, pp 68–72; Gilbert, 1879, vol. 1, p. 374.
4. Royle, 2004, p. 118.
5. Aidan Clarke in Moody, Martin and Byrne (eds), 1978, pp 280–85.
6. Harold O'Sullivan, 'The Magennis Lordship of Iveagh in the Early Modern Period, 1534 to 1691' in Proudfoot (ed.), 1997, pp 169–79; Gillespie, 1985, pp 98–9, 136.
7. Gillespie, 1985, pp 122–4; O'Sullivan in Proudfoot (ed.), 1997, p. 170.
8. Gillespie, 1985, pp 118–20; Gillespie, 2006, p. 140.
9. Ohlmeyer, 1993, pp 28–30.
10. Ibid., pp 61–3.
11. Perceval-Maxwell, 1994, pp 32–5, 42; Gillespie, 1985, p. 74.
12. Perceval-Maxwell, 1994, p. 41.

13. Ibid., p. 43; Gillespie, 1985, p. 82.

14. Bardon, 1992, p. 135.

15. Raymond Gillespie, 'The murder of Arthur Champion and the 1641 rising in Fermanagh,' *Clogher Record*, vol. 14, 1993, no. 3, pp 53–9.

16. John B. Cunningham, 'The Blennerhassets of Kesh,' *Clogher Record*, vol. 16, 1999, no. 3, pp 123–5.

17. Gilbert (ed.), 1879–80, vol. 2, pp 465–6.

18. Perceval-Maxwell, 1994, p. 218.

19. Hilary Simms, 'Violence in County Armagh, 1641' in Mac Cuarta (ed.), 1993, pp 133–8.

Chapter 13 (pp 279–316)

1. Patrick J. Corish in Moody, Martin and Byrne (eds), 1978, pp 299–316.

2. Perceval-Maxwell, 1994, pp 214–16; McGettigan, 2010, p. 41.

3. Curl, 1986, p. 91; Stevenson, 1981, pp 53–4; McGettigan, 2010, p. 38; Elliott, 2000, pp 101–4.

4. Stevenson, 1981, pp 104–6, 112; Hayes-McCoy, 1969, p. 179.

5. Patrick J. Corish in Moody, Martin and Byrne (eds), 1978, pp 299–308.

6. Hayes-McCoy, 1969, p. 193; Stevenson, 1981, p. 233.

7. Lacy, 1990, pp 107–9.

8. Patrick J. Corish in Moody, Martin and Byrne (eds), 1978, p. 340.

9. Bardon, 1992, pp 140–41.

10. Berresford Ellis, 1975, pp 30–31.

11. Ibid., pp 69–73.

12. O'Sullivan in Proudfoot (ed.), 1997, pp 189–90.

13. McGettigan, 2010, pp 47–50; Elliott, 2000, pp 112–14.

14. Elliott, 2000, pp 133–4.

15. Berresford Ellis, 1975, p. 249.

16. Reid, 1867, vol. 2, pp 260–9.

17. W. Macafee and V. Morgan, 'Population in Ulster, 1660–1760' in Roebuck (ed.), 1981, pp 47–9.

18. Ohlmeyer, 1993, pp 249–50, 259–65.

19. O'Sullivan in Proudfoot (ed.), 1997, p. 191.

20. Elliott, 2000, p. 114; William Roulston, 'Castles, churches and country houses: The lost architecture of County Fermanagh in an age of improvement, c. 1700–c. 1750' in Murphy and Roulston (eds), 2004, pp 171–3.

21. Holmes, 2000, p. 39.

22. T. C. Smout, N. C. Landsman and T. M. Devine, 'Scottish emigration in the seventeenth and eighteenth centuries' in Canny (ed.), 1994, p. 87.

23. W. Macafee and V. Morgan, 'Population in Ulster, 1660–1760' in Roebuck (ed.), 1981, pp 52–6.

24. Young, 1898, pp 24–31; Quinn, 1966, pp 39–41; Hill, 1873, pp 381–2.

25. Livingstone, 1980, p. 137.
26. Elliott, 2000, p. 116; O'Sullivan in Proudfoot (ed.), p. 193.
27. Steel, 1984, pp 125–6; Macafee and Morgan in Roebuck (ed.), 1981, p. 58.
28. Wilsdon, 2010, p. 99; Perceval-Maxwell, 1973, p. 346.
29. T. C. Smout, N. C. Landsman and T. M. Devine, 'Scottish emigration in the seventeenth and eighteenth centuries' in Canny (ed.), 1994, pp 80–86.
30. Raymond Gillespie, 'Scotland and Ulster: A Presbyterian perspective, 1603–1700' in Kelly and Young (eds), 2009, pp 84–5.
31. Macafee and Morgan in Roebuck (ed.), 1981, pp 58–9.
32. Elliott, 2000, map 6 and p. 131.
33. Reid, 1867, vol. 3, pp 68–70.
34. Agnew, 1996, pp 2–17.
35. Gillespie, 2007, p. 91.
36. Ibid., p. 92.
37. Agnew, 1996, pp 16–17; Gillespie, 2007, pp 97–117.
38. Agnew, 1996, p. 63.
39. Ibid., p. 110.
40. Benn, 1877, pp 317–19.
41. Lacy, 1990, pp 149–51.
42. Murray and Logue, 2010, pp 16–19; Canavan, 1989, pp 70–75; Camblin, 1951, pp 49–51; Bardon, 1992, pp 200–201.
43. Jonathan Bardon, in Parkhill (ed.), pp 4–7; Jonathan Bardon, pp 13–14, Tom Duncan, pp 16–21, David McCreedy, pp 83–7, Ivor Edgar, pp 117–21, Richard Bennett, pp 169–76, and Canon David Crooks, pp 218–22, in Duncan (ed.), 2008.
44. Curl, 2000, p. 206.
45. Bardon, 1992, p. 189.

Chapter 14 (pp 317–46)

1. Karl S. Bottigheimer, 'Kingdom and colony: Ireland in the westward enterprise, 1536–1660' in Andrews, Canny and Hair (eds), 1979, p. 55; Smyth, 2006, pp 422–31.
2. Nicholas Canny, 'The permissive frontier: Social control in English settlements in Ireland and Virginia, 1550–1650' in Andrews, Canny and Hair (eds), 1979, p. 21; Smyth, 2006, p. 422; Bardon, 1992, pp 120, 128.
3. Canny in Andrews, Canny and Hair (eds), 1979, pp 25–9.
4. Bottigheimer in Andrews, Canny and Hair (eds), 1979, p. 53.
5. Smyth, 2006, pp 427–9.
6. Ibid., p. 428.
7. MacMaster, 2009, pp 40–57.
8. Smyth, 2006, p. 439.
9. MacMaster, 2009, p. 73.

10. Bardon, 1992, pp 178–9.
11. Bardon, 2008, pp 248–51; David Dickson, *Arctic Ireland: The Extraordinary Story of the Great Frost and Forgotten Famine of 1740–41*, Belfast 1997, pp 20–33, 35–8, 46–52, 69.
12. Bardon, 1992, pp 177–8.
13. Desmond McCourt, 'County Derry and New England: The Scotch-Irish migration of 1718' in O'Brien (ed.), 1999, p. 305.
14. MacMaster, 2009, pp 51, 79, 138–49.
15. Bardon, 1992, pp 209–10.
16. Smyth, 2006, p. 429.
17. Ibid., p. 442.
18. Harris, 1744, p. 98.
19. Bardon, 1992, p. 283.
20. Ibid., pp 223–7.
21. Ibid., p. 226.
22. Bardon, 2008, p. 328.
23. Bardon, 1992, p. 238.
24. Bardon, 1982, pp 66, 83.
25. Ibid., p. 108.
26. Bardon, 1992, p. 350.
27. Hill, 1877, p. 590.
28. Bardon, 1992, pp 242, 240.
29. Ibid., pp 344–8.
30. See Bell, 1988; Bardon, 1992, pp 400–401; and information supplied by Aodán Mac Póilin, Ultach Trust, on English as a surname.
31. Bardon, 1992, p. 382.
32. Ibid., p. 447.

BIBLIOGRAPHY

— Aalen, F. H. A., Whelan, Kevin, and Stout, Matthew (eds), *Atlas of the Irish Rural Landscape*, Cork, 1997.

— Aalen, Fred, and Hunter, Robert J., 'Two early 17th century maps of Donegal,' *JRSAI*, 94:2 (1964).

— Agnew, Jean, *Belfast Merchant Families in the Seventeenth Century*, Dublin, 1996.

— Akenson, Donald Harman, *The Irish Diaspora: A Primer*, Toronto and Belfast, 1996.

— Akrigg, G. P. V., *Letters of James VI & I, edited with an introduction*, London and California, 1984.

— Allingham, Hugh, *Captain Cuellar's Narrative of the Spanish Armada and His Adventures in Ireland*, London, 1897.

— Andrews, J. H., *Plantation Acres: An Historical Study of the Irish Land Surveyor and his Maps*, Omagh, 1985.

— Andrews, K. R., Canny, N. P., and Hair, P. E. (eds), *The Westward Enterprise: English Activities in Ireland, the Atlantic and America, 1480–1650*, Detroit, 1979.

— Bagwell, Richard, *Ireland Under the Stuarts and During the Interregnum*, 3 vols., London, 1909–16.

— Bagwell, Richard, *Ireland Under the Tudors*, 3 vols., London, 1885–90.

— Bardon, Jonathan, *A History of Ireland in 250 Episodes*, Dublin, 2008.

— Bardon, Jonathan, *A History of Ulster*, Belfast, 1992.

— Bardon, Jonathan, *Belfast: An Illustrated History*, Belfast, 1982.

— Barnard, Toby C., *A New Anatomy of Ireland: The Irish Protestants, 1649–1770*, New Haven and London, 2003.

— Barnard, Toby C., *Cromwellian Ireland: English Government and Reform in Ireland, 1649–60*, Oxford, 1975.

— Barnard, Toby C., *Making the Grand Figure: Lives and Possessions in Ireland, 1641–1770*, New Haven and London, 2004.

— Bell, Robert, *The Book of Ulster Surnames*, Belfast, 1988.

— Benn, George, *A History of the Town of Belfast from the Earliest Times to the Close of the Eighteenth Century*, Belfast, 1877.

— Berresford Ellis, Peter, *Hell or Connaught!: The Cromwellian Colonisation of Ireland, 1652–1660*, London, 1975.

— Bossy, John, and Jupp, Peter (eds), *Essays Presented to Michael Roberts*, Belfast, 1976.

— Bottigheimer, K. S., *English Money and Irish Land: The 'Adventurers' in the Cromwellian Settlement of Ireland*, Oxford, 1971.

— Brady, Ciarán, *The Chief Governors: The Rise and Fall of Reform Government in Tudor Ireland, 1536–1588*, Cambridge, 1994.

— Brady, Ciarán, and Gillespie, Raymond (eds), *Natives and Newcomers: The Making of Irish Colonial Society, 1534–1641*, Dublin, 1986.

— Buckley, J., 'Report of Sir Josias Bodley on some Ulster fortresses in 1608,' *Ulster Journal of Archaeology* 14:1 (1910).

— Camblin, G., *The Town in Ulster*, Belfast, 1951.

— Canavan, Tony, *Frontier Town: An Illustrated History of Newry*, Belfast, 1989.

— Canny, Nicholas, *From Reformation to Restoration: Ireland, 1534–1660*, Dublin, 1987.

— Canny, Nicholas, *Kingdom and Colony: Ireland in the Atlantic World, 1560–1800*, Baltimore (Md), 1988.

— Canny, Nicholas, *Making Ireland British, 1580–1650*, Oxford, 2001.

— Canny, Nicholas, *The Elizabethan Conquest of Ireland: A Pattern Established, 1565–76*, Hassocks (Sussex), 1976.

— Canny, Nicholas (ed.), *Europeans on the Move: Studies on European Migration, 1500–1800*, Oxford, 1994.

— Carr, Peter, *'The Most Unpretending of Places': A History of Dundonald, County Down*, Dundonald, 1987.

— Connolly, S. J., *Contested Island: Ireland, 1460–1630*, Oxford, 2007.

— Connolly, S. J., *Divided Kingdom: Ireland, 1630–1800*, Oxford, 2008.

— Connolly, S. J. (ed.), *The Oxford Companion to Irish History*, Oxford, 1998.

— Cosgrove, Art (ed.), *A New History of Ireland, II: Medieval Ireland, 1169–1534*, Oxford, 1987.

— Crawford, W. H., *Domestic Industry in Ireland: The Experience of the Linen Industry*, Dublin, 1972.

— Cullen, L. M., and Smout, T. C., *Comparative Aspects of Scottish & Irish Economic and Social History, 1600–1900*, Edinburgh, 1977.

— Cunningham, John B., 'The Blennerhassets of Kesh,' *Clogher Record*, vol. 16, 1999, no. 3.

— Curl, James Stevens, *The Honourable the Irish Society and the Plantation of Ulster, 1608–2000*, Chichester, 2000.

— Curl, James Stevens, *The Londonderry Plantation, 1609–1914*, Chichester, 1986.

— Devine, T. M., and Dickson, David (eds), *Ireland and Scotland, 1600–1850*, Edinburgh, 1983.

— Dickson, David, and Ó Gráda, Cormac (eds), *Refiguring Ireland: Essays in Honour of L. M. Cullen*, Dublin, 2003.

— Dickson, R. J., *Ulster Emigration to Colonial America, 1718–1775*, London, 1966.

— Docwra, Henry, 'A narration of the services done by the army ymploye'd to Lough-Foyle,' *Miscellany of the Celtic Society*, John O'Donovan (ed.), Dublin, 1849.

— Dudley Edwards, R. (ed.), 'Letter book of Sir Arthur Chichester, 1612–14,' *Analecta Hibernica*, 8 (1938).
— Duffy, Patrick J., 'Farney in 1634: Thomas Raven's survey of the Essex Estate,' *Clogher Record*, 11:2 (1983).
— Duffy, Patrick J., Edwards, David, and Fitzpatrick, Elizabeth (eds), *Gaelic Ireland: Land, Lordship and Settlement, c. 1250–c. 1650*, Dublin, 2001.
— Duncan, Tom (ed.), *The 1608 Royal Schools Celebrate 400 Years of History, 1608–2008*, Aghalee, 2008.
— Dunlevy, Mairéad, *Dress in Ireland: A History*, Cork, 1989.
— Edwards, David, Lenihan, Pádraig, and Tait, Clodagh (eds), *Age of Atrocity: Violence and Political Conflict in Early Modern Ireland*, Dublin, 2007.
— Elliott, Marianne, *The Catholics of Ulster*, London, 2000.
— Ellis, Steven G., *Tudor Ireland: Crown, Community and the Conflict of Cultures, 1470–1603*, London, 1985.
— Falls, Cyril, *Elizabeth's Irish Wars*, London, 1950.
— Faulkner, John, and Thompson, Robert (eds), *The Natural History of Ulster*, Holywood (Co. Down), 2011.
— Fitzgerald, Patrick, and Ickringill, Steve (eds), *Atlantic Crossroads: Historical Connections between Scotland, Ulster and North America*, Newtownards, 2001.
— Ford, Alan, *The Protestant Reformation in Ireland, 1590–1641*, Dublin, 1997.
— Fraser, Antonia, *The Gunpowder Plot: Terror and Faith in 1605*, London, 1996.
— Fraser, George MacDonald, *The Steel Bonnets: The Story of the Anglo-Scottish Border Reivers*, London, 1971.
— Gailey, Alan, *Rural Houses of the North of Ireland*, Edinburgh, 1984.
— Gilbert, J. T. (ed.), *History of the Irish Confederation and the War in Ireland*, 7 vols., Dublin, 1882–9.
— Gillespie, Raymond G., *Colonial Ulster: The Settlement of East Ulster, 1601–1641*, Cork, 1985.
— Gillespie, Raymond G., *Conspiracy: Ulster Plots and Plotters in 1615*, Belfast, 1987.
— Gillespie, Raymond G., 'Continuity and change: Ulster in the seventeenth century,' in C. Brady, M. O'Dowd and B. M. Walker (eds), *Ulster: An Illustrated History*, London, 1989.
— Gillespie, Raymond G., *Early Belfast: The Origins and Growth of an Ulster Town to 1750*, Belfast, 2007.
— Gillespie, Raymond G., 'Harvest crises in early seventeenth-century Ireland,' *Irish Economic and Social History*, 11 (1984).
— Gillespie, Raymond G., *Seventeenth-Century Ireland*, Dublin, 2006.
— Gillespie, Raymond G., 'Small towns in early modern Ireland,' in P. Clark (ed.), *Small Towns in Early Modern Europe*, Cambridge, 1995.
— Gillespie, Raymond G., 'The murder of Arthur Champion and the Rising of 1641 in Fermanagh,' *Clogher Record*, 14 (1993).

— Gillespie, Raymond G., 'The origins and development of an Ulster urban network,' *Irish Historical Studies*, xxiv, 93 (1984).

— Gillespie, Raymond G., 'The small towns of Ulster, 1600–1700,' *Ulster Folklife*, 36 (1990).

— Gillespie, Raymond G., *The Transformation of the Irish Economy, 1550–1700*, Dundalk, 1991.

— Hamlin, Ann, *Historic Monuments of Northern Ireland*, Belfast, 1983.

— Harkness, David, and O'Dowd, Mary (eds), *The Town in Ireland*, Belfast, 1981.

— Harris, Walter, *The Antient and Present State of the County of Down*, Dublin, 1744.

— Harris, W. F., 'The Commission of 1609: Legal aspects,' *Studia Hibernica*, 20 (1980).

— Harris, W. F., 'The rebellion of Sir Cahir O'Doherty and its legal aftermath,' *Irish Jurist*, 15 (1980).

— Hayes-McCoy, G. A., *Irish Battles: A Military History of Ireland*, London, 1969.

— Hill, G., *An Historical Account of the Macdonnells of Antrim, Including Notices of Some Other Septs, Irish and Scottish*, Belfast, 1873.

— Hill, G., *An Historical Account of the Plantation in Ulster at the Commencement of the Seventeenth Century, 1608–1620*, Belfast, 1877.

— Hill, G., *The Montgomery Manuscripts, 1603–1706, Compiled from Family Papers*, Belfast, 1869.

— Holmes, Finlay, *The Presbyterian Church in Ireland: A Popular History*, Blackrock (Co. Dublin), 2000.

— Hughes, A. J., and Nolan, William (eds), *Armagh: History & Society*, Dublin, 2001.

— Hunter, R. J., 'Plantation in Donegal,' in W. Nolan, L. Ronanyne and M. Donlevy (eds), *Donegal: History and Society*, Dublin, 1995.

— Hunter, R. J., 'Sir Ralph Bingley, c. 1570–1627: Ulster planter,' in Peter Roebuck (ed.), *Plantation to Partition: Essays in Ulster History*, Belfast, 1981.

— Hunter, R. J., 'Sir William Cole, the town of Enniskillen and Plantation Co. Fermanagh,' in E. M. Murphy and W. J. Roulston (eds), *Fermanagh: History and Society*, Dublin, 2004.

— Hunter, R. J., 'Style and form in gravestone and monumental sculpture in County Tyrone in the seventeenth and eighteenth centuries,' in H. A. Jefferies and C. Dillon (eds), *Tyrone: History and Society*, Dublin, 2000.

— Hunter, R. J., 'Ulster plantation towns,' in D. Harkness and M. O'Dowd (eds), *The Town in Ireland: Historical Studies XIII*, Belfast, 1981.

— Hutchison, W. R., *Tyrone Precinct*, Belfast, 1951.

— Jefferies, H. A., 'George Montgomery, first Protestant bishop of Derry, Raphoe and Clogher (1605–10),' in H. A. Jefferies and C. Devlin (eds), *History of the Diocese of Derry from Earliest Times*, Dublin, 2000.

— Jefferies, H. A., and Dillon, C. (eds), *Tyrone: History and Society*, Dublin, 2000.

— Johnston, John D., 'The Plantation of County Fermanagh, 1610–1641: An Archaeological and Historical Survey,' MA thesis, Queen's University, Belfast, 1976.

— Kearney, Hugh F., *Strafford in Ireland, 1633–41: A Study in Absolutism*, Manchester, 1959.

— Kearney Walsh, Micheline, *An Exile of Ireland: Hugh O'Neill, Prince of Ulster*, Dublin, 1996.

— Kearney Walsh, Micheline, *'Destruction by Peace': Hugh O'Neill after Kinsale*, Armagh, 1986.

— Kelly, William (ed.), *Docwra's Derry: A Narration of Events in North-west Ulster, 1600–1604*, Belfast, 2003.

— Kelly, William P., and Young, John R. (eds), *Scotland and the Ulster Plantations*, Dublin, 2009.

— Kerrigan, Paul M., *Castles and Fortifications in Ireland, 1485–1945*, Cork, 1995.

— Lacy, Brian, 'Londonderry City,' *Excavations Bulletin*, 1977–9.

— Lacy, Brian, *Siege City: The Story of Derry and Londonderry*, Belfast, 1990.

— Lacy, Brian, 'The archaeology of the Ulster Plantation,' in Michael Ryan (ed.), *Irish Archaeology Illustrated*, Dublin, 1997.

— Lee, Maurice, *Great Britain's Solomon: James VI and I in His Three Kingdoms*, Urbana, 1990.

— Lenihan, Pádraig, *Consolidating Conquest: Ireland, 1603–1727*, Harlow (Essex), 2008.

— Lennon, Colm, *Sixteenth-Century Ireland: The Incomplete Conquest*, Dublin, 1994.

— Logue, Paul, 'Archaeology of post-medieval Derry and Londonderry,' in Audrey Horning et al. (eds), *Post-medieval Archaeology of Ireland*, Dublin, 2007.

— Lowry, T. K., *The Hamilton Manuscripts, Containing Some Account of the Settlement of the Territories of the Upper Clandeboye, Great Ardes and Dufferin in the County of Down*, Belfast, 1867.

— Lydon, James (ed.), *England and Ireland in the Middle Ages*, Dublin, 1981.

— Lynch, Michael (ed.), *The Oxford Companion to Scottish History*, Oxford, 2001.

— Lyttleton, James, and Rynne, Colin (eds), *Plantation Ireland: Settlement and Material Culture, c. 1550–c. 1700*, Dublin, 2009.

— McBride, Ian, *Eighteenth-Century Ireland*, Dublin, 2009.

— McCall, Timothy P. J., 'The Gaelic background to the Settlement of Antrim and Down, 1580–1641,' MA thesis, Queen's University, Belfast, 1983.

— MacCarthy-Morrogh, Michael, *The Munster Plantation: English Migration to Southern Ireland, 1583–1641*, Oxford, 1986.

— McCavery, Trevor, *Newtown: A History of Newtownards*, Belfast, 1994.

— McCavitt, John, *Sir Arthur Chichester, Lord Deputy of Ireland, 1605–16*, Belfast, 1998.

— McCavitt, John, *The Flight of the Earls*, Dublin, 2002.

— McCracken, Eileen, 'Charcoal burning ironworks in seventeenth- and eighteenth-century Ireland,' *Ulster Journal of Archaeology* 20 (1957).

— McCracken, Eileen, *The Irish Woods since Tudor Times: Their Distribution and Exploitation*, Newton Abbot, 1971.

— Mac Cuarta, Brian, *Catholic Revival in the North of Ireland, 1603–41*, Dublin, 2007.

— Mac Cuarta, Brian, 'The Plantation of Leitrim, 1620–41,' *Irish Historical Studies* 32 (2001).

— Mac Cuarta, Brian (ed.), *Reshaping Ireland, 1550–1700: Colonisation and its Consequences*, Dublin, 2011.

— Mac Cuarta, Brian (ed.), *Ulster 1641: Aspects of the Rising*, Belfast, 1993.

— MacCulloch, Diarmaid, *Reformation: Europe's House Divided, 1490–1700*, London, 2003.

— McGettigan, Darren, *The Donegal Plantation and the Tír Chonaill Irish, 1610–1710*, Dublin, 2010.

— McGurk, John, *Sir Henry Docwra, 1564–1631: Derry's Second Founder*, Dublin, 2006.

— MacLysaght, Edward, *Irish Life in the Seventeenth Century*, Cork, 1939, New York, 1969.

— MacMaster, Richard K., *Scotch-Irish Merchants in Colonial America*, Ulster Historical Foundation, Belfast, 2009.

— Macrory, Patrick, *The Siege of Derry*, London, 1980.

— Mallory, J. P., and McNeill, T. E., *The Archaeology of Ulster*, Belfast, 1991.

— Maxwell, Constantia, *Irish History from Contemporary Sources (1509–1610)*, London, 1923.

— Montgomery, Michael, *From Ulster to America: The Scotch-Irish Heritage of American English*, Belfast, 2006.

— Moody, T. W., 'Sir Thomas Phillips of Limavady, Servitor,' *Irish Historical Studies* 1:3 (1939).

— Moody, T. W., *The Londonderry Plantation, 1609–41: The City of London and the Plantation in Ulster*, Belfast, 1939.

— Moody, T. W., 'The treatment of the native population under the scheme for the Plantation of Ulster,' *Irish Historical Studies* 1 (1938).

— Moody, T. W., 'Ulster Plantation Papers, 1608–13,' *Analecta Hibernica* 8 (1939).

— Moody, T. W., Martin, F. X., and Byrne, F. J. (eds), *A New History of Ireland, IX: Early Modern Ireland, 1534–1691*, Oxford, 1978.

— Morgan, Hiram, 'The colonial venture of Sir Thomas Smith in Ulster, 1571–75,' *Historical Journal* 27 (1985).

— Morgan, Hiram (ed.), *Political Ideology in Ireland, 1541–1641*, Dublin, 1999.

— Morgan, Hiram (ed.), *The Battle of Kinsale*, Bray, 2004.

— Moryson, Fynes, *An History of Ireland, from the Year 1599 to 1603*, London, 1617; repr. Dublin 1735.

— Mullin, T. H., *Coleraine in By-gone Centuries*, Belfast, 1976.
— Murphy, Eileen M., and Roulston, William J. (eds), *Fermanagh: History and Society*, Dublin, 2004.
— Murray, Emily, and Logue, Paul (eds), *Battles, Boats & Bones: Archaeological Discoveries in Northern Ireland, 1987–2008*, Belfast, 2010.
— Nicholls, Kenneth, *Gaelic and Gaelicised Ireland in the Middle Ages*, Dublin, 1972.
— Nolan, William, Ronayne, Liam, and Dunlevy, Mairéad (eds), *Donegal: History & Society*, Dublin, 1995.
— Northern Ireland Environment Agency, *Dunluce Castle*, Belfast, 2010.
— O'Brien, Gerard (ed.), *Derry & Londonderry: History and Society*, Dublin, 1999.
— O'Clery, Lughaidh, *The Life of Hugh Roe O'Donnell, Prince of Tirconnell (1586–1602)*, ed. Denis Murphy, Dublin, 1893.
— O'Donovan, John (ed.), *Annála Ríoghachta Éireann: Annals of the Kingdom of Ireland by the Four Masters, from the Earliest Period to the year 1616*, 2nd ed., Dublin, 1856.
— Ohlmeyer, Jane, *Civil War and Restoration in the Three Stuart Kingdoms: The Career of Randal MacDonnell, Marquis of Antrim, 1609–83*, Cambridge, 1993.
— O'Neill, Brendan (ed.), *Irish Castles and Historic Houses*, London, 2002.
— Ó Siochrú, Micheál (ed.), *Kingdoms in Crisis: Ireland in the 1640s*, Dublin, 2001.
— O'Sullivan, H. C., 'The Magennis Lordship of Iveagh in the early modern period, 1534–1691,' in Lindsay Proudfoot (ed.), *Down: History and Society*, Dublin, 1997.
— O'Sullivan, H. C., *Ireland from Independence to Occupation, 1641–1660*, Cambridge, 1995.
— Pakenham-Walsh, W. P., 'Captain Josias Bodley, Director-General of Fortifications in Ireland, 1612–1617,' *Royal Engineers Journal* 8 (1908).
— Parkhill, Trevor (ed.), *The Castle and the Crown: The History of Royal School Dungannon 1614–2004*, Dungannon, 2004.
— Pawlisch, Hans S., *Sir John Davies and the Conquest of Ireland: A Study in Legal Imperialism*, Cambridge, 1985.
— Perceval-Maxwell, M., *The Outbreak of the Irish Rebellion of 1641*, Dublin, 1994.
— Perceval-Maxwell, M., *The Scottish Migration to Ulster in the Reign of James I*, Belfast, 1973.
— Prendergast, J. P., *The Cromwellian Settlement of Ireland*, London, 1865.
— Quinn, David Beers, 'Sir Thomas Smith (1513–1577) and the beginnings of English colonial theory,' *Proceedings of the American Philosophical Society* 89 (1945).
— Quinn, David Beers, *The Elizabethans and the Irish*, Ithaca (NY), 1966.
— Reid, J. Seaton, *History of the Presbyterian Church in Ireland*, 3 vols., Belfast, 1867.

— Robinson, Philip, *The Plantation of Ulster: British Settlement in an Irish Landscape, 1600–1670*, Dublin and New York, 1984.

— Roebuck, Peter (ed.), *Plantation to Partition: Essays in Ulster History in Honour of J. L. McCracken*, Belfast, 1981.

— Roulston, William J., 'Exploring and understanding the Ulster Plantation' (typescript draft).

— Roulston, William J., 'Memento mori: The seventeenth-century monumental inscriptions,' *Familia* 14 (1998).

— Roulston, William J., 'Seventeenth-century manors in the barony of Strabane,' in J. Lyttleton and T. O'Keefe (eds), *The Manor in Medieval and Early Modern Ireland*, Dublin, 2005.

— Roulston, William J., 'The provision, building and architecture of Anglican churches in the north of Ireland, 1600–1740,' PhD thesis, Queen's University, Belfast, 2004.

— Roulston, William J., 'The Ulster Plantation in the manor of Dunnalong, 1610–70,' in H. A. Jefferies and C. Dillon (eds), *Tyrone: History and Society*, Dublin, 2000.

— Roulston, William J., *Three Centuries of Life in a Tyrone Parish: A History of Donagheady from 1600 to 1900*, Strabane, 2010.

— Rowan, A., *The Buildings of Ireland: North West Ulster*, Harmondsworth (Middx), 1979.

— Royle, Trevor, *Civil War: The Wars of the Three Kingdoms, 1638–1660*, London, 2004.

— Silke, John J., *Kinsale: The Spanish Intervention in Ireland at the End of the Elizabethan Wars*, Liverpool, 1970.

— Simms, Katharine, *From Kings to Warlords*, Woodbridge (Suffolk), 1987.

— Smout, T. C., *A History of the Scottish People, 1560–1830*, Glasgow, 1969.

— Smyth, T. S., *The Civic History of the Town of Cavan*, Dublin, 1938.

— Smyth, William J., *Map-making, Landscapes and Memory: A Geography of Colonial and Early Modern Ireland, c. 1530–1750*, Cork, 2006.

— Steel, Tom, *Scotland's Story: A New Perspective*, London, 1984.

— Stevenson, David, *Scottish Covenanters and Irish Confederates: Scottish-Irish Relations in the Mid-Seventeenth Century*, Belfast, 1981.

— Story, George, *A True and Impartial History of the Most Material Occurrences in the Kingdom of Ireland during the Two Last Years*, London, 1691.

— Treadwell, Victor, *Buckingham and Ireland, 1616–28*, Dublin, 1998.

— Treadwell, Victor, 'The survey of Armagh and Tyrone,' *Ulster Journal of Archaeology* 23 (1960).

— Treadwell, Victor (ed.), *The Irish Commission of 1622*, Dublin, 2006.

— Turner, Brian S., 'Distributional Aspects of Family Name Study Illustrated in the Glens of Antrim,' PhD thesis, Queen's University, Belfast, 1974.

— Turner, Brian S. (ed.), *Migration and Myth: Ulster's Revolving Door*, Downpatrick, 2006.

— Wilsdon, Bill, *Plantation Castles on the Erne*, Dublin, 2010.

— Woodward, Donald, 'The Anglo-Irish livestock trade of the seventeenth century,' *Irish Historical Studies* 18 (1973).

— Young, Arthur, *A Tour in Ireland, 1776–1779*, 2 vols, ed. A. W. Hutton, London, 1898.

INDEX